The Cold War and After

Critical Introductions to World Politics

Series Editors: Alejandro Colás (Birkbeck College, University of London)
Richard Saull (Department of Politics, Queen Mary, University of London)

Also available:

Ray Kiely
EMPIRE IN THE AGE OF GLOBALISATION: US HEGEMONY AND
NEOLIBERAL DISORDER

Susanne Soederberg
GLOBAL GOVERNANCE IN QUESTION:
EMPIRE, CLASS, AND THE NEW COMMON SENSE IN MANAGING
NORTH-SOUTH RELATIONS

THE COLD WAR AND AFTER

Capitalism, Revolution and Superpower Politics

Richard Saull

Pluto Press
LONDON • ANN ARBOR, MI

First published 2007 by Pluto Press
345 Archway Road, London N6 5AA
and 839 Greene Street, Ann Arbor, MI 48106

www.plutobooks.com

British Library Cataloguing in Publication Data
A catalogue record for this book is available from the British Library

Hardback
ISBN-13 978 0 7453 2095 3
ISBN-10 0 7453 2095 3

Paperback
ISBN-13 978 0 7453 2094 6
ISBN-10 0 7453 2094 5

Library of Congress Cataloging in Publication Data applied for

10 9 8 7 6 5 4 3 2 1

Designed and produced for Pluto Press by
Chase Publishing Services Ltd, Fortescue, Sidmouth, EX10 9QG, England
Typeset from disk by Newgen Imaging Systems (P) Ltd, Chennai, India
Printed and bound in India

To L. B.

Contents

Series Introduction

Critical Introductions to World Politics

Series Editors: Alejandro Colás (Birkbeck College, University of London)
Richard Saull (Department of Politics, Queen Mary, University of London)

World politics in all its socio-economic, cultural, institutional and military dimensions affects the lives of billions across the globe. Yet international relations is still an area of study associated with the 'high politics' of statecraft, strategy and diplomacy, or with distant and seemingly uncontrollable global flows of money, people and commodities. Critical Introductions to World Politics aims to reverse this prevailing elitism by illuminating and explaining the causes and consequences of these diverse aspects of international relations in an accessible way, thereby highlighting the impact of international processes and developments on the lives of ordinary people. The series will bring together a range of theoretical and empirical studies into the workings of world politics, while also identifying areas for political intervention by those seeking not just to interpret the world, but also to participate in political struggles to change it.

The series engages with key areas, providing succinct, informative and accessible overviews to central debates in global affairs. It draws mainly, although not exclusively, on Marxist approaches to international relations concerned with the analysis of, among other issues, transnational class formation, the role of international organisations in sustaining global capitalist hegemony, the sources of violent conflict and war, and the nature and evolution of state sovereignty. Empirically, it focuses on such issues as the origins of the modern international system, the Cold War and the consequences of its end, globalisation, and the character of American global power.

Critical Introductions to World Politics builds on a new, distinctly historical-materialist approach to global affairs, serving as a key reference point and resource for those studying and teaching international relations from a critical perspective, as well as those involved in the various movements for a more just, equal and sustainable world.

Acknowledgements

I would like to thank Alejandro Colás for his very useful and probing comments on the whole manuscript. I would also like to thank Roger van Zwanenberg, the Publisher at Pluto Press, for his support and, above all, patience in seeing this project through to completion. There are many other people, too numerous to mention, with whom I have discussed different aspects of the argument in this book at conferences, workshops and over a drink, for which I am also very grateful. Finally, I would like to thank my partner, Liza Burdett, for her support throughout this project.

1

Introduction: History and Theory in the Cold War

This book provides a theoretically informed historical survey of the Cold War and the nature and consequences of its end. It seeks to offer a distinct contribution to the theorisation of the Cold War as a form of international (social) conflict, as well as providing a comprehensive examination of the principal historical developments within the Cold War. Further, the book seeks to trace and explain the origins of contemporary resistance to US global power, particularly as manifested by the rise of Islamist movements and their violent/terrorist offshoots, by highlighting the paradoxical character of the Cold War's end. The argument outlined in this book challenges the intellectual consensus on the understanding of the Cold War within the disciplines of International Relations (IR) and Diplomatic History in four ways:

- through offering an alternative periodisation of the Cold War understood as the 'short twentieth century', 1917–91;
- by stressing how geopolitical conflict between the superpowers was primarily a consequence of their contrasting domestic socio-economic properties;[1]
- by arguing that the Cold War was a form of global social conflict associated with the revolutionary and communist consequences – in the form of political movements and states – of a shifting, contradictory and uneven capitalist development;
- by arguing that the Cold War did not have a singular ending focused on the collapse of the Soviet communism in 1989–91, but rather had a *series of ends* in time and space, associated with the *differentiated* containment and defeat of historical communism as a political and socio-economic challenge to capitalism.

The principal intellectual justification for the book is a dissatisfaction with prevailing accounts of the history of the Cold War and the theoretical assumptions that have tended to dominate such accounts.

The theoretical understanding of the Cold War and the explanation of its end have been dominated by the debate between scholars drawing on a Realist theoretical framework and ideational approaches. For Realists[2] the Cold War is understood as the bipolar (superpower) relationship based on strategic competition, which was a consequence of the geopolitical arrangements brought about by the Second World War. In this understanding the Cold War is classified as a typical great power conflict based on the utility of military power and distinguished by the strategic currency of nuclear weapons.[3] From this perspective ideological and socio-economic factors are seen as largely subordinate to the material (military and economic) interests of each superpower; having more explanatory significance for accounts of the domestic political relations of each rather than their respective international relations.[4]

Consequently, the end of the Cold War occurred because the USSR was forced to make strategic concessions (withdrawal from east-central Europe, arms control concessions and ending political-military support for allies) to preponderant US material power. Following this explanatory logic, the social and political developments within the Soviet bloc that altered the domestic socio-economic, ideological and political character of communist states are seen as being of secondary import.

Ideational approaches[5] share with Realist-informed scholars some key theoretical assumptions about the Cold War: that it was a post-war conflict derived from the consequences of the Second World War, and that it was a conflict centred on the conflicting post-war objectives of the superpowers. Both, then, understand the Cold War as the diplomatic history of the post-1945 Soviet–US relationship. However, in contrast to Realists, ideational approaches emphasise the importance of domestic political ideas, values and ideology on superpower behaviour and, consequently, take much more seriously the ideological character of the Cold War conflict and the way in which domestic political factors (and change) conditioned the bipolar relationship. In this respect, perception or misperception played a key role in fomenting conflict as much as conflicting objective material interests.

Further, domestic political change and the way in which ideas evolved within each of the superpowers are seen as ultimately determining for the evolution of the Cold War and its end, highlighted by role of Mikhail Gorbachev's 'new thinking' on Soviet foreign policy changes in the late 1980s. It was a change in the subjective view of the world of the Soviet leadership, ushered in by the generational and ideological changes of Gorbachev, that triggered the end of the Cold War through the impact of domestic political change on Soviet foreign relations. The Cold War system, then, is not a product of the post-war configuration of geopolitical power, but rather a social-ideological construction founded on distinct perceptions of self-identity and the social construction of an enemy.[6] However, this recognition of the importance of ideas and values in superpower relations and the Cold War is rather limited in the sense that it tends to separate the role of ideology on leadership decision-making rather than examining the way in which ideological values were rooted in social and political structures within society and state, which structured and conditioned the determining currency of ideology on decision-making and politics more generally.

Accordingly, the mainstream understanding of the Cold War – Realist or ideational – rests on reducing the explanatory significance of the socio-economic properties of the superpowers and the wider social systems (communism and capitalism) that each was part of. Consequently, both approaches tend to separate the bipolar political–military relationship from wider transnational political, economic and ideological processes associated with the spread and/or contraction of the rival social systems of capitalism and communism and the international and geopolitical consequences of the expansion of each social system. The argument of this book tries to unite these two conceptual areas – the strategic/military with the socio-economic and ideological – thus providing an historically richer and more sociologically informed account of the Cold War through anchoring military power and geopolitical relations in the contrasting socio-economic properties and ideological structures of states.

RADICAL THEORIES OF COLD WAR[7]

The neglect of the socio-economic dimensions of the Cold War in mainstream theories has been tackled by a number of radical theories of Cold War informed, to varying degrees, by a Marxist understanding of international relations. There are two strands to these arguments.

The Cold War and Intra-Systemic Conflict

The first emphasises socio-economic conflict *within* each of the superpower blocs to varying degrees, claiming that it was primarily *internal* conflict that shaped the evolution of the Cold War rather than the external superpower conflict. Thus, although there was antagonism between the superpowers and the social systems that each led,[8] there were also intense socio-economic contradictions within the political relations of each bloc, which the intensification of the external Cold War conflict helped resolve. This approach outlines a radically different perspective on the Cold War from mainstream arguments, playing down external geopolitical and ideological conflict and emphasising internal/intra-bloc conflict.[9]

With their focus on internal conflict such approaches obviously questioned the socio-economic distinctiveness of the USSR and other types of revolutionary state with some Marxists going as far as describing the USSR as a form 'state capitalism', and in this respect the Cold War is seen as a form of inter-imperialist conflict between different, antagonistic forms of capitalist state.[10] In this sense these arguments can be seen as being about imperialism, and in particular attempts to revise Lenin's classic statement[11] on imperialism and inter-imperialist conflict. The prevailing assumption within such perspectives is the organically, conflictual, violent and war-like tendencies or consequences of capitalist development, and the way in which the existence of the post-war liberal peace was in part contingent on the Soviet communist threat. What flows from this is that without the functional role of the Soviet threat towards the unity of the capitalist world under US leadership, the stabilisation of post-war capitalism would have been much more problematic.

Ultimately, according to this 'internalist' perspective, the driving force for international conflict was not between the two superpowers and the social systems that they led, but rather emerged from within each bloc. Thus, the Soviet threat and the way in which the USSR consolidated its power over east-central Europe after 1945 was a fundamental factor – a kind of *deus ex machina* – in bringing together the advanced capitalist states under US leadership. Further, the continuation of US hegemony over the advanced capitalist world – those states that were and are the main economic rivals of the US – required the continuation of the Soviet threat as it was this that gave the US particular leadership privileges over its economic rivals, and which helped ensure that economic tensions did not escalate into political conflict because of the way in which the advanced capitalist world – through institutions such as NATO – was dependent on the military protection of the US. For the Soviet Union and the ruling elements within it, and the socio-economic constituencies that were allied with such elements, the domestic stability of authoritarian communist rule required the continuation of an external context of threat and insecurity that helped justify not only domestic power structures, but also the character of its political presence with east-central Europe.

Through focusing on the priority of internal socio-economic and political dynamics these approaches also suggest that the superpowers, to varying degrees, were less concerned about the expansion of the social system that each led and more concerned about their respective survival in a way that ensured the political status quo within each bloc. In a word, both superpowers, and especially the USSR, were conservative in their international orientation and averse to pursuing policies that threatened to jeopardise the 'systemic status quo' upon which their power and leadership rested. The upshot of this is that the USSR is seen not only as a conservative power but in some respects a counter-revolutionary power understood as pursuing policies that subverted and undermined the prospects of realising socialist revolution by non- (pro- Soviet) communist forces in other parts of the world, when such developments threatened to jeopardise the ideological power of the Soviet leadership. This argument is most strongly associated with the state-capitalist argument[12] and derives from the critique and hostility towards Stalinism based on the defeat of the left-opposition within the USSR by the late 1920s and the construction of a Stalinist – as opposed to socialist – Soviet state.

The argument that Stalin betrayed the Bolshevik Revolution, transforming the USSR from a revolutionary to a counter-revolutionary state, is based on his creation of a dictatorship defined by political terror and an economy organised upon the dominance of the party-state bureaucracy rather than democratic workers' power. This internal betrayal is seen as being mirrored by an international betrayal of revolution evident – according to such approaches – by the failure to mobilise workers effectively against the rise of Nazism in Germany, the failure properly to aid, and the attempts to limit, the revolutionary socialist character of the Spanish Revolution between 1936 and 1939, the Molotov–Ribbentrop Pact of 1939, and the failures of the USSR to support socialist revolution in the post-Stalin era.

Whether or not one agrees with the interpretation of the history of the Bolshevik Revolution and the character of Stalinism, these arguments highlight important aspects of the history of the Cold War largely neglected by the mainstream debate. The internal socio-economic and class dynamics of each social system are important for tracing the domestic sources and causes of the foreign policies of the superpowers. Further, the argument that the Cold War was a struggle, in the words of David Horowitz, between 'imperialism and revolution', and not between the USSR and the US, highlights the significance of revolutionary movements and change realised *without* Soviet assistance, which highlights the 'autonomous revolutionary' sources of Cold War.[13]

However, these analytical and explanatory strengths are tempered by the failure to connect the way in which the domestic socio-economic constitution of each superpower (and the blocs that they led) determined their *form* of international relations, and also the failure to recognise fully the significance of the Soviet role in support of international revolution. With respect to the first issue, there were major, indeed fundamental, differences in the way that each superpower related to the wider world and social system that each led, and the differences derived from their contrasting domestic socio-economic properties. This was significant not only in the role of force and coercion in the reproduction of the political power within their respective blocs – its centrality in the reproduction of Soviet-communist power and its more limited role in the reproduction of the (internal) social relations within the advanced capitalist world – but also in the expansion of each social system.

The Cold War and Inter-Systemic Conflict

The second strand of Marxist-informed theories of the Cold War locates the dynamic of Cold War conflict less in the internal contradictions within each bloc and more in the international antagonism and conflict between the two social systems – hence the Cold War is seen as inter-systemic conflict. This approach is associated with the work of Isaac Deutscher[14] and Fred Halliday,[15] and it is this theoretical framework that has most informed the conceptualisation of Cold War outlined in this book and elsewhere.[16] Deutscher's work is distinct from that of those Marxists who focus on *intra*-systemic conflict, because he argued that the USSR and its social system operated according to a different socio-economic logic – though far from meeting the socialist idea of democratic workers' control of the means of production – from that of capitalism. In this respect, world politics after 1917 was characterised by a 'great contest' between two rival social systems for global socio-economic supremacy based on the relative and comparative economic performance of each.

Though far from uncritical of the Soviet regime, Deutscher's understanding of the Soviet system recognised its revolutionary and socialist character reflected in the abolition of the private ownership of the means of production, the organisation of production, consumption and exchange through the five-year state plan, and the significant improvements in the material living standards of the Soviet people that this system had helped secure. Further, Deutscher's understanding of Soviet socialism was imbued with a significant dose of idealism in two senses. First, through his hope and expectation that it could be reformed from within and, second, that the authoritarian and coercive aspects of the system – most associated with Stalin and his political and economic legacy – could be removed or reduced.

These 'idealistic' hopes about the possibilities of extending socialism within the USSR combined with the Marxist-Leninist assumption that an economic system based on state planning would inevitably out perform a capitalist system characterised by a history of crisis, slump, depression and war. The degree to which these two elements of the great contest – the prospects for reforming the Soviet system and the inherent contradictions and tendency towards crisis with capitalism – were interrelated was not fully resolved by Deutscher, as he did not live to see the economic stagnation that characterised the Soviet bloc's economic performance in its latter years, nor the transformation in the nature of capitalist development, such that the economic crises that ended the long boom in the early 1970s did not trigger major political conflict between the advanced capitalist states or moves towards socialism within these states.

Whilst Deutscher recognised systemic differences between the two superpowers and their respective blocs and a relationship based on competition he saw this as separate from the military-strategic competition of Cold War. By downplaying the Soviet role in support of international revolution and its apparent focus on domestic economic-material development – the essence of 'the great contest' – Deutscher shared with the American Cold War Revisionists the assumption that US responses to revolution were in large part exaggerated and misplaced.

Fred Halliday's work draws on Deutscher's idea of the great contest and, by integrating this with the post-1945 dynamic of the arms race and military competition, provides a more substantial theory of Cold War as inter-systemic conflict involving global competition between the two social systems combined with the other notable attributes of Cold War – ideological conflict and military competition. Although he gives some ground to those Marxists that emphasise the significance of intra-bloc conflict for the international relations of each superpower during the Cold War, Halliday argues that both superpowers did, to varying degrees, attempt to expand their respective social systems and consequently there was a genuine international conflict between capitalism and communism not reducible to the internal political dynamics within each bloc.

In this respect, then, the Cold War was about the expansion and retraction in each social system principally through the way in which the periodic convulsions of revolutionary transformation in the third world after 1945 – involving communist and pro-Soviet radical nationalist forces – saw the creation of states opposed to capitalism that institutionalised political and economic structures that drew on the Soviet experience and supported – politically, economically and military – by the USSR.[17] Thus, whereas Deutscher tended to separate the role of the arms race and military competition between the two superpowers from the competition between capitalism and communism, Halliday links them by recognising the Soviet role in support of revolutionary change in other parts of the world, and the third world in particular after 1945, by arguing that the superpowers tended to support rival political forces associated with specific social constituencies – classes – in their political and military interventions in the third world.[18]

However, whilst Halliday does connect the domestic socio-economic properties of each superpower with the character of their international relations, particularly with respect to international revolution, he distinguishes periods of Cold War from 'other' periods in post-war international history,[19] and in this sense, like Deutscher, continues to separate the socio-economic and ideological dimensions of inter-systemic conflict from that of military power. In summary, those periods of reduced military tension – most evident in détente during the early 1970s – are not periods of Cold War in spite of the continuation of the socio-economic and ideological aspects of antagonism because of the removal of military competition and threat from such antagonisms.

Consequently, Halliday has to outline a military logic/dynamic of Cold War separate from the socio-economic properties of each superpower, and in doing so ends up disconnecting inter-(social)-systemic conflict from military competition based on the individual state interests of each superpower. Thus, whilst he recognises the socio-economic antagonism between the USSR and the West after 1917 this was not a Cold War because of the separation of the geopolitical and military character of world politics during the inter-war period. In distinguishing different levels of conflict – social and military – Halliday concedes too much to a Realist conceptualisation of the superpower relationship by granting an explanatory primacy to the arms race and military power as, in the last instance, constitutive of Cold War. This not only ends up separating social conflict and the socio-economic constitution of each superpower from geopolitical conflict, which is seen to operate autonomously from the former, but also fails to recognise fully how military conflict and the arms race were the manifestation of the most intense forms of social conflict in the Cold War. Consequently, it was revolutionary socio-economic change that engendered geopolitical crises involving the superpowers. Further, military power was central to the preservation and expansion of each social system: for the US as the ultimate means to deter Soviet political expansion and as a way of disciplining and undermining Soviet power; for the USSR as a means to ensure internal political order.

THE COLD WAR AS A GLOBAL SOCIAL-SYSTEMIC CONFLICT

In this final section of the Introduction I will outline the theoretical framework that guides the historical discussion in the following chapters. This section seeks to build on the critique outlined above – particularly of the mainstream debate on the Cold War – and in doing so better integrate military power and geopolitical conflict with the socio-economic dimensions of the Cold War. I will do this by highlighting: first, how the socio-economic constitution of the superpowers (and of other states that participated in the Cold War) was conditioned by the role of coercive and militarised social relations, and how this was the primary source of the military competition and geopolitical conflict that dominated the Cold War; and second, how the international political dynamic of the Cold War was located in the shifting and periodic eruptions of revolutionary socio-economic change, and how the social and political character of such change and the construction of revolutionary states – carried through by particular constellations of social forces and political movements – provoked geopolitical crises involving the superpowers.

The Socio-Economic Sources of Geopolitical Conflict

The mainstream debate on the Cold War locates the source of geopolitical conflict in either the ideological preferences of each superpower leadership and the Soviet leadership in particular or the working-out of the balance of power highlighted in the competition for spheres of interest and the arms race. Neither of these positions gives adequate attention to how the domestic socio-economic properties of the superpowers and their allies contributed to geopolitical conflict. In what ways, then, was the domestic constitution of political power within each superpower a source of geopolitical conflict?

The answer lies in the way in which the socio-economic constitution of each superpower was associated with or founded upon institutions, structures and relations conditioned by coercive and military power, and the degree to which such forms of power determined the international relations of each superpower, and the international expansion of the socio-economic system of which each superpower was a part. The domestic role of militarised relations of power, then, conditioned the *form* of each superpower's respective international relations and effectively determined whether or not the international relations and international expansion of each superpower, and its social system, would have geopolitical ramifications.

As I have suggested, the domestic politics and socio-economic systems of superpowers were not only different but mutually antagonistic in the sense that the domestic and international reproduction of each was threatened by the other, because the socio-economic properties of each were mutually antithetical.[20] The international expansion of one system necessarily threatened the political security and social existence of the other and the social constituencies that benefited from each social system. On this level, then, as Mervyn Leffler has recognised, the socio-economic properties of the USSR were seen as a threat to the well-being of the American way of life based on liberal-democratic capitalism,[21] and a geopolitical threat when the Soviet social system threatened to expand. Whilst the expansion of the Soviet system posed a political challenge to the US, so the expansion and challenge of liberal capitalism were seen as a political threat to the USSR as any capitalist encroachment into the USSR and/or the Soviet bloc threatened to undermine and challenge the political arrangements based on the communist party's monopoly of political and economic power. The opening up of Soviet-type societies would not only challenge the organisational and political characteristics of these societies – through the establishment and expansion of a social space autonomous of the party-state authorities – but would also mobilise and benefit different social constituencies, which is what happened with the fall of communist power in 1989.

The coercive and militarised character of the USSR was a result of two interrelated factors: first, the forceful and violent way in which the USSR attempted to construct the material foundations of socialism from a position of material and social backwardness, particularly under the doctrine of 'Socialism in One Country'; and second, the geopolitical hostility that confronted the USSR at its birth and throughout most of its history, particularly highlighted by the devastating human and material impact of the Second World War. In this sense military power and coercive militarised relations were defining of the USSR through the role of state-sanctioned command and coercion in the organisation and operation of the Soviet economy,[22] and also through the way in which the Soviet economy was subordinated to the production of the *matériel* of military power.[23]

Such socio-economic arrangements were problematic for the maintenance of a stable political order in two key respects. First, because economic activities were explicitly political as they involved the state and political authorities directly (from the planning ministry in Moscow to the local factory manager and trade union representative on the shopfloor) and economic questions and problems were directly related to the state and communist party rule. Consequently, economic conflict between workers and managers or producers and consumers was always political and had the potential – particularly evident in the periodic eruptions of crises within east-central Europe – to challenge the continuation of communist party rule and the social reproduction of the Soviet-style system.

Second, because of the highly militarised character of its international relations and the hostile geopolitical environment within which the USSR found itself throughout its history, to secure 'geopolitical autonomy' – national security and the ability to project itself internationally – the USSR needed to build up and maintain its military strength in line with those states hostile to it, which obviously undermined the ability of its economy to meet the social and economic needs of the people. In successfully achieving geopolitical autonomy after 1945, the USSR ended up undermining its domestic political stability and legitimacy in the long term by sacrificing the socio-economic needs of its people to the requirements of the arms race and geopolitical competition.

In two respects, then, the nature and social reproduction of the Soviet political order were founded on coercive and military power: the organisation and functioning of the economy which continued throughout the history of the USSR in spite of the episodes of de-Stalinisation; and second, in the *systemic requirement* for the use of the oppressive and militarised apparatus of the state to ensure the maintenance of party rule, without which communist rule, especially within east-central Europe, would in all likelihood have been overthrown before 1989.

However, in spite of this mutual political antagonism, what was defining of the geopolitical conflict of the Cold War was the fact that the expansion of the Soviet social system – either directly as occurred during the Second World War into east-central Europe or 'autonomously' through the successful revolutionary transformations carried out by a number of revolutionary and communist movements after 1945 – required the physical destruction of the socio-economic and political structures of those societies through coercive-military force.[24] The preservation and expansion of the US capitalist social system did not.[25]

The differences in the socio-economic properties of the superpowers and the consequences thereof for their respective international relations and geopolitical conflict were most evident in the ways in which each superpower realised its respective project of national security after the Second World War in Europe. Whilst US power and security concerns were realised by allowing *and* promoting significant levels of domestic political autonomy[26] within Western Europe and establishing deep socio-economic and cultural forms of political influence over West European states through the multiple forms of political agency[27] located in (an international) civil society, Soviet security was realised and power institutionalised by imposing a top-down revolutionary transformation of societies and states in east-central Europe. Whereas the US allowed a significant degree of political autonomy[28] and realised its influence and political objectives through a range of mechanisms and agents, most of which were not directly associated with the US state and its coercive apparatus, that reflected the socio-economic properties of US politics, the USSR realised its objectives in a manner that reflected the constitution of Soviet domestic politics. Simply put, there were no autonomous sources of political and

economic influence, only the political, administrative and coercive mechanisms of the Soviet state backed by the Red Army. Consequently, as much as
US influence and power in Western Europe revealed the distinct socio-economic
characteristics of US international relations and the social constituencies –
primarily capital – that benefited from such relations, so did Soviet influence
and power in east-central Europe.

It was the combination of the coercive and militarised nature of the Soviet
form of politics and the manner of its international expansion into east-central
Europe, then, which was a significant factor in accounting for the Western
European 'invitation' for a permanent US military presence in Europe and the
geopolitical containment of the USSR, as West European states were unable
and unwilling to distinguish the internal use of Soviet military power to uphold
communist rule within the Soviet bloc from the possible international use of
that power either to intimidate and threaten other European states or expand
Soviet power, as had occurred after 1945. Whilst Soviet security concerns were
legitimate after the devastation wrought by the German invasion, the political
means by which those security concerns were realised – through imposing
communist power in east-central Europe backed by the Red Army – would
inevitably provoke a militarised response to counter the expansion of that power.

Because of the way in which Soviet power was constituted, necessarily, a
militarised response was always likely and this would remain the case until the
coercive and militarised foundations of that power were fundamentally transformed as Gorbachev attempted to do in the late 1980s. Geopolitical conflict,
then, was not *primarily* a product of the ideological predisposition of the Soviet
leadership, nor was it a product of the Soviet political leadership pursuing its
national interest, nor the working-out of the balance of power. Instead, it was a
product of the international consequences of the socio-economic constitution of
Soviet power and the way in which it related to the world and expanded.

Consequently, the reasons for Soviet hesitancy and inconsistency – *contra*
those scholars associated with an intra-systemic argument – in support of
international revolution throughout the history of the USSR after 1917[29] – not
just during Stalin's rise to power – were not a product of domestic political
concerns associated with struggles between different factions and personalities
over questions of domestic power, but the result of the geopolitical risks associated with supporting international revolution. This explains why Soviet support for international revolution was primarily concerned with subordinating
other revolutionary states and movements into Soviet political and geopolitical
discipline rather than opposed to revolutionary change as such. Further, the
USSR did provide support to international revolution, and the success of revolutionary movements and the survival of revolutionary states in a context of US
military hostility was to a significant degree because of the USSR *not* in spite
of Moscow. Soviet support may have come at the cost of local political
and economic autonomy, but to imply – as some Marxist critics of the USSR

did – that Vietnam could have withstood US military power without Soviet (and Chinese) support, or that Cuba could have withstood US and regional hostility – political, economic and military – without Soviet assistance is fanciful at best.

Diplomacy, leadership change and ideological flexibility could and did have an impact on the way in which other states responded to the USSR, however, as long as Soviet power was institutionalised and reproduced through a political order based on coercive and militarised relations, then the geopolitical containment of Soviet power would always take precedence over all other international relations. In large part then the Cold War was a product of how the capitalist great powers sought to deal with the problem of a (revolutionary) state organised in a very different way.

Uneven Capitalist Development, Social Revolution and Cold War

Whilst the superpower relationship was a defining element of the Cold War and source of geopolitical conflict, the socio-economic sources of this conflict were also present more widely in world politics (before and after 1945) and consequently were also major sources of Cold War in themselves, and in the way that socio-economic change that led to the establishment of Soviet-like communist and revolutionary states conditioned the superpower relationship, provoking the most important and dangerous geopolitical crises of the Cold War. The Vietnam War and Cuban Missile Crisis were the two main examples of how autonomous socio-economic sources of Cold War – revolutionary social transformations carried through by revolutionary nationalist and communist movements – triggered geopolitical crises involving the superpowers.

Such revolutionary changes witnessed the overthrow of pro-western (developing) capitalist societies and states integrated, to varying degrees, into the US-led international capitalist order, and the construction of states whose socio-economic properties were antagonistic to US capitalism in a way similar to the socio-economic properties of the Soviet bloc. Further, these states were defined by a heavy dose of coercive military power, particularly Vietnam. Such developments in themselves were enough to generate geopolitical concerns for the US, but their political and military connections with the USSR, thus contributing to the international expansion of Soviet influence, were the key element which ensured geopolitical conflict and, in the case of Cuba, a situation developing between the superpowers that brought the world to as close that is has ever come to a nuclear exchange.

The significance of revolutionary change as a factor in the Cold War highlights a number of issues that the mainstream debate on the Cold War – and some Marxists – have neglected. First, it highlights the shifting and uneven – in time and space – geopolitical consequences of revolutionary change. In this sense we can identify a connection between the Bolshevik Revolution and the emergence of the USSR in 1917 with subsequent bouts of revolutionary change. The link between 1917 Russia and post-war Vietnam and Cuba, amongst others, is located in the fact that although there were significant differences between these episodes of revolution, they emerged out of contradictions and conflicts associated with their capitalist socio-economic development.

These revolutions emerged from conflicts involving the mobilisation of different social classes whereby subaltern social classes – the poorer peasantry, the proletariat, elements of the petit bourgeoisie and radical intelligentsia united by a communist and/or radical nationalist ideology – confronted traditional ruling classes – landlords and the bourgeoisie (local and metropolitan), aided by the capitalist great powers. All of these states had been integrated into the structures and operations of the capitalist world economy through forms of imperial experience, and it was the consequences and contradictions of this experience from which revolutionary conjunctures and struggles emerged.

Each revolution was a product of the very local and particular forms of historical capitalist development whereby pre-capitalist social structures and relations co-existed in an uneasy relationship with capitalist socio-economic structures, some of which were directly tied to external metropolitan markets and involved significant external political interference in the domestic affairs of these states.[30] Consequently, the revolutionary movements that emerged were, above all else, committed to a project of national independence and sovereignty based on the expulsion of the foreign and imperial political and economic presence within their states. Hence, political independence could only come through degrees of social revolution as the imperial presence within these societies was located in the social relations of production and exchange, i.e. how large numbers of ordinary people lived, as much as it was through the formal political and military connections between the local state and metropolitan capitalist powers.

The new revolutionary states that emerged, though less defined by the experience of war than the USSR, constructed socio-economic structures – based on the mobilisation and support of particular social forces – and state institutions very similar to those which emerged within the USSR after 1917 and this was even more apparent when these states formed political, ideological and economic relations with the USSR. In this respect, the politics and historical experience of the USSR was symptomatic, though defining, of a wider social systemic phenomenon not confined to the USSR. Soviet-like states (and communist movements) emerged elsewhere after 1917 and 1945, thus perpetuating (globalised) social systemic conflict. Whilst these revolutions did not occur in the advanced capitalist world – though they threatened to in parts of Western Europe in the early years after the First World War and 1945 and in Portugal in the early 1970s – their occurrence in the third world permitted the Soviet social system and Soviet political influence to expand, thus challenging the geopolitical strength of the US and punching holes in the international capitalist order by establishing state-society structures antithetical to US capitalism.

However, it is also important to recognise the differences in the character and international consequences of the shifting episodes of revolutionary change that occurred in the third world after 1945, as there was a good deal of variety in the 'Soviet-like' revolutionary states that contributed to the Cold War notably between 'communist' and 'revolutionary nationalist' movements and states. Whilst all of them were founded on some use of coercive force to push through socio-economic and political change and erected political barriers to western and capitalist penetration of their respective societies – denoting their hostility towards the social interests of metropolitan capital – the Soviet and communist influence within these societies varied.

Thus, whilst a number of states, such as Vietnam and Cuba, institutionalised communist power structures modelled on the USSR and were committed to the construction of socialism cemented by external military links, others, such as Egypt and Syria, constructed state-society structures that either marginalised or limited the influence of communist parties and implemented relatively less far-reaching socio-economic and political transformations.[31] In effect, these states became embroiled in the Cold War less because of the revolutionary character of the domestic changes they implemented, and more because of the ideological character – anti-imperialism and Arab nationalism – of their foreign policy. Further, in the case of some revolutionary states (such as China and Egypt), after periods of domestic revolutionary change and external confrontation with US imperialism, these states moved out of the Soviet ideological and geopolitical orbit and shifted their internal social development away from a statist-socialist direction towards an opening up to the world market.

What all these qualifications suggest is that whilst the Soviet experience and form of state could be considered as symptomatic of the revolutionary challenge, we also need to recognise the differences amongst revolutionary states and the degree to which they could be seen as part of a wider Soviet bloc. The inner core of the revolutionary challenge to Western capitalism consisted of the USSR and Soviet occupied east-central Europe followed by other communist-ruled states, such as China, until the early 1970s, North Korea, Vietnam, Laos, Cuba and Afghanistan, with the outer core of states that came to power through revolutionary change in the decades after 1945 (Angola, Mozambique, Ethiopia, Egypt, Iraq, Syria, Libya, Nicaragua and South Yemen) more characterised by a revolutionary nationalism and, consequently, more distantly associated with the Soviet bloc. In the chapters that follow these distinctions and their impact on the evolution of the Cold War will be made clearer.

The periodic eruptions of revolutionary change highlight the autonomous sources of political agency – revolutionary movements, communist parties and armed guerrillas supported by particular social classes – in the Cold War that condition and qualify the impact of the superpowers and the USSR in particular on the evolution of the Cold War and the sources of geopolitical conflict. The dynamic of the Cold War – the social and political struggles associated with revolutionary change and the establishment of communist and revolutionary states – was due to the actions of collectivities of ordinary men and women mobilised and organised into revolutionary movements committed to specific socio-economic and political objectives which put them at odds with the social constituencies associated with the American-led international capitalist order. As long as ordinary people were organised in such movements and committed to programmes of revolutionary socio-economic and political transformation that were at odds with the social constituencies that benefited from the rule of capital, the Cold War would continue. It was only when such movements had been fragmented, weakened and crushed that the Cold War ended, as the dynamic of social systemic conflict that had propelled it since 1917 gave way to new sources of resistance and antagonism to American imperialism.

2

The International Impact of the Bolshevik Revolution and the Early Cold War, 1917–45

INTRODUCTION

Most studies of the Cold War, beginning as they do with a discussion of the breakdown of the anti-fascist grand alliance between 1945 and 1948, tend to overlook the impact of the 1917 Bolshevik Revolution on the international system and historical developments between 1917 and the end of the Second World War. In spite of the Bolshevik Revolution, the establishment of a new type of state and the creation of an international revolutionary movement – the Communist International (Comintern) in 1919 – the scholarly consensus assumes the absence of Cold War during the interwar years for two main reasons: first, because the USSR was not seen as an international threat to the major capitalist powers due to a combination of its relative economic and military weakness and Stalin's preoccupation with domestic political issues; and second, because, by the early 1930s, the defining ideological and geopolitical fracture in the international system was not one between communism and liberal capitalism and, correspondingly, between the US and the USSR, as it was to be after 1945, but between liberal (capitalism) and fascism, or what Marxists term inter-imperialist conflict.

Both claims are difficult to dispute. Furthermore, the conventional analyses are also right in identifying the Second World War as the event that ended up producing a geopolitical and ideological transformation in the international system through the geopolitical vanquishing of Western Europe as a major source of global power and its replacement by the superpowers, and the international competition for *global* ideological primacy between liberal capitalism and communism.

At first glance, an understanding of the Cold War does not seem to require an analysis of the international relations of the inter-war period and, specifically, the relations between the USSR and the major capitalist states. My general contention in this book, and in this chapter in particular, argues the contrary. My examination of relations between the USSR and the US and the other major capitalist powers after 1917 up to the onset of the Second World War suggests a significant degree of similarity with the relations between the USSR and the capitalist great powers after 1945, whilst the international responses of the major capitalist states to the outbreaks of social revolution and the activities of the international communist revolutionary movement more broadly during the inter-war period also resemble the responses to revolutionary change involving communist forces after 1945. Consequently, although the post-1945 world *was* different, a *form* of Cold War could be seen to exist after 1917 evidenced in:

- the diplomatic hostility between the USSR and the capitalist great powers prior to June 1941 and the USSR's entry into the war against Nazi Germany;
- the incidents of crisis and social revolution in Europe and beyond, which witnessed political and military clashes between anti-capitalist revolutionary forces involving the international communist movement and various capitalist great powers;
- the continuity in the constitution and character of Soviet relations with the outside world, with respect to communist movements and states and capitalist states.

The account that I will outline recognises the significance of the conflict between fascist-militarist states (Germany, Japan and Italy) and liberal capitalist states (Britain, France and, later, the US) and the USSR that came to dominate inter-war international relations in the 1930s. It will also recognise the transformatory impact of the Second World War on relations between the USSR and the major capitalist powers and amongst the leading capitalist states as well. However, rather than reducing or marginalising the 'inter-systemic' social conflict between communism and capitalism during this period, I will highlight how this conflict contributed to the onset of war due to the ongoing diplomatic suspicion and hostility between the USSR and the liberal capitalist powers *in spite of* the growing threat of fascism. Consequently, the anti-communism of the capitalist great powers was a major factor in the outbreak of war in 1939.[1] Indeed, it was ultimately war and the struggle for political survival that brought the USSR and the liberal capitalist states together in an alliance of enmity towards the common threat to both liberal capitalism and Soviet communism.

The chapter is organised in the following way. It begins with an overview of the socio-economic and political constitution of the USSR after the 1917 Bolshevik Revolution and, in particular, the imprint left on the USSR by the 'Stalinist Revolution'. It then analyses the international relations of the Soviet state with the outside world, concentrating on its relations with and the behaviour of the major capitalist states towards the USSR. After concentrating on the impact of the Soviet state on international relations, I shift my attention to the eruptions of crisis and social revolution from central Europe to the Caribbean and the involvement of the international communist movement and the USSR in these revolutions. The chapter ends with a discussion of the 'Cold War within the World War', or how the simmering political and ideological conflict between communism and (liberal) capitalism was played out during the Second World War in the common struggle against fascism.

THE BOLSHEVIK REVOLUTION AND THE CONSTITUTION
OF THE SOVIET STATE

The revolutionary political and economic changes unleashed after the 1917 Bolshevik Revolution and, in particular, Stalin's 'revolution from above' after 1928 created a form of state that was to have profound consequences for the way in which the USSR related to the world beyond its borders, and also how capitalist states perceived and related to the USSR. Accordingly, the tensions and conflicts that emerged between the wartime allies after the Second World War were primarily about the way in which the domestic socio-economic con-stitution of Soviet power determined the way in which the USSR realised its international political objectives after the war. The breakdown of the wartime alliance was not, then, simply a consequence of the clash of interests between the US and the USSR after the war, or their opposing ideological visions, but rather the fact that the realisation of each superpower's political and security objectives, and the manner in which such objectives were realised, made a clash inevitable. Consequently, the only way that conflict between the USSR and the capitalist powers after the war could have been prevented was if one of the protagonists – and the USSR in particular – was domestically transformed (i.e. no longer the same kind of state that it was before the war) during the war.[2] An account of the nature of the Soviet state and why and how it emerged is, then, crucial to any understanding of how the USSR behaved after 1945.

Political and Economic Developments and the
Creation of the Soviet State

The character of the Soviet state was determined by two sets of processes, one international, the other domestic. The former concerned the pervasive hostility of the capitalist great powers after the revolution, most evident in the armed inter-ventions against the revolution in support of the 'White' counter-revolutionary forces between 1918 and 1920, and the emergence of fascist-militarist states in Germany and Japan in the early 1930s. The latter concerned the socio-economic contradictions that confronted the Bolsheviks in their attempts to construct socialism in the USSR after the end of the civil war and the way in which they – and Stalin in particular – sought to overcome them.

The important point to stress is that these two sets of processes were closely interlinked. The international hostility towards the USSR was in large part directed towards the domestic revolutionary political character of the Soviet state, whilst the direction and nature of domestic socio-economic and political change were strongly conditioned by the international context: the absence of an international revolutionary ally that would assist in the socio-economic transformation of the USSR as much as helping in its military defence, and the way in which any project of domestic socio-economic transformation had to incorporate preparations for the military defence of the revolution. The interrelationship of these two sets of processes was not in itself *fully* responsible for the emergence of the highly coercive and militarised dictatorial state evident by the early 1930s, however. For that we have to include the way in which Stalin used the instruments of dictatorship and terror to secure his leadership and power within the USSR from the late 1920s onwards, as well as recognising the way large sections of the peasantry opposed the economic policies implemented after the late 1920s.

The emergence of a highly coercive and militarised form of state was not then an inevitable outcome of the Bolshevik Revolution. Rather, it was a product of a combination of political contingencies – the failure of the expected international revolution after the Bolsheviks seized power (itself a product of chance and opportunity) and the outcome of the post-Lenin leadership and ideological struggles within the Bolshevik party – and objective historical circumstances of socio-economic backwardness vis-à-vis the capitalist great powers and the hostility of these powers.

The interrelationship and conditioning importance of domestic and international factors varied in the period between 1917 and 1928. Initially, the character of the revolution was determined by the political and military hostility that it had to deal with from both within and without. Hence, civil war and international counter-revolution were major stimulants to the creation and promotion of coercive and military institutions in the form of the rapid mobilisation of workers and demobilised soldiers into a new Red Army and the establishment of the forerunner to the KGB, the Cheka (the All-Russian Extraordinary Commission) which ended up eclipsing the 'democratic spring' of free and open political debate, assembly and decision-making that characterised the early months of the revolution.

With the defeat of the White armies by 1920 and the evacuation of hostile foreign forces the revolution was secured from armed overthrow.[3] Consequently, whilst international and political factors continued to condition the progress of the revolution, henceforth its outcome was to be shaped much more by domestic and socio-economic developments. In this respect the key issues that were to determine the type of state and society that would emerge within the USSR were how the Bolsheviks would deal with the simmering socio-economic tensions present within the revolution after the civil war, and the type of socialism the Bolshevik leadership would attempt to construct and the methods they would employ to do this.

The simmering economic tensions concerned the clash between the socio-economic objectives of large swathes of the peasantry – and the richer peasants in particular – and the Bolsheviks and the urban workers whom they saw as their primary social constituency. The period after the initial seizure of power and the civil war had seen a number of important economic developments that would play a major part in the future direction of the revolution. First was the introduction of state control over large areas of economic activity in the summer of 1918 in response to the military exigencies of civil war, what Lenin termed 'war communism'. War communism had two main elements that were to play a much more important, indeed defining, role in Soviet economic history than was originally anticipated when they were initially introduced: (1) the concentration of economic authority and power in the hands of state authorities through centralised control and management of production and planning; and (2) the effective elimination of market mechanisms in the distribution of goods and services based on fixed prices and state-directed rationing.[4]

The second defining element which stood in stark contradiction to the first was the social and economic consequences of the revolution in the countryside. During the early phase of the revolution the peasantry had provided a major constituency of support for the revolution derived largely from the Bolsheviks' policy of ending participation in the war (thus ending the collective sacrifice of the peasantry who made up the vast majority of the Russian army) and the Bolsheviks' hostility towards the traditional landlord class. However, during the revolution the peasantry not only overthrew the rule of quasi-feudal landlords, but also went about laying the foundations of petty-commodity and capitalist agriculture by seizing land and setting up private landholdings.

The primary source of tension between these two developments concerned the following. First was that state control of the economy would allow the Bolsheviks to use the state apparatus and, if necessary, the coercive power of the state to achieve their economic objectives. Socialism and industrialisation could be constructed using state power as a surrogate for the class forces that were not sufficiently present or developed to carry through the task of socialist construction, particularly in the countryside. The institutions of war communism, then, fundamentally threatened the ability of peasants to control their own means of production – private landholdings – and determine how and what they would produce. Second, the interests of the peasants in securing access to land and carrying out production did not necessarily correspond to the interests of urban workers who were dependent on food produced by the peasantry. Whilst workers (and the Bolsheviks) wanted cheap, plentiful and stable supplies of food to feed the cities and to produce a surplus on which industrialisation could be based, peasants were concerned with determining what they produced and providing foodstuffs for the market at prices that they considered appropriate.

The defining contradiction, which was to shape the character of the Soviet state, concerned the socio-economic interests of the peasantry and the ideological and political interests of the Bolsheviks with the socio-economic interests of the urban proletariat. The management of this contradiction between town and country, peasant and worker, state socialism and agrarian capitalism pre-occupied the Bolshevik leadership throughout the 1920s as they juggled with the competing demands of political stability, economic growth, industrialisation and military security, and – after Lenin's death in 1924 – the way in which these issues became imbricated in the personal struggles amongst the leading Bolsheviks for leadership of the party.

Under Lenin's guidance, the tensions were initially addressed with the introduction of the New Economic Policy (NEP) in March 1921. The NEP reflected the fragile social and political situation that the Bolsheviks confronted after the civil war,[5] combined with the pressing need to stimulate economic activity in the countryside to feed the cities. The Bolsheviks faced a choice: either make concessions to the peasantry and encourage them to produce foodstuffs for the cities; or confront the peasantry using armed force, compelling them to produce foodstuffs at the point of a gun. Whilst the former was likely to stimulate economic growth by appeasing the peasantry, thus reducing in the short term political instability, it would come at the cost of allowing capitalist social interests in the countryside to strengthen, thus jeopardising in the medium term any moves towards the construction of socialism. On the other hand, taking the latter option would have been highly risky. It would have meant class war against the peasantry, testing to breaking-point the military resources of the Bolsheviks and the loyalty of the Red Army after war and civil war, and it would have also in the short term aggravated the urban situation as food supplies would continue to be disrupted. In effect, the Bolsheviks had only one choice – the NEP.

With the introduction of the NEP economic growth was stimulated as peasants were encouraged to produce an economic surplus for the urban market through market mechanisms rather than state requisitions.[6] Consequently, agricultural production increased and this had a knock-on effect on the wider economy. However, the economic benefits – and short-term political benefits – contrasted with the strengthening of capitalist social forces – food wholesalers (the nepman) in the cities and large peasants (Kulaks) in the countryside, both of whom posed a challenge to any future moves towards socialism. Furthermore, although the NEP stimulated economic growth, it did not resolve urban–rural, bourgeois–worker tensions. These tensions began to trouble the Bolshevik leadership with the so-called 'scissor crisis' in the summer of 1923.[7] The result of this was the abandonment of fixed prices, which triggered a doubling of the price of crops between the end of 1924 and mid-1925. The delicate balance between the economic interests of the two sets of social forces – workers in the cities and peasants in the countryside – further deteriorated in 1925 where grain prices were being driven up by the competition for scarcer amounts of grain by urban-based wholesalers, in part a consequence of larger peasants – the Kulaks – hoarding grain. It was this deteriorating situation – in some senses an inevitable consequence of the mixed economy of the NEP – that confronted the collective Bolshevik leadership (Kamenev, Bukharin, Trotsky, Zinoviev and Stalin), the resolution of which was to determine the character of the Soviet state for the rest of its history.[8]

The problems of the NEP, the leadership of the party and what type of 'socialism' would be constructed within the USSR were 'resolved' with Stalin's victory over his leadership rivals and the onset of the Stalinist trans-formation of Soviet society after 1928. After 1928 and under Stalin's direction the USSR pursued a policy of forced collectivisation and industrialisation within the context of Socialism in One Country – the construction of socialism in conditions of autarchy. Forced collectivisation and industrialisation moved to abolish market relations in the town and country and replace them with the social relations of force based on the physical compulsion of state power and terror organised through the five-year central plan. The state expropriated agricultural land and equipment from the peasantry and forcibly – at the point of a gun – organised peasants into state-run collective farms, or *Kolkhozes*. By 1934 over 70 per cent of peasants' households had been collectivised at a brutal and devastating human cost with peasant resistance and obstruction. A former communist official summed up the nature of the struggle between the peasantry and the regime:

A ruthless struggle is going on between the peasantry and our regime ... It's a struggle to the death. This year was a test of our strength and endurance. It took a famine to show them who is master here. It has cost millions of lives, but the collective farm system is here to stay. We've won the war.[9]

Robert Service estimates that between 4 and 5 million peasants perished in 1932–33 from 'de-kulakization' and grain seizures.[10]

With respect to industry, production was organised through the five-year plan drawn up by *Gosplan*, which determined 'credit and production targets to factories, mines and construction sites'.[11] The Soviet economy had become socialist, then, in the sense that private property had been abolished and economic activity was regulated by public political power in place of the market and competition amongst firms. However, this was not a socialism that Marx and most Marxists would recognise. The workers did not control the means of production and did not have effective or democratic mechanisms to determine how production would be organised, what would be produced, and how the economic benefits of production would be distributed amongst the population. The party-state determined the questions of 'what' and 'how' with respect to production and until Stalin's death in 1953 – but less so after – the production goals of the USSR were not primarily concerned with the social and economic well-being of the Soviet people, but rather with the objective of rapidly catching up with the industrial might of the capitalist great powers[12] and ensuring the USSR's military security.

The need to overcome the USSR's relative economic and social backwardness as quickly as possible drove Stalin and the USSR to squeeze as much as the party-state could out of the Soviet people's collective labour power in the years after 1928. The collective commitment and sacrifice of the people were spurred on by the ideological propaganda of building socialism. However, the propaganda of persuasion was matched by the widespread use of brutal techniques of labour 'discipline' and slave labour in the gulag system.[13] Thus, the full forces of the coercive and militarised machinery of party-state were deployed to achieve the realisation of plan targets, thus ensuring that Soviet economic backwardness would be short-lived. The consequence was that the Soviet people were treated as instruments, like any other factor of production, to be exploited and sacrificed for the good of the plan.

The Soviet state became highly coercive because it was determined to push through a revolutionary socio-economic transformation based on a new *modus operandi* in the economic relationship between agriculture and industrialisation, whereby agricultural production and development would be subordinated to industrialisation. In all likelihood – Stalin or no Stalin – such radical change would have triggered resistance amongst some sections of the peasantry, resulting in the state using coercive measures. However, the reasons why these changes came to rely on state-sanctioned terror and the militarisation of the Soviet state were because Stalin insisted upon a rapid and intense transformation towards heavy-militarised industrialisation, carried through by the state.[14] Consequently, it was *external necessity* – Stalin's belief in the inevitability, sooner rather than later, of capitalist military aggression[15] – that propelled the speed and focus of change alongside the way in which such methods facilitated Stalin's *personal* ambition of creating a personalised dictatorship based on an apparatus of terror.

The Constitution of the Soviet State and the Character of its International Relations

By the late 1920s, then, the USSR had evolved into a very different kind of state with respect to the leading liberal capitalist powers (Britain, France and the US) and also the emerging fascist-militarist regimes (Italy, Germany and Japan). In socio-economic terms the remnants of the rule of capital had been broken alongside the USSR's entanglements with the international capitalist economy. Yet, Soviet autarchy and centralised state planning were not free from the power of capital in the form of the political challenge and military threat of the more advanced capitalist great powers and, consequently, the drive towards the construction of socialism within the USSR under Stalin and thereafter was preoccupied with surpassing the economic and military advances of the capitalist powers. Politically, the USSR had become a highly coercive form of state, dominated by the suppression and crushing of political dissent and the supremacy of the ideology and institutions of the party-state in all spheres of social life.

The domestic character of the Soviet state had profound implications for the way in which the USSR related to the outside world. Because of the absence of civil society and a capitalist economy in the USSR, the only way that the USSR could engage in international relations was through the structures and institutions of the party-state. In contrast to the liberal capitalist states, private, non-state relations across borders between individuals, businesses, cultural and political associations were nonexistent, as the Soviet state monopolised all spheres of domestic society and, correspondingly, international relations.

The domestic political *form* of the Soviet state effectively determined the way in which it related to the rest of the world, friend and foe alike. Thus, relations with capitalist states were premised on the antagonistic domestic socio-economic properties of each state respectively, and were complicated, as I will detail below, by the presence of social and political forces within capitalist states loyal to the USSR and committed to the political transformation of their states in a direction that emulated the experience of the USSR. The socio-economic expansion of each form of state threatened the political security of the other as such expansion necessitated a fundamental revolutionary alteration in existing political arrangements.

The relations that became pronounced and determining of world politics after 1945 were, then, present during the inter-war period. The USSR was the same kind of state (as was the US) after 1945 as it had been before the war. Its international objectives and the way in which it sought to realise them were also the same. What changed for the USSR was the geopolitical environment that conditioned its international behaviour. Geopolitical circumstances or, more precisely, conjunctures of geopolitical crises and transformation, effectively determined the character of its international relations – ambition or hesitancy[16] – throughout the USSR's existence. Thus, the USSR emerged and consolidated in the geopolitical context of inter-capitalist conflict between 1917 and 1918. It was strengthened and expanded through the geopolitical vanquishing of Europe during and immediately after the Second World War and it was geopolitically most adventurous during the 1970s – the only time during the Cold War when it was a strategic match for its capitalist foes and when its leading opponent, the US, was unable to deploy external military forces to contain Soviet power as it had done previously.

Accordingly, the state created under Stalin was dominated by coercive-militarised relations from within and, correspondingly, conditioned by coercive-militarised relations from without. A transformation in its domestic socio-economic properties resulting in the removal of the institutions and relations built on state-sanctioned coercion and force within the USSR would necessarily alter the international environment and thus relations of the USSR, whilst reductions in the conditions of external military threat provided the key opportunities for Soviet international expansion.

It was this relationship between the domestic politics of the USSR and the shifting geopolitical context that conditioned Soviet international relations and the evolution of the Cold War. It suggests a remarkable continuity in the form and substance of Soviet international relations from the late 1920s until its collapse over 60 years later. I will discuss Soviet foreign policy in the next two sections, where these themes will be developed. I turn first to relations between the USSR and the major capitalist states between 1917 and the Second World War before assessing the impact of international revolution in the inter-war period and the responses to revolution of the USSR and the major counter-revolutionary powers.

THE USSR AND THE CAPITALIST GREAT POWERS, 1917–41

I have divided this section into three parts, each of which reflects the specific geopolitical context within which Soviet foreign policy was made.

International Revolution and Counter-Revolution, 1917–21

The significance of the failure of international revolution by the early 1920s and the survival of the USSR after the civil war in a sea of enmity meant that the USSR had to ensure that its domestic political economy provided a solid basis for its external defence and also that the USSR would be forced to engage in diplomatic relations, through the policy of 'peaceful co-existence', with capitalist states. Fortunately for the USSR, its capitalist foes were split – a legacy of the First World War and the Versailles peace treaty – and this division in the capitalist world provided an opportunity for the USSR to cultivate relations with different capitalist states as a way of ensuring its security. Speaking in November 1920, Lenin outlined how the USSR should deal with its capitalist opponents:

[U]ntil the final victory of socialism throughout the world ... exploit the contradictions and antagonisms between the two imperialisms, between the two systems of capitalist States [sic], inciting them one against the other. So long as we ... remain weaker than the rest of the capitalist world, so long shall we keep to that rule: [i]f we had not kept to that rule, we should long ago have all been hanging from the lamp-posts – to the gratification of the capitalists ... [B]y making concessions to one form of imperialism, we at the same time fenced ourselves off from persecution by both imperialisms ... But as soon as we are strong enough to fight the whole of capitalism we shall at once take it by the neck. Our strength is growing and very quickly too.[17]

This contrasted with the post-1945 situation where the leading capitalist states were united under US leadership and where Soviet victories in the Second World War had transformed its external security environment to its advantage.

This split within the capitalist world was at its most acute at the time of the Bolshevik Revolution; indeed, we might say that the conflict between capitalist states after 1914 was a major cause of the revolution. After seizing power the Bolsheviks had to move quickly to address the greatest threat to their survival – the presence of a large, advancing German army on Russian soil. In signing the punishing peace of Brest-Litovsk in March 1918, the Bolsheviks 'neutralised' the threat of their military annihilation by the German army, but in doing so incurred the wrath of the already suspicious Western allies. The consequence of this was that the Western allies led by Britain and France and, in a less committed fashion, the US, decided to intervene militarily in Russia with relatively small detachments.[18] Initially, the allies were concerned to try to maintain Russian involvement on the Eastern Front. This put them at loggerheads with the Bolsheviks, especially after they had signed a separate peace, which quickly led to a significant increase in the military pressure from Germany on the Western Front.

Although hostile towards the Bolsheviks and dedicated to their overthrow, the Western allies were racked by divisions. Whereas Britain and France were committed to a more aggressive military intervention to destroy the Bolshevik Revolution at birth by supporting the White Russian counter-revolutionaries, the US, under Woodrow Wilson, was hesitant in its support for what Wilson saw as reactionary and equally unpopular political forces who wanted to restore the *ancien régime*, as well as remaining unconvinced as to the utility of force in responding to revolutions.[19] These arguments over how best to deal with the Bolshevik menace dominated the deliberations at Versailles in 1919.[20] The lack of wholehearted US support for military intervention was crucial in alleviating external pressure and undermining support for the Bolsheviks' domestic military foes. With Britain and France concerned as much about post-war Germany as Russia, and with sections of their respective populations, particularly in the trade unions, sympathetic to the new Bolshevik government, Allied intervention quickly petered out by 1920 and with it the defeat of the Whites.

Whilst domestic and international counter-revolution threatened to strangle Bolshevism at birth because of the splits amongst the capitalist great powers, it also afforded moments of opportunity, which the Bolsheviks were quick to seize. In what was to be a rehearsal of events between 1939 and 1945 in east-central Europe, the Red Army took advantage of Poland's attempt at territorial conquest of the western Ukraine and Allied-endorsed counter-revolution to counter-attack and use the Red Army as a vehicle of territorial conquest and social revolution. The Red Army failed to achieve its goal due to a combination of military overstretch and the absence of sufficient support from the Polish working class, who failed to greet the Red Army as liberators when it reached the outskirts of Warsaw.[21] This episode highlights the relationship between revolutionary military power and social revolution from below where the former undermined the latter by stoking Polish nationalism rather than class struggle, which was marshalled by the Polish army to drive out the Reds. The failure in Poland contrasted with the success of Bolshevik military power in the Caucases and Mongolia in the early 1920s with the spread of social revolution through territorial annexation, a formula which was to be used with effect after the defeat of the *Wehrmacht* in 1944 in east-central Europe.

Western intervention in the civil war reinforced the ideological expectations of the Bolsheviks of how their class enemies would seek the destruction of the first 'Workers' Revolution'. It also set the tone for future relations, which were to be plagued by suspicions and fluctuating bouts of hostility. The political impact of this hostility, however, was muted by the ongoing divisions within the capitalist world. Such divisions, which provoked crises and conflicts, were crucial to the history of the Soviet Republic. The Bolshevik Revolution would not have occurred without inter-imperialist war after 1914, and the survival and early consolidation of the revolution was secured, in large part, because of the continuation of inter-imperialist war, which the Bolsheviks were able to take advantage of, and the subsequent conflicts of interest in the post-war plans of the Western allies. The USSR was able to take advantage of limited diplomatic and economic links after the war, particularly with Germany, because of Germany's estrangement from the French-led European international order.

Inter-capitalist divisions, then, were paradoxical. On the one hand, continued divisions gave the USSR some political space, which allowed it to consolidate communist power and also develop limited links with (potentially hostile) neighbours, thus securing the USSR's external borders and contributing to the internal consolidation of Bolshevik rule through economic relations. On the other hand, the divisions, crises and conflicts, particularly in Europe after 1918, helped produce situations of revolutionary crises, which implicated the USSR – a state that emerged from similar circumstances – and also because of the perceived revolutionary threat from local communist movements, which were seen as being closely associated, if not controlled, from Moscow, thus undermining the diplomatic advances made by the USSR and jeopardising its external security. It was exactly this type of situation that helped bring Nazism to power in 1933 and with it a rabidly anti-communist/Soviet regime, which posed a new order of military threat to the USSR.

The Contradictions of Soviet Diplomacy and Peaceful Co-existence, 1921–33

The end of the civil war corresponded with the beginnings of a period of stability in Europe after the crisis and turmoil of war and the threat of the spread of the revolutionary 'contagion' of Bolshevism. The initial period of

Soviet international relations had, then, come to an end by the early 1920s. Though intact with the defeat of the counter-revolution and the evacuation of foreign forces from its soil, the USSR was isolated and weak. The international revolution had failed with the defeat of the German Revolution through a combination of military suppression and the coming together of the forces of conservatism and social democracy against communist revolution.[22] The split within the left between social democrats and communists that characterised the post-1945 era, then, had its origins in the international response to the Bolshevik Revolution with the non-communist left throwing its weight behind support for liberal-constitutional government rather than the forceful overthrow of capitalism.

From the early 1920s until the early 1930s and the emergence of Nazism, the USSR implemented the doctrine of peaceful co-existence as the prospects for a new wave of international revolution receded. The bourgeois powers, though hostile to the USSR to varying degrees, did not threaten to destroy the USSR, as they suggested they might do in the early years of the revolution. Although antipathetic to the character of the Soviet state and to communism more generally, because of the relative strategic weakness of the USSR, (the USSR did not have the economic or military power to threaten the security of any of the major capitalist states at this time), Britain, France and the US were more concerned with the domestic implications of the communist threat than with any geopolitical threat.[23]

During this period the USSR sought to take advantage of the divisions within the capitalist world, which were a legacy of the war, and the Versailles peace settlement in particular. Thus, in spite of the revolutionary disturbances in Germany, which continued into the 1920s with the October 1923 communist rising in Hamburg,[24] the USSR developed its closest diplomatic relations with the other major state that was hostile to the Versailles settlement, Germany. These relations developed out of the Treaty of Rapallo signed in May 1923 where Germany established diplomatic and trade relations with the USSR and also secret military contacts.[25] With London establishing diplomatic relations with Moscow in February 1924 (followed by other European states), the USSR had managed to break its diplomatic isolation.[26]

However, these diplomatic successes were hostage to wider domestic and international developments. Thus, whilst Germany was willing to develop its relationship with the USSR this was largely because of its continued estrangement from the Western powers and France in particular, which was underlined by France's co-opting of the new states in east-central Europe as a *cordon sanitaire* around Germany. What was ultimately to determine the character of German relations with the USSR were domestic political developments within Germany itself, specifically, the degree to which the German government could distinguish the diplomatic gains from its relationship with Moscow from the spectre of social revolution and their perception of the power of the KPD.

In spite of the KPD increasingly accommodating itself to the imperatives of Soviet foreign relations – even when such behaviour undermined the struggle to prevent the Nazis from coming to power in Germany in the early 1930s – the German ruling class could not bring itself to trust the KPD to contain any revolutionary aspirations amongst the German working class.

Similarly, relations with Britain were subject to fluctuation derived from the suspicions the British ruling class had towards the Soviet regime, combined with its paranoia about the potential for communist revolution within Britain. British policy was also concerned about Comintern activity within the Empire. The UK made it clear that the 1921 Anglo-Soviet Trade Treaty was contingent on Moscow refraining from encouraging anti-imperialist forces within the Empire.[27] The fragile nature of Anglo-Soviet relations was highlighted by the 1926 General Strike in Britain. Though the vast majority of strikers and their trade unions were not motivated by thoughts of social revolution, the British ruling class thought they were, as did Comintern. With Soviet trade unions offering financial support for British strikers, the Conservatives latched on to a tactic that would serve the British ruling class well throughout the Cold War: associating the revolutionary left, communist and non-communist, with Moscow. It seemed to work, as the election after the General Strike brought the Conservative Party to office under Stanley Baldwin, who announced the severing of diplomatic relations with Moscow in May 1927.[28]

The Fascist Threat and the Road to War, 1933–41

The diplomatic gains made by the USSR during the 1920s, which compensated for the decreasing likelihood of international revolution and which allowed the USSR to focus on increasingly serious domestic political and concerns, were of a fragile and insecure nature. It was clear that the ruling classes of capitalist Europe remained implacably hostile to the USSR and all it stood for, and that the relations European states established with Moscow were subject to change, depending on domestic political developments that Moscow was unable to determine, despite trying through directing the activities of local communists. Whereas the early period after the revolution had been characterised by fear mixed with a measure of hope and expectation, and the 1920s with a satisfaction that the USSR had managed to play the diplomatic game to its advantage, the 1930s were characterised by growing Soviet concern and worry about how the shifting international circumstances were beginning to pose a serious threat to its security.

The threats to the USSR's security came from both the east and west in the form of the militarist-imperialist states of imperial Japan and Nazi Germany. With respect to Japan, the threat emanated from Japan's imperial expansion, initially in Manchuria (north-east China) after 1931 and later, in 1937, with Japan's full-scale invasion of China. With the establishment of the Japanese-dominated 'puppet state' of Manchoukuo in February 1932, tensions between

Moscow and Tokyo intensified as the Japanese and Soviet forces (based in Mongolia) met each other at the border. Disputes over the exact location of the border triggered clashes on the Amur river, which escalated into a full-scale battle in 1938 for control of the border heights at Changkufeng. The results of these hostilities were inconclusive. Whilst serving to indicate the threat of Japanese military power in the east, a combination of the geography of the USSR – the fact that the locus of Soviet political and economic power was centred thousands of miles in the western region of the USSR – and the Japanese getting bogged down in 'pacifying' resistance to its invasion in China, as well as Japan's primary concern with dealing with the challenge to its imperial ambitions from the US, served to minimise the level of threat from the east.

This was not to be the case with respect to the threat from Nazi Germany. The significance of Nazi Germany for the Cold War and international history more generally is such that most scholars have argued that the geopolitical fault-line produced by Nazism makes any talk of Cold War in the inter-war period misplaced. Thus, in spite of the hostility towards the USSR, what was to become the deciding axis of international conflict in the inter-war period was the unfinished business of Germany's quest for imperial dominance over Europe and how this challenged the Anglo-American international order, thus reducing the geopolitical significance of Bolshevism and the USSR. The upshot is that for the inter-war period, fascism trumps communism as the principal axis of conflict in the international system, and because of this we cannot speak of a Cold War between the USSR and the major capitalist powers after 1917.

Though this is the case, at least in geopolitical terms – offensive German power came very close to reconfiguring the international system – we also need to recognise that Soviet relations with the West were not transformed 'from within', but rather as a consequence of the actions of Nazi Germany, particularly after its invasion of the USSR in June 1941, which established a common objective between Moscow and London and, soon afterwards, Washington in the defeat of fascism – something that had been extremely difficult to achieve in the preceding years.

Prior to this, the suspicion and hostility between Moscow and the Western powers was such that even after the rise of Nazism and the forewarnings of the threat posed by it – highlighted by a series of aggressive acts by Nazi Germany in the 1930s (the re-militarisation of the Ruhr, the *Anschluss* with Austria, the annexation of the Sudetenland and the occupation of Czechoslovakia) – the Western powers could not bring themselves to forge an alliance with the communist foe. What this suggests is that, without the benefit of hindsight, the rulers of Western states were willing to trust and tolerate fascism much more than they were willing to lower their guard towards the USSR and the threat of international communism. Such perceptions and actions were characteristic of Cold War. Whereas the key actors opposing the USSR after 1945 may have shifted places in geopolitical ascendancy and ideological complexion, the essence of the character of relations was very similar. Thus, whereas the traditional ruling classes in Britain, France and the US thought that Hitler could be made 'to play his game according to their rules',[29] such assumptions obviously did *not* apply to the USSR prior to June 1941, which was seen to be a *fundamentally* different form of state embodying a qualitatively different kind of political challenge. Arguably, then, until 1939 inter-systemic conflict trumped inter-imperialist conflict as defining in the relations between the great powers.

The behaviour of the Western powers in the 1930s and their inability to ally themselves with the USSR in an anti-fascist pact provides evidence of 'inter-systemic' conflict. However, it is important to recognise that the substance of inter-systemic conflict went beyond the formal diplomatic relations the USSR had with the outside world. This is important because in recognising the non-Soviet and domestic-localised eruptions of inter-systemic conflict and crisis, we are able to explain not only the Cold War but also the rise of fascism and the causes of the Second World War.

The geopolitical threat from fascist militarism, particularly with respect to Germany, emerged from inter-systemic conflict, as played out in the 'resolution' of revolutionary crises that afflicted a number of states in Europe after 1918.[30] The 'general crisis' that characterised the attempts to construct a viable and stable domestic and international political order after 1918 saw embryonic and weak liberal-constitutional states mortally wounded by the political and economic challenges they were forced to confront. Fascism, then, came to power in the context of a revolutionary crisis invoked by the spectre of communism,[31] but *not* through revolution. Whereas a revolution *requires* a political vacuum to emerge through the collapse of the coercive and administrative power of the state, (i.e. a fundamental weakening if not collapse of state power), the fascist 'conquest of the state'[32] saw fascist political movements inherit the extant apparatus of the state. With the administrative and coercive instruments of the state in their hands, they went about prosecuting a counter-revolutionary terror against the left, communist and non-communist alike, and in doing so, crushed any hopes of socialist revolution, as well as destroying any remaining residue of the liberal legal-constitutional order.[33]

The importance of this for inter-war international relations was that as much as the new fascist states were committed to the overthrow of the Versailles settlement, they were also committed to counter-revolution against the USSR and international communism. Indeed their emergence, growth and ultimate success derived from the communist-revolutionary threat. As much as these same social and political forces had been marshalled to prosecute counter-revolution and anti-Bolshevism after 1917 in and outside Russia,[34] so they were mobilised in the 1930s in response to a new conjuncture of crisis. In this sense, the fascist–communist relationship within states (particularly where they jostled for power within weak liberal states – Germany, Italy, Spain and, to a lesser extent,

France), and at an international level, principally between Germany and the USSR, could be seen as a form of international civil war and inter-systemic conflict, between the forces of revolution and counter-revolution.

The emergence of a fascist-militarist threat reversed the orientation of Soviet foreign policy. Seeing a change in its external environment and the emergence of a new threat Moscow shifted from siding with Germany and its contestation of the legitimacy of the post-1918 order to embracing the Versailles system.[35] In September 1934 the USSR joined the League of Nations, formally adopting collective security, and in May 1935, after Hitler had announced German rearmament in March – thus explicitly challenging the Versailles system – it signed a mutual assistance pact with France. This diplomatic shift went hand-in-hand with a *volte-face* in Comintern strategy with the discarding of ultra-leftism, which was officially predicated on the expectation of a new wave of revolutionary crisis in capitalism and implacable hostility to the 'social fascists' of social democracy. Ultra-leftism was replaced by the strategy of popular front, which was 'agreed' at the August 1935 Comintern Congress.

Any doubts that Stalin might have had about the wisdom of trying to forge links with the West to counter the Nazi threat were to be dismissed in 1936 as Hitler spoke of the Ukraine and Siberia as *Lebensraum* at Nuremberg rallies and the signing of the anti-Comintern pact by Germany and Japan in November 1936. However, the success of Stalin's cultivation of France and Britain necessitated a fundamental reorientation in the attitude and perceptions of the French and British ruling classes towards the USSR which was not forthcoming. Whilst Britain made no formal commitment to the USSR, France did, but the alliance never really amounted to anything other than paper commitments; the two militaries did not develop any joint planning and, in spite of the popular front strategy paying off with communist support for a socialist-led government in 1936, French commitment to the alliance remained at most distant. The hesitancy in France's willingness to join forces with the USSR was brought home over the Czechoslovak crisis in the autumn of 1938 when France and Britain caved in to German demands over the Sudetenland. The Anglo-French capitulation and spurning of Soviet offers of joint military action effectively destroyed the popular front strategy and laid the foundations for a further *volte-face* in Soviet and Comintern policy with the signing of the Nazi–Soviet pact in August 1939.[36] Drawing on recently released evidence from Soviet archives, Geoff Roberts suggests that Stalin was 'forced' into the Nazi–Soviet pact because of the failure of Britain and France to respond to his offers:

'We would have preferred an agreement with the so-called democratic countries', Stalin conceded to his closest associates, and 'we entered negotiations with them, but Britain and France wanted us to be their hired hand ... and without pay'.[37]

The shifts in Stalin's foreign policy in the 1930s, at first glance, seem to reflect a crass opportunism and desperation, which, taken together with Soviet policy towards the rise of Nazism in Germany before 1933 and the Spanish Republic in the civil war between 1936 and 1939, suggest an almost deliberate sabotaging of international revolution. Whilst it is clear that Comintern and local communist parties were increasingly dominated by the USSR's security concerns, it is less evident that Stalin was guilty of counter-revolution rather than short-sightedness and gross miscalculation. As Deutscher rightly remarked, if Stalin made colossal errors of judgement, then so did the British and French leaderships with regard to judging the threat from Hitler,[38] *as well as* the German social democrats.

What better explains the failure of Soviet policy is the contradictory interplay between Soviet foreign policy and Comintern doctrine with social and political developments within a number of crisis-ridden capitalist states. As much as the success of Soviet diplomacy in the 1920s rested on the assumption of capitalist stabilisation and domestic social peace thus reducing the spectre of revolution and any link, real or imagined, with Moscow, so it was to be in the 1930s. Try as they might, Stalin and the Comintern could not control social and political developments in other countries, or paper over the deep socio-economic and political fractures that increasingly dominated them. Consequently, 'popular frontism' failed to ease social and political tensions, most notably in France, where it appeared it might succeed; nor was it able to transform the perception of the ruling classes in Britain, France and the US towards the communist threat. Thus, the socio-economic and political developments that gave rise to communist agitation and the perception of a revolutionary threat from within by capitalist ruling classes were autonomous of the actions and policies of the USSR.

In this context developments in Spain were to be crucial. The revolution and civil war in Spain are seen as providing clear evidence of Stalin's treachery towards international revolution through the way that Soviet/Comintern policy undermined the revolutionary coalition from within. This, however, is a rather simplistic reading of both Soviet policy and the character of the Spanish Revolution. The first thing to note is the character of the Spanish Revolution itself. It was not a revolution in the classical sense of state collapse, but rather the defence of a liberal-democratic republic against armed fascist counter-revolution after a left-wing coalition government, had been elected to government, combined with a wave of strikes and land seizures, which threatened to push the new government towards revolution. The civil war is better understood, then, as a product of counter-revolution in the sense of an attempt by social forces located in the Roman Catholic hierarchy, the military, landlords and the big bourgeoisie to prevent radical, democratic social, economic and political reforms. Second, the challenge that the Republic faced was essentially military, particularly after Italy and Germany began to intervene on the side of the fascists.

The international response to the civil war, particularly the response of Britain and France, was crucial and ultimately determined how the civil war ended, much more so than Soviet policy.[39] The hostility to radicalised social reform within a bourgeois-democratic framework, let alone a communist revolution, was such that Britain and France would not come to the aid of the Spanish government. It was in this context that Stalin made policy. In light of Soviet concerns to avoid antagonising Hitler and damaging the prospects for 'popular frontism' *qua* collective security with Britain and France, after months of deliberation Moscow decided to provide military aid to the Republic but avoid any hint of the 'Sovietisation' or 'communisation' of Spain. Stalin, then, was obviously primarily concerned with the security of the USSR, and his policy towards Spain was premised on the Soviet objective of establishing an anti-fascist pact with the Western powers. Stalin wanted to reduce any political fall-out associated with communist and Soviet involvement in Spain within France and Britain that might give political ammunition to the anti-Soviet forces within these countries. Stalin obviously did not want to see the Republic defeated, but neither did he want to be associated with a social revolution in Spain that would only serve to further the cause of anti-communism and counter-revolution in Europe, of which the USSR was likely to be its principal victim.

The failure of this policy reflected Stalin's inability to understand the nature of political developments within Britain and France, and in Spain as well. Thus, the attempts by Comintern agents to uphold a popular front line of prioritising the military defeat of fascism came into conflict with those, mainly anarchist and Trotskyist groups, who advocated social revolution 'from below' as the primary means of struggle against fascism. Ironically, the ultra-leftism that Trotskyites had accused the Comintern of pursuing in Germany between 1928 and 1933, which 'opened the door' to fascism through splitting the anti-fascist camp, was now inverted, as the Comintern pursued a strategy that singled out fascism as the primary threat, thus requiring collaboration with *all* democratic forces, whilst the anti-Stalinists preached social revolution, in effect splitting the anti-fascist coalition and assisting fascist *military* victory.

Despite Soviet military support, which was crucial to the Republic's fighting potential, it was defeated by superior military power. Soviet support, then, helped and hindered the Republican cause in equal measure. Stalinist politics – the extension of the Stalinist terror launched in the USSR at the same time – most evocatively described in George Orwell's *Homage to Catalonia*, did enormous damage to the political strength and unity of the Republican cause. Yet, the Comintern line of a popular front combined with a unified and efficient army provided the best hope of victory.[40] A combination, then, of insufficient international support – largely the fault of Britain and France – and the civil war within the Republican side were the ultimate causes of the Republic's defeat.

Stalin's policy towards Spain, and in other cases during the inter-war period, reflected a tendency within Soviet foreign policy that continued into the post-1945 era under other Soviet leaders based on the need to ensure that Soviet support for any revolutionary cause would not undermine the USSR's external security situation. However, the critique of Soviet policy from the non-communist revolutionary left overlooks the primary issue that, as much as the Bolshevik Revolution (and other successful revolutions) survived due to favourable internal *and* external military circumstances, the instances of revolutionary failure and counter-revolutionary success have largely occurred because of unfavourable military circumstances. Consequently, the only way that the Spanish Republic could have been saved was through greater military power, which, in the absence of intervention from other powers, would have required Soviet military intervention, the political consequences of which these same critics would have baulked at.

The gyrations in Soviet foreign policy in the years after 1917 and leading up to the Second World War reflected the interplay of domestic and international factors. The key determinant of Soviet international relations, however, was the nature of political and economic developments outside Soviet borders. Here, it was the consequences of shifting and fluctuating inter-systemic conflict that determined the degree of hostility towards the USSR and the possibilities for revolution. Despite the spectre of revolution that hung over bourgeois Europe during the inter-war period (as it had done over pre-1914 Europe), particularly in the minds of the traditional ruling class, the prospects of social revolution were limited in the absence of externally induced (war) state collapse. The revolutionary wave of communism, then, was contingent on war. Just as Bolshevism emerged triumphant out of state collapse produced by systemic war, the absence of this meant that the structural conditions of social revolution reduced the likelihood of successful revolution during the inter-war period. Trotsky recognised this as much as Soviet party state *apparatchiks*. With systemic war after 1939, a new wave of revolution was unleashed.

THE CONTRADICTIONS OF CAPITALIST DEVELOPMENT
AND INTERNATIONAL REVOLUTION

In the final section of this chapter I will discuss the role played by communist and revolutionary movements in world politics after 1917. The significance of these movements for our understanding of the Cold War (inter- and post-war) is that:

- Many of them were associated with the Bolshevik Revolution and the USSR through their membership of Comintern, and consequently were a significant factor in Soviet foreign policy.
- Many of the revolutionary movements that emerged after 1917 were to play important roles in the post-war Cold War as they took advantage of the consequences of the Second World War to make bids for political power as in the cases of China, Indochina/Vietnam, Korea and elsewhere.

- Many of these revolutionary movements, particularly those that were officially communist, shared the same ideology, organisational features and political objectives as the Bolsheviks. In many respects they also confronted the same domestic and international problems. In this respect, we could consider communism as a specific form of politics in movement, not just confined to its manifestation in the Soviet or other revolutionary states.
- Most of the revolutionary movements that emerged in the shadow of the Bolshevik Revolution drew support from similar social constituencies (the poorer peasantry, the proletariat and the radical-nationalist intelligentsia) and were opposed by similar social forces (the traditional/landlord class, the big bourgeoisie – foreign and local – and the middle class), and also emerged out of capitalist socio-economic structures and crises very similar to that which characterised Russia before 1917.
- Finally, whilst the USSR was limited in its international reach and preoccupied with domestic and security issues, inter-systemic conflict continued as communist/revolutionary movements remained active and committed to revolutionary change and the openings afforded them by the autonomous workings of capitalist development and the periodic eruptions of crises, regardless of Soviet and/or Comintern doctrine. In this respect the inter-systemic or social conflict of the Cold War was largely carried out by social and political movements autonomous of the USSR though associated with it and committed to achieving the same historical objectives that the USSR had committed itself to. Furthermore, the activities of these movements put them on course for political and military clashes with the major capitalist powers, which had an impact on political developments where such clashes took place, but also on perceptions of the USSR – guilt by association.

I have already mentioned the role played by communist and revolutionary movements in the inter-war period in my analysis of Soviet foreign policy. In the immediate period after the 1917 revolution, Lenin and the Bolshevik leadership saw these social and political forces as providing the best opportunity, not only for the spread of revolution beyond Russia, but also for ensuring their long-term political survival.

With the failure of international revolution the role of social forces and political movements inspired by the 1917 revolution on Soviet foreign policy became more paradoxical. On the one hand, the USSR was officially committed to the spread of revolution, which required the USSR to support and encourage revolutionary forces, but at the same time it had to balance this with the imperative of developing diplomatic relations with states, particularly when the emerging consensus within the Bolshevik leadership was that the prospects of international revolution had significantly dimmed. Even Trotsky, the one individual within the Bolshevik leadership most associated with support for international revolution, was moved to say at the Third Congress of

Comintern in June 1921, 'We told ourselves back in 1919 that it [world revolution] was a question of months, but now we say that it is perhaps a question of several years'.[41] The USSR had, then, to make strategic and tactical judgements as to the prospects of political advances for revolutionary forces in Europe and beyond. The problem for the USSR was that even with Soviet diplomatic and security interests taking precedence over those of local communist parties after 1928, which effectively meant that the Comintern instructed member parties not to participate in activities that might jeopardise Soviet diplomacy,[42] the USSR was still unable to control socio-economic and political developments and the activities of revolutionary forces *and* the perceptions of anti-communist/revolutionary opinion.

This perception was as marked in the inter-war period as it was after 1945; as much as Washington detected the machinations of Moscow behind any political moves in a radical or revolutionary direction after 1945, so the British and French detected Bolshevism behind any sign of social or political militancy in the 1920–1930s. In this respect, in spite of Soviet moves towards accommodation highlighted by the popular front policy of the early 1930s and détente in the early 1970s, the activities of the revolutionary left, a product of developments that the USSR could not control, ended up undermining Soviet diplomacy.

Revolutionary and communist movements played an autonomous role throughout the Cold War. The significance of this for the inter-war period, as much for the post-war period, was that the social-systemic conflict of Cold War continued even when Soviet diplomacy sought to limit or subordinate revolutionary movements to its strategic interests, which, as in the 1930s, resulted in the USSR playing down any talk let alone support for revolution.[43]

The key point, then, with respect to the relationship between inter-systemic conflict *on the ground* and Soviet/Comintern policy is that they were, to a significant degree, divorced from each other. This had negative and positive consequences for the working-class revolutionary movement. In the former, the distance between Comintern's dogma of 'class against class' and 'social fascism' between 1928 and 1933 with the socio-economic and political reality on the ground (particularly in Germany) led the KPD effectively to assist in the victory of Nazism in 1933.[44] This contrasts with the more positive development of the popular front, particularly in France in 1934–36. In this case, the shift in Comintern tactics away from 'ultra-leftism' to the 'popular front' was partly influenced by a 'bottom-up' shift amongst French communists from hostility towards social democrats, as stipulated by Comintern policy, to joining forces with them in an anti-Fascist front after Hitler's success in Germany. However, the distance between Comintern policy objectives and the reality of class struggle on the ground was that whereas Comintern policy was meant to reassure formerly hostile anti-communists (and not just social democrats), and the French ruling class in particular, that French communists were not about to launch social revolution, but rather were committed to preserving bourgeois democracy from the threat of fascism, it had precisely the opposite effect. The popular front period initiated a wave of worker militancy and class struggle, which appeared to presage a workers' revolution.[45] This was not to be, as the objective/structural circumstances for social revolution were not in place, but it was enough to dash any hopes that the popular front in France would produce an international dividend for Moscow in a substantive French commitment to an anti-fascist pact with the USSR.

Where and what were the instances of inter-systemic conflict and how did they have an impact on the Cold War and Soviet relations with the capitalist world during the inter-war period? Whereas the post-1945 era was characterised by a much more intense pattern of inter-systemic conflict establishing itself (largely through eruptions of revolutionary crisis) outside of Europe in the global South, at least by the late 1940s with the consolidation of new political dispensations in divided Europe, the inter-war period saw inter-systemic social conflict dominate European domestic and international politics. The initial revolutionary upsurge that saw Soviet 'governments' established, albeit briefly, in Vienna, Budapest, Munich, Hamburg, Turin and Berlin, were quickly crushed by the forces of the counter-revolutionary right. However, revolutionary and communist movements continued to play an important role, as political agent and as imagined spectre, throughout the 1920s and 1930s. I have discussed these above, but to recapitulate, inter-systemic conflict involving class struggle and the political forces of socialism against those of capitalism and reaction occurred in Spain, reaching its height during the civil war of 1936–39, in France especially after 1936, in Germany in the late 1920s and early 1930s, and in Italy between 1918 and 1922. The outcome of these struggles and crisis was fascism and world war.

Inter-systemic conflict also established itself outside of Europe in a number of locales that were to become highly significant for post-war Cold War in Cuba, Vietnam, China and elsewhere. In China, inter-systemic conflict evolved into a three-way political struggle involving Chinese communists led by Mao Zedong, Chinese nationalists (the Kuomintang) led by Chiang Kai-shek and Japanese imperialist forces. In Indochina the struggle pitted a fledgling nationalist movement led by the Indochinese Communist Party against French colonial authorities. And in the case of Cuba, and Latin America more generally, a range of nationalist revolutionary movements with varied communist involvement struggled against US imperial power. None of these struggles was resolved before the Second World War, though all of them, especially the first two, were deeply affected by the geopolitical consequences of the Second World War.

In all three cases (and others), inter-systemic social conflict was played out within the struggle for national independence or what the Comintern called the national-democratic revolution. Thus, whereas the inter-systemic conflicts in Europe were primarily concerned with issues of domestic class power, in the

South, the primary objective of revolutionary movements was the eviction of external imperial domination. However, such nationalist projects could not be disentangled from class struggle because of the specific class basis of imperial domination and the role of traditional local ruling classes in the imperial project. In the three cases just mentioned local-traditional ruling classes (landlords) were either co-opted into the imperial project through securing political privileges and/or economic concessions or cowed into accepting imperial domination should indigenous subaltern classes challenge their economic wealth and power. The upshot was that alternative sources of anti-imperialist resistance emerged that sought not only to end foreign domination but also the economic exploitation carried out by local as well as foreign landlords and capitalists. Let me look at each 'revolutionary locale' – China, Indochina and Cuba – in a little more detail.

The Chinese Revolution

During the inter-war period, as much as the international context was unhelpful for revolution in Europe after the extinguishing of the revolutionary flame by 1921–22 so it was to be in Asia. The clearest evidence of this was in China. As part of Comintern's strategy of support for anti-imperialist national revolution, which amounted to a revolutionary strategy based upon a cross-class national alliance against foreign-imperial domination, the Chinese communists were a junior partner in the Kuomintang – a nationalist movement that set itself the task of uniting the disparate and fragmented elements of China and removing foreign influence. However, as events were to unfold, in an unpredictable fashion, the social contradictions within the Chinese nationalist revolution quickly revealed themselves.

Tensions between the communists and the Kuomintang were evident in the different responses to peasant revolt in Hunan in 1925–26 with the communists wanting to side with the peasants whilst the dominant right wing of the Kuomintang wanted to crush it.[46] The eruptions of peasant revolt combined with growing communist influence amongst the workers in Shanghai[47] concerned not only Chiang Kai-shek but also the British authorities in China, who announced a number of concessions to try to wean the right wing of the Kuomintang away from the communists.

The outcome was a split in the cross-class alliance, which revealed that the domestic socio-economic concerns of the Kuomintang highlighted by the threat from a communist-led worker and peasant revolution took precedence over the struggle to expel foreign interference in China, as well as highlighting the unsustainable nature of official Comintern doctrine. Consequently, a Comintern-supported workers' insurrection in Shanghai, organised and led by the CCP between February and April 1927, was crushed and following it communist militants were massacred by Chiang's forces, effectively eliminating the CCP's social base in the heart of the Chinese urban proletariat.[48]

The anti-Stalinist revolutionary left, inspired by Trotsky's critique of Comintern policy in China and paralleling its attack on Comintern policy in Spain between 1936 and 1939, blamed the Comintern for the débâcle in Shanghai in 1927 through its insistence on the Chinese communists subordinating themselves to a nationalist struggle led by the Kuomintang rather than a socialist revolutionary one. The Comintern's insistence on the 'united front' policy did put the CCP into a subordinate and ultimately vulnerable position; however, this in itself does not explain the disastrous consequences of the Shanghai insurrection. At the heart of the matter was the wider domestic and international context that was, to put it mildly, inopportune for communist-led revolution at this time.[49] The communists were small in number and concentrated in a few urban centres with no significant military force, which would allow them to challenge local warlords, much less the Kuomintang or foreign forces in China. In this sense both the Comintern and local communists were at fault. The clash with Chiang's Kuomintang brought to the surface the social conflict within the Chinese national democratic revolution, but it also exposed the absence of a revolutionary conjuncture. Until such circumstances were to change – through the combination of a shift in communist strategy, notably mobilising the peasantry, and the defeat or weakening of the external powers involved in China – the possibility of national, let alone socialist, revolution in China would not be propitious.

These developments could have destroyed communism in China but instead led to the emergence of a more independent revolutionary strategy under Mao Zedong's direction, based on mobilising the huge reservoirs of the Chinese peasantry. Under Mao, the CCP developed an independent class analysis and strategy for revolution in China. However, the doctrinal and tactical shifts were in themselves insufficient to produce social revolution. For this to occur the external and political context in which communists operated would have to change. This it did with the Japanese intervention in Manchuria and then its invasion of China in 1937. This was a prelude to inter-imperialist war with the US, the consequences of which – Japan's defeat – provided the favourable objective circumstances that made communist revolution possible.

During the Sino-Japanese war of 1937–45 the social characteristics of the conflict were also present as civil war was waged within the struggle to expel the Japanese. Whilst both nationalists and communists struggled against the Japanese occupiers, it was the communists who took the lead in the guerrilla struggle, whilst the nationalists, particularly after Pearl Harbor, waited for Japan's defeat by the US, thus preserving their forces to see off the communists.

The point here is that inter-systemic conflict, as encapsulated in the coming together of national and social revolution in China under communist leadership, was a major factor in inter-war international relations in Asia where social contradictions and conflict intersected with anti-imperialism, and where imperial powers, at least the British (and later the Americans), supported particular social forces against other social forces because of the differing (revolutionary) political objectives of each. This was to be a feature of the Cold War, with the US supporting national-democratic, as opposed to radical nationalist and/or communist, anti-colonialism. As the British had sought to isolate the Kuomintang from the communists in the 1920s, recognising the different social constituencies that each represented and the likely character of the socio-economic and political changes that each would or would not make, so the US followed, committing itself to support the Kuomintang's national rather than social revolution.

The Indochinese Revolution

The situation in Indochina bore great similarities with China, with Indochinese communists playing a leading role in anti-imperialist struggle against French colonial rule. Similarly, as much as the international conjuncture was crucial to the fortunes of Chinese communism, so it was in Indochina, with the French colonial authorities unable to re-institute pre-war French colonial power after their defeat by Japanese forces during the war and the advances made by the communists during and immediately after the war.

The nationalist struggle was strongly conditioned by social conflict – the product of the uneven penetration of capitalist social relations under French colonial rule.[50] The communist party was founded in 1930 after a period of working-class unrest in the mid–late 1920s.[51] Its influence, and the broader impact of anti-capitalist class struggle on Indochinese anti-colonialism, increased considerably during the great depression, as workers suffered the consequences of a collapse in the prices of primary exports (particularly rice and rubber) in the early 1930s.[52] Class struggle revealed itself in the spontaneous revolt that took place across Indochina in 1930–31, which severely tested the coercive resources of French colonial power.[53]

The French managed to crush the revolt and did so in a manner which quashed any hopes that the communists might have had of intensifying their anti-colonial struggle. However, this defeat did not alter the social dimension of Indochinese nationalism or the role of inter-systemic conflict in that struggle. In contrast to China where the traditional ruling class of landlords and bourgeoisie gravitated towards the Kuomintang, in Indochina after the early 1930s the nationalist struggle was increasingly dominated by the communists based on the mobilisation of workers and, increasingly, peasants. Whereas the Kuomintang was nominally committed to anti-imperialism and national unification, in Indochina the traditional ruling class was tied to the political structures of the colonial state. This was a product of the nature of capitalist penetration of Indochina, which effectively prevented the emergence of an indigenous bourgeoisie under French colonial rule combined with the dependence of indigenous landlords on the colonial state to suppress peasant revolt and land seizures. Consequently, as much as social systemic conflict in the inter-war period in China was encapsulated in the peasant/land question (after the CCP had thrown off the straitjacket of Comintern doctrinal orthodoxy), so it was in Indochina, and because the landlord class required the upholding of this iniquitous social order by force, they ultimately depended on the political forces that would ensure this – the Kuomintang in China and the French in Indochina.

The impact of social systemic conflict in south-east Asia, however, was of limited significance during the inter-war period and would become of global significance only after the French withdrew from Indochina in 1954. The reason why Indochina became one of the defining crises of the post-war era was precisely because of the social dimension of anti-imperialist struggle, something which emerged in the 1920s and which directly related to the creation of an international communist movement – Comintern – which took the lead in campaigning against imperialism in Asia. Whilst the principal opposition to national and social revolution came from French colonial power until the early 1950s, after 1954 it came from the US with its commitment to mould and create a 'free', non-communist nationalism in the South. Unfortunately, the social base of the South Vietnamese state, resting as it did on the traditional landlord class, which had signally failed to take any leading role in the anti-colonial struggle due to its political dependence first on the French and then the Americans, proved too narrow and weak a foundation upon which to build a viable state.

Social Conflict in Latin America, the Cuba Revolution and US Imperialism

Thus far my discussion of inter-war international relations as an episode of Cold War has made only very fleeting reference to the US, one of the two principal state participants in the Cold War after 1945. The absence of the US from European affairs in particular reflected its decision to disengage from Europe after 1918–19 and the continuing, though declining, strength of the European great powers. However, in the case of the international politics of Latin America, the defining role of the US made for a very different story.

The geographical distance from Europe and the USSR in particular was a major factor in Washington's perception of the rather limited geopolitical challenge posed by the USSR in contrast to the European capitalist powers. This did not, however, prevent the US from taking significantly longer to establish diplomatic relations with Moscow. The US was, then, implacably opposed to communism, but its concern was much less with the USSR than with the perceived menace from communist political subversion from within the US[54] and also the threat to US political and economic interests from revolutionary forces – communist and non-communist – in its 'regional backyard'.

In this sense Leffler[55] is right to distinguish the nature of the communist threat that concerned Washington prior to the Second World War, but he is wrong to imply that the nature of inter-war US anti-communism was substantively different from the anti-communism that guided US policy after 1945.

Although US anti-communism was given a geopolitical formula – containment – which it did not have in the inter-war era, in response to the increased international power of the USSR after the Second World War, US anti-communism, indeed, Washington's hostility to radical socio-economic change more broadly, was concerned with the same thing before the war as it was after the war – the fear of what the US saw as the 'Sovietisation' of the US and/or its neighbours through the activities of domestic and local communists/revolutionaries.[56] Furthermore, as much as the USSR was unable to challenge the US geopolitically in the western hemisphere before the Second World War so its post-war challenge was also fundamentally limited. It was not until the late 1960s that the USSR developed a naval capacity which allowed it to project itself beyond the Eurasian landmass and when it did offer a geopolitical challenge to the US in 1962 (over Cuba) it could do so only because of the consequences of domestic revolutionary upheaval. The Cold War in Latin America, then, as elsewhere was about the consequences of domestic socio-economic and political change, as this was the prerequisite for any geopolitical challenge to US power.

Prior to the 1917 Bolshevik Revolution the US, like other capitalist great powers, had shown itself to be suspicious, if not hostile, to revolutionary social change. This was clearly expressed in 1898 when the US intervened with military force at the end of the Cuban War of Independence against Spanish colonial rule.[57] The US intervention prevented the Cuban people from organising their post-colonial affairs themselves and suggested that the US had emerged as an 'imperial anti-colonial power',[58] committed to ensuring that US external power would play an increasingly influential role in shaping the domestic affairs of the region. This more intrusive and coercive policy was nakedly expressed with the US effectively drafting the constitution of the newly 'independent' Cuba and inserting the infamous Platt Amendment in 1901 which provided it with a legal cover for military intervention should political events in Cuba turn against US interests.

The intervention in Cuba was to establish a pattern of US military interventions in the region in response to domestic political instability and the threat of socio-economic transformation, in Mexico, Panama, Cuba, Nicaragua, El Salvador and Haiti. In most if not all of these cases of political instability, communist parties did not play a leading role,[59] but this should not prevent us from recognising the centrality of social conflict, not only in provoking domestic political crises in these states, but also as the primary reason for US intervention. Communist parties had to compete with pre-existing indigenous sources of revolutionary ideology and struggle dating from the anti-colonial experience of the people in the region. Furthermore, as members of Comintern, communists also implemented Comintern doctrine, which, at certain junctures, prevented them from taking advantage of and playing a leading role in local eruptions of social crisis and leading revolutionary struggle. In many respects, then, US post-war policies of intervention against revolution that dominated

US foreign policy and US presidential doctrines from Truman to Reagan orig-inated in the western hemisphere decades before 1947. The geographical and geopolitical context was different, but the ideological and social substance behind intervention remained constant.

The inter-war period, as much as the post-1945 period, then, saw the US committed to a strategy of counter-revolution in Latin America in response to the intensification of social conflict and periodic moments of revolutionary cri-sis. One of the most significant eruptions of social conflict that did involve a communist party and which was to foreshadow post-war developments in the region concerned the revolutionary crisis in Cuba between 1930 and 1933. The US role in establishing an 'independent' Cuba between 1898 and 1902 initiated a relationship that typified the more assertive US role in Latin America. US involvement went beyond the collusion of the island's political elite with US political interests, by amounting to a quasi-colonial economic and cultural relationship through the pervasive influence of US commerce and popular cul-ture on the island, and US control of most of the island's productive assets. Just as the traditional dominant classes in Indochina were effectively dependent on the French colonial state and thus incapable of organising and leading anti-colonial struggle, so the Cuban bourgeoisie and landlord class were deeply enmeshed in relations with US capital and the US state, and consequently inca-pable of ridding Cuba of the US's neo-colonial hold over the island.

The social contradictions at the heart of Cuba exploded in the revolutionary crisis of 1930–33. The crisis emerged out of economic turmoil precipitated by the Great Depression. The trigger to the explosion of social conflict originated in the US response to the collapse in world agricultural prices with the passing of the Smoot–Hawley Act in 1930, which increased the excise duty on Cuban sugar. Following this, the Cuban share of the US market, upon which Cuba was almost completely dependent, declined from 49.4 per cent in 1930 to 25.3 per cent in 1933; sugar production fell by 60 per cent and exports by 80 per cent.[60] With the Cuban political leadership inert, Cuban workers in the form of CNOC (*Confederacion Nacional Obreros de Cuba*) organised a general strike in August 1933, which resulted in the seizure of a large number of American-owned sugar mills and the establishment of 'soviets'. With the capitalist social order under threat and with it the US economic *and* political presence on the island, the US dispatched Assistant Secretary of State Sumner Welles to the island to try to bring an end to the crisis and the momentum of social revolution. The outcome was a US-endorsed military coup which brought to power the dictatorship of Fulgencia Batista, who was to play a dominant role in policing Cuba for local and US capital until his regime was overthrown in 1959.

The significance of these events in Cuba is that they revealed the social contradictions typical of many state-society complexes integrated into the world capitalist economy through colonial and neo-colonial relationships dur-ing the inter-war period and also after 1945. The consequence of these social contradictions was class conflict and political instability which challenged not only the power of the traditional Cuban social and political elite but also the US social presence on the island.

The Cuban communist party played an ambivalent role in the revolutionary crisis of 1930–33. Whilst playing an important part in initiating the general strike through its influence in the CNOC, it was also instrumental in bringing the crisis to an end by accommodating itself and its cadres to the Batista regime and the social concessions made by Batista. The communist accommodation with the military dictatorship reflected the many other instances where communist parties, usually following doctrinal pronouncements from Moscow, found themselves on the margins of class struggle being waged by social constituencies – workers and peasants – that communist parties supposedly represented.

Furthermore, the developments in Cuba in the 1930s, but also more widely in Latin America (the revolutionary struggles led by Augusto Sandino in Nicaragua and Agustín Farabundo Martí in El Salvador), highlight the presence of inter-systemic social conflict and US hostility and intervention against revolution before the official onset of the Cold War after 1945. In these cases, as in Cuba in 1959, Guatemala in 1954 and Nicaragua and El Salvador in the 1970–1980s, revolutionary struggle was a product of local social contradictions which implicated the US, but not the USSR. Cold War then could involve *dramatis personae* that did not always include the USSR or the US (as was the case in areas beyond the western hemisphere) prior to the end of the Second World War.

What this suggests is that Cold War conflict was a social conflict between forms of socio-economic system and how these systems rested on particular social constituencies and mobilisations. States (and the superpowers) were obviously manifestations in an organisational, administrative and coercive sense of class power, but the social antagonism of Cold War was not confined to states. Rather it concerned, as these and other examples indicate, constellations of social interests competing for control of state power. What made these episodes of social conflict 'inter-systemic' was that they rested on rival visions of socio-economic organisation, with the struggle 'from below' waged by revolutionary movements whose organisational form, ideological basis and political strategy was largely inspired by the 1917 Bolshevik Revolution in the social, economic and political tasks that these movements set themselves and how they related to the major capitalist powers.

CONCLUSIONS: WORLD WAR AND SOCIAL CONFLICT

The inter-war period was dominated by explosions of social conflict contributing to waves of revolutionary crises across the world and, ultimately, world war. The sources of conflict derived from the social contradictions of capitalist development within and between states as antagonistic social constituencies struggled to control state power and/or reconstitute the socio-economic basis of the state and as rival states competed to secure and dominate spheres of interest, economic resources, markets and strategic access points. It was this competition for *global* hegemony that caused the Second World War.

Domestic social conflict played a key role in bringing the world to war. In particular the establishment of fascist-military states was a product of a series of domestic political crises, where states were taken over by fascist movements committed to domestic and international counter-revolution against the communist- revolutionary threat and military-dominated territorial-economic conquest and expansion. The war brought together the USSR and the two leading liberal-capitalist states, Britain and the US, in common cause against fascism. This alliance between formerly antagonistic states – the USSR and Britain had considered military conflict with the other prior to 1939 and between August 1939 and June 1941 were on opposing sides in divided Europe – hid deeper social and political tensions between all three powers below the surface of unity in response to the threat from fascism.

These tensions concerned not only the prosecution of the war against fascism, in particular over which state would carry the biggest military burden in the defeat of fascism and Nazi Germany,[61] the most powerful of the fascist enemies, in particular, but also the differing and conflicting visions of the post-war world. Thus, whereas Britain was fighting to keep its empire as much as ridding the world of fascism, the US was fighting to ensure that the post-war world would be based on a political and economic vision encapsulated in the internationalisation of the domestic political-economy of the US. In this sense the US post-war vision was at loggerheads with both Britain, which wished to maintain its system of imperial preferences, the supremacy of sterling as the currency of international trade and restrictions on the economic activities of other capitalist states within the empire, all of which fundamentally contradicted the US vision of open and 'free' international economic exchange,[62] and the USSR, with its objective of securing itself from future military threats by expanding its communist party-state model to east-central Europe, and thus eliminating non-Soviet sources of political and economic influence and power.

The differing priorities that each state had and the method each advocated for the defeat of fascism, and each state's post-war vision, also reflected distinct social interests. For Britain the war was first and foremost a defence of the survival of the British bourgeoisie and second a war to ensure the continued strength and prosperity of British capital as a global social force. For the US, the war had provided 'salvation' for US capitalism, gripped as it was by almost a decade of economic stagnation and rising social tensions, but also a way of expanding US local economic power by replacing Britain and the other European colonial powers as the state responsible for managing the international economy. Finally, for the USSR the war was to preserve the specific social interests associated with the party-state's monopoly of political and economic power and its primary goal of developing the productive forces of the USSR.

The war also had a significant impact on social and political relations within the three main anti-fascist states. The mobilisation of society and economy by the state for total war effectively terminated capitalist economic relations in the spheres of production, distribution, exchange and consumption as most areas of economic activity were determined by the political imperative of national survival and victory. This was already the case in the USSR where a command, state-directed economy had been established after 1928 and which played a pivotal role in the defeat of Germany. It was much more pronounced in Britain than in the US. Thus, there was less rationing in the US and although the state played an increasingly 'hands-on' role in directing war production, the level of state-socialisation of economic activity was much less than in Britain, where the rule of capital was replaced by the rule of state-capital with the co-opting of the organised working class into the heart of the capitalist state. Such developments were to play a crucial role in the social advancements of the British working class and the concessions made by British capital between 1945 and 1950.

The significance of these developments is that they reflected a struggle between different social interests. Thus, although war in many respects suppressed the social contradictions of capitalist development that had dominated inter-war international relations, the war did not eliminate them. The fundamental clash between capital and labour was a factor in wartime production in both the US and the UK, with workers using the threat of strike action to secure material concessions from a resentful capitalist class. Social tensions of a different kind were evident in the USSR,[63] mainly expressed through nationalist hostility towards communist dictatorship and with significant numbers of non-Russians siding with the Nazis.

Social conflict was also present in the numerous popular liberation struggles that took place in all the theatres of the war. This was most evident in the role played by nationalist, anti-colonial movements in Asia. For these social forces, the war was primarily about the end of colonial occupation – Japanese or European. The defeat of Japan in August 1945 provided a crucial platform for nationalist forces to gain the upper hand in the areas formerly under European administration before the Second World War. National revolution combined with social revolution, particularly in those cases where revolutionary movements were inspired by communist revolution, as in Korea, Indochina, China and the Philippines.

In these countries the impact of the war was felt differently by different social classes and their political representatives, and this was a primary factor in support that different anti-colonial movements sought to mobilise both during and after the war. This was also the case in Europe where class mobilisations played an important role in the anti-fascist resistance in the Balkans, France and Italy. Communist partisans played a leading role in harrying German occupying forces and, in the cases of Yugoslavia and Greece, class conflict spilt over into civil war during the war, culminating in the victory of Tito's communist partisans over the nationalist (Serbian) *Chetniks* and

(Croatian) *Ustashe*, and after the war in Greece with the civil war, where British forces came to the aid of right-wing pro-Royalist forces against the communists (supported by Tito but not by Moscow). In these cases, and Greece in particular, Cold War social conflict could not have been clearer.

The war had an uneven impact on different social constituencies. Capital had been weakened in Europe, but not defeated, whereas workers and peasants had borne the brunt of the war as victims and participants, they had also gained power through their role in the war effort of the key Western allied powers, particularly through the expansion of state control over the economy and also in those countries where local nationalist resistance to fascism had been led by communists mobilising workers and peasants. It was these developments that signalled the continuation of social struggle and Cold War during the Second World War and which contributed to the balance of social and political forces at the war's end, which was to play an important role in the developing geopolitical antagonism between the US and the USSR, which I will turn to in Chapter 3.

3

The Cold War Transformed: Geopolitical Restructuring and a New Wave of Social Revolution, 1945–49

INTRODUCTION

In the previous chapter I argued that a Cold War existed in the period from the foundation of the USSR in 1917 up to and including the Second World War. The sources of inter-war Cold War were twofold:

- the emergence of the Soviet state and the hostility towards it from the major capitalist powers; and
- the persistence of inter-systemic social conflict involving the USSR (through its growing domination of Comintern), but also, and more importantly, local communist and revolutionary movements against the social forces of local and international capital.

These two elements were transformed by the Second World War. Through its overcoming of German military power and occupation of east-central Europe, the USSR emerged as a geopolitical power of the first rank earning it the sobriquet of 'superpower'. Whilst the USSR had prospered geopolitically, the consequences of the war also altered the balance of social forces in Europe and elsewhere. Prior to the war, the revolutionary left, particularly in Europe, had been severely weakened and in some cases physically eliminated by the rise of fascism. However, through their leading role in the resistance to fascist occupation, and the weakening and/or destruction of the administrative and coercive capacities of a number of capitalist states by the war, communist-revolutionary forces ended the war in a position of considerable political advantage. The strengthened position of the USSR and the social forces of communist revolution contrasted with the vulnerability of the European capitalist classes and the towering military and economic power of the United States. The end of the Second World War, then, *re*produced patterns of inter-systemic competition and conflict evident after 1917 but in a slightly altered *form*, which was to frame post-war international history and determine the character and outcome of the Cold War.

The competition and antagonism between the US and the USSR – the superpower/bipolar conflict – over how the post-war world would be reordered and which state's global political vision would prevail have dominated the literature on the Cold War. However, there were other important relationships and sources of conflict that this concentration on the superpower relationship has tended to overlook. Inter-capitalist/imperialist conflict had been a major cause of the two world wars out of which two waves of revolutions emerged. However, in contrast to the post-1918 period, the post-1945 era saw a fundamental transformation of the capitalist world as it was 'united' under US leadership. Capitalist stability contributed to political stability within and between the major capitalist states and the decline of revolutionary expectations. The significance of this was not only that one of the most fundamental ideological assumptions of Marxism-Leninism,[1] upon which Soviet domestic and foreign policy rested, became effectively redundant, but it also made even more acute the pressures upon the USSR's domestic political economy, as its objective of surpassing the productive potential and capacity of the major capitalist states assumed the continuation of ever more severe and damaging economic crises that would result in either economic stagnation and/or socialist revolution. The post-war stabilisation of the advanced capitalist world was, then, an outcome of the Second World War as significant as the bipolar distribution of geopolitical power. Indeed, in terms of *world historical development*, it was to prove to be more momentous.

The third defining international relationship of the post-war Cold War era was that between communist/revolutionary movements (and states) with the capitalist world (not just the US) and the USSR. These sources of social conflict were a continuation of the inter-systemic social conflict of the inter-war period. However, whereas Europe had been the crucible of social conflict and revolutionary crisis during the inter-war period, after the stabilisation of bourgeois order in Europe by the late 1940s, the axis of social conflict and revolutionary crises moved to the south, providing the dynamic for the shifting crises and geopolitical confrontations of the post-war era. Furthermore, as much as the actions of communist movements in the inter-war period had highlighted the geopolitical constraints on Soviet support for international revolution so it was to be in the post-war era *in spite of* the geopolitical strengthening of the USSR. Whereas Soviet geopolitical weakness had been mitigated by splits and conflicts between the major capitalist states during the inter-war period, the unification of the advanced capitalist world under US leadership, combined with the commanding advantage of US strategic power over the USSR, countered Soviet wartime geopolitical gains.

The Second World War, then, produced a new geopolitical constellation centred on the USSR and the US, a reordered capitalist world economy managed by the US and a new wave of social conflict and communist revolution spreading beyond the borders of Europe. Whilst the war had seen the USSR defeat its most serious military threat, in Nazi Germany, and through the Red Army's victories saw the expansion of the Soviet social system into east-central Europe, the war also left it facing a very different *form* of capitalist foe. Whilst one does not have to accept the ideologically-loaded characterisation of the US as a bastion of 'freedom', 'democracy' and 'liberty' in contrast to the 'totalitarian' Soviet Union, US capitalist power and the capitalist world economy that it reordered after 1945 were significantly different from the imperial(ist) order that preceded it. This was significant for two reasons:

- The relations within and between the major capitalist states developed into a pattern different from earlier eras. Whereas (world) war had been the means of resolving the contradictions and conflicts amongst the leading capitalist states in the past, because of a combination of the military dominance of the US and the way in which it organised and managed the international economy after 1945, through multilateral institutions and inter-governmental co-operation, inter-capitalist relations became much more stable and, where tensions and conflicts emerged, they were not resolved through inter-capitalist war. In sum, the capitalist world, after riding out the initial post-war years of instability and economic crisis, mainly a consequence of the devastation and chaos caused by the war, quickly moved towards unity, stability and prosperity.
- The capitalist world as a collective entity, and the individual states within it, that the USSR now confronted were also quite different from the capitalist world from which the USSR emerged out of systemic crisis and revolution in 1917. Whereas the USSR met and defeated the militaristic capitalist challenge in the form of fascism between 1941 and 1945 and 'prospered' in a world of imperial-capitalist blocs riven by inter-imperialist contradictions and conflict, these political and economic strengths were to prove to be a source of vulnerability and weakness by the 1980s. The transformed nature of capitalism and its leading states was significant for the USSR not only in transforming the nature of international competition between Soviet socialism and US-led capitalism, but also with the dismantling of the European colonial empires, (American) capitalist social relations and capitalist forms of state could be maintained and expanded without requiring direct and formal political domination, highlighted by US support for decolonisation and national self-determination. This contrasted with both the formal and directly coercive, indeed, militarised nature of imperialist capitalist expansion of the previous epoch, and the expansion – on the back of the Red Army – of the Soviet social system in east-central Europe.

Discussion of the post-war period of Cold War has been dominated by the debate amongst (mainly American) diplomatic historians over the origins and causes of the Cold War focusing on the question(s): Who was to blame or who caused the Cold War? My concern in this chapter is less with apportioning blame for the breakdown of the wartime alliance or trying to adjudicate in this debate amongst historians. Rather, I will discuss the key developments, centring on Europe, in the ending of the wartime alliance and the move towards geopolitical confrontation between the USSR and the US and its Western allies. Briefly, my explanation for the collapse of the wartime alliance will focus on the clash between two forms of state, arguing how the different socio-economic properties of each superpower made diplomatic accommodation, ultimately, impossible in the same way that it had been unattainable prior to the Second World War. In this sense, what needs explanation is not the emergence of the post-war antagonism between the USSR and the US,[2] the communist and capitalist social systems, but rather their accommodation and alliance in the defeat of fascism. The history of inter-war international relations and the character and manner in which the war was prosecuted made (the renewal of) Cold War highly likely. However, the drive towards Cold War was not solely a product of increasingly conflictual bilateral diplomacy between Moscow and Washington, as most diplomatic historians would have us believe, but also – as was the case after 1917 – due to the explosions of social conflict and the spectre of revolutionary crisis. The implication of the USSR in these crises, in Italy, France, Germany and elsewhere, even where the USSR had disassociated itself from such revolutionary struggles, as in Greece, was sufficient to undermine fundamentally the wartime relationship between the USSR and the western capitalist states.

The chapter is organised in the following way. First, I will discuss the geopolitical consequences of the war and the attempts by the 'big three' to order post-war Europe. This section will highlight the different, antagonistic visions of post-war Europe and will also engage with some of the arguments in the historical debate over the 'origins of the Cold War'. The second section will discuss the relations between the capitalist states, the degree of conflict and how this contributed to the consolidation of Cold War after 1945. The final section discusses the renewed bouts of intensified social conflict and revolutionary crisis and how this had an impact on the superpowers and their bilateral relationship.

THE GEOPOLITICAL CONSEQUENCES OF WAR

The geopolitical changes wrought by the Second World War and its consequences have provided the historical facts from which explanations and theories of the Cold War have been based. Simply put, the new socio-economic, political and ideological borders within Europe, which were to last until 1989, were determined by the furthermost points of advance of the Allied armies: the Red Army in the east and Anglo-American forces in the west.[3]

The Orthodox-Revisionist Debate on the 'Origins of the Cold War'

The debate on the origins of the Cold War has focused on why Europe emerged out of 1945 divided in this way and why this 'territorial division of spoils' was to cause the disintegration of the wartime alliance and decades of hostility between the USSR and the US. The 'orthodox' or traditional account[4] of the Cold War blames the USSR, and Stalin in particular, for the deterioration in intra-allied relations and Cold War. The essence of the orthodox argument is that US policy was largely reactive to Soviet acts of aggression in east-central Europe reflected in the creeping Sovietisation of the region after 1945. The division of Europe and the expansion of Soviet power through military coercion, political intimidation and subversion caused US hostility and the policy of containment, to prevent any further expansion of Soviet power. The key orthodox assumption is that whereas the USSR had a preconceived plan for the domination of east-central Europe and Soviet expansion, the US did not. Instead, the US, and President Roosevelt in particular, assumed that the USSR would join with the Western allies in the newly established United Nations to manage world affairs on the basis of the anti-fascist alliance.

The orthodox account dominated US diplomatic history throughout the 1950s[5] largely due to the bipartisan political consensus around anti-communism that had emerged by the late 1940s in the US, combined with the impact of McCarthyism, which provided a political and intellectual context highly unfavourable to the criticism of this consensus. The emergence of a very different account of the causes of the Cold War emerged in the 1960s, reaching the peak of its influence at the high point of US involvement in Vietnam in 1968. As much as the social and political context of the late 1940s and 1950s had promoted the conservative account of the origins of the Cold War so the radicalised social and political context of the 1960s helped produce an account that was much more critical of US actions.

The Revisionist or radical account of the origins of the Cold War turns the spotlight of critical attention and blame away from Moscow and towards Washington.[6] Whereas the orthodox account emphasises the USSR's use of force and coercion in east-central Europe after 1945 the Revisionist account emphasises the significance of US economic power[7] and how the US attempted to use its superiority to try to undermine Soviet influence in east-central Europe through the Marshall Plan and other economic instruments. The orthodox account identifies the combination of traditional Russian expansionism and communist ideology as being the main reason for the outbreak of Cold War, while the Revisionist account identifies the tensions and contradictions within US capitalism, which necessitated the dismantling of (political) restrictions on open international exchange, trade and investment.

Revisionist scholars base their accounts, to varying degrees, on the idea of an American 'open door' empire and imperial 'anti-colonialism' associated with the work of William Appleman Williams. Gabriel Kolko's work is the most explicit in this regard; he argues that US post-war foreign (economic) policy was based upon securing access to new markets and raw materials to benefit the interests of capital and also to reorder the world economy after the crisis of the inter-war period. The key obstacles to the US realising such objectives were, in order of significance, anti-capitalist revolutionary movements, the British Empire and the USSR. The importance of this is that Kolko plays down the substance of the USSR as a cause of, or even significant factor in, the Cold War by emphasising the autonomous nature of revolutionary movements, and also the role of inter-capitalist conflict between the US and Britain. The upshot is that the Cold War is regarded as a conflict between US imperialism and global anti-capitalism, increasingly located in the third world.

As much as we can criticise the orthodox account for its rather one-dimensional explanation, so we can with the Revisionist argument.[8] Consequently, as much as the USSR did use coercion and intimidation to consolidate its political hold over east-central Europe after 1945, we also need to recognise the role of *defensive* security concerns in Soviet expansion into east-central Europe. Although the USSR won the war it did so at an immense human and economic cost.[9] The imperative of post-war reconstruction and security was, then, a key factor in motivating Stalin's policy in east-central Europe as much as political expansion.

However, we also need to recognise the significance of the character of the Soviet state and the type of international relations it was capable of constructing as a way of expanding its influence and power. In contrast to the US, which could and did deploy private and economic sources of influence in Western Europe, as a way of ordering the international and domestic political economy of post-war Western Europe and, in doing so, consolidating US influence and power in the region,[10] the USSR deployed explicitly political and military sources of power to secure its hegemony in east-central Europe. In this sense the form of Soviet international expansion was directly political and coercive, and was tied to the extension of Soviet political and coercive institutions and relations, which in effect transformed the nature of state power in the areas where Soviet expansion took place, in contrast to the 'American Empire' in Western Europe, which effectively preserved the character of state power there or refashioned it according to the principles of capitalist liberal democracy.

The issue of the character of the Soviet state – its method of expansion – and its *legitimate* defensive security needs after two devastating wars, also relate to the problem of realising its security concerns in east-central Europe and Poland in particular with western political and ideological concerns. In light of the history of Polish nationalism, the Nazi–Soviet pact, the massacre of Polish officers by the NKVD in 1940 and the failure of the Red Army to come to the aid of the Warsaw uprising in 1944, there was little prospect of the Polish people choosing to form a security alliance with the USSR after 1945, Stalin's key objective. Furthermore, because of the way that the Soviet Union was politically constituted, Stalin could have faith in the loyalty of Poland (and this also applied to the areas of the USSR that had been under German occupation between 1941 and 1943) only through the extension of communist power, i.e. the construction of a party-state in Poland modelled on the structure of the USSR. The alternative of independence or 'neutrality' based on a liberal democratic political system, as the Western allies desired, risked two things: the possibility of an anti-Soviet government coming to power which might again threaten the security of the USSR; and, how an independent Poland (and east-central Europe) might not 'co-operate' in the post-war reconstruction of the USSR.

We need to see the Soviet expansion into east-central Europe after 1945 as reflecting the *form* of Soviet international relations *combined with* its security needs. The US had security needs of a political, military and economic nature too with regard to Europe after 1945, though we might qualify such needs in light of the US's vastly different wartime experience and its *strategic* military and economic strength in 1945. However, because of the way that it was domestically constituted as a capitalist state, US security needs and post-war political-ideological objectives were at odds with those of the USSR. For the US, security rested upon the maintenance and spread of 'American-like' political and economic systems, as this was the best, indeed the only, way not only of maintaining a favourable external security context, but also of preserving the domestic political and economic character of the US. As much as fascism was a threat to the US security – economic and military in equal measure – through its closing off of large areas of the world to 'open' international economic exchange by militarist expansion, so were Soviet actions in east-central Europe and revolutionary seizures of power in China and elsewhere after 1945.

The significance of this for our understanding of post-war developments between the US and the USSR is that whereas US security was enhanced by the (re)establishment of liberal capitalism in Western Europe, which did not require a US or, for that matter, a local-national state political-military presence, over the societies of Western Europe,[11] Soviet-communist security necessitated quite the opposite, a political-military presence over and within society. Both sides *politically* expanded after 1945 in the two halves of Europe to the furthest points of each respective army and in this sense Stalin was absolutely right in stating that '[w]hoever occupies a territory also imposes on it his own social system. Everyone imposes his own social system as far as his army can reach'.[12] However, whereas Soviet expansion took the form of the domestic character of the Soviet state – centralised, authoritarian, coercive and militarised and centred on the communist party's monopoly of socio-economic and political power – US expansion took the form of the US state – resting on the bourgeois separation of state and economy permitting political influence and power through international capitalist economic relations.

Whereas any encroachment of the liberal-capitalist form of state and politics into east-central Europe threatened to undermine the security of the Soviet *communist* state (as it did in 1956, 1968, 1980–81 and 1989) so did any intrusion of communist influence – Soviet or otherwise – into Western Europe (as in Italy and France, in particular between 1945 and 1947) threaten to undermine US security. In this sense, then, both Revisionist and orthodox accounts of the Cold War are partly correct, but not for the reasons that each set of scholars suggest. The realisation of one side's security contradicted the other. However, what the Revisionists do recognise (and what, in the main, the orthodox account does not) is the significance for particular social interests of the realisation (or not) of US liberal-capitalist and Soviet-communist security. US security preserved the capitalist class in Western Europe, whilst Soviet security in east-central Europe required the elimination of the capitalist class and the social property relations upon which its class rule rested. This social aspect of the rival conceptualisations of 'security' was not made explicit in the discussion of post-war Europe, but it was at its heart none the less, as US power concerned itself with preserving and expanding the rule of capital and upholding private property rights and consequently the social interests which benefited from this. In contrast the USSR saw capitalism as a threat to the security of the party-state's monopoly of political and economic power.

What this account also suggests is the inevitability of conflict between Moscow and Washington after 1945 – a renewal of the conflict that characterised relations between the USSR and western capitalist states prior to the Second World War. This is not to be deterministic, as there was always the possibility of political change on either side triggering a transformation in relations, but rather to focus on the character of each side's form of state and how the different, antagonistic forms of politics and state were incompatible.

The Sovietisation of Poland and East-Central Europe

The two key conferences of 1945 to decide the post-war future – in February at Yalta (in the Crimea) and between late July and early August at Potsdam (a suburb of Berlin) – and the ongoing diplomatic negotiations involving the 'Big Three' quickly brought these antagonisms to the surface. The flashpoints that emerged at the war's end were the nodes of geopolitical friction over Poland (and Soviet-occupied east-central Europe), Germany/Berlin, Iran and Turkey.

With respect to Poland, forewarnings of post-war disagreement between the USSR and the Western allies were apparent before Yalta and Potsdam after the USSR broke off diplomatic relations with the (London-based) Polish government-in-exile in 1943.[13] With the crossing of the Red Army into what was pre-1939 Polish territory in 1944 Moscow refused the claims of the London Poles of the right to administer liberated Poland. Instead, Stalin established an alternative Polish government, the so-called Lublin Committee (named after the town in eastern Poland in which it was based), which was dominated by pro-Soviet communists. Furthermore, and which spoke more tellingly of Stalin's intentions towards Poland, the USSR undermined the Western allies' efforts to back the Warsaw uprising of August 1944 by refusing to allow British or American planes to land on Soviet-controlled territory. Without external support, the uprising was brutally crushed by the Germans. For Stalin, the uprising had not altered his preoccupation with the destruction of the *Wehrmacht*, and although Soviet (in)action had shocked his admirers in the West,[14] for Stalin it seemed a political price worth paying as the defeat of the Warsaw uprising ensured that Soviet power in 'liberated' Poland was unlikely to be contested by Polish armed force.

Developments in Poland mirrored those elsewhere in Soviet-occupied east-central Europe. In 'liberated' east-central Europe the pattern established with Soviet direction saw pro-Soviet and communist elements control ministries responsible for the police and army laying the foundation for a series of 'revolutions from above' which consolidated Stalinist control by the late 1940s across all of east-central Europe. Whilst ostensibly committed to the continuation of anti-fascist politics based on coalition governments including non-communists,[15] the *Allied* commitment to the purge of fascists from the government and administration of newly liberated territories benefited communist elements as the most organised anti-communist elements had been those most associated with fascism. Furthermore, under Soviet direction, anti-fascist campaigns became campaigns targeting whole social groups rather than individuals, using coercive and administrative means rather than due legal process. Mazower also highlights how in Hungary during negotiations to establish a provisional government, even before Germany's defeat, the Soviets insisted on a wide-ranging anti-fascist purge that went much further than the pro-Nazi Arrow Cross movement, but also included 'the "full liquidation of feudal structures" and measures against "reactionaries" in state and society'.[16]

Without *directly* using force, then, the Soviets gradually engineered the steady augmentation of local communist power in east-central Europe through a mixture of intimidation, electoral fraud and a rather zealous interpretation of anti-fascism. With the gradual escalation of tension between Moscow and Washington after 1945 and with the US making its intention clear – in opposing communist seizures of power and subversion of liberal democracy – with the announcement of the Truman Doctrine in March 1947, the tendencies evident in Soviet behaviour in east-central Europe in the early months after liberation became much more marked as non-communists were removed from political office and communist party-state monopolies were established.[17]

The Division of Germany

The division of Europe paralleled the division of Germany. Although the Allies had agreed to preserve the unity of Germany at Yalta and Potsdam with the establishment of the Allied Control Council, this formal consensus hid underlying differences.[18] This was evident in the USSR's unilateral alteration of Germany's eastern border with Poland by transferring all the territory east of the Oder and Niesse rivers to Poland (after the USSR had annexed former Polish territory further east) along with the forced expulsion of the German population from these areas. Territorial change was also accompanied by the effective transformation of Soviet-occupied Germany with the dismantling of German industry and its shipment to the USSR to replace the factories and machinery laid waste by the *Wehrmacht*.

Whilst the Soviets set about the economic plunder of eastern Germany as reparations for its wartime losses, and as a means to realising its vision of post-war security, the Western allies, and the US in particular, began to pursue contradictory policies in their zones of occupation. At Potsdam, Britain and the US rejected Soviet demands for joint control of the Ruhr, Germany's industrial heartland, which was situated in the western zone, and US Secretary of State Byrnes had ensured that reparations to the USSR from the American sector in Germany would be limited so as not to impede Germany's post-war reconstruction.[19] The socio-economic interests at the heart of both sides' visions of post-war Germany (as for all of Europe) soon began to make a mockery of the idea of a unified Germany. The USSR's confiscation of private property and seizure of economic assets rankled with the US vision of an economically reinvigorated Germany based on the sanctity of private property, which the US saw as integral to its plans for a stable and prosperous post-war international capitalist economy. The result of these contradictory policies was the suspension of reparation payments to the USSR from the American/Western zone in May 1946.

By the middle of 1947 the three western zones (British, French and American) began to implement a common set of economic policies. The *de facto* division of Germany, in spite of new Soviet proposals, tabled by Molotov, the Soviet foreign minister in July 1946, for a neutral but united Germany, was more or less sealed in March 1948 with the introduction of a new currency in the western half. With a common currency it seemed only a matter of time before the western sectors were politically united. Containing almost three-quarters of the population and the bulk of its industrial plant, the prospect of a separate West Germany associated with the US set alarm bells ringing in Moscow.

It was in this context that the USSR decided to apply pressure on the most vulnerable point of the western presence in Germany – the western half of Berlin deep inside the Soviet zone of occupation. The 'Berlin Blockade' of June 1948 to May 1949 – the severing by the USSR of all western land links to west Berlin – was meant to exert leverage on the West to return to negotiations over the future of Germany. It turned out to be a grave miscalculation on the part of Stalin.[20] Instead of producing the desired response and thus, at least in the short term, preventing the creation of a separate West German state, it did precisely the opposite. The Western allies responded with an airlift to west Berlin, thus challenging the Soviets to risk war if they attempted to impede it.

The airlift required a huge logistical effort, but was successful and, with the Soviets lifting the blockade in May 1949, exposed the limitations of Soviet coercive power. Rather than preventing the creation of a West German state it accelerated it. In May, Germany was divided as two new German states emerged, one in the east, one in the west, and with it a piercing capitalist thorn – in the form of west Berlin – in the heart of Soviet-occupied Germany which was to be source of future crisis in the Cold War.

In retrospect the division of Europe appears an inevitable by-product of the irreconcilable differences between the US and the USSR and the social systems that each represented. However, the way in which the division occurred and the character of that division was not predetermined. What effectively caused the division to be so sharp and confrontational, to the point that by the mid-1950s thousands of soldiers and weaponry organised by NATO in the west and the Warsaw Pact in the east confronted each other in a central European 'face-off', was the character of Soviet political power in east-central Europe combined with its limitation to a politics of threat and coercion as a way of securing its objectives.

Geopolitical Tensions in the Near East

The use of military power and diplomatic coercion by the USSR to realise its security objectives after the war was not confined to central Europe, it was also apparent in the geopolitical fault-lines of the eastern Mediterranean and what US diplomats called the 'northern tier'[21] – the countries (Iran in particular) that bordered the southernmost parts of the USSR. The main area of tension in the eastern Mediterranean concerned the USSR's goal of addressing the possible threat of future invasion from the south, and in this respect as much as the USSR was concerned to have friendly and 'loyal' states on its borders in east-central Europe so it was the case with respect to access to the Black Sea through the Dardanelles Straits.[22] With no military forces in Turkey and with few if any levers with which it was able to manipulate domestic political developments in Turkey in its favour, the USSR was forced to deploy a diplomatic strategy of intimidation and threat to try and exact concessions from Turkey.

In March 1945 Molotov handed the Turkish ambassador in Moscow a diplomatic note demanding major revisions to the 1925 Turko-Soviet Treaty of Friendship and Neutrality. By June the Soviets had been granted a number of concessions, including the 'return' of territory acquired by Turkey after the First World War which had been ceded to Tsarist Russia in 1878, revision of the 1936 Montreux Convention which governed shipping in the Dardanelles Straits and, of most concern to Turkey, the leasing of military bases.[23] Soviet demands were backed by hostile commentary in the Soviet press and troop movements near the Turkish border. Although the Soviets argued that the demands were for defensive reasons, the Western allies saw them not only as a form of diplomatic intimidation, but also a threat to their strategic and economic interests in the region, particularly oil. In this respect it was not only the way in which developments in the primary theatre of Cold War conflict – central Europe – fed into western thinking over Soviet behaviour towards Turkey but also, and probably more significant, the perception of Soviet actions elsewhere in the region, notably in Iran, and also the simmering civil war involving communist forces in Greece, which I will discuss below.

Iran had been divided during the war, with British forces in the south and the Red Army in the north, with the expectation that both sides would withdraw at the war's end. The crisis in Iran began over Soviet claims to oil in the north of Iran together with secessionist tendencies in the Iranian province of Azerbaijan in the Soviet zone of occupation. With troops on the ground and a local pro-Soviet communist party, the *Tudeh*, which it could manipulate combined with genuine local demands for provincial autonomy the Soviets seemed to be in a strong position to secure their objectives. Using tactics that would work in east-central Europe, the Soviets encouraged the *Tudeh* to organise an insurrection against the Iranian government in November 1945. This resulted in the election of a *Tudeh*-dominated local assembly, which the Soviets used as a bargaining chip to ensure that the oil concessions they demanded would be granted.

The degree to which the USSR instigated a conflict between Iranian Azeris and the central government has been a matter of argument, but the view from London and Washington was that, in the light of Soviet policy towards Turkey at the same time, the USSR was using its military strength to force the Iranian government into an economic agreement that it did not want to make. As in the case of Turkey, western concerns were less to do with the 'independence' of Iran and Turkey and more to do with the character of Soviet behaviour and the consequences – economic, political and strategic – of Soviet success. The western response to these crises was, then, to challenge Soviet objectives diplomatically and militarily, i.e. meet what they saw as Soviet coercion with their own threats. Thus, the Western allies mounted a vigorous diplomatic campaign in the UN to put pressure on the Soviets to evacuate Iran, which they did in May 1946, and in September 1946 – after Turkey had received another diplomatic note from Moscow reiterating Soviet claims – made a *de facto* military commitment to Turkey by announcing the dispatch of part of the US Mediterranean fleet to Turkey where it would be permanently based.[24]

The pattern of Soviet behaviour after 1945, to secure advantages from its improved geopolitical position at the war's end, reveals a strong element of consistency. In conditioning and in some cases determining the political orientation of the territories that it occupied, the USSR realised its security goals in the only way that it could. To have acted differently, to have sought different goals, would have required a transformation in the domestic social and political character of the USSR, something that Stalin's policy after 1945 was primarily aimed at preventing. As much as a liberal-capitalist Russia would have wanted similarly constituted states on its borders, so an authoritarian-coercive communist USSR required a combination of politically incorporated and militarily pliant states as its immediate neighbours. The realisation of Soviet objectives rested upon a challenge to and the undermining of the liberal-capitalist security objectives of the US in particular. Whereas the USSR required political-military supremacy, the US required political and economic openness that would not only acquiesce to US military hegemony in the West but also uphold wider US security objectives.

INTER-CAPITALIST RELATIONS AND COLD WAR

As much as the post-war era of Cold War was dominated by geopolitical change and conflict, highlighted by superpower antagonism and the division of Europe, it was also influenced by the transformation in the socio-political relations within and between the major capitalist states. The Cold War, in the form of the emergence of Bolshevism – as a territorial state and international political movement – was a product of an international crisis amongst the leading capitalist states reflected in the 1914–18 war. The Second World War provided the second major international conjuncture of systemic capitalist crisis, from which the USSR and international revolution prospered. If one includes the breakdown of the Bretton Woods system in the early 1970s and the crisis this produced in the capitalist world, terminating the long boom and initiating a period of economic stagnation and intensified social conflict within and between the leading capitalist states, the three conjunctures of systemic crisis in the capitalist world implicating the leading capitalist states, all provided the context for waves of social revolution and the expansion of Soviet power. What this suggests is a symbiotic relationship between Cold War and the character and consequences of capitalist development and how the strengthening of the Soviet and revolutionary 'correlation of forces' was *dependent* upon inter-capitalist crisis and conflict.

In 1945 the capitalist world was in a paradoxical state. The old order, centred on the European-imperial capitalist powers and Britain in particular, had been brought to its knees by the consequences of two world wars and the inter-war economic crisis within the space of two generations. On the other hand, the US, the leading capitalist *economy* prior to the war, emerged from the war in a position of unparalleled political, economic and military advantage over the other capitalist states. Furthermore, whereas the US had decided to remain aloof from the responsibilities of managing the world economy after 1918, during the war the US political leadership and capitalist class had united on the need for the US to reconstruct the international capitalist order. The war had transformed US perceptions of itself, and had also produced political and economic circumstances that provided an opportunity for the US to reshape the world in its own image. The presence of US troops on three continents, the weakness of the other major capitalist states and the huge global economic imbalance that had emerged by the end of the war almost necessitated US leadership.[25]

The Politics of Bretton Woods

Leading economic policymakers in the US wartime administration and particularly those that attended the Bretton Woods conference had concluded that the absence of US political leadership in the management of the world economy after 1918 had been a major cause of the inter-war economic crisis that precipitated war[26] and, consequently, the key objective of US policymakers after 1945 was to prevent the return of economic nationalism and with it national, regional and imperial economic trading blocs – in a word, economic autarky – as had occurred during the 1930s in response to the great depression. US policymakers firmly believed in the sanctity of liberal, open markets and the need to limit the degree of state interference over economic activity through non-discrimination, and equal access to raw materials. As Truman wrote in October 1946, '[s]ound and healthy trade, conducted on equitable and non-discriminatory principles, is a keystone in the structure of world peace and security'.[27] However, American leaders' faith in 'free markets' and fostering international economic exchange was also balanced by a concern to limit the possibilities for instability and crises to emerge, as occurred in the 1929 Wall Street Crash through the activities of financial speculators. To some degree, then, US officials recognised the need for some public-governmental regulation of capitalism, both domestically and internationally, and this was reflected in the nature of the capitalist order that the United States sought to construct after 1945.

Plans for the management of the post-war world economy were laid at the Bretton Woods conference in July 1944 with the creation of the so-called Bretton Woods institutions:

- the International Monetary Fund (IMF), which was to be responsible for managing the international monetary system and to help prevent the recurrence of the currency and financial instability that had plagued the inter-war world economy contributing to the great depression; and
- the International Bank for Reconstruction and Development (the World Bank), which was to be responsible for providing funds to assist post-war economic reconstruction.

These two institutions were to provide the multilateral foundations for the post-war management of the capitalist world economy. They were significant because they were emblematic of the US model of hegemony or leadership after 1945. Thus, membership of the two organisations was open and decisions were made after discussion amongst members, but because of the differentiated weighting of votes on the management boards of each institution, the US, unsurprisingly – given its huge accumulation of gold and foreign exchange during the war – had the largest proportion of votes (17.5 per cent).

The Bretton Woods institutions and the overall character of the post-war world economy that the US sought to establish after 1945, then, enshrined US hegemony and were founded upon strongly anti-statist and anti-protectionist assumptions. Subsequent political and economic developments within Western Europe, however, would see these two institutions marginalised by 1948, replaced by the Marshall Plan and the European Recovery Programme. However, what is important to recognise is the political basis of the Bretton Woods agreement and the degree to which the agreement and the two institutions that emerged from it reflected US economic interests. This was apparent in the negotiations, and also after the Bretton Woods conference in the bilateral talks between Britain and the US over a loan to Britain. With respect to the negotiations at Bretton Woods, the British, led by John Maynard Keynes, argued for a much more ambitious (and less economically liberal) IMF, the upshot of which would have been the creation of a truly multilateral institution, in which the US would not have had a controlling stake, and where the US would have had to 'donate' the bulk of its accumulated gold and foreign exchange reserves to the institution to fund it. Unsurprisingly, the US rejected what it saw as an overly bureaucratic institution that would have had too much power over markets and would have prevented the US from using its financial resources as a source of political leverage over other states, and Britain in particular, to dismantle its Empire.

Economic relations with Britain were a significant source of friction in the early post-war period, particularly as the US saw imperial trading blocs[28] in general and the British Empire's system of imperial preferences and the 'Sterling area' in particular, as major obstacles to its goals of a multilaterally managed liberal world economy based on open international exchange and free trade. The clash of economic interests between British national-imperial capital and American liberal capital, highlighted in the rejection of Keynes' proposals for the IMF at Bretton Woods, were also apparent in the negotiations between London and Washington for a post-war loan to Britain. As Pollard suggests, the Anglo-American Financial Agreement of December 1945, which replaced Lend-Lease, saw Britain forced to make a number of painful economic concessions to American liberal capital.[29] In particular, the British were expected to abolish import controls on American goods and end the restrictions in the 'Sterling area' (the British Empire) on the convertibility of sterling to US dollars.[30]

The objective of US policy highlighted in the hard bargaining with the British over the loan saw the US deploy its economic power to 'persuade' Britain to pursue economic policies that would not only benefit the interests of US capital but would also result in a significant weakening of the capacity of the British state to regulate and manage the imperial economy, but also the

British domestic economy. The realisation of sterling–dollar convertibility in July 1947 triggered capital flight and saw a plunge in the value of sterling, thus contributing to the 'famine of dollars', further undermining any prospects of economic recovery dependent as it was in Britain (and the rest of Europe) on US imports.[31]

The early months and years after the end of wartime hostilities, then, brought to the surface tensions over rival, antagonistic socio-economic interests not only between the US and the USSR but also between the US and the other major capitalist states. It was this conflict and its consequences 'on the ground', in the shattered economies of Western Europe, that provided opportunities for the re-emergence of nationalist-statist blocs or Soviet-style autarchy. This is exactly what happened between 1945 and 1947. West European economies pursued state-led bilateral trade agreements as a way of coping with the massive imbalance in the world economy and their lack of foreign currency.[32] The upshot was that economic growth was negligible and US hopes of creating a liberal, open and multilateral international economy seemed likely to falter. This was a concern for the Truman administration, because such economic arrangements not only threatened to alter the political-economic character of Western European states (bringing them much closer to the USSR's form of political economy) but, as Leffler suggests, the domestic socio-economic character of the US as well, as the US government would inevitably have to respond politically to any moves towards autarky in Western Europe.[33]

The Marshall Plan

The post-war economic crisis in Europe came to a head during the winter of 1946–47. With a severe chill, demands for coal soared depleting stocks, which led to factory closures and the prospect of major social and political instability. Briefly, the plans laid out at Bretton Woods for the post-war economy were inadequate to deal with the economic problems in Europe caused by the war. The principal source of the economic crisis, which had gripped Europe soon after the war's end, was a dollar shortage. European economic recovery required liquidity – cash, and specifically US dollars – to fund trade and to pay for imports of American goods. The only source of dollars was the US and with the announcement of the Marshall Plan in June 1947, the US realised that it would have to compromise on its vision of a liberal-market-led post-war recovery if it was to prevent the collapse of liberal capitalism in Europe and the triumph of statism, trading blocs and autarky.

The Marshall Plan rested on two elements.[34] The first was the commitment to pump cash into the (Western) European economies (US$13 billion flowed into Western Europe between 1948 and 52[35]) and, in doing so, overcome the dollar shortage. The second was the political-institutional condition upon which European countries would receive US funds. This latter element was crucial, as it was a major contributing factor towards future European economic integration, which was initiated in 1951 with the European Coal and Steel Community,[36] and also because it forced European governments to abandon economic bilateralism and nationalism and embrace (liberal) multilateralism in the form of the OEEC (Organisation for European Economic Co-operation), created in April 1948 to administer, co-ordinate and dispense Marshall Aid.

The Marshall Plan, then, was not primarily an American response to a perceived Soviet[37] political threat to the security of Western Europe, but rather a response to the growing possibility that socio-economic developments in Europe would severely undermine US post-war plans for reconstructing the capitalist world economy, which would have had serious political and economic implications for the US. However, although we need to recognise that Marshall Aid was reactive to an economic crisis in (Western) Europe resulting in the shelving of the initial Bretton Woods post-war model, it also provided considerable means for the US to secure its political and economic interests through influencing the domestic and regional political economy of the participating states. As Carew[38] has shown, the US continually used the leverage of financial aid, by emphasising that the flow of aid was conditional on performance and not need, to press European governments, responding to popular demands, to scale back welfare measures and limit state encroachments, through nationalisations of industries, on the functioning of the market economy.

The introduction of the Marshall Plan went beyond dealing with the 'dollar gap' and promoting liberal multilateralism, as it also included the US abandoning the Bretton Woods goal of the rapid convertibility of European currencies (this had to wait until 1958). Furthermore, and more disconcerting for economic liberals, the US also accepted a limited degree of European and Japanese trade protectionism as a way of facilitating industrial development, which contributed to the so-called post-war 'economic miracles' in West Germany and Japan.[39]

The Marshall Plan helped construct a set of international economic circumstances[40] that went much further than overcoming the immediate economic and, correspondingly, impending social and political crisis within Europe in 1947–48, to provide the foundations for the so-called 'long boom'. This refers to the period between 1952 and the early 1970s, which saw the longest and most widespread growth of national capitalist economies and the international capitalist economy as a whole in world history. The long boom not only restored economic health to a war-devastated Europe and Japan, it also helped promote political stability within and between capitalist states and facilitated the political and economic integration of state societies at the regional (the European Community) and global levels.

The Class Basis of Capitalist Stabilisation and Anti-Communism

The significance of the changes in the character of the post-war international capitalist economy went beyond the balance of trade and payments and the level of protectionism between Western Europe and the US. At its heart, as Mark Rupert (drawing on the work of Charles Maier and Robert Cox[41]) has shown, was a major class dimension, which had significant implications for the Cold War. The consequence was that whereas the US was willing to make short-term concessions to deal with the crisis it confronted in 1947, it was also committed to a project of social engineering as a way of combating communist influence in Western Europe and building a social coalition, or what Cox calls a 'historical bloc', in support of liberal multilateralism and liberal-capitalist policies to promote economic growth – what Maier terms the 'politics of productivity'.[42]

Thus, at two levels, the domestic and international,[43] US foreign economic policymakers, working through the Economic Co-operation Agency (ECA), helped construct the social basis for the new international economic order. This was crucial to bind together formerly warring states (like France, Italy, Britain and Germany) and to integrate them into US-led international economic institutions and, domestically, to bring together formerly antagonist social interests – primarily capital and labour – into a new socio-political consensus. Whilst, in the inter-war period, conflicts between antagonistic social interests had threatened revolution and produced aggressive and warlike states based on the 'emergency politics' of fascism, after 1947 the new socio-political consensus helped produce social and political stability, economic growth and, importantly, inculcated strong anti-communist tendencies within major sections of organised labour and the working class. Whereas European workers had been the primary constituency of (potential) social revolution in the inter-war period, after 1945 a sizeable – indeed dominant – portion of the working class became a pillar of the prevailing social order by securing a greater material stake in that order.[44]

The 'politics of productivity' rested on a compromise, which saw capital grant material and political concessions to organised labour and its trade union representatives, which amounted to a restructuring of the socio-political bases of the major capitalist states devastated by war.[45] The basis of this new socio-economic consensus was the commitment of labour to economic growth as capital accumulation rather than social justice, on the basis that economic growth and prosperity would secure improved living standards for workers who would be able to benefit from productivity gains and participate in bargaining over the distribution of the fruits of economic growth.[46] By bringing organised labour 'in from the cold', the new constellation of social power made the trade unions pillars of the anti-communist social order rather than enemies of it. Rupert sums it up thus:

Empowered by their predominance in the global division of labor, American state managers, capitalists, and organized labor leaders sought to foster economic recovery and interdependence among the major capitalist powers as part of an explicit strategy of global order.[47]

Labour was very much a junior partner in this social coalition,[48] as the interests of capital, expressed in the form of the accumulation of profit, took precedence over social justice claims. Nevertheless, on the back of the long boom, the European working classes secured significant social and economic advances between 1947 and the early 1970s. Thus, full employment, the creation of a welfare state, sustained increases in real wages and recognition of the centrality of trade unions in managing industrial relations helped establish social peace and consequently eliminated the prospects for social revolution and communist political advance.

The success of the Marshall Plan and the overall health of the post-war international capitalist order required the refashioning of societies and the working class in particular. The central field of ideological struggle were trade unions, those bodies that had grown in strength from the 1930s and particularly during the war and whose cooperation and loyalty were imperative if social peace was to be maintained and economic growth restored. In the lead in the US strategy to isolate revolutionary and communist elements from trade unions and the working class were American trade unions: the AFL (American Federation of Labor) and the CIO (Congress of Industrial Organizations). As Rupert shows, even before the end of the war, the leadership of American unions had committed itself to a liberal vision of the post-war international economic order, which they saw as the best way of protecting jobs and improving wages through access to export markets.[49] By 1948 the AFL's support for reciprocal trade agreements was understood as 'part of the American foreign policy counterattack against Soviet Communist imperialism and its menace to peace and freedom'.[50]

As well as supporting US international trade policy the leading American unions were also directly involved (primarily through the FTUC [Free Trade Union Committee], established in 1944) in an intra-class ideological war to undermine the social and political power of communist trade unions such as the *Confédération Générale du Travail* (CGT) in France and the *Confederazione Generale Italiana de Lavoro* (CGIL) in Italy. The FTUC worked with the CIA and used government funds to promote 'free' over communist trade unionism by tarnishing communist trade unions as Soviet stooges. Rupert documents how the activities of the FTUC were instrumental in splitting the CGT in 1947–48 with the formation of the anti-communist *Force Ouvrière* (FO) in France and with the creation of the anti-communist *Libera Confederazione Generale Italiana de Lavoro* (LCGIL) in Italy in 1948.[51]

American anti-communist 'class collaborationist' trade unionism played a crucial role, alongside other US state and non-state agencies, in the construction of a social consensus that helped stabilise post-war capitalism and marginalise communist influence. Rupert cites a CIO publication of the time that leaves little room for doubt as to the ideological objectives of American unionism and how it contributed to the Cold War,

> Free world labor, organized in the growing ranks of the ICFTU [International Confederation of Free Trade Unions], stands today as the only firm and reliable bulwark against further infiltration of red totalitarianism among the masses of workers both in the industrial nations of western Europe and in the awakening lands of the Middle and Far East.[52]

The success of the post-war restructuring of international capitalism rested, then, on a mixture of US economic largesse and an orchestrated campaign to build a cross-class alliance that not only tied workers into supporting the capitalist system after 1945, but also helped eliminate the political threat from European communism. In effect, the Cold War – understood as social conflict between the social forces associated with capitalism and the social forces organised in a Bolshevik-communist movement committed to social revolutionary transformation – was over in Western Europe by the late 1940s. Revolutionary-communist movements, as agents of political transformation, were marginalised and the socio-political contexts or structures out of which they could prosper – moments of systemic capitalist crisis – no longer emerged as capitalist states and social classes were bound together by a combination of anti-communism and 'welfare capitalism'. The ideology and politics of anti-communism were key elements in helping to overcome domestic and international divisions that would have made the task of capitalist restoration and stabilisation much more difficult. In this respect the actions of Stalin and the USSR in east-central Europe provided a crucial external ideological and political context and 'threat' that helped the realisation of Washington's objectives both internationally – in creating a US-led multilateral system – and domestically, in the US, where public opinion and Congressional lawmakers were successfully convinced of the necessity of US 'hands-on' international engagement and leadership by the 'Soviet threat'.

A NEW WAVE OF SOCIAL REVOLUTION AND COMMUNIST EXPANSION

With the end of the war, in a number of different locales from Western Europe to south-east Asia, conditions looked propitious for revolutionary change and the restructuring of state–society relations. As should be evident from what I have said, world war provided the geopolitical *and* social context for social revolution and communist advance. However, as much as the revolutionary consequences of 1914–18 were uneven and ultimately decided by military force, so were the prospects of turning a series of revolutionary crises brought about by the Second World War into successful communist expansion after 1945.

Prospects for Revolution in Western Europe: The
Communist Threat in France and Italy

In many respects the social, economic and political circumstances within Western Europe, and France and Italy in particular, after the war seemed highly favourable to a *form* of revolutionary anti-capitalist transformation. The reasons for this I have already indicated – the weakness of conservative and pro-capitalist social forces in contrast to the strength of the left and communists in particular.[53]

Why, then, did revolutionary change not occur in France and Italy between 1945 and 1948? A number of scholars, particularly those on the radical left, such as Gabriel Kolko, have argued that the failure of revolutionary forces to take advantage of a 'revolutionary conjuncture' immediately after the war was because of the inherently conservative or, more precisely, Stalinist tendencies within the two major West European communist parties, which followed political directions from the Kremlin. In effect, the USSR and its loyal servants – Thorez in France and Togliatti in Italy – scuppered any hope of revolutionary transformation in France and Italy.

There is a good deal of truth in this argument. As had been the case prior to the war, Stalin's enthusiasm for supporting revolutionary struggle tended to decrease the greater the distance a revolutionary crisis was from the walls of the Kremlin and the armed power of the Red Army. The significance of this insight and how far it accounts for the failure to realise revolutionary change in France and Italy, however, can only be judged by an assessment of other international factors that shaped developments in France and Italy and also the specific character of 'revolutionary dynamics' within these two countries.

With the end of the war both the Italian and French communist parties continued the policy of the 'united front', signaling, at least in the short term, a prioritisation of political stability and consolidation over revolutionary adventurism. In France the PCF joined a coalition government led by Charles de Gaulle (until his resignation in January 1946) and in Italy, the PCI joined a short-lived government led by a former close ally of Mussolini, Marshal Badoglio. At first glance such behaviour suggests that both parties, or at least their respective leaderships, were guilty of an extreme form of compromise, and a momentous failure to seize a unique historical opportunity to initiate revolutionary change. However, it is possible to see a 'revolutionary' logic at work in these actions which reflected the specific social, political and military context in which both communist party leaderships found themselves. In short, the immediate post-war conjuncture presented an historic opportunity for the radical left, communist and non-communist, to become 'hegemonic', yet it also presented complex and challenging strategic and tactical issues over how to achieve this.

Both parties confronted a rather curious revolutionary conjuncture, at least in contrast to the revolutionary crises that had emerged before and after the war in other parts of the world. Both parties quickly became mass parties at the war's end with growing roots, through their influence in trade unions, and in the wider social fabric. Furthermore, the political context was one of an externally (allied) policed peace, alongside a commitment by the Anglo-American occupying powers to establish liberal democratic government. The significance of this was that the weaknesses of reactionary and pro-capitalist forces, combined with a mechanism for enabling communists to get their hands on the levers of power and the foreclosure of the insurrectionary option through the presence of the military power of the Western allies, made the constitutional-parliamentary road to power highly attractive.

The risks and dangers associated with the 'insurrectionary path' to revolutionary change were made all the more apparent with the vicious civil war in Greece which erupted in the summer of 1946 between Greek communists against a British and subsequently US-backed right-wing government, which was to see collaborators with the fascist occupation in Greece return to serve the anti-communist cause as 'patriots' and 'democrats' against 'Soviet-controlled' communists.[54] The assumption, then, of the French and Italian communist leaderships and, by extension, Stalin as well, was that the two communist parties could come to power and implement social transformation through the ballot box and in this respect they should not act to undermine their respective chances of winning democratic elections, or the prospects for the western powers acquiescing to the ensconcing of Soviet power in east-central Europe.

Certainly, other factors suggest that the French and Italian leaderships were not made from the same revolutionary mould as Lenin, Trotsky or Mao. Both parties disbanded their armed wings after the defeat of the *Wehrmacht* and both, in an attempt to emphasise their moderate and democratic credentials, committed themselves to industrial policies that promoted post-war productivity over concerns about questions of property ownership and the distribution of wealth.[55] The consequence of this kind of policy meant that communists in position of authority found themselves in conflict with the demands of sections of the working class, and indeed some of their own members, as they supported economic reconstruction.

A strategy based on the 'parliamentary road' at a time of simmering social conflict as workers were encouraged to make sacrifices to preserve a system that many of them saw no benefit in saving, as a way of securing a wider coalition of support to ensure communist success in parliamentary elections, posed severe strains on the relationship between communist parties and working people. In retrospect, the strategies of the PCF and PCI look naïve. As much as the USSR would not tolerate anti-Soviet social and political forces coming to power in the east, so it would have been the case in the western half of Europe had either of these parties come close to gaining power. As it was, the contradictions within the strategy between leaders and the rank and file, rightly emphasised by Marxist-informed analyses of this period such as Kolko, combined with the manoeuvrings of other non-communist political groupings and the not insignificant role of US (CIA) secret finance and propaganda, particularly in Italy, closed off the parliamentary road to communist power.

The foreclosure of the parliamentary road was not only a product of domestic political developments and western manipulations, but also, as Michael Cox has rightly stressed, the lengthening shadow of Soviet domination in east-central Europe.[56] Stalin's combined security and political concerns about ensuring Soviet domination of east-central Europe helped undo – though they did not cause – the electoral prospects of West European communist parties. Not only did Soviet actions alert the US to the 'Trojan horses' of the PCI and PCF, they also fundamentally undermined the liberal democratic credentials of the PCF and PCI in the eyes of the wider French and Italian publics, destroying any hope of power through the ballot box.

By mid- to late 1947, it was evident to the French and Italian communist leaderships that the parliamentary road was blocked with the formation of coalition governments, which pitted formerly antagonistic political forces in common cause (with the support of the Western allies) in keeping the communists from power. With the announcement of the Truman Doctrine in March 1947 it had become virtually impossible to isolate domestic political struggles involving communists from the growing tensions between Moscow and the Western allies. Furthermore, with the launching of the Marshall Plan in June 1947 and the subsequent Soviet rejection of any participation in it weeks later, Moscow, via the newly established Cominform (September 1947), instructed Thorez and Togliatti to mount a campaign of opposition to Marshall Aid, which destroyed any remaining ambiguity over the political loyalties of the French and Italian communist parties.

With increasing Cold War tensions and their inability to secure popular ascendancy via the route of party competition and liberal constitutional politicking, the French and Italian communist parties belatedly endorsed a more militant, though hardly revolutionary, strategy. Communist ministers were dismissed from the French government in May 1947 after failing to support the government's austere wage policy and got behind a series of strikes involving car workers, dockers, railway, electricity and gas workers in June. Further strikes broke out in November and reached a peak at the beginning of December involving over two million workers.[57] However, with a parliamentary majority and the loyalty of the armed forces of order, a combination of rapidly introduced anti-union legislation and police and army batons cowed the strikers and with it any hopes of an extra-parliamentary challenge to the new French state. Further industrial unrest the following autumn, led by miners, was met by even more force, with troops occupying mining areas and the police arresting hundreds of strikers.[58] As much as the USSR could use force, then, to ensure that its post-war political and economic objectives were secured in east-central Europe, so could West European liberal democratic states, though in this case what confronted the French state was not an attempt by workers and communists to overthrow the state but rather a militant strategy to secure wage increases.

In Italy developments followed a similar pattern. After losing its toehold in the state with the formation of a new government under the liberal Alicide de Gasperi in May 1947, the PCI, like the PCF, turned to support labour militancy against government austerity. A series of PCI-supported strikes broke out in the autumn of 1947 culminating in the CGIL calling a general strike in December.[59] As in France, the strike was primarily concerned with economic issues – wage increases – yet this did not prevent the state, as in France, invoking the spectre of communist-inspired insurrection to use the iron fist of police and armed forces to crush the strike. When, in July 1948, after an assassination attempt on Togliatti, communist militants and workers took over factories and came out on the streets, the de Gasperi government again used force, leading to 16 fatalities and over 200 wounded, to destroy any hopes of insurrection.[60]

By the end of 1948, then, the 'forces of order' had seen off the communist challenge and with it the Cold War in Western Europe was effectively over. Frustrated by parliamentary-constitutional politicking, aided and abetted by US financing and propaganda for anti-communists, and lacking the means and will (and prospect of success) to seize power through force, the French and Italian communist parties – the only organisations that could have 'delivered' revolution – were confined to the margins of post-war politics. Both parties made tactical mistakes, however. The suggestion that the actions of the PCI and PCF leaderships and, by implication, Stalin, prevented revolution overlooks the particular social and political context that each party confronted at the war's end, as well as what would have been the definitive factor had France and Italy succumbed to revolution: the intervention of Anglo-American military power.

Revolution and Civil War in Greece

The political and constitutional manoeuvrings that were largely responsible for preventing communists from coming to power in France and Italy contrasted with the determining role of force and the more direct involvement of Anglo-American military power in preventing a communist advance in Greece between 1945 and 1949. As in many other parts of fascist-occupied Europe (Greek) communists (the KKE) had taken a leading role in the anti-fascist resistance through their dominance of the EAM (the National Liberation Front) and its armed wing, ELAS (the National Popular Liberation Army). This contrasted with those social forces associated with the traditional and pre-war political elite that had, to varying degrees, either acquiesced to or actively collaborated with the occupation.

Up to the closing stages of the war, the Western allies, and Britain in particular, pursued a contradictory policy which could be seen as a microcosm of the wider wartime alliance with the USSR – a policy that unravelled with the EAM, as it was to do with Moscow after the military objective of defeating Nazi Germany had been achieved. Whilst providing military support to the communist-dominated ELAS as the principal means of sapping the military strength of the fascist occupation, they also maintained diplomatic relations with the rabidly anti-communist Greek government-in-exile in Cairo. The tensions in the relations were finally brought into the open in September 1943 with the breakdown of relations between the British and the EAM over British support for the restoration of the monarchy in post-war Greece.[61] These tensions over the political future of Greece were also reflected in armed clashes between ELAS and the pro-monarchist resistance, the EDES (conservative National Republican Greek League) in late 1943.[62]

With the war drawing to an end, the question of the future of Europe and Greece in particular – a key strategic outpost in the eastern Mediterranean – became increasingly influenced by external actors and the diplomacy of the USSR and Britain in particular. With British forces responsible for expelling the *Wehrmacht* from Greece, Stalin conceded to Churchill in a geopolitical quid pro quo, otherwise known as the 'percentages agreement' of October 1944 where the USSR committed itself to pressing the KKE to join a royalist-led coalition government, with Greece remaining within the British sphere of influence, whilst Britain recognised Soviet preponderance in Bulgaria.[63] In concluding this agreement, Stalin signalled his willingness to sacrifice the KKE and the prospects of a communist seizure of power in Greece on the altar of Soviet geopolitical and ideological interests.[64] To have done differently, that is, to have actively encouraged the KKE to seize power, through force of arms if necessary, would have risked a major diplomatic and, possibly, military confrontation with Britain at the war's end, in effect jeopardising the future of Soviet gains in the rest of Europe as a result of the war.

However, Stalin's policy was guided not only by a geopolitical calculus but also by ideological considerations. Unless the USSR directly intervened in Greece through the Red Army, the only way that it could have supported the cause of Greek communism would have been by providing support to the Greek communists, in effect, contributing to the establishment of communist power in Greece outside the direct control of the Kremlin. With the benefit of hindsight we can see how this concerned the ideological interests of the USSR, and Stalin in particular, and how such ideological considerations had geopolitical consequences too. Developments in Yugoslavia[65] after 1945, and China much later, highlight how the emergence of 'autonomous' sources of communist power challenged the political and ideological leadership of the USSR within the international communist movement and, geopolitically, exposed the USSR to political and military confrontations with the West through the 'irresponsible' or 'reckless' behaviour of these states.[66]

Soviet policy towards Greece reflected a general policy to those parts of post-war Europe where it lacked a political-military presence on the ground (as it had been for most, if not all, of the period after the Bolshevik Revolution) and was based upon the limits imposed on Soviet behaviour by the geopolitical context combined with political and ideological concerns about the future direction of the international communist movement and the USSR's leadership of it, particularly if another centre of communist power emerged outside Soviet control.

With Stalin prioritising Soviet dominance in east-central Europe based on the Red Army's presence, the situation in Greece was seen as troublesome, both geopolitically and ideologically.[67] Consequently, the KKE had two options: follow directions from Moscow and accommodate to the restoration of a bourgeois order, which would mean the postponement of any hopes of revolutionary change; or go against Moscow (with Yugoslav support) and confront British-backed right-wing forces in Greece – a strategy of revolutionary war.

The signing of the Varkiza Agreement in February 1945, which brought a pause to the fighting between the communists and British-backed government forces (which had erupted in December 1944 after police had fired on a large EAM demonstration in Athens on 3 December) saw the KKE reluctantly take the first option. The agreement demanded the demobilisation of the ELAS and the surrendering of its *de facto* control of large parts of Greece in exchange for legal recognition, the promise of parliamentary elections, a plebiscite on the future of the monarchy and the promise of a purge of fascist sympathisers in the police and armed forces.[68]

Whereas the French and Italian communist parties managed to adapt to the post-war constitutional order and were accepted, with qualifications, as 'legitimate' political forces by their political opponents, the social conflict within Greece and the blood-letting during and immediately after the war, prevented the establishment of a liberal constitutional democracy. Within weeks of Varkazia, violence again erupted with a wave of assassinations of EAM and KKE members by right-wing groups. Between spring 1945 and summer 1946 the violence between both sides escalated as the right-wing government, backed by London and, to a lesser extent, Washington, reneged on the commitment it had made at Varkazia. In a climate of increasing intimidation and violence the left boycotted the election that took place in early 1946 which returned right-wing forces to power. The right's electoral success triggered a more intensified wave of violence, which effectively forced the KKE leadership to launch armed struggle against the government.

With civil war the contradictions in western policy and the deep divisions within Greece came to the fore. Whereas Britain and, after the spring of 1947, the US supported the Greek government,[69] Yugoslavia, and to a lesser extent Albania and Bulgaria, provided some military support to the communists. Moscow provided no aid to the Greek communists[70] and became increasingly irritated at Yugoslavia's support for the KKE.[71] The divisions within the international communist movement between Moscow and Belgrade were played out within the Greek communists as 'civil war' took place within the KKE between Stalinists and Titoists,[72] which was reminiscent of the violent conflict between Comintern communists and other leftists in Spain between 1936 and 1939. Although one should recognise the significance of these divisions, which certainly undermined the communists in the civil war, as in the case of Spain, what ultimately decided the civil war was not the divisions within the 'revolutionary cause' but the superior military strength, backed by external military support, of right-wing/conservative forces which secured their victory in October 1949.

The first military conflict of the Cold War, then, saw a victory for western-backed forces and established a political-military template for future western and US policy in particular. When confronted with communist power – armed or otherwise – the US would provide political and economic support to anti-communist forces and, if necessary, military support with the possibility of direct involvement, to crush communist forces. The significance of the Greek civil war, however, was not only about the practical implementation of the Truman Doctrine, but also how local communist forces, products of shifting fronts of revolutionary crises outside of the control of Moscow, and driven by local dynamics, emerged as Cold War flashpoints. The Greek civil war was a key crisis of the early post-war Cold War *in spite of* the absence of Soviet support for the Greek Revolution. We may condemn the blinkered anti-Soviet attitudes of British and US policymakers who could find no concrete evidence of Soviet involvement in Greece yet refused to accept this fact at the time, but this should not blind us to the reality of a genuine communist threat (from the KKE and Belgrade's plans for communist confederation in the Balkans) and the consequences of a communist victory in Greece for western power in the Balkans and eastern Mediterranean (and with this, access to oil reserves in the Middle East) and the landlords and bourgeoisie in Greece.

Revolution in Asia

The social and political turmoil, and with it the prospects for communist expansion, were even greater in Asia. The war had seriously weakened the coercive and administrative capacities of the main colonial powers, and in those colonies – French Indochina, the Dutch East Indies (Indonesia) and British Malaya – that had been overrun by Japanese forces in 1941, European colonial power was effectively dismantled. These weaknesses, combined with the growth of anti-colonial and nationalist sentiment, encouraged by the Japanese, left nationalist movements in a much stronger position, militarily and ideologically, than they had been prior to the war.

In the Dutch East Indies (Indonesia) the nationalist movement, which was to be successful in driving out the returning Dutch colonial forces between 1946 and 1949, was led by non-communists. In Malaya, the war had strengthened communist forces, which launched an insurgency in 1948 (which was only finally defeated in 1960). In the Philippines a communist-dominated anti-imperialist guerrilla army, – the *Hukbalahap*, was established in 1942 which launched an insurgency against the US-backed government in 1948 that simmered on for years.[73] And in Indochina the communist-led Vietminh began a guerrilla war in 1946 against the restoration of French colonial power through to 1954.

This upsurge of national and social revolution emerged within the trans-formed geopolitical circumstances brought about by war. In this sense war was very much the 'midwife of revolution'. The Pacific War ended abruptly in early August 1945 with the devastation and horror unleashed by the detonation of atomic weapons over Hiroshima on 6 August and Nagasaki three days later, forcing the Japanese into unconditional surrender. The geopolitical situation was rendered thus: the USSR had made small advances[74] through Manchuria and had managed to gain a foothold in the north of the Korean peninsula and northern China. In contrast US military power controlled most of the islands of south-east Asia and would soon be the sole occupying force in Japan. In (French) Indochina the end of the war created a political vacuum with the surrender of Japanese troops and the absence of French or western military forces to 'maintain order' for a month until the arrival of British forces in early September, and in China the Japanese defeat left the country split between areas of communist and Kuomintang control with no agreement on who would assume power over the country as a whole.

The war, then, had left the European colonial powers seriously weakened and confronting better organised and stronger nationalist-revolutionary forces. Because of the USSR's limited participation in the Pacific War and Stalin's preoccupation with developments in Europe,[75] the US had a relatively free hand as the key external power in the region. However, its military preponderance was not matched by a political freedom to re-order the region as it saw fit. Until the end of 1949, US policy was based on the assumption that China would emerge as a stable pro-western partner to manage the region. The US was also nominally committed to the independence of colonial territories and their incorporation as 'independent' states into a US sphere of independent nations bound together by liberal democracy and open markets. Both goals were to be frustrated. The hopes centred on China collapsed in late 1949 with the triumph of communist forces in the civil war and the massive advancement of communist power in the region. With respect to establishing independent post-colonial states in the region, US objectives were complicated by the leading role of communist parties in a number of nationalist movements, combined with the US prioritising its concerns over Western

Europe and the need to help stabilise and strengthen countries such as France as pillars of Western Europe's defence against Soviet communism.[76] This meant that rather than putting pressure on the European metropoles to transfer political power to local political forces, the US ended up facilitating the return of colonial power and, with respect to France, financing its war with the Vietminh between 1950 and 1954.

Two of these post-war revolutionary 'fronts' – in Indochina and China – were to play a defining role in the post-war Cold War. Twelve days after the Japanese surrender the communist leader, Ho Chi Minh, declared a general insurrection,[77] instructing the Vietminh to seize control of as much of Vietnam as possible. By 22 August most of North Vietnam was under Vietminh[78] control as communist cadres with local support filled the power vacuum created by the Japanese surrender. The Vietminh had taken advantage of the chaos produced by the Japanese surrender as the only indigenous political force capable of organising a national insurrection in a way comparable to the Bolsheviks' 'storming of the Winter Palace' in October 1917. However, whereas the Bolsheviks' military limitations were not to be fully tested because of the continuation of world war, the Vietminh's exercise of political authority in Vietnam was to be short-lived.

In September British forces arrived in the south of the country and quickly took control of Saigon whilst Kuomintang forces filtered into the north, resulting in the squeezing of Vietminh power. The Vietminh, recognising the changing and unfavourable military situation, opted for a united front policy, calling for national independence rather than social revolution, and even went as far as officially dissolving the communist party in November 1945, as a way of currying favour with moderate and non-communist elements within Vietnam and the US internationally.[79]

However, with the return of French forces by early 1946 hopes of independence were to be frustrated. Although negotiations took place between the French and the Vietminh, which led to an agreement in March 1946 where the French 'agreed to recognise the Democratic Republic of (North) Vietnam as a free state',[80] with French military forces increasing in strength it soon became clear to Ho Chi Minh that the French were committed to the restoration of colonial rule and that the only way that Vietnam would achieve independence was through force of arms. The deterioration in relations between France and the Vietminh reached breaking point and war was triggered in November 1946 when French naval forces shelled Haiphong harbour killing thousands.[81] The escalating violence between the two sides saw the French gradually take control of the major urban areas throughout the country and the Vietminh retreat into the countryside to launch a combined political-military strategy of guerrilla war and peasant social revolution.

The Vietnamese Revolution, then, emerged out of a transformed geopolitical context, which allowed the socio-economic tensions and contradictions – most evident in the famine that gripped parts of the country in 1945–46 – that had been built up under French colonial rule to reveal themselves politically with the communists momentary seizure of power in August–September 1945. The revolution's progress was also to be conditioned by the geopolitical context and with the return of superior French military power, the revolutionary tide was temporarily turned until the communist triumph in China in late 1949, which was to prove decisive in influencing the progress of national and social revolution in Vietnam.

The impact of the war on China was to be decisive in transforming the fortunes of the communist party in its struggle with the Kuomintang for ascendancy over all of China. On the surface, both parties put aside their differences in the name of national unity and formed a united front against Japan. However, as in an earlier period of cooperation (the mid-1920s) against another imperialist presence, formal unity masked the continuation of socio-economic conflict and shifts in the balance of forces which would prove to be decisive at the war's end.[82]

Simply put, the war benefited the communists and undermined the Kuomintang. Whilst before the war the Kuomintang had been seen as the primary instrument of national unification and independence, and had controlled the major population and industrial areas, the Japanese invasion had forced it to evacuate the locations of its 'natural' social constituencies – the Chinese urban middle class and large and petty-capitalists. It was not only that the Kuomintang was detached from its popular social base, but Mao's strategy of peasant revolution, developed after the 'Long March', was perfectly suited to anti-Japanese struggle based on guerrilla war. Consequently, the most effective means of challenging the Japanese presence was facilitated by the social transformation of the peasantry through destroying the semi-feudal nexus of exploitation between peasants and landlords (many of whom were associated with the Kuomintang). This contrasted with the Kuomintang, whose ideology and social base were anathema to transforming the social relations between peasants and landlords.[83] Thus, whereas the social bases of Kuomintang strength were weakened by the Japanese invasion, the social bases and areas of territory controlled by the communists were extended between 1937 and 1945[84] and with these changes the CCP was transformed in the eyes of the millions of Chinese peasants not only as a movement of national liberation but also one of social betterment, in contrast to the Kuomintang.

However, in spite of the advances made by the CCP during the war, it was far from clear that this momentum would be sufficient to triumph over the Kuomintang. With the end of the war, the Kuomintang was no longer constrained by the Japanese presence and, furthermore, was seen by both the

USSR and the US as the legitimate government of China. The absence of Soviet support for the CCP after the war, which contrasted with the military support afforded to Chiang Kai-shek by Washington,[85] combined with the much greater military strength of the Kuomintang, in spite of the growth of the Red Army during the war, seemed to suggest that the Kuomintang would triumph.

The eventual triumph of the communists in 1949 was as much a product of the corruption, incompetence and leadership failure of the KMT[86] as it was the political and military tactics of the CCP. The strategy of the communists, in defiance of Moscow's advice and interest in not wanting to jeopardise Soviet gains elsewhere in Asia[87] and east-central Europe, reflected not only the local sources of Cold War but also the contradictions within the international communist movement and its form of expansion, something that would come to dog Sino-Soviet relations, particularly after Stalin's death in 1953. Thus, in the same way that Stalin was not willing to risk the geopolitical instability that would have followed any significant direct military intervention on behalf of communist forces in Greece, or indirectly through the provision of *matériel*, alongside the ideological consequences of the establishment of a centre of communist power outside the discipline of the Soviet party-state machinery, so Moscow adopted a conservative and risk-averse stance towards the prospect of communist success in China.

The absence of Soviet support put a very different geopolitical complexion on the Chinese civil war, in contrast to the Cold War in Europe. This was not sufficient, however, for the US to question its hostility towards any prospect of communist success and support for the Kuomintang,[88] but it did mean that the level of US involvement in China was significantly less than its attention to and concern over the future of Europe. The US was concerned to prevent the outbreak of civil war in China after the war, knowing full well that it would find it very difficult to secure the support of the American public for any military intervention in China. Truman dispatched former Secretary of State George C. Marshall to China in December 1945 to facilitate negotiations between the two sides.[89] Although Marshall managed to secure a truce in January 1946 he was not able to bridge the gap between the two sides and in early 1947 he returned to the US.

Whilst talking of peace the US prepared its ally for war, continuing to supply the Kuomintang with military aid.[90] However, the US was not uncritical of Chiang, and throughout the post-war period until the communist victory, pressured him to reform his administration by clamping down on corruption and inefficiency and implementing political and economic reforms to loosen the grip of neo-feudal landlord interests in the Kuomintang and cultivate popular support amongst the Chinese masses.[91]

The US, then, confronted a dilemma, much like the one it was to confront in Vietnam in the 1960s. Although committed to preventing communist victory in the civil war it was well aware of the weaknesses and failings of its local ally. However, other than directly intervening in the civil war with tens of thousands of troops and, in effect, usurping the leadership role of the Kuomintang and, at the same time, appearing as yet another colonial power meddling in Chinese affairs, there was little the US could do to alter the direction of the civil war.

The nature of US involvement in China between 1945 and 1949 reflected the political divisions within the US between those who were suspicious of the Kuomintang and the seriousness of the communist threat, and those who came to blame the Truman administration for the 'loss of China' after 1949. These divisions were all the more significant as similar divisions – which the Truman administration had to navigate – also existed over US policy towards Europe and the provision of economic and military support for Western Europe after 1947. US domestic politics, then, played an important role in conditioning US involvement in China after 1945, as they did throughout the Cold War. The US was unable to prevent communist expansion in China because the form of international politics that the US sought to cultivate after 1945 (and before) – independent capitalist liberal democracies – could not be constructed in China in contrast to Western Europe. The alternative was full-scale military intervention, something that the US came to rely on to a much greater degree after the loss of China, but which would prove equally problematic in realising US political and economic objectives.

CONCLUSIONS: THE UNEVEN SOCIO-ECONOMIC CONSEQUENCES OF GEOPOLITICAL TRANSFORMATION

As I have explored in this chapter, the mainstream focus on the diplomatic relations between Washington and Moscow and the attempt to apportion blame for 'causing' the Cold War has tended to miss a crucial, one might argue defining, element of the Cold War, as significant as the nuclear stand-off and arms race between the superpowers, in our understanding of the meaning of Cold War. The point that I have emphasised in analysing the post-war conjuncture is that all geopolitical change has socio-economic sources and consequences. As much as geopolitical change is in some sense produced by the evolving and sometimes convulsive arrangements between socio-economic structures and social-economic agency, so it is the case with the geopolitical consequences of the Second World War and the 'origins' of the Cold War. It is in this *qualified* sense that we can say that the Cold War began after 1945.

The war produced a new geopolitical context within which the two social systems of capitalism and communism, and their political agents, tried to consolidate and expand. However, this was not, as the mainstream debate tends to assume, a struggle waged between states alone and the superpowers in particular, but rather a struggle between social forces within states and also outside of the state in the form of guerrilla armies, revolutionary movements and organised, politically conscious social classes. Whilst war had strengthened (in different and uneven ways) the power of the US and the USSR – the major victors of the Second World War it had also shattered the power of many other states and territories (colonies), and it was in these spaces that the socio-economic consequences of the war and, consequently, the socio-economic dynamics of the Cold War were most pronounced.

What this also suggests is a continuation of the relationship between socio-economic crisis and conflict and geopolitical change evident in the 1917 Bolshevik Revolution and the character of inter-war international relations. As much as the success of communist revolution in 1917 was determined by the catalyst of war and geopolitical circumstance, so was a new wave of social revolution after 1945. The significance of this was that although the strengthening and, in some cases, successes of communist revolutionary movements was a product of geopolitical change, it was not a product of Soviet strength or behaviour. Consequently, the sources of Cold War crises and flashpoints remained as they were after 1917 – revolutionary crisis within varied forms of capitalist state and how revolutionary movements might seize power. The 'revolutionary moments' in parts of Europe and Asia after 1945 could be seen as new waves of revolution similar to those that emerged elsewhere after 1917. The sources of Cold War remained essentially the same – revolutionary communist movements seizing the opportunity of a crisis of state power at a national and international level – produced from geopolitical transformation.

However, the political consequences of the opportunities for socio-economic change brought about by geopolitical transformation were also uneven and paradoxical. Whereas in the colonial hinterland new geopolitical circumstances fused with local revolutionary forces to promote waves of crisis that were to dominate the post-war Cold War and see communist movements come to power, in the most economically and socially advanced zones of the world, and Western Europe in particular, the political consequences were quite different. Here, a combination of internal political and economic weakness and geopolitical vulnerability with Soviet power now bordering Western Europe, allowed for political and economic transformation. Unlike in the South, the US was able to work with well-established political and social forces to restructure the operations of the world economy and domestic political and economic structures and to isolate and marginalise communists, who were tainted by association with the USSR, to produce a truly epochal international political transformation – a zone of peace and prosperity in Europe.

The Cold War, understood as the international consequences of revolutionary crises, could then be said to have begun and ended at the same time. By the late 1940s the prospect of revolutionary-communist expansion into Western

Europe by internal (local communist parties) or external (absorption into the Soviet sphere) forces had passed, whilst at the same time the prospects for communist expansion elsewhere looked highly likely. In this sense, claiming that the Cold War originated in the post-war conjuncture is to miss the point that its origins lay in something all the more complex and paradoxical, though conditioned by geopolitical transformation.

4

The Militarisation of Cold War: The Containment of the USSR and the Emergence of New Revolutionary Fronts, 1950–62

INTRODUCTION

The pattern of social and geopolitical relations established within and between the two social systems and geopolitical blocs between 1945 and 1949 and the position of the superpowers – as they looked inwards towards the bloc they each led and outwards at each other – was to remain more or less fixed until the early 1970s. The political reach of Soviet communist power was effectively confined to the Eurasian landmass and in this sense the USSR was an 'incomplete' superpower, not only in the sense of its economic limitations in comparison to the US,[1] but also spatially; for it was unable to penetrate areas beyond the territory that the Red Army had occupied between 1944 and 1945.

The *potential* for Soviet expansion westwards had been checked by US military power, through the combination of nuclear deterrence *and* intimidation, based upon the US technological lead in the development and manufacture of strategic nuclear weapons, and the establishment of a network of military alliances from the late 1940s onwards (NATO, 1949; ANZUS, 1951; SEATO, 1954) which encircled the USSR and permitted a US global reach that the USSR was never able to equal. The military reach of the US was to be matched by its global economic expansion through public and private overseas investment and the development of a multilateral liberalised trading system. The external (military) context that prevented any further Soviet advances in Europe also reinforced the prevailing tendencies within the Kremlin based on Stalin's overriding concern with consolidating and strengthening communist power within the USSR and the Soviet bloc and not risking the gains of the victory over Nazism that a war with the US would jeopardise.

Whereas the Cold War conflict was stabilised, albeit through two opposing military alliance systems – the Warsaw Pact and NATO – each side effectively accepted the division of Europe and did little to try to alter it. This contrasted with ripening sources of social conflict across the third world and in the declining European colonial empires which laid the foundations for successive waves of revolutionary crises and, from them, political-military confrontations involving the superpowers and the US in particular. Whilst Europe, then, remained a crucible of Cold War, it was one where the agents were principally states (and the superpowers in particular) and where the currency of conflict was confined to diplomatic denunciations and occasional military tensions. This contrasted with the earlier phases of Cold War in Europe dominated, as they were, by social classes and political movements committed to revolutionary change; in most cases in a communist direction. The linkage that had been broken in Europe between communist movements, socio-economic crisis, revolution and military conflict was much more pronounced in the third world, making it a region where the dynamic of Cold War was to become most marked.

The paradox was not only in the differentiation between Gaddis's[2] superpower 'long peace' in Europe and the eruptions of conflict, violence and war in the third world, but also in the much more marginal role the USSR played in the third world until the 1960s. What this suggests is that the conceptual framework of bipolarity or a 'Cold War system' dominated by the superpower relationship does not accurately reflect the historical or empirical reality of a significant part of the post-war Cold War, where only one superpower was a global actor. Furthermore, even the reach of the US was constrained by the continuing presence and influence of Britain and France in much of the third world throughout the 1950s. Finally, with the emergence of communist China in 1949, the Cold War, arguably, could be seen as multipolar rather than bipolar, at least in east Asia, as Soviet involvement in the Korean and Indochina wars was of secondary import after China in the 1950s and, in the case of Vietnam, until the mid-1960s.

This chapter will analyse the evolution of the Cold War from 1950 until 1962. It begins and ends, then, with a focus on two of the defining crises and conflicts of the Cold War – the Korean War and the Cuban missile crisis, both of which involved the superpowers, but also which originated *not* out of superpower strategic plotting but rather the outcomes of localised social-political conflict involving revolutionary and communist movements. This chapter will concentrate on developments in the third world, specifically the attempts by communist-revolutionary forces allied to though autonomous from the USSR to secure revolutionary social transformations, and how such change threatened US designs for the post-war international order and provided opportunities for the expansion of Soviet international power and, in doing so, led to geopolitical confrontations between the superpowers.

What this chapter seeks to highlight is the significance of local/domestic sources of Cold War understood as products of social conflict emanating from the legacies of imperialist and capitalist penetration of particular societies in the third world and how and why the US responded to these developments militarily. It also seeks to address how these local agents of revolutionary change not only provided the sole means of expanding Soviet power at this time, but also exposed the core contradiction at the heart of Soviet international relations – how Soviet support for international revolution threatened to provoke a military-nuclear confrontation with the US at a time when the US held an advantage in strategic nuclear weapons.[3] Finally, the chapter seeks to examine the emerging tensions within the Soviet-communist bloc with respect to Soviet relations with east-central Europe and China, and how the tensions within these relationships, particularly in the latter case, contributed to the dynamic of the Cold War.

The chapter begins with a discussion of the consolidation of the superpower blocs in Europe during the 1950s. This is followed by an analysis of the crisis that erupted within east-central Europe in the mid-1950s and the emerging Sino-Soviet split. The chapter ends with an examination of new fronts of revolutionary crisis in Korea, Indochina and Cuba and how they provoked superpower geopolitical confrontations.

EUROPE'S 'LONG PEACE': THE CONSOLIDATION OF COLD WAR BLOCS AND THE MILITARISATION OF THE COLD WAR

With the implementation of the Marshall Plan in Western Europe in 1947 and western moves towards the establishment of a West German state in June 1948, the consolidation of a divided Europe around two opposing political-geographical blocs under superpower leadership was clear. The USSR had responded to the Marshall Plan with the creation of Cominform (Communist Information Bureau) in September 1947, as a way of instilling ideological and political direction and co-ordination amongst communist leaderships in the Soviet bloc and Comecon (Council for Mutual Economic Assistance) in 1949 to organise trade and other economic links between the USSR and the east-central European 'satellites'.

The Creation of NATO and the Warsaw Pact

With the 'seeing off' of each bloc's respective internal political threats through the marginalisation and electoral defeat of communist parties in Western Europe, and the coercion and repression of non-communists in east-central Europe, the only way that the political map of Europe could be redrawn would be through a change in the military-geopolitical framework that 'governed' Europe's post-war political development. This was made explicit with the formation of NATO in April 1949 and the Warsaw Pact[4] in May 1955. The creation of the Warsaw Pact was formally in response to German rearmament and membership of NATO, but as with NATO (though to a much lesser degree) the Warsaw Pact was, or became, much more an organ for upholding Soviet-communist power in east-central Europe and ensuring the militaries of its east-central European communist allies were integrated and loyal to the USSR. This is something that I will discuss below. Suffice to say, the Warsaw Pact formalised the Red Army's integral place in the institutionalisation of (Soviet) communist power in the region which was already evident through the use of the Soviet coercive power in establishing communist dominance in the region after 1945.

The need for the USSR to institutionalise its social-political presence in east-central Europe through military power rather than through the institutions of a capitalist economy, civil society and bourgeois democracy provided an important source of political legitimacy not only for NATO but also German rearmament. The cycle that began with Marshall Aid triggered a tightening of the Soviet grip on east-central Europe evident in the Czech *coup* of 1948, which in turn strengthened calls for a US military commitment to Western Europe on both sides of the Atlantic.

Although the creation of the Warsaw Pact could be seen as a legitimate response to German rearmament, especially since it occurred at a time when the ravages of German military aggression were still fresh in the minds of the Poles and Czechoslovaks in particular, it was very much a Soviet-inspired creation which contrasted with NATO, which reflected to a much greater degree the *external* security concerns of western European leaders.[5] As history would have it, neither NATO nor the armies of West European states were deployed to suppress an internal political threat to the post-war liberal capitalist order. This is not to suggest that given the emergence of such a threat military force (including US military power) would not have been used, as in France in May 1968 had the French police not been able to deal with the combined student–worker insurrection, and as was planned for Italy with the CIA-organised P-2 Gladio network which was to be enacted if and when the PCI came to power. Instead, it merely underlines the different way social and political power was constituted in the western half of Europe and the disengagement of direct political coercion from the maintenance of social order within *advanced* capitalist societies, and how the bouts of intensified social conflict that erupted during the post-war decades never threatened the power of the capitalist state.

Whereas NATO was primarily a product of developments in east-central Europe and Western European calls for a US military presence, the Warsaw Pact was much more a product of internal political developments; indeed, it was a 'natural' consequence of the Soviet form of political power in east-central Europe. Without it, that is, without Soviet military dominance and the subservience of the armies of east-central Europe to Soviet objectives, Soviet-communist power would have unravelled much earlier than 1989.

The Problem of German Rearmament

The militarisation of Cold War Europe at least in the form of two military alliances facing each other, however, was far from inevitable, even after

Western European fears about Soviet military power had become much more pronounced after 1948. An important stumbling block in this regard was how far Western European governments, committed to some kind of national economic welfare, could convince their populations of the necessity of rearmament and how this might undermine such welfare objectives – the 'guns over butter' dilemma. More importantly, however, was the scope of Western European rearmament and what role, if any, the newly created West German state should play in it.

This was particularly problematic for the French. Any meaningful military alliance in Western Europe, unless it was going to be based upon the permanent garrisoning of hundreds of thousands of US troops, something both the US Congress[6] and Western European public would not allow, required the involvement of the two major continental powers – West Germany and France. Yet any suggestion that so soon after the end of the Second World War Germany would be rearmed set alarm bells ringing in Paris. Although suspicions and fears remained, it was political and military developments in east and south-east Asia that played a key role in reducing French hostility to German rearmament. The North Korean attack on South Korea in June 1950 and subsequent war combined with increasing French dependence on US military aid in its struggle with the Vietminh in Indochina contributed to a shift in French security concerns away from Germany towards the USSR. In the same way that the perception of Soviet aggression in east-central Europe between 1945 and 1948 had contributed to the declining fortunes of the French and Italian communist parties and the political division of Europe, so the perception of Soviet-directed military aggression *across borders* in Asia assisted those willing to accept German rearmament and make the fundamental shift in French strategic thinking by seeing the USSR as a greater threat to France than Germany.

Discussions over how to integrate a rearmed West Germany into the embryonic institutions of West European security revolved around US concerns to maintain its leadership of NATO but without having to carry the military burden of providing NATO's military teeth through deploying large numbers of troops in Europe[7] and French concerns to ensure that a rearmed Germany would be integrated and subordinated within a European alliance system that it would lead. The tensions that fluctuated throughout the history of the post-war transatlantic alliance during the Cold War and after (most obviously over the 2003 Anglo-American invasion of Iraq) originated, then, over these different strategic and political concerns.

After accepting the need for West German rearmament the French attempted to ensure that they, or Europeans, as the British were invited to participate, would effectively control the strategic consequences of a rearmed West Germany. This was what the announcement of the Pleven Plan in October 1950 by the French premier, René Pleven, hoped to achieve. Pleven's proposal drew on the framework of the Schuman Plan,[8] which had been announced in May, whereby German (military) power, as opposed to its coal and iron production, would be integrated into a European military alliance, led by France rather the US. For the US, any hesitation over the Pleven Plan based upon the potential for a European or French challenge to its alliance leadership (which was a possibility should the Pleven Plan become operational) was overcome by the urgent need to boost European rearmament, and also to maintain French resolve and success against threatened communist expansion in Indochina.

In May 1952 six states, one of which was West Germany, signed the treaty establishing the European Defence Community (EDC). However, after months of arguments and deliberations the French parliament failed to ratify the treaty in August 1954 mainly due to Britain's refusal to commit its military forces fully to the EDC. With the failure of the EDC the problem remained of how to organise the required increased European contribution to the Atlantic Alliance. The solution came from Britain, who proposed admitting West Germany and Italy to the Brussels Pact of 1948. Unlike the failed supranational EDC this was a conventional military alliance and it already provided for a significant British commitment and military presence to Western Europe's defence. This was enough to persuade the French, and the Brussels Pact was transformed into the eight-member Western European Union in October 1954.

In less than a year West Germany acceded to NATO in May 1955. The dilemmas and conflicts within the transatlantic alliance had been resolved, with the Europeans shouldering a greater part of the military burden of NATO with German participation, whilst the alliance had been turned into what was a paper military entity in 1949 to one with significant military bite by 1955. Furthermore, and politically significant, France had failed to obtain a European military framework autonomous of the US, under its leadership, and Washington had secured a more dominant position within the alliance through its diplomatic leverage over Germany, as its principal external guarantor from Soviet aggression, and its deployment of more troops in Europe.

The significance of these developments went beyond Europe. The spectre of a global communist military threat orchestrated by the Kremlin apparently indicated by the announcement in 1950 of the Sino-Soviet Alliance, the USSR's acquisition of atomic weapons in 1949 and the communist 'aggression' in north-east and south-east Asia were key developments in shifting European and US political opinion towards militarising the alliance and containing the USSR and communism militarily. In this sense the moves in Europe towards militarisation reflected a shift on the part of the US towards a much greater emphasis on military power to deal with the Soviet/communist threat. Consequently, without the developments just mentioned, particularly the Korean War, the militarisation of the Western Alliance and the projection of US global power might not have emerged, at least not in the form that they did. Thus, local eruptions of intense (i.e. militarised), social and political conflict involving communist forces committed to revolutionary transformation, even without Soviet sanction[9] or involvement, *always had geopolitical consequences* tending to provoke a militarised response from the West. This was a persistent feature of the Cold War.

NSC'68: The Militarisation of Containment

The key document and decision in the militarisation of US foreign policy was NSC'68, a paper commissioned by President Truman in January 1950 to review national security policy after the shock of the earlier than anticipated successful detonation of an atomic device by the USSR in August 1949.[10] NSC'68 was accepted as the basis for US military and strategic policy by the Truman administration in May 1950. Truman's acceptance of its proposals settled the nature and orientation of post-war US foreign policy from the ambiguity over the nature and scope of its commitment to defend Western Europe from (Soviet) aggression and, more fundamentally, in committing the US to a global struggle combining the full political, ideological, moral and economic resources of the US against the Soviet Union and international communism, and in defence of the 'free world'. Once communist forces had crossed one Cold War boundary – the 38th parallel on the Korean peninsula in June 1950 – it became much easier for the Truman administration to convince Congress and the public of the possibility that something similar might occur in Europe. Without this *casus belli* things might have been rather different.

NSC'68 launched US and transatlantic alliance rearmament, and in doing so communicated in clear, unambiguous language that the USSR could not afford to test the military resolve of the US. Leffler states that US military production in early 1953 was seven times the level it had been in June 1950. Whilst the Korean War had been an obvious stimulus to increased war production, only a small proportion of the increased military production went to Korea; most went to Western Europe and elsewhere, highlighting that the consequences of NSC'68 were global in scope rather than just focused on east Asia. Furthermore, the US sought to extend its lead in strategic nuclear weapons by successfully testing a hydrogen device in 1952 and increasing the production of nuclear warheads with the aim of having over five times the number of warheads that the USSR had by 1955.[11]

The Post-Stalin 'Thaw'

However, whilst a 'strategic dynamic' in the Cold War was escalating military competition and threat, the leaderships in Washington and Moscow changed: Eisenhower replaced Truman in January 1953 and two months later Stalin died. The consequence of Stalin's death was obviously more significant, particularly when it was far from clear who would replace him. Much has been written[12] about the so-called 'lost opportunity' that Stalin's death and a new leadership in the Kremlin provided in a similar fashion to the way in which Gorbachev was seen as a very different Soviet leader from his predecessors and how this was recognised by the West, which was crucial to bringing the Cold War to an end. The consequences of Stalin's death and his public repudiation by Khrushchev in February 1956 proved to be paradoxical, however, as I will show.

Whilst we need not accept the assumption that a change of leadership in the USSR in 1953 (and at other times) was enough to signal a transformation in superpower relations and the Cold War, we do need to recognise that the new Soviet leadership did manage to signal a shift in foreign policy. For one, the new leadership put pressure on Pyongyang to agree an armistice to end the Korean War and, along with the Chinese, also pressured the Vietminh to accept the division of Vietnam at the Geneva conference in July 1954 to end the 'first' Vietnam War.[13]

These 'accommodations' could be seen to reflect the concern of the new Soviet leadership over the consequences of military conflict with the West.[14] These concerns were encapsulated in the idea of 'peaceful co-existence', which Khrushchev adopted as his foreign policy mantra. Peaceful co-existence amounted to a renunciation of the assumption, associated with Stalin and the 'early' Lenin, that war between capitalist and communist states was inevitable. Instead, Khrushchev did the eminently rational thing[15] in a world of nuclear weapons – and where military conflict could trigger nuclear annihilation – of making it clear that competition and conflict between the two social systems did not have to lead to military conflict and that communism could expand peacefully.[16] It was this shift, in rhetoric at least, that suggests that the early post-Stalin period resembled what in the 1970s would be called détente.

The intensification of militarised Cold War between 1949 and 1953 gave way to a brief de-escalation of military tension in the mid-1950s, and in July 1955 a summit in Geneva, which achieved little of substance, indicated the possibilities of superpower agreement on controlling nuclear weapons, highlighted by Eisenhower's 'open skies' proposals for the aerial inspection of each side's nuclear weapons, which were to bear fruit in the late 1960s and early 1970s. However, with the Soviet response to the Hungarian Revolution of 1956 and the nagging problem of Berlin's status unresolved from 1949 after the lifting of the Soviet blockade, diplomatic and military tensions increased in Europe and between the superpowers in the late 1950s.

The Second Berlin Crisis, 1958–61

Berlin, or more precisely the status of West Berlin deep inside East Germany and the concerns this raised for the East German regime and Moscow, provided an issue which reignited military tensions and diplomatic conflict. The principal problem was the flow of people and skilled workers to the West[17] through the porous frontier of East–West Berlin and the way in which the presence of a western zone in East Germany cemented West Germany's military alliance with Washington deep in the heart of the Soviet bloc. This had become particularly acute for Moscow with the prospect of imminent West German nuclear armament, which made the attainment of the USSR's goal of a demilitarised Germany more remote than ever.[18]

The haemorrhaging of skilled and productive labour had a devastating impact on the East German economy. An economic solution – that is, economic inducements based on increased Soviet aid, to persuade people to stay – was ruled out, as the USSR did not have sufficient resources to address the gravity of the East German regime's demands. This, as Zubok and Pleshakov[19] suggest, was probably the decisive factor in pushing Khrushchev, prodded by the East German leader, Walter Ulbricht, to try to force a solution to the 'Berlin problem'.

In November 1958 Khrushchev demanded that the Western powers (Britain, France and the US) and the USSR negotiate a peace treaty with divided Germany, and end the division of Berlin. The demand was accompanied by a threat that unless such a treaty was concluded within six months the USSR would hand over control of access to West Berlin to the East German government, which would threaten another blockade of West Berlin. The second Berlin crisis had begun. Negotiations revolving around Soviet proposals for the withdrawal of West and East Germany from NATO and the Warsaw Pact respectively and the internationalisation of Berlin began, whilst the US proposed a unified Germany with free elections to decide the nature of its government, confident that the communists would be routed.

The negotiations dragged on and Khrushchev's deadline passed. However, with a new President (John Kennedy) in the White House, Khrushchev sought to turn up the pressure by reinstating the six-month deadline. Kennedy responded by calling Khrushchev's bluff – not for the only time – that the US would resist with force any change in the status of West Berlin, which was followed by a war of nerves, with both sides strengthening their military forces in Berlin, highlighted by the image of a US and Soviet tank facing each other at the crossing point 'Checkpoint Charlie'. The increased tension provoked by the crisis increased the flow of people westwards and with no intention of starting a war with the US, the Soviets agreed to Ulbricht's call to seal East Berlin's border with the construction of the Berlin Wall in August 1961. This stemmed the tide of migrants, but came at a propaganda and military price for the two communist states. The wall was a serious blow to the social and political legitimacy of the East German regime, and Khrushchev's failure to carry out his threat at a node where the Western Alliance was, militarily, most exposed highlighted the problematic nature of the USSR's 'military hand' by having to risk war, and a nuclear one at that, to force Western concessions, when the USSR's strategic-nuclear posture was at a disadvantage vis-à-vis the US.

The military containment of the USSR was brought home in the outcome of the second Berlin crisis. Without a strategic-geopolitical opening for the USSR, such as those which emerged between 1944 and 1948 and in the early–mid-1970s, the USSR's dependence on coercive-militarised power was always limited by the possibility of gambling that Soviet moves would not provoke a US military response, something the Soviet leadership wanted to avoid at all costs.

TENSIONS WITHIN THE COMMUNIST WORLD: THREATS TO SOVIET POWER IN EAST-CENTRAL EUROPE AND THE DEVELOPING SINO-SOVIET SPLIT

Challenges to Soviet-Communist Power in East-Central Europe

The tensions that resurfaced between the superpowers over the status and political orientation of Berlin and Germany between 1958 and 1961 were intimately connected with the stability of communist power in east-central Europe and the decisions of the post-Stalin leadership in the USSR. The early post-Stalin period between 1953 and 1956 was characterised by a power struggle inside the Kremlin,[20] instability in east-central Europe and East Germany, Poland and Hungary in particular and, by the end of the decade, the emergence of a major schism between the two great communist powers, China and the USSR.

The sources of these tensions and crises were largely endogenous, associated as they were with the nature of communist power. Communist power was based on eliminating alternative sources of ideological legitimacy, including dissident 'anti-party' ideological and political currents, and promoting economic development through highly centralised and coercive methods. With the end of the Stalinist era, both issues surfaced as sources of disagreement and conflict, not only within the Soviet bloc but also between Moscow and Beijing. With respect to ideology, the key personalities within the Soviet leadership jockeying for power – Khrushchev, Molotov, Malenkov and Beria – disagreed over how far future Soviet policy at home and abroad should be based on explicitly Stalinist formulas. Disagreement over ideology also translated into differences over economic policy and the method of constructing socialism and what the social and material bases of socialism were. Under Stalin there was little ambiguity over these issues. The material basis of socialism was the establishment of heavy industry at breakneck speed to provide the foundations for a war economy necessary to deter and fight the imperialist aggressors. Immediately after the war this translated into the subordination of the economies of east-central Europe to the post-war reconstruction of the USSR's shattered industrial base through the plundering of plant and machinery.

Such policies severely undermined the ideological and economic viability of implanting (Soviet) socialism in east-central Europe. The political legitimacy of communist power, then, was undermined by both the political and economic nature of communist power: politically, in that it was externally imposed and openly based on coercive-militarised power, and economically, in that economic assets had been seized by the USSR and economic activity was subordinated to Soviet objectives and prescriptions.

Khrushchev's doctrine of peaceful co-existence rested on a combination of domestic and foreign policy changes that were to be mutually reinforcing. Indeed, Khrushchev's objective of stimulating economic development within the USSR and Soviet bloc through a loosening of the command economy and a focus on the production of consumer goods required a transformation in the external military-geopolitical context in a similar fashion to the way in which Gorbachev's domestic reform programme of *glasnost* and *perestroika* necessitated 'new thinking' in foreign policy and in relations with the West and the US. Similarly, Gorbachev's reform programme, like Khrushchev's, was highly risky in that it faced opposition from within the Soviet leadership, and in significant elements within the Soviet party-state bureaucracy, as well as from some east-central European communist leaders, many of whom were committed to Stalinism.

The greatest risk was that the relaxation of centralised and coercive power would undermine Moscow's supervision and 'control' over east-central Europe, if not the USSR, as social and political forces took advantage of the increased autonomy from the centre and developed institutions, relations and social spaces that would implicitly test the limits of pluralism and diversity within the Soviet bloc and challenge communist power therein. This is exactly what happened. Whereas in 1989 the release of such social and political forces led to the collapse of communist power between 1953 and 1956 it led to the deployment of the Red Army to maintain communist power.

The first signs of instability emerged in East Germany three months after Stalin's death. Although not directly caused by the end of the Stalin era, developments within East Germany were connected with the different positions towards the 'German problem' of the key personalities in the Kremlin – Khrushchev, Molotov, Malenkov and Beria. Indeed, as Mark Kramer[21] has convincingly argued, it was the turn of events in East Germany that played a crucial role in the leadership struggle leading to Beria's downfall in June 1953 and execution six months later. Beria had been instrumental in the 'looting' of eastern Germany after the war, and after Stalin's death suggested that the USSR should accept a unified and neutral Germany even if it was capitalist[22] as the best way of consolidating Soviet power. When, in June 1953, workers in East Germany launched an uprising against communist rule, Beria's position on the 'German question' became the focus of severe criticism and contributed to the decision by Khrushchev and Malenkov to move against him.[23]

The East German uprising was the first major challenge to Soviet-communist power since 1945. It emerged out of the policies initiated by the Ulbricht leadership and approved by Stalin in 1952 for the forced and rapid construction of socialism in East Germany. The programme followed the classic Stalinist formula of top-down centralised coercion over the economy of channelling investment towards heavy industry, eliminating small businesses, collectivising agriculture (the disruption of which caused food shortages in the spring of 1953),[24] and clamping down on religious and other forms of social activity. Significantly, it also rested on workers working longer hours for less pay, i.e. making sacrifices to lay the material foundations for socialism. The goal was not only to integrate East Germany further into the Soviet bloc and eradicate the remaining 'bourgeois' elements within East Germany, but to do so in a way that underlined Stalinist goals of centralised-coercive state power. The results were disastrous: economic activity slowed, particularly in the provision of consumer goods, causing a flood of refugees to the West.[25] With the East Germans receiving emergency Soviet aid and Soviet fears of civil unrest and/or mass exodus, Moscow demanded that Ulbricht abandon the Sovietisation programme and relax state repression of dissidents.

However, although the East German leadership announced the introduction of a 'New Course' in early June 1953, reversing most of the policies associated with Sovietisation, it was done in such a rushed way that it caused a major split within the East German party, mainly because the membership was not consulted. The confusion and divisions within the leadership and between the leadership and membership were evident in the contradictory reports concerning the New Course in the 14 June 1953 edition of the East German party's paper, *Neues Deutschland*. In this context of political confusion, splits in the regime, public criticism of the leadership by Moscow and widespread workers' discontent, tens of thousands of East German workers took to the streets of East Berlin and elsewhere in the country to challenge communist rule. On 16–17 June it is estimated that approximately half a million East German citizens marched against the communist regime throughout the country, with some attacking party offices.[26] With the East German party in turmoil the vulnerability of the regime was exposed and without the intervention of the Red Army on 17 June Ulbricht would have been ousted and possibly communist power as a whole.

The crisis in East Germany exposed how economic problems, combined with splits in the local communist leadership and between East Berlin and Moscow, provided the spark for popular hostility towards the communist regime which could not be contained or channelled elsewhere without challenging communist rule. Not for the last time Soviet military intervention rescued an east-central European communist regime.

The next major crisis of Soviet-communist power in east-central Europe occurred in the second half of 1956 in Poland and Hungary. As in East Germany, the sources of the crises stemmed from the consequences of leadership change in the Kremlin and how this altered relations within the Polish and Hungarian communist parties and in their relations with Moscow, combined with the context of severe economic problems associated with the pursuit of Stalinist economic policies in each country.

Whereas in East Germany in 1953 the process of criticising and changing a number of aspects of Soviet policy closely identified with Stalin – de-Stalinisation – had only just begun, by 1956 Khrushchev's campaign of de-Stalinisation was in full swing. The key moment in the attack on Stalin's legacy was Khrushchev's 'secret speech' (the contents of which quickly became very public) denouncing Stalin at a closed session of the twentieth congress of the Soviet communist party in February 1956. Khrushchev's main concern was to consolidate his power within the USSR by attacking and weakening Stalinists opposed to his reform programme within the party-state, but because of the direct links between the Soviet party and communist parties in east-central Europe, and the fact that similar struggles between reformers and Stalinists were also taking place within these parties, the speech provided a further catalyst to de-Stalinisation in east-central Europe and with it increased political instability.

In Poland the crisis consisted of two elements, one involving the challenge from workers 'on the street', in June 1956, the other involving the challenge from a new leadership in the Polish (Communist) United Workers' Party (PZPR) in October of the same year. The crisis initially erupted in late June when industrial workers in Poznan launched a protest that turned into a riot. The protest was primarily in response to the introduction of new and higher work targets as part of a wider programme of Sovietisation launched by the Polish leadership. The protests were violently put down by the security forces, who continued to be heavily influenced by Soviet officers, resulting in the death of over 50 protesters and with hundreds injured.[27] Out of this context, a new challenge emerged in early October 1956 with the return of Wladyslaw Gomulka[28] to the PZPR and the prospect that he would quickly secure the party leadership. This reflected the growing strength of anti-Stalinist reformers within the Polish party who were committed to economic reforms in tune with some of the concerns of the Poznan workers.

In the context of communist authorities having recently violently suppressed a workers' insurrection, the Kremlin was worried that Gomulka might act on his 'Titoist' (national communist) sympathies by taking Poland out of the Soviet bloc. Such fears were given credence by Gomulka's calls for the withdrawal of Soviet officers in the Polish army and the removal of the Polish defence minister, Konstantin Rokossowksi, who was an officer of the Red Army.[29]

The crisis came to a head on 19–20 October just before a PZPR central committee meeting that seemed likely to elect Gomulka as leader. A politburo delegation led by Khrushchev came to Warsaw to warn Gomulka that Moscow would not tolerate Poland's withdrawal from the Soviet bloc. This was backed up by the advance of Soviet military units based in Poland towards Warsaw.[30] With some Polish armed forces commanded by pro-Gomulka elements in the Ministry of the Interior prepared to fight, and with Soviet troops advancing on

Warsaw, the prospect of civil war and a Polish–Soviet war seemed increasingly likely. Such an outcome would not only have been bloody, it would also have had a devastating impact on Soviet-communist power in east-central Europe. As it was, Gomulka reassured the Soviet delegation that he had no intention of taking Poland out of the Soviet bloc, particularly with respect to Poland's membership of the Warsaw Pact and the stationing of the Red Army in Poland, but he insisted on the right of Poland to follow its own path towards socialism.[31]

The 'resolution' of the crisis in Poland was influenced by the emergence of a new and much more serious threat to Soviet power in Hungary in late October. Political developments there had revolved around post-Stalin turmoil within the leadership of the Hungarian (Communist) Socialist Workers' Party, which involved Moscow and the shifting balance of power between Khrushchev and the other personalities I mentioned earlier. In June 1953 the Stalinist Rakosi was replaced by Imre Nagy, whose reputation as an anti-Stalinist reformer helped quell simmering social discontent reflected in the outbreak of social disorder throughout parts of Hungary in the spring of 1953.[32] However, Nagy, who was seen by the Kremlin as allowing anti-Soviet currents in and outside the HSWP to flourish and appearing too close to Tito, was replaced by an ally of Rakosi in the spring of 1955.[33]

With Stalinist forces back in leadership positions, Khrushchev's 'secret speech' was enthusiastically greeted in Hungary with a revival of reformist and radical elements demanding political and economic reform. The events in Poland in June and October further galvanised opposition forces in and outside the HSWP, highlighting what Halliday has labelled the 'demonstration effect' of radical or revolutionary political change in one country triggering similar developments in neighbouring countries.[34] On 23 October thousands demonstrated throughout the country demanding the government's resignation. When Hungarian security forces opened fire on a crowd trying to enter the radio station in Budapest to broadcast their demands, the situation rapidly deteriorated, unleashing an armed rebellion. This triggered the first Soviet military intervention, involving over 30,000 Soviet troops, as local security forces struggled to contain the rebels.

Under pressure from reformist elements within the Hungarian leadership grouped around Nagy, and after a number of Hungarians had been killed, Soviet forces were withdrawn from Budapest and other flashpoints on 30 October, as Moscow hesitated about the use of brute force to resolve the situation and placed its hopes in the hands of Nagy to salvage the situation. Nagy had been readmitted to the party on 13 October and appointed prime minister on 23 October. However, violence continued, as did popular demands for Nagy to go beyond a policy of autonomy within the Soviet bloc. Nagy gave in to these pressures and on 1 November announced Hungary's withdrawal from the Warsaw Pact. Alongside his commitment to multi-party democracy, Nagy had differentiated himself from other reformist currents elsewhere in east-central Europe, especially Poland, and on 4 November a massive Soviet army of 250,000 troops and armour returned to Budapest and other major Hungarian cities. Intense and bloody fighting ensued, leading to thousands of casualties, including over 5,000 deaths. Nagy was deposed, replaced by Janos Kadar and was subsequently executed in November.[35]

The significance of events in Hungary was that the Kremlin and other communist leaderships, particularly in East Germany, Czechoslovakia and Romania, were aware that developments in Hungary were being followed by reformist and anti-Soviet elements which might also rebel against Soviet-communist power should Hungary succeed in breaking away from the Warsaw Pact. Student-led demonstrations in support of the rebellion in Hungary took place in Bratislava and other cities in Czechoslovakia and in a number of cities in Transylvania, the Romanian border area with Hungary. Not implausibly, then, the crisis in Hungary threatened the whole of Soviet power in east-central Europe and even, though to a much lesser degree, social and political stability in the USSR.[36]

The three crises and challenges to Soviet-communist power in East Germany, Poland and Hungary between 1953 and 1956 all emerged out of the nature of communist power in east-central Europe, in particular, in that socio-economic and political power was monopolised by the party-state and identified with a foreign power. The immediate causes of crises, however, related to the coming together of popular demands for economic improvements with splits in the local and Soviet leaderships during a period of transition. A similar context was to produce the collapse of Soviet and communist power in east-central Europe in 1989.

For the future of Soviet power in east-central Europe, the Kremlin realised that if it was to avoid a recurrence of such crises and the need to use brute force, a new pattern of relations was required between Moscow and the Soviet satellites. This was given official blessing, ironically, at the height of the Hungarian crisis with the 'Declaration on the Principles of Development and Further Strengthening of Friendship and Co-operation Between the USSR and Other Socialist Countries'. What this amounted to was not only increased co-ordination and deliberation over policies amongst the members of the Soviet bloc rather than Moscow determining things itself,[37] but also a recognition that east-central European states could diverge from Soviet orthodoxy in some elements of economic policy alongside a flow of funds and subsidies into the 'satellites' from the USSR, the goal being to address economic discontent and 'buy off' any political challenges to communist power. For the next 20 years this would prove to be effective in overcoming the contradictions of Soviet-communist power.

The Emergence of the Sino-Soviet Split

Tensions and crises within the communist world were not confined to the management of the post-Stalin transition in east-central Europe, but also in the wider international communist movement between the USSR and the newly established People's Republic of China as well. Tensions existed even before the communists seized power in 1949, largely due to the legacy of the calamitous consequences for the Chinese communists of following Soviet advice and doctrine in the mid-1920s, and because of Stalin's lack of whole-hearted support for the Chinese communists in their war with the Kuomintang between 1945 and 1949.

The signing of the treaty establishing the Sino-Soviet alliance in February 1950, after a protracted period of negotiations (over two months) between the two communist leaderships, appeared to the West, and the US in particular, as evidence of communist unity and the expansion of the Moscow-directed communist monolith. The outward show of unity and mutual hostility towards the West, however, masked continuing tensions between the two countries.[38] The substance of the alliance reflected Stalin's jealously guarded supreme leadership of the international communist movement and Mao's implicit recognition of China's junior status within it. This was revealed in the hard bargaining involved in negotiating the treaty; the USSR agreed to provide limited economic aid[39] to China whilst maintaining, though for a reduced period, some of the territorial concessions in China that it had secured from the previous treaty between the USSR and Chiang Kai-shek.[40]

The first test of the alliance came with the outbreak of the Korean War in June 1950 and the unexpected US-led intervention in September of that year, which I will discuss in more detail in the following section. Briefly, the war exposed tensions between Moscow and Peking over who should shoulder the burden of confronting US military power on the Korean peninsula and the consequences of such military calculations for the political relationship between not only China and the USSR, but also the broader issue of leadership of communist revolution in Asia. In a nutshell, China's military lead in confronting US forces in contrast to the USSR's actions to distance itself from direct combat with the US strengthened Mao's political position within the international communist movement vis-à-vis Moscow. The intricacies of how the Korean War influenced the Sino-Soviet alliance and the way in which the North Korean leader, Kim Il Sung, tried to play off Mao and Stalin for his own objectives is brilliantly relayed in the publications of the Cold War International History Project.[41]

Regional (and global) political developments in Korea and south-east Asia and the impact they had on the USSR and China, particularly with respect to their respective relations with the US, were bound to challenge the unity of the Sino-Soviet alliance. Such externally induced tensions associated with the geopolitical consequences of revolutionary social change combined with contrasting domestic political, economic and ideological agendas after 1950 to put further strains on the alliance, particularly when such agendas, along with foreign policy, determined domestic political battles amongst different leadership factions within both states. However, as the documents released during the last decade or so also show, personalities, and the clash between Mao and Khrushchev after 1953, point to this as a not insignificant factor in accounting for the emergence of a public split between the two communist giants by the early 1960s.[42]

The death of Stalin and the ushering in of a new phase in Soviet domestic and international politics centred on the personality of Khrushchev, and his programme of de-Stalinisation and highlighted by the 1956 'secret speech' in particular, were to be crucial developments in the gradual unravelling of the Sino-Soviet alliance. The changes in Soviet policy initiated by Khrushchev not only sparked conflict with Stalinist hardliners within the USSR and Soviet bloc, but also with Mao. It was not only the fact that Mao was upset at not having been consulted in advance about the content of Khrushchev's 'secret speech' but, more importantly, the direction of Soviet policy at home and abroad (with the doctrine of peaceful co-existence suggesting a reduced role for military conflict in the spread of communism) clashed with the domestic and international preoccupations of Mao.

The tensions that emerged between the two communist powers, then, were a product of the contradictions that sprung from the constitution of social and political power within each communist state and how the two leaderships sought to overcome them. With respect to the USSR, Khrushchev decided that domestic and bloc stability demanded a change in economic strategy and a reduction in geopolitical tension with the US, whereas Mao's continued dominance within the Chinese leadership required precisely the opposite:[43] a programme of Stalinist-like top-down, centralised and coercive socio-economic transformation of the Chinese countryside and peasantry introduced in January 1958, epitomised in the (disastrous) 'Great Leap Forward', and a policy of geopolitical confrontation with the imperialist powers.

The significance of the ideological differences associated with the divergent views on the correct path for building socialism and anti-imperialism was that both Khrushchev and Mao were vulnerable to internal critics and opponents who sided – ideologically at least – with an external communist leadership. This was revealed in November 1957 during Mao's visit to the USSR where some of the ideas he outlined in speeches during the visit bore marked similarity to the ideological arguments of the recently defeated 'anti-Party group'.[44] Such an ideological faux pas by the Chinese leader was returned in kind in 1964, but more directly, when leading figures within the Kremlin encouraged a visiting Chinese delegation to remove Mao as Chinese leader.[45]

What was at stake in the developing ideological and political conflict between Moscow and Beijing after 1956 was not only the political standing (and personal survival) of particular communist leaders within their respective states, but also the overall direction of the international communist movement. The Soviet communist party considered itself as the leading/directing force of socialist construction and revolutionary class struggle not only within the USSR, but in the communist world as a whole. Mao and China's divergence from the (revised) ideological-doctrinal path established by Khrushchev was an implicit challenge, which was to become explicit by the early 1960s.

Domestic political factors within the USSR and China played an important role in sowing discord between the two sides. However, international developments also played a crucial role in creating the split. Indeed, because of the potential for international crises and conflict with the US to lead to nuclear confrontation, the consequences of such developments between 1953 and 1962 could be seen, arguably, as decisive in causing the Sino-Soviet split. Whereas the Korean War had been a joint enterprise directly involving Moscow, a number of crises, notably the (second) Quemoy crisis of August–October 1958 and the Sino-Indian border conflict of October 1959, saw China initiating conflict. This reflected Mao's attempt to consolidate his leadership position through external crisis, which at the same time posed serious challenges to Khrushchev's policy of peaceful co-existence.[46]

The Quemoy crisis related to the unfinished business of the Chinese civil war and the Kuomintang's continued occupation of a number of offshore Chinese islands, including Quemoy and Matsu. Although, on one level, Mao's quest to unite the offshore islands with the communist-controlled mainland was a domestic matter, it was to have significant international repercussions, not least in contradicting Khrushchev's emphasis on the avoidance of using force to settle international disputes. However, Mao's resort to force also stemmed from his more belligerent and reckless posture towards the West based on his (misplaced) confidence in the USSR's strategic nuclear advantage over the US after the test of an ICBM (Intercontinental ballistic missile) in August 1957 and the successful launch of the Sputnik satellite mission in October. Consequently, whereas Khrushchev spoke of the necessity of avoiding (nuclear) war and moved towards *nuclear* détente with the US, Mao spoke of the US as a 'paper tiger' which would not risk provoking a nuclear war with the USSR. Further, he argued that should a nuclear war occur, the greater populations of the combined communist powers would ensure that they would ultimately prevail over the imperialists.

The Chinese Peoples' Liberation Army (PLA) began a bombardment of Quemoy and Matsu in August 1958. The USSR supported China's goal of 'liberating' the islands from Kuomintang rule and sent military supplies and advisers to the Chinese in August.[47] However, with the US dispatch of a heavily armed naval taskforce to the Taiwan Straits to defend Chinese Nationalist territory, China's aggression quickly turned into a Cold War flashpoint. With US intervention, Mao, in spite of his belligerent rhetoric (and Khrushchev's announcement in early September that any attack on China would be considered an attack on the USSR), was forced to abandon his military operations by October.

Although the Quemoy crisis never really came close to a nuclear confrontation between the superpowers, the way in which the Chinese reacted caused serious concerns in Moscow, which was to have long-term consequences for the alliance and the outbreak of the split. The nub of Moscow's concern was the degree of autonomy that China could have in its use of force and the consequences of such action on Soviet–US relations. Soviet concerns were raised by a comment made by the Chinese foreign minister, Zhou Enlai, during the crisis in September that the USSR would not need to become involved in any conflict that might break out between the US and China involving the use of tactical nuclear weapons. Rather, the USSR should only become involved if and when the US used strategic nuclear weapons.[48] Moscow interpreted this as a possibility that it would be Chinese and not Soviet actions that would decide whether or not the USSR became involved in a nuclear war with the US. Zhou Enlai's words and China's actions had exposed the problem at the heart of the Sino-Soviet alliance: an increasingly autonomous and belligerent China challenging the implicit division of power and responsibility 'agreed' in 1950 when China ceded strategic leadership to the USSR, the consequence of which was that China risked drawing the USSR into a nuclear war with the US.

The fall-out of the Quemoy crisis also affected nuclear co-operation between the two sides. Between 1955 and 1956 a number of agreements were reached on nuclear co-operation, culminating in the October 1957 New Defence Technology Agreement (NDTA), which committed the USSR to support China's strategic nuclear weapons programme.[49] However, even before the Quemoy crisis, Khrushchev had decided that the USSR could not afford to be as generous in sharing its nuclear technology with China. China's conduct during the Quemoy crisis merely reinforced the concerns over the advisability of helping its nuclear weapons programme and how this might undermine Soviet international power and leadership.

What, from a Chinese perspective, appeared to be evidence of the USSR reneging on the Sino-Soviet alliance was given added weight between July and October 1959 with the military clashes between Chinese and Indian troops over the disputed border between the two countries. Chinese actions again challenged the USSR's peaceful co-existence doctrine, particularly when the USSR had developed warm relations with India as a way of securing influence in the Non-Aligned Movement.

The rising tensions over nuclear co-operation, the Sino-Indian conflict with Moscow calling for a peaceful resolution of the conflict, and over new Soviet reservations over the use of force to resolve the Taiwan problem came to a head in Khrushchev's visit to Beijing in October 1959. The disagreements over policy were combined with increasing personal friction between the two leaderships and on his return to Moscow Khrushchev authorised the withdrawal of Soviet scientific and technical advisers from China, which was announced in July 1960.[50]

The official reasons given by Moscow for the withdrawal of its advisers centred on accusations that the Chinese authorities had pressured them to embrace
Beijing's doctrinal positions.[51] These positions were outlined in an article titled
'Long Live Leninism', published in the Chinese communist daily *Remnin
Ribao* (Peoples' Daily) in April 1960. The article accused the Khrushchev leadership of revisionism and denounced the policy of peaceful co-existence as the
appeasement of the imperialist powers.[52]

The split between Moscow and Beijing took on a greater degree of gravity
in 1962 during and after the Cuban Missile Crisis. Prior to this, the growing
ideological dispute between Moscow and Beijing was played out as each side
sought to court the new Cuban regime and justify its ideological stance through
its analysis and policy towards the Cuban Revolution. However, with the outbreak of the Missile Crisis in October 1962 after the US had found Soviet intermediate nuclear missiles on the island, and Khrushchev's decision to withdraw
the missiles to avoid risking a nuclear exchange with the US, the Sino-Soviet
relationship reached a point of no return.

In desperate need of Chinese support in a time of acute tension, the Soviets
decided to revise their 'neutral' position on the Sino-Indian border dispute with
an article in *Pravda* on 25 October supporting Chinese claims about the
inequity of the border. The Soviet leadership hoped that this would bury the
hatchet and shore up the communist alliance at a time when war with the US
looked a distinct possibility.[53] The Chinese response, the last time Beijing officially praised Soviet policy, merely endorsed Soviet policy. As
Prozumenschikov argues, the outcome of the crisis would have an important
bearing on the ideological dispute between Moscow and Beijing. If the US
backed down, then it would support Mao's claim that the US was a 'paper
tiger' and if the Soviets backed down, it would vindicate Chinese accusations
of revisionism and appeasement.[54] With the crisis ending in Krushchev's
humiliation and cries of betrayal from Cuba, the Chinese launched a propaganda offensive attacking the Soviet 'capitulation' comparing Cuba's situation
after Khrushchev's decision to withdraw the missiles with that of
Czechoslovakia in 1938 after the Munich agreement.[55]

By the early 1960s, then, the Sino-Soviet alliance was coming apart and the
disputes over ideology and tactics that had been shielded from public view
were now in the open. With the moves towards a limited form of nuclear
détente between the US and the western nuclear powers with the 1963 Nuclear
(Atmospheric) Test Ban Treaty, the Chinese again accused Moscow of appeasing the imperialist powers at the expense of strengthening the military power
of the socialist camp by making it much harder for China to develop its nuclear
weapons programme. By the mid-1960s, the fraternal ties between the Chinese
and Soviet parties were cut and the communist movements were split between
factions sympathetic to the Soviet or Maoist line. The ideological dispute
became a military one in the late 1960s with armed clashes over the

Sino-Soviet border[56] to the point that the USSR even targeted some of its nuclear forces on China. And with the rapprochement in Sino-US relations marked by Nixon's visit to Beijing in 1972, the Alliance was effectively dead.

GLOBAL SOCIAL CONFLICT AND NEW REVOLUTIONARY FRONTS

In this section I will discuss a number of developments in the third world – the Korean (revolutionary) War, revolution and war in Indochina, and the Cuban Revolution and Missile Crisis – to demonstrate how socio-economic transformation carried out by communist-revolutionary forms of political agency contributed to geopolitical conflict between the superpowers. These developments indicate that the momentum of Cold War was, to a significant extent, largely a product of socio-economic and political developments outside of the direction of the superpowers. Arguably, then, superpower relations were, to a considerable degree, determined by localised social and political developments that not only had an impact on their external/bilateral relations but also their internal domestic politics; the domestic impact of Vietnam on the US and Afghanistan on the USSR are testament to this. Furthermore, the moments when the superpowers came closest to nuclear war were not products of directly bipolar tension and conflict, but instead were products of how each superpower responded to localised revolutionary change as in Korea, Indochina and Cuba.

These episodes of revolutionary transformation in the third world were associated with the broader fabric of Cold War in two senses. First, they were products of a series of crises centred on the reproduction of a specific pattern social and political relations based on capitalist development. This is not to suggest that each locale replicated the historical trajectory of other capitalist states in the third world or elsewhere because no capitalist state follows the pattern of another. Rather, it is to suggest that the crises that confronted a number of states in the third world after 1945 reflected a pattern of historical development based on their establishment as states and their populations' incorporation into the social relations of a capitalist world economy via forms of imperial domination. The consequence was that local-national economic development was determined by the production of commodities (usually primary and/or agricultural products) for the world market, which served the economic interests of particular social constituencies, and those in the 'imperial power' in particular, to the disadvantage of the overwhelming majority of the population and the development of the national economy as a whole.

This structural socio-economic similarity with other cases of revolutionary change, such as Russia and China, was matched by a social and political similarity with the failure of traditional ruling classes to establish more equitable, balanced and independent forms of economic development, mainly because these social groups, unsurprisingly, tended to benefit from the socio-economic status quo. The consequence was that political movements emerged which were committed to challenging the established pattern of external domination, which required the overthrow of the traditional ruling class and the ejection of the imperial presence. The success of these revolutionary movements – communist and radical-nationalist in complexion – was in large part based on their ability to mobilise the mass of the population (workers and peasants) to struggle for revolutionary transformation. Communism, then, was not just a form of state power, but also a product of a particular and *historically distinct* social and political crisis, committed to *historically specific* political tasks – national political independence – based on severing links with the source of external domination and constructing a modern industrialised economy that served the economic interests of a national cross-class alliance rather than the former domestic and metropolitan bourgeoisie.

In both ways – economic and political – revolutionary developments in the third world showed similarities to the revolutions in Russia and China. Third world revolutionary movements, to varying degrees, identified with the anti-imperialism of the Bolshevik Revolution and the Soviet state. The states that they established in Cuba, Vietnam and elsewhere, though defined by the historical and cultural specificities of each, to a significant degree resembled the Soviet-communist form of state with respect to an authoritarian (militarised) party-state's domination of society and economy tasked with establishing a nationally autonomous and industrialised political-economy beyond the tentacles of US capitalism. Furthermore, as much as the Bolsheviks were able to take advantage of the way in which world war fundamentally weakened the coercive power of the Russian state (and other imperial states), so were revolutionary movements in the third world, during and immediately after the Second World War, able to take advantage of a weakening and/or collapse of local-imperial state power. Thus, it was a global-systemic crisis reflected in world war that provided the key catalyst to revolutionary crises in the third world as a similarly global-systemic crisis had done between 1914 and 1918. War, then, was indeed the 'midwife of revolution' and its absence would prove to be equally decisive in the evolution of revolution and Cold War.

The second way in which local eruptions of revolutionary crisis and transformation were part of the broader fabric of Cold War was in their consequences. Revolutionary transformation – both the process, usually through armed conflict, and the state-form that emerged – saw the restructuring of economic relations based on the expropriation of local and metropolitan capital and land by the new revolutionary state, acting on behalf of the new social interests which it served. The relations of *international* (western) capitalist domination were broken. The degree to which this occurred varied from case to case, as reflected in the emergence of what is best described as a form of national-state capitalism in a number of states in the Middle East (Egypt, Iraq and Syria) where 'revolutions' were dominated by radical-nationalists within the armed forces leading popular revolt and the more limited socio-economic and political transformation witnessed in these states. These contrasted with the profounder revolutionary changes that occurred in China, North Korea, Vietnam and Cuba where the break with the capitalism and the world market was more comprehensive and the construction of non-capitalist socio-economic forms more evident.

The elimination of capitalist social relations was of more than economic significance. Economic transformation had profound political consequences. For one, in a number of cases, western property was expropriated, which sparked demands for compensation or restitution by the social groups affected. However, more significantly, the transformation of the economy effectively remodelled the nature of the state and the character of its international relations, as (bourgeois) autonomous and external sources of socio-economic power were no longer able to condition political developments within these states, at least in the *economic* manner they had done prior to the revolution.

However, the changes produced by social revolution went beyond the loss of western economic assets and political influence. The new regime and its ideology were committed to international change and the overthrow of those same social groups that revolutionary forces had just disposed of in neighbouring states. Although revolutionary regimes had mixed success at best in 'exporting' their revolution beyond their borders, their attempts at revolutionary internationalism served to destabilise neighbouring states and contributed to the spread of the threat of revolution. With respect to China, the establishment of the Peoples' Republic in 1949 had a major impact on revolutionary developments in Indochina and the Korean peninsula. At a very local level, then, revolutionary change within a state was of international significance for its neighbours and their external allies.

Where revolutions were carried through by communist movements, the ideological and organisational links with the USSR were sufficient to invoke western hostility. External hostility from the US in particular became militarised, however, because of the way in which these new states were politically constituted, based on state forms dominated by a coercive-militarised apparatus. Statist-militarised regimes committed to regional transformation through (revolutionary) armed struggle – Nasserism in the Middle East, Maoist communism in east and south-east Asia – were sufficient to incur a militarised response from the US. Such dynamics produced geopolitical consequences. However, the militarised response of the West to these new revolutionary states was also a consequence of the manner in which the USSR related to these states and sought to incorporate them into its political orbit. Because of the way that the USSR was constituted, its means of international expansion, unlike US capitalism, rested on relations of external political domination. Military power, then, as in east-central Europe, was used to ensure the maintenance of Soviet 'discipline' and international revolutionary leadership. And, in the case of Cuba in 1962, local revolutionary change was seen as a way of directly altering the strategic balance between the superpowers through the placing of intermediate-range nuclear weapons on the island.

Revolutionary crises and transformation in the third world after 1945 reflected the dynamic nature of the Cold War which emerged from the social relations of uneven capitalist development. In creating different forms of state removed from the clutches of the US-led global capitalist economy, these new states threatened the US project of constructing a liberal capitalist inter-national economy with the US at its heart. In severing links with the US-led international capitalist order, revolutionary states jeopardised the economic interests of the dominant social groups within the US by promoting an alterna-tive form of political economy that, if able to spread and prosper, threatened, as Leffler[57] recognises, the character of the US domestic political economy and the social interests it served. US hostility, then, was not just because of the militarised character of revolutionary states – this was why the US policy of containment became militarised – but because the spread of these different non-capitalist forms of economic development threatened the reproduction of the social relations of the US domestic political economy and, in particular, with respect to access and control of raw materials, access to external markets, and the consequences for the US's *liberal* political economy of increasing militarisation to meet the political challenge of these statist-militarised states backed by the USSR.

The Korean War, 1950–53

The Korean War was the first major military confrontation of the post-war Cold War. Indeed, the Korean War saw armed conflict between US and Chinese military forces and also, for the first and only time in the Cold War, armed combat (in the air) between Soviet and US military forces over the Korean peninsula. As I mentioned above, the war in Korea had an impact well beyond the peninsula and east Asia. The decision by North Korea, with the support of both Moscow and Beijing, to unite the peninsula under communist rule through the invasion of the south in June 1950 was a major factor in ensur-ing that the proposals for militarising US foreign policy, embodied in NSC'68, were implemented by the Truman administration. Furthermore, as part of this move towards militarisation, and in part due to the need to send thousands of troops to Korea, the US pressed for the rearmament of West Germany and its incorporation into NATO, as well as taking on a much greater role in support-ing the French in their struggle with the Vietminh in Indochina (and sowing the seeds of its much greater involvement in Vietnam in the 1960s).

The Korean War was seen by the Truman administration and scholars sym-pathetic to an 'orthodox' interpretation of the origins of the Cold War as an act of aggression directed and planned by Moscow, as part of its global strategy. However, as Bruce Cumings has convincingly argued, local-domestic factors were the primary causes of the war[58] and in this sense the Korean War originated in the rival projects of national unification and social-economic transformation drawing on different social constituencies. On the one hand, concentrated in the north and assisted by the Soviet military occupation between August 1945 and December 1948 were Korean communists led by Kim Il Sung. On the other hand, were anti-communist Korean nationalists and social elements that had collaborated with the Japanese colonial occupation (1905–45), who were assisted by the US occupation authorities between August 1945 and June 1949, and led by Syngman Rhee.

With the end of the war the Potsdam summit agreed the division of Korea into two zones of Allied occupation at the 38th parallel, with US forces moving into the political-military vacuum in the south and the Soviets in the north on the basis that this division would be temporary until a trusteeship to direct Korea towards unity and full independence could be agreed.[59] However, as in Europe/Germany, the political-military division, though officially committed to future unification, served to entrench partition, as rival political groupings took advantage of the political sympathies of each occupation administration to carve out antagonistic political and economic structures. Thus, under the nose of the US occupation authorities, indeed, in part encouraged by the US occupation chief, Lieutenant-General John Hodge, the US recruited former collaborators and anti-communists to assist in the administration of the south. These social elements predictably persecuted leftist nationalists and communists and suppressed demands for land reform and other measures that threatened the social power of the traditional ruling class.[60] In contrast, in the north, communists carved out a new regime based on the persecution of non-communists, the expropriation of property and the creation of a Soviet-equipped army.[61]

By 1949, then, with US–Soviet tensions out in the open, prospects of Korean unification seemed distant, other than through force of arms.[62] It is important to emphasise, as Cumings does, that both newly established regimes – Kim in the north and Rhee in the south – were committed to unification through force and both pressed their superpower patrons to support them to this end. The crucial difference was that whereas Washington remained opposed to facilitating Rhee's aggressive intentions, Soviet policy shifted from one of opposing Kim Il Sung's plans for a 'war of unification' to endorsing it. The primary cause of the Korean War, then, was a clash of rival projects of national and socio-economic transformation. What turned civil war into an international war was Stalin's (and Mao's) decision to support Kim Il Sung's plan for national unification and social revolution through war.

Most scholars, particularly after the publication of a large number of Soviet documents over the last decade or so relating to Soviet decision-making towards Korea, recognise that Kim Il Sung was primarily responsible for the war in persuading Stalin and Mao to support his plans. A number of factors contributed to Stalin's *volte-face* from opposing Kim's plans for unification through war in 1949 to agreeing to support him in April 1950, though on the condition that the Chinese also agreed to support North Korean plans. The most important factor, then, in shifting Soviet policy was the emergence of communist power in China and Mao's commitment to supporting the unification of Korea through force of arms.[63] It was the prospect of China taking the lead in determining the outcome of political-military developments on the Korean peninsula that was a major factor in shifting Stalin's position. With Moscow failing to provide support for the Chinese communists in their victory over the Kuomintang, the USSR could not afford for another pole of communist power to be established outside of its sphere of political-ideological influence. Chinese success in Korea without Soviet involvement would, then, further undermine Soviet 'revolutionary credibility' and leadership of the international communist movement.[64]

Other considerations were also important in revising Soviet policy. The successful explosion of an atomic device in August 1949 strengthened the strategic position of the USSR providing a source of confidence for the deployment of Soviet military power and a means of countering the US strategic advantage in nuclear weapons. Finally, the speech by US Secretary of State Dean Acheson to the National Press Club in Chicago in January 1950, which failed to include the Korean peninsula within the US's strategic perimeter in east Asia, indicated that the US would not intervene militarily to prevent a North Korean conquest of the south. This assumption was supported by the fact that the US had not intervened to prevent the defeat of their allies in China – a much more significant political and strategic prize than Korea. The USSR's perception of the geopolitical context in east Asia was that it was much more opportune for the spread of communist power than in other parts of the world – Europe in particular – where the US appeared to be much more forthright in containing communism and Soviet power.

It seems clear, then, that Stalin's decision to support the use of force by North Korea (and provide arms and advisers to the North Koreans) was premised on the assumption that the US would not intervene with military force[65] in response to North Korean aggression and that communist victory would be swift.[66] This highlights the cautious nature of Soviet foreign policy and particularly over the consequences of the use of force. However, it also highlights, in the same way that the Soviet externally imposed 'revolution from above' in east-central Europe did, that given a favourable geopolitical context the USSR would use force (or support its use by an ally) to expand communist power and Soviet influence. The risks in depending on coercive and military power rather than economic relations to expand the borders of communist power were clearly exposed in the Korean War, particularly when US forces were commanded by a belligerent anti-communist, General Douglas MacArthur, who pressed his political superiors to use tactical nuclear weapons against Chinese targets.

With US and western intervention, the gamble by the three communist leaders blew up in their faces, exposing the tensions between the three leaders and the risks associated with revolutionary war, and the North Korean regime managed to survive thanks only to massive Chinese intervention. The war was to drag on until 1953, ending in stalemate and the restoration of a divided peninsula at the 38th parallel. The war reinforced US and western fears of Soviet-directed aggression, thus playing a major part in the military strengthening of NATO and the implementation of the call for rearmament contained in NSC'68.[67] The war highlighted the problematic nature of expanding communist power outside of a geopolitical context of global systemic crisis and war and tested the Sino-Soviet alliance, bringing to the surface tensions that would play themselves out over the next decade. Finally, the Korean War highlighted the geopolitical consequences of domestic socio-economic change. The basis for the North Korean attack was national and social revolution and the expansion of a communist form of political authority ideologically and strategically linked to Moscow.

Revolutionary War in Indochina and the Origins of US Intervention, 1950–60[68]

War as a means to revolutionary transformation was not confined to the Korean peninsula. In Indochina, at the time of the North Korean invasion of the south, French colonial forces were engaged in counter-insurgency against communist guerrillas, the Vietminh, who were fighting to expel the French colonial presence and establish a national and social revolution throughout Indochina. With the communist victory in China, arms and support began to flow across the border, providing much needed assistance to the Vietminh. This was particularly important as with the outbreak of war in Korea the US became much more involved in assisting the French.

Prior to the Korean War US policy towards south-east Asia had been focused on encouraging decolonisation and the construction of a new, US-led political and economic edifice to replace the weakened colonial order. As in Western Europe, US policy rested on the twin pillars of establishing an open and liberal network of international economic relations as a way of promoting economic development and US security interests in the region backed up by the second pillar of US geopolitical ascendancy.

With the loss of China the US turned to Japan as the centre of its regional system, and with the outbreak of the Korean War Japan became a hub of US military and economic activity in the region.[69] Indochina, along with the rest of south-east Asia, was seen as important as part of a regional sphere central to Japan's post-war economic construction as an open liberal political economy.[70] The US, then, was committed to reordering social and political relations within the region, through the establishment of liberal-capitalist states in place of colonial political forms and, in doing so, promoting social interests (new ruling classes in the region) committed to such goals.

The problem for the US with respect to Indochina was that the leading social and political force opposed to colonial rule and committed to re-ordering patterns of economic development and political power in Indochina was the communist-dominated Vietminh who drew their support from the peasants, workers and nationalist intellectuals and who were opposed to the type of social and political arrangements the US had in mind. Without a local political agent and social constituency with which to construct new political and economic arrangements and in the wider context of communist expansion in China and aggression in Korea, the US was forced to back-pedal on its demand that France act on its commitment to grant independence to the three constituent parts of Indochina (Laos, Cambodia and Vietnam), and recognised the Vietnamese 'puppet' government of Bao Dai in 1950. US policy towards French Indochina was also constrained by the need to ensure France's involvement in the emerging western security architecture in Europe.

With communist aggression in 1950 the US was pushed further towards prioritising the struggle against communist movements and, consequently, supporting the defence of French colonial power in Indochina to the extent that by 1954 the US was financing three-quarters of the French war effort.[71] Whilst in the short term US support helped contain the spread of communist power in Indochina, in the longer term it undermined its broader goal of building an independent and capitalist Vietnam as its support for French rule helped destroy the prospects of an anti-communist nationalist movement emerging to counter the Vietminh's project of national liberation. When the US came to assume the role of 'defender' of South Vietnam in the early 1960s, the social and political forces it had to work with to defeat the communist-led National Liberation Front (NLF) guerrillas were those same social and political forces that had benefited from French colonial power, particularly the landlord class who acquiesced to French rule, as it was the coercive power of the colonial state that upheld the social property relations in the countryside from which the landlords benefited, which the Vietminh were committed to overthrowing. Furthermore, in spite of US pressure during the 1960s, the political representatives of the South Vietnamese landlords continued to frustrate land reform, which, along with napalm, helped drive the South Vietnamese peasantry into the arms of the NLF.[72]

In spite of increased US financial support for the war, French casualties mounted.[73] With the humiliating defeat of the French garrison by communist forces at Dien Bien Phu in May 1954, the French government was forced to sue for peace. A peace agreement was signed in Geneva in July 1954 resulting in France's withdrawal and the creation of three independent states – Laos, Cambodia and Vietnam – all of which would eventually fall to communist forces. With respect to the latter, French forces withdrew from north of the 17th parallel and the Vietminh evacuated their positions south of the 17th parallel, with agreement that elections were to take place within two years to reunite North and South Vietnam.

The division reflected the strength of communist forces in the north in contrast to the south, where the French had managed to hang on to a larger area under the nominal leadership of Bao Dai. However, most political observers agreed that had elections followed within two years Ho Chi Minh would have been the most likely winner, thus unifying Vietnam under communist rule. Ho and the Vietminh had been pressed into accepting the French terms by Moscow and Beijing, both of whom had decided to try to reduce tensions with the US (the so-called 'post-Stalin thaw') after three years of war in Korea and both were concerned at the threats of an escalation in US military intervention should the Vietminh reject the peace agreement.

However, the Geneva agreement quickly unravelled, particularly because the Bao Dai government in the south was replaced in 1955 by the American-backed Ngo Dinh Diem. With the Saigon regime and its external guarantor refusing to abide by the Geneva agreement the stage was set for the continuation of revolutionary war, now involving the US rather than the French. Taking his cue from the successful military containment of North Korea, Eisenhower based US policy on the so-called 'domino theory', claiming that if Indochina fell to communism, the rest of south-east Asia would follow and with it US hopes for a liberal-capitalist political economy in the region.

US concern to contain communism in Indochina was linked to its wider concern with regional security and, in particular, the relationship between war and communist-revolutionary expansion. Consequently, the US pledged itself to strengthening the military power of South Vietnam and committed itself to the defence of the region from external (i.e. Soviet/communist) aggression with the establishment of SEATO (South-East Asian Treaty Organisation) in September 1954. Through this, as with NATO, the US identified the expansion of the communist socio-economic system as a strategic threat. This reflected the means by which communist power had expanded in the past through armed struggle and the nature of the states that emerged, based as they were on abolishing the relatively autonomous sphere of a capitalist economy and (liberal) civil society, thus preventing the forging and means of securing externally induced domestic political change through the currents of international socio-economic relations based upon private property, and instead a coercive-militarised state form.

The state-building mission that the US embarked upon in South Vietnam was, then, concerned to strengthen the internal and external military capacity of the South Vietnam to the detriment of the liberal democratic civil, economic and political dimensions of the state. As Borer highlights, prior to the US commitment of combat troops to South Vietnam in 1965, 78 per cent of US economic assistance to Saigon went towards South Vietnam's military budget.[74]

With the passing of the two-year deadline for unification elections in the summer of 1956 and increases in US military aid to the South, Ho Chi Minh sought and received approval from Moscow for his plans to 'liberate' the south in 1957. He also authorised the formation of communist military units in the south to prepare for a new wave of revolutionary guerrilla war.[75] The decision to launch revolutionary war in the south was a product of the growing opposition, and not just from communists, to the increasingly corrupt and repressive Diem regime. In this respect, although North Vietnam (DRV, the Democratic Republic of Vietnam) encouraged and supported anti-Diem activities in the south, the political initiative, at least at the beginning of the 'second' Vietnam War, lay with an alliance of leftist forces in the south who were responding to local socio-economic and political developments. A coalition of groups, created the National Liberation Front in December 1960, committed to overthrowing the Diem regime and carrying through revolutionary change in the South. The DRV quickly extended support through the demilitarised zone and the porous borders of Laos in particular.[76] Thus, on entering the White House in January 1961, President Kennedy confronted the prospect of a new guerrilla war in South Vietnam and US support for a corrupt and unpopular regime in Saigon. Developments after 1960 will be discussed Chapter 5.

The Cuban Revolution and Missile Crisis, 1959–62[77]

Perhaps the most serious crisis of the Cold War, when the superpowers came closest to a nuclear exchange, was over the installation of Soviet intermediate range nuclear missiles on Cuba during October–November 1962. The nuclear-strategic crisis emerged from the complex interactions involving the Cuban revolutionary leadership and the superpowers between 1959 and 1962. The crisis originated from the consequences of revolutionary socio-economic and political transformation in Cuba launched in January 1959 with the overthrow of the Batista regime carried through under the leadership of the Movement of 26 July.

The overthrow of the brutal and corrupt Batista dictatorship was greeted with widespread approval in Cuba, uniting a wide range of social classes; even Washington greeted the revolution with a cautious welcome.[78] It was not clear what direction the revolution would take; although the Movement of 26 July was led by the radical nationalists Fidel Castro and Ernesto 'Che' Guevara, communist influence – at least from the Cuban communist party – was limited, and the USSR's political and ideological presence in the western hemisphere was negligible.[79] This situation was not to last.

Within months developments within Cuba would see the fragmentation of the cross-class and multi-party political coalition that had celebrated Batista's overthrow and growing hostility from Washington. The revolution's turn towards socialism and Moscow reflected the response and encouragement of the Movement of 26 July to social mobilisations in favour of major socio-economic transformation.[80] Although Castro and the Movement of the 26 July were sympathetic to such demands for redistributing wealth and renegotiating the foreign (largely US) capitalist presence on the island, what was crucial in turning these sympathies into action was the support and demands for such changes by the social constituencies of the urban and rural proletariat throughout Cuba between 1959 and 1961. Thus, whereas the revolution had begun as a 'national democratic revolution' uniting all progressive social forces against the Batista dictatorship, the dynamics of class conflict within Cuba between workers, peasants, landowners and capitalists quickly fractured the revolutionary coalition as the Movement of 26 July sought to locate its support within the most radicalised class constituencies. This brought it into conflict not only with the liberal, bourgeois and middle-class elements within the revolution that wished to maintain the rule of law and the sanctity of private property rights and a limited state, but also the US.

Ever since Cuban independence at the turn of the twentieth century, Cuba's political and economic development had been dominated by the 'imperial' presence of the US.[81] This was particularly evident in the structure and ownership patterns of the Cuban economy, where the US had an overwhelming *material and social* presence within Cuban society.[82] The problems and contradictions prevailing within Cuba, and which were a key ingredient that helped spark the revolution, were, then, directly related to the nature and consequences of the US capitalist-imperial presence in Cuba since 1898. Consequently, the initiation of any major socio-economic and political change within Cuba would obviously affect the US's social and political presence on the island, and when those changes were concerned to meet the socio-economic needs of the Cuban people, a clash with the US became inevitable.

In moving towards the expropriation of private and US property within Cuba the 'Fidelistas' embarked on a state-orchestrated class struggle against local and US capital, leading to political confrontation with the US. It was within this international context that the Movement of 26 July joined forces with the pro-Soviet Cuban communist party as a way of strengthening the organisational basis of the revolution within Cuba and, externally, moved towards an alliance with Moscow to balance the threat from growing US hostility.[83] Internally-driven socio-economic change and class struggle provided the dynamic which initiated the Cuban Missile Crisis, as the Cuban revolutionary leadership, all too conscious of the power of the US, its increasing hostility towards Havana and the many historical cases[84] of US military intervention to prevent revolutionary socio-economic change solicited Soviet support to defend the revolution.

Cuban concerns over the US response to the revolutionary transformation underway on the island were realised in April 1961 with the attempted invasion of Cuba at Playa Giron (the Bay of Pigs) by Cuban exiles based in Miami and trained and equipped by the US. The invasion proved to be a disaster. The new Kennedy administration was less enthusiastic about associating the US, – by committing US forces, to the invasion, and with the absence of air support in particular, Cuban revolutionary forces routed the invaders. The decision by the US to endorse a form of military solution to the Cuban problem reflected the failure of alternative measures, principally the strategy of diplomatic isolation and pressure that the US pursued through the Organisation of American States (OAS), and the economic measures through its capitalist-material presence on the island from late 1959 to 1961. Whilst the US secured strong backing through the OAS in isolating Havana, it was not able to gain a mandate from other states in the region for military intervention to topple the regime – hence the support for a 'Cuban solution' and the hesitancy about the US being directly associated with the invasion, which risked fatally undermining the OAS as an anti-communist and anti-Soviet system, based as it was on the fiction of legal equality and the upholding of the rule of law and political consensus in the diplomatic relations of the region.

With respect to using the levers of capital,[85] with the expropriation of US capital, the US effectively lost its political presence in Cuba, as the end of its *economic* presence paralleled the end of its *political* presence through the institutions, parties and apparatus of the post-independence Cuban state and political system. Whilst the continuation of capitalist social relations provided powerful sources of economic and political influence in Cuba as elsewhere, with a state committed to breaking the power of capital, and supported domestically by significant sections, if not the majority of the population, combined with the external economic support of the USSR,[86] the expropriation of capital and introduction of non-capitalist relations of production, exchange and consumption, eliminated the possibility of economic measures halting revolutionary developments in Cuba.

With the Cuban Revolution moving from a national democratic and anti-imperialist orientation to socialism and with the growing confrontation with the US, Moscow began to take an increasing interest in developments. The Cuban Revolution was significant not only because of its geographical location and the possibility that it offered a 'revolutionary bridgehead' for channelling Soviet influence into a region where, prior to the revolution, Soviet influence had been marginal at best, but also because the Cuban Revolution potentially threatened Khrushchev's doctrine of peaceful co-existence and the downgrading of armed struggle in spreading (communist) revolution. Indeed, at first glance, which Khrushchev and the Kremlin were all too aware of, developments in Cuba seemed to vindicate Mao's analysis of the anti-imperialist struggle. Soviet interest in Cuba, then, was complex and went beyond extending Soviet influence in the western hemisphere to being a major factor in the developing Sino-Soviet schism and, moreover, with Khrushchev's failure to resolve the Berlin problem in Moscow's favour and with his domestic economic policies coming under critical scrutiny,[87] Cuba seemed to offer the possibility of political success which would consolidate Khrushchev's position within the Kremlin and Moscow's leadership of the international communist movement.[88]

However, with its proximity to the US and the evident hostility of the US to Cuba, which had shown itself in military form in the 'Bay of Pigs' invasion, any move by the USSR to develop closer links with Cuba and bring it into the Soviet bloc would not only pose serious risks to the Cubans, by providing ammunition for those elements within the US who were arguing for an invasion to crush the revolution, it would also pose risks to the USSR itself. The geographical distance between the USSR and Cuba made it almost impossible for the USSR to defend Cuba from invasion. Furthermore, the absence of a loyal communist party tied to Moscow organisationally, ideologically and personally exposed the problem that emerged in relations between Moscow and Beijing over the (second) Quemoy-Matsu crisis in 1958, whereby the possibility existed that 'reckless' actions by Havana in its attempts to spread revolution throughout the western hemisphere might provoke a US military response that would put Moscow in an extremely problematic position.

Whereas Havana approached Moscow to secure economic support (which was subsequently to become dependence) thus allowing it to pursue its socio-economic objectives in the face of US opposition, and as a way of deterring further US or US-sponsored military aggression, the USSR approached Cuba to defend the revolution from possible US aggression, but also to bring Cuba into the discipline and ideological-political objectives of the Soviet bloc, thus uniting the objectives of seeing off the Chinese ideological challenge (and elements within the Kremlin) and, with a presence in the western hemisphere, gaining a significant improvement in its geopolitical position vis-à-vis Washington.[89]

The decision to place Soviet nuclear missiles in Cuba ('Operation Anadyr') was agreed in the summer of 1962 after a secret visit to Moscow by Raul Castro in July. The decision to deploy the missiles was reached to secure Cuba militarily from a US attack, as well as increase Soviet *political-ideological*[90] (as much as military) influence over Cuba and, with the hope that the missiles could be made operational before a US response, a major strategic advantage secured against the US. In effect, then, the USSR was using its military power, and its nuclear weapons in particular, to expand the borders of Soviet communism and to challenge US power. Without doubt it was a highly risky decision, yet it was also the only way that the Soviets could secure Cuba and, at the same time, ensure continued Soviet leadership of the international communist movement. Had, Khrushchev and the USSR not acted they would have risked being seen as betraying a revolutionary ally threatened by 'imperialist aggression'. This would have had consequences beyond the Caribbean; alternatively they might have become involved in a military confrontation with the US through the reckless actions of its Cuban ally. Thus, 'Operation Anadyr' was at the same time reckless and rational, as the USSR had limited means of disciplining a revolutionary ally, yet could not afford to see the Cuban Revolution destroyed.

The USSR began to dispatch the nuclear missiles in late September 1962. On 14 October the CIA informed the White House that aerial reconnaissance of Cuba had identified the construction of Soviet nuclear bases stocked with

150 missiles. On 22 October Kennedy made public that the US knew about 'Operation Anadyr' and indicated that the US would not tolerate the presence of Soviet missiles in the western hemisphere, with the announcement of a quarantine of Cuba by the US Navy and the interdiction of all vessels sailing to and from Cuba. The Kennedy administration had acted with a degree of restraint considering the domestic pressure it was under to launch an invasion from right-wing elements in Congress led by Senator Barry Goldwater.[91] However, the quarantine and, in particular, not knowing what the Soviet vessels sailing towards Cuba would do, along with whether or not the Soviets would dismantle and remove the missiles already on Cuba, left open the continuing possibility of superpower nuclear conflict.

As it was Khrushchev, as before over Berlin, blinked first and facing the prospect of US military action agreed to remove the missiles after an exchange of notes with Kennedy between 24 and 28 October. Khrushchev's backing down was a public humiliation. With Castro seething about betrayal and sniping from Beijing, Khrushchev's political credibility at home and abroad was seriously dented and the outcome of the crisis was a major factor in his removal from office in 1964. However, Khrushchev did secure the Cuban Revolution by getting a commitment from Kennedy that the US would not invade Cuba, as well as the secret agreement that the US would withdraw Thor and Jupiter nuclear missiles based in Turkey.

The crisis had a number of consequences. It gave an impetus to arms control that was to gain momentum by the end of the decade and the setting up of the so-called 'hotline' between Moscow and Washington in January 1963, as a confidence-building measure and a means of 'crisis management' should a situation like that over Cuba occur again. For the Soviets, the crisis exposed their continuing strategic disadvantage vis-à-vis the US and, consequently, the Soviet leadership that replaced Khrushchev embarked on a massive programme of increasing the number of Soviet ICBMs and a much bigger naval capacity better to project Soviet military power.[92] These changes would be a major factor in the Cold War during the 1970s.

For Cuba, in spite of the public attacks on Moscow, Havana remained dependent on Soviet economic aid, though it continued to carve out a distinct revolutionary position in the western hemisphere[93] based on armed struggle, the so-called 'foco theory' of revolution.[94] Cuba, in the western hemisphere at least, challenged Soviet doctrine (though with little concrete success in exporting revolution), highlighting the increasingly 'polycentric' nature of international communism, though it never sided with the Chinese in their dispute with the Soviets.[95]

CONCLUSIONS

The period of Cold War covered in this chapter has highlighted a number of key themes that the overall argument of this book seeks to convey as to how we should understand the nature and evolution of the Cold War. First, the US was militarily and strategically dominant during this phase of the Cold War. This is most evident in the relative ease and autonomy in its use of force and the success of militarised containment against attempts at revolutionary and Soviet expansion, particularly in north-east and south-east Asia. Although the US was constrained in its use of military force, ironically, in a 'theatre' of Cold War conflict as close – in the Caribbean – as the Cold War was ever to come to the US mainland, its strategic nuclear advantage forced a humiliating public Soviet climbdown, which was to have profound consequences for the future of the Cold War and the long-term health of the Soviet economy in particular. In many respects, then, in spite of Khrushchev's 'reckless adventurism' in Cuba and his sabre-rattling rhetoric over Berlin, the international reach of Soviet communist power was effectively confined to the Eurasian landmass.

In this respect, during this phase of the Cold War, there was only one super-power with a global reach and record of global interventions. This further underlines the way in which the (socio-economic) constitution of power within each superpower conditioned the international relations of each and the limits to Soviet expansion in a context of geopolitical adversity.

The uneven geopolitical character of the Cold War during this period, which suggests that the abstract idea of bipolarity is not particularly illuminating in explaining the Cold War, also highlights the shifting causal dynamic of the Cold War and the different, non-state forms of political agency engaged in the Cold War struggle. With respect to the former, as much as the evolution of the Cold War reflected US concerns and responses to Soviet policies, the history of the Cold War and US containment policy was also in response to localised attempts at revolutionary seizures of power – sometimes not involving communist forces, at least in leadership positions – and/or the initiatives of other communist revolutionary states, sometimes against the strategic interests of Moscow. The structure of Cold War conflict and the agency involved were, then, much more complex and shifting than traditional theoretical frameworks recognise.

With respect to the latter, revolutionary successes, as in the Middle East, south-east Asia and the Caribbean, highlighted the importance of non-state forms of political agency in the evolution of the Cold War and, consequently, the need to recognise that the revolutionary/communist form of politics was not confined to the political power of the Soviet state and that the challenge that the US confronted extended to the mobilisation of particular social forces in the pursuit of specific *and* antagonist socio-economic goals to the class objectives that the US and its allies sought to uphold and expand after 1945. These incidences of social revolution, as they did before and were to after, highlighted how the Cold War was about how states and societies should be organised and, in particular, the degree to which political, state-organised coercion, should determine the character of the state-society relationship.

Chapter 5 continues the theme of this and previous chapters by highlighting the non-superpower sources of Cold War and the relationship between localised socio-economic struggles and state transformations with geopolitical crises involving Moscow and Washington. However, whilst the early phase of the Cold War after 1945 witnessed the successful military containment of the USSR and the successful use of military power by the US to contain revolutionary forces in the third world, the deployment of massive US military power to prevent the communist-revolutionary unification and transformation of Vietnam was to reverse the pattern of the Cold War, witnessed in the combination of Soviet and revolutionary 'offensives' in the third world during the mid- to late 1970s.

5

The Final Gasp of Cold War: The Decline of US Military Superiority and the Expansion of International Communist Power, 1962–80

INTRODUCTION

The period from the end of the Cuban Missile Crisis until 1980 was marked by a number of major transitions in the character and dynamic of Cold War. Whilst the US had secured a strategic victory through the withdrawal of Soviet nuclear forces from Cuba in late 1962, by the end of the 1960s it confronted the prospect of political defeat and humiliation in the jungles of south-east Asia at the hands of Vietnamese communist forces, backed by the USSR. The failure to prevent communist expansion in south-east Asia and the consequences for the ability of the US to continue to rely on militarised containment were major factors in the succession of revolutionary victories and Soviet geopolitical advances throughout the 1970s. The continuation of militarised containment as the basis of US Cold War strategy in the early 1970s was also challenged by recognition on the part of the US that the USSR had finally reached approximate parity in its strategic nuclear arsenal. Finally, the long boom that had laid the foundations for the post-war restoration of capitalism was about to enter a decade of crisis and recession that would undermine the social and political coalitions upon which US anti-communism had been built after 1945. In sum, the pattern of international relations that had prevailed since 1945 was, by the late 1960s, about to be overturned.

The 'conjuncture of the 1970s' was the third and final international conjuncture of the Cold War within which Soviet geopolitical power expanded on the back of political advances by revolutionary forces across the third world. In this respect it could be seen as the last gasp of the Cold War, understood as the communist and revolutionary consequences of international capitalist crisis. The 1973–79 period thus bore similarities with the earlier periods of structural crisis within the international capitalist system from which the USSR emerged in 1917, and when Soviet power, and that of the social forces of communist revolution, expanded between 1939 and 1945. However, whilst in the two earlier episodes the USSR confronted the prospect of military strangulation by a range of capitalist powers (the Western allies and Wilhelmine Germany in 1917–21, and Nazi Germany in 1939–44), during the 1970s it faced a more geopolitically opportune external environment.

This chapter focuses on each of these transformations in the Cold War, seeking to link the different strands that constituted the sources of transformation. As in previous chapters the historical analysis will engage with theoretical explanations of the Cold War and in doing so develop the main theoretical argument of the book: that the Cold War was a shifting and uneven form of global social conflict, which emerged from the communist-revolutionary outcomes of capitalist development. The chapter begins with a discussion of the failure of US military intervention in Indochina, followed by a brief discussion of the diplomacy of détente and arms control. It then moves on to an analysis of the consequences of the end of the long boom, highlighted by the dismantling of the Bretton Woods managed exchange rate system between 1971 and 1973, and ends with an examination of the revolutionary offensive and Soviet expansion during the 1970s, which culminated in the Soviet intervention in Afghanistan in December 1979.

VIETNAM: THE REVOLUTIONARY DEFEAT OF MILITARISED CONTAINMENT[1]

US involvement in Vietnam[2] began with the provision of financial support and military advice to the French in their unsuccessful struggle against the Vietminh from 1950. With the end of French colonial power as a result of the July 1954 Geneva agreement, the US took it upon itself to construct an anticommunist state linked to its regional security system (based on SEATO) and integrated into the capitalist world economy through a 'regional hub', centred on Japan. From the outset, then, US involvement in Vietnam was part of a wider regional strategy of containment, which was to become highly militarised with the expansion of communist power through the Chinese Revolution, the attempt by Korean communists to unify the peninsula through military force in 1950, and the revolutionary wars of national liberation within different parts of Indochina raging during the 1950s.[3]

US intervention was militarised partly because of the political character of the communist threat that it confronted. Diplomatic, political and economic instruments of containment were ineffectual against social forces and political movements committed to a revolutionary transformation of their societies through force. Although the USSR from the early 1960s, and China after 1949, played a significant military role in the Vietnam War – without which Ho and Giap's strategy of a 'people's war' would not have been able to withstand the

US military assault – the source of the conflict between the US and revolutionary communism was local and specific to Vietnam and the political form and objectives of the Vietnamese communists.

The militarised nature of US intervention after 1954, and especially after 1962, however, also reflected the weak social and political foundations of the South Vietnamese state. From within, military power was required to ensure that the new US-backed South Vietnamese state secured and maintained a monopoly on the means of violence after the combined evacuation of French forces (by 1956) and Vietminh forces (to the north) against remaining rival sources of power in the south at the end of the first Vietnam War. This was never to be realised, as the policies of US-backed governments in the south from Diem onwards not only failed to secure the acquiescence of the rural population in particular but actually antagonised and alienated them, so sowing the seeds for a revival of communist-led revolutionary insurgency with the formation of the National Liberation Front (NLF) in December 1960. Thus, in contrast to US experience in other parts of the world, and particularly Western Europe, where US-backed post-war 'nation-building' could draw on widespread social support and political legitimacy (partly because of the authoritarian and militarised character of Soviet policies in east-central Europe), which permitted containment *within* Western Europe to take on a largely political and economic rather than a militarised form, this was not possible in South Vietnam.

From without, military power was seen as essential for the new state as the US and its southern ally assumed that the greatest communist threat to South Vietnam was through a North Vietnamese invasion, as had occurred in the divided Korean peninsula some years earlier. Further, the character of the communist form of politics and state, resting on explicitly coercive instruments to carry through revolutionary transformation, in some senses necessitated a coercive response. Although US assumptions about the 'external'[4] involvement of the North Vietnamese armed forces in the war from October 1964 were borne out, it was not until after the 1968 Tet Offensive that North Vietnamese forces began to dominate communist military operations in the south.

From the outset, then, and which the US implicitly recognised in its refusal to hold a referendum on unification in July 1956 (as stipulated in the Geneva Accords), the South Vietnamese state rested on very narrow democratic and social foundations. Military power could not alter this fact; indeed, the increasing militarisation of US intervention, and with it the South Vietnamese state, merely exacerbated these weaknesses. What was required was a major overhaul of the socio-economic structure of South Vietnam, primarily through land reform, to break up the large agrarian estates built up and protected by French rule and the political power of the landlord class, which the Vietnamese communists had began to do in the north. In short, a democratic Vietnam after 1954 would in all likelihood have been a communist Vietnam, an outcome the US would not tolerate.

Thus, just as the French had failed to realise the political fiction of local political autonomy and popular legitimacy under their protégé Bao Dai after 1948, so the US was unable to convert the formal/fictional trappings of South Vietnamese political sovereignty, first under their charge, Ngo Dinh Diem, and, after his assassination in November 1963, a succession of military leaders. Consequently, as scholars such as Gabriel Kolko and Marilyn Young[5] have recognised, the outcome of the Vietnam War and US intervention was ultimately decided by the balance of social forces that supported the rival projects of national liberation and state formation associated with each local political leadership in Hanoi and Saigon respectively. Whilst the US and its local South Vietnamese allies managed to kill a far larger number of communist forces[6] (both NLF/Vietcong southern-based guerrillas and regular North Vietnamese troops) between 1965 and 1973, they were not able to build a state in the south that held the political loyalty or reflected the political aspirations of South Vietnamese people.

The situation in the South on the eve of the evacuation of French forces was chaotic, with no obvious political heir-apparent to the French colonial state. It was in this situation that the US committed itself to helping to construct a new, anti-communist South Vietnamese state through Diem.[7] Whilst the French had managed to maintain control of most of the major urban areas in the south, the countryside, in spite of the Vietminh withdrawal, continued to be dominated by political currents sympathetic to the Vietminh, mainly due to the economic reforms and land redistribution carried through by communist forces during the war with the French. Thus, whilst Diem – with US support – moved in to fill the political vacuum produced by the end of French rule, the political situation in the countryside remained much less favourable.

The problem for Diem and the US was that securing the support of the majority of South Vietnamese (who happened to live in the countryside) required radical socio-economic changes that went against the interests of one of Diem's principal sources of support: the traditional landlord class. Although US administrations from Eisenhower through to Kennedy and Johnson pressured their South Vietnamese allies to implement land reform, the socio-economic structure within the South Vietnamese countryside remained largely unchanged[8] throughout the war, as landownership remained concentrated in the hands of the traditional landlord class, with most peasants having little or no land of their own.

The pattern of relations between the US and its 'client' South Vietnam in the area of political and economic reform that was established under the Diem regime persisted throughout the period of US intervention. The land reform measures proposed by the US reflected very modest goals, which were very different from the far more ambitious and transformatory measures proposed and enacted by the communists. Yet even these modest measures (only landholdings over 115 hectares would be subject to confiscation and redistribution[9]) were never fully implemented. Consequently, a negligible amount of the large landholdings were broken up and the highly hierarchical, iniquitous and exploitative social relations of the countryside continued. Further, the failure to provide a capitalist alternative to the communists was compounded by landlords using the South Vietnamese army and police to evict peasants forcibly from the land and the arbitrary violence associated with the South Vietnamese state in its campaign through the late 1950s to root out remaining communist political influence in the countryside, which saw deportation, torture and the killing of suspected communists.[10]

Arbitrary violence increased through the 1960s as the war in the countryside intensified and involved US forces more directly as they took the lead in combat operations against communist forces after 1965. Thus, peasant village communities were forcibly uprooted through the ill-advised 'strategic hamlet programme', based on the classic counter-insurgency formula – inverting Mao's maxim 'to drain the water [the civilian population] from the fish [the guerrillas]'. The upshot was that peasants were moved with no compensation and little infrastructure support, which meant that these new settlements were unviable and soon infiltrated by communists.[11] Alongside this the introductions of napalm and biological warfare[12] in the early 1960s and the 'free fire zones'[13] served to destroy any hopes of building a state in South Vietnam that had popular legitimacy and roots in social constituencies other than the traditional ruling class, and those in urban areas that benefited from US economic largesse through the Commercial Import Programme, which effectively funded the budget of the South Vietnamese state.[14]

The moderation in US-backed proposals on land reform reflected the socioeconomic paradigm of US policy: promoting a capitalist agriculture tied to a regional and global capitalist export structure. In broader terms, however, US policy – except in the military sphere where it retained a good deal of autonomy over the South Vietnamese state, especially between 1965 and 1968 – was mediated and, to a large degree, thwarted by the political interests of the leading elements within the South Vietnamese state. Thus, although South Vietnam survived only with the aid of US dollars and military support, because the US was committed to creating an independent South Vietnamese state and not a colony, it was forced to work with and through local political forces and structures, and to try to build them up. Yet in doing so, it propped up social constituencies and socio-economic structures that prevented South Vietnam from gaining wider social and political support, and instead consolidated the power of those social forces at the heart of the problem. The only area where the US had autonomy was in military operations, a sphere where these social contradictions were made more acute.

With the authorisation from Hanoi in 1959 for armed struggle and the establishment of the NLF in December 1960 (largely in response to the increasing violence against suspected communists in the south) the political and military vulnerabilities of the South Vietnamese state were to be severely tested. As the NLF became bolder and more effective in its military operations throughout the early 1960s, the US became increasingly involved in counter-insurgency, playing a more direct role,[15] mainly through the use of helicopter gunships in support of ARVN[16] ground forces to compensate for the shortcomings of the South Vietnamese army.

The political crunch for US policy in Vietnam came in 1963 in response to increasing evidence of the unpopularity of the Diem regime[17] and the problems of using economic pressure – cutting off aid – on the war effort against the NLF. With prompting from the US ambassador in Saigon, Henry Cabot Lodge, and with little or no hope that the Diem regime could be reformed, the Kennedy administration endorsed a military *coup d'état* in November, which resulted in the assassination of Diem[18] and a new regime, a military junta, under the leadership of General Duong Van Minh. Within a couple of months, Minh was replaced by another general, Nguyen Khanh, more in tune with US concerns, further underlining the contradictions in the relationship between Washington and Saigon, as a government that appeared to be less dominated by US strategic concerns – as Minh's early announcements suggested – was likely to secure wider acceptance amongst the people of South Vietnam, yet at the price of antagonising its US paymaster and economic benefactor.

With new leaderships in both Washington and Saigon, and the former moving towards a much greater involvement in the conflict, the war quickly escalated with the momentous decisions to dispatch US combat troops and bomb the north. US combat troops arrived in Danang in March 1965 following on from the launching of 'Operation Rolling Thunder' (the aerial bombing of North Vietnam) a month earlier.[19] As in the past, the momentous decisions to make Vietnam a US war required Congressional approval and, implicitly, the endorsement of the American public. Congressional endorsement (virtually unanimous), the so-called declaration of war without a formal declaration, came in August 1964 with the Gulf of Tonkin Resolution. This unofficial declaration of war followed an incident that took place between 2 and 4 August 1964 when, according to the Johnson administration, North Vietnamese naval forces launched unprovoked attacks on two US Ships, the *Maddox* and *Turner Joy*, in the Gulf of Tonkin.[20]

With the escalation of the war, not only did North Vietnamese forces become more involved, so did their communist allies, particularly the USSR (to be discussed below). Further, the war quickly became a domestic political issue within the US. As the war dragged on, the US extended the draft (after 1965) and casualties mounted, the anti-war movement became an increasingly important factor in US policy. With the Americanisation of the war, the state that the US was supposedly defending and helping to build became even more dependent on its ally. When domestic developments in the US shifted after 1968 (largely in response to the political humiliation inflicted on US forces by the joint North Vietnamese/NLF Tet Offensive in January 1968) and particularly after the last US combat troops were evacuated in March 1973, the weaknesses of the south's military power were rapidly exposed.

With the periodic bombardment of North Vietnam and the 'Ho Chi Minh trail' (the main supply route from North Vietnam to communist forces in the south which traversed the Vietnamese–Laotian border) the US attempted to use massive conventional air power to destroy the material base and political will of the North Vietnamese. The material and human toll on North Vietnam was huge. However, the political will of the North Vietnamese leadership and people, combined with support – not just in military supplies – from Moscow and Beijing, allowed North Vietnam to withstand the US air onslaught. In the south US forces took the lead in combat operations to crush the insurgency through superior technology and military force.[21] The US followed this strategy because the communist forces in the south – Vietcong and North Vietnamese – had got the better of the ARVN in military engagements, and because US policy in the political and economic sphere came up against the contradiction of dealing with a state that was unable to address the social and political issues at the heart of the conflict. The resort to military power, then, reflected political weakness and the frustrations of US policy towards Vietnam. Further, in judging its success by how many Vietcong it had killed, the US ended up killing the very people in the South Vietnamese countryside upon whom any political salvation of the South Vietnamese state rested. In this sense US military power was abstracted from a political strategy to win the war. The logic was that the only way that the US could be victorious was by eradicating the population base from which the NLF drew its support.[22] General William Westmoreland, commander of US forces in Vietnam, admitted as much in that the massive use of firepower in Vietnam served to 'deprive the enemy of the population'.[23]

The relationship between South Vietnam's political weakness and overwhelming US military strength was exposed in the Tet Offensive at the end of January 1968. The wider political context, particularly within the US, of Tet was that the US was supposedly winning the war. Tet highlighted something very different. In an audacious and co-ordinated attack, NLF forces, for the first time, brought the war to the cities, attacking five of the six largest cities in the South and 36 of the 44 provincial capitals. In Saigon, Young[24] documents how an NLF force of 1,000 tied down 11,000 US/ARVN troops, occupying the heavily fortified US embassy. The dialectic between political and military power in the Vietnam War once again revealed itself in Tet and its consequences. Militarily, the Tet Offensive saw huge losses inflicted on the NLF from which it was never fully to recover, leading to a much greater northern involvement in the war. Politically, the offensive did not result in a revolutionary insurrection in the cities occupied by the NLF, and from this point of view it could be seen as a setback for the NLF political strategy to end the war.[25]

For the US and its ARVN ally, Tet saw the successful deployment of over-whelming military power, but at a significant political cost. The images of NLF cadres in the US embassy in Saigon and the cold-blooded killing of a hand-cuffed and unarmed prisoner by the head of the South Vietnamese police broadcast in US homes not only exposed the lie parroted by Westmoreland, that the US was winning the war, but also that they were fighting a just war. These political problems, highlighted in polls showing further falls in support for the US presence in Vietnam, were compounded by Westmoreland's call for 200,000 more troops to 'win the war'. In a post-Tet context where the US mil-itary in Vietnam was boasting that it had killed tens of thousands of Vietcong, suggesting that fewer US forces would continue to be required, Westmoreland was demanding more. The Johnson administration refused Westmoreland's request; the highpoint of US military involvement in Vietnam had been reached. With this, the US effectively recognised that it could not win the war through military means.[26] The question now was what political settlement it could reach to preserve the South Vietnamese state.

Although US military operations intensified immediately after Tet,[27] with the election of Richard Nixon in November 1968 the US moved towards negotiations with Hanoi and the Vietnamisation of the war.[28] Peace talks began in Paris in January 1969 and in June of that year Nixon announced the withdrawal of 25,000 US troops. However, although the US moved towards negotiations and a reduced role on the ground, these elements of de-escalation were paralleled by an intensification of the air war and the Phoenix programme.[29] However, Nixon and Kissinger's attempts to secure 'peace with honour' and a US withdrawal, leaving behind a non-communist south, were under increasing pressure from an impatient anti-war movement at home. Anti-war demonstrations across the US peaked dur-ing 1969–70, with massive demonstrations in October–November 1969 involving hundreds of thousands across the US, providing crucial pressure on the Nixon administration to show concrete results of its so-called peace strategy.

The degree to which the anti-war movement reflected the will of the major-ity of Americans and caused the US withdrawal from Vietnam is arguable. What is clear, however, is that the mass demonstrations indicated that the US was a deeply divided nation, which posed a serious threat to the post-war Cold War consensus. In short, combined with emerging economic difficulties – to a significant degree caused by the economic costs of the war[30] – US society was about to enter a period of political and economic crisis.[31] One major expression of that crisis was the growing movement of anti-militarism, which helped break the Cold War consensus over the role of military power in containment policy. This was to be given Congressional expression between December 1970[32] and 1976[33] in legislative attempts to reassert its control – signed away in the blank cheque of the 1964 Gulf of Tonkin Resolution – over executive privilege in foreign policy, particularly over the deployment of US forces overseas and, in the case of Vietnam, by cutting off funds for the war effort.[34]

However, in spite of pursuing Vietnamisation the Nixon–Kissinger strategy was not willing, initially at least, to end the war if it resulted in the collapse of its South Vietnamese ally, as this was the key to preserving a very battered US prestige. Peace talks, then, continually stalled, interrupted by periods of intense US bombing and communist military offensives such as in the spring of 1972, until negotiations resumed in the summer of 1972 that led to the peace agreement in January 1973 signed by all four parties: North and South Vietnam, the US and the NLF.[35]

With the passing of the War Powers Resolution in November 1973, combined with the Watergate scandal, Nixon's promise of rescuing the south should Hanoi breach the peace agreement unravelled, and with the Saigon government refusing to act on the stipulations of the agreement on negotiations to bring the NLF into government, Hanoi decided to use military force to break the impasse in the spring of 1975, culminating in North Vietnamese troops capturing Saigon on 25 April 1975 and bringing the Vietnam War to an end. The fall of Saigon was quickly followed by the fall of the other Indochinese dominoes to communist forces in 1975. Yet wider south-east Asia and the key state of Indonesia remained resolutely anti-communist. The US had lost Vietnam but had made North Vietnam and the Vietnamese people pay a dreadful price to secure national and social liberation.

A number of factors contributed to the US defeat. The anti-war movement in the US, assisted – as the Republican right would have it – by a 'treacherous liberal media', and the reassertion of Congressional authority over foreign policy and executive power, all played a significant role in the US 'losing the war on the home front'. The role of the communist powers in supporting Hanoi and the Vietnamese people in their struggle were also crucial factors; the provision of aid and the deterrent to a full-scale US invasion of the north or use of nuclear weapons.[36] However, the key to the US defeat was local and based on the character of the two political forms that emerged from the first Vietnam War in 1954. The South was not a viable state in the sense of the social forces that supported it at its foundation and the US dependence on a military solution to a social and political problem further weakened the *political* strength of South Vietnam. As I mentioned earlier, the political logic of US strategy was the physical destruction of the South Vietnamese peasantry. In itself this was a barbaric policy; politically, it was catastrophic. However, this strategy of US militarism was defeated only because of the political will of Hanoi and hundreds of thousands of NLF cadres and others in the south who were willing to make the supreme sacrifice to realise national and social liberation.

The Communist Powers and the Second Vietnam War[37]

The USSR and China[38] played a major role in supporting the Vietnamese communists in their struggle, and the growing intensity of the Sino-Soviet dispute through the 1960s[39] also had a major impact on the role of the communist powers in the war. Thus, prior to the massive escalation in US involvement in 1964–65, Soviet involvement in the Vietnamese conflict had been secondary to the Chinese role.[40] This stemmed from the legacy of Chinese involvement in the first Vietnam War and the similar ideological perspectives on the use of force in the anti-imperialist struggle shared by Beijing and Hanoi, which clashed with the Soviet idea of peaceful co-existence associated with Khrushchev.[41]

As much as the geopolitical context of US military power had conditioned the policies of Beijing and Moscow in 1954 towards Hanoi in pressuring Ho to accept the Geneva Accords to ward off the prospect of US military intervention, so the policies of the USSR and China during the 1960s were conditioned by US military involvement in Vietnam (and its possible escalation) as much as they were by the deterioration in their bilateral relations. In this sense, Vietnam became a major factor in the Sino-Soviet dispute. Whilst the character of the conflict in the early 1960s suggested a vindication of the political-ideological stance of the CCP of revolutionary guerrilla war, exposing the US as a 'paper tiger', after the commitment of US combat troops in 1965 the political-ideological dimensions within the international communist movement were inverted.

After 1965 the Chinese yet again, faced the reality of a large US military presence on their regional doorstep and the prospect of direct conflict with the US. Further, such a scenario clashed with the domestic objectives of Mao, on the eve of the launching of the 'Great Proletarian Cultural Revolution' against his ideological opponents within the CCP. Finally, any military clash between the US and China over Vietnam would necessarily involve the USSR and expose the strategic vulnerabilities of China.[42] For the USSR, the escalation in US involvement highlighted the risks of the strategy of revolutionary war as well as the folly of Mao's description of the US as a 'paper tiger'. Further, it highlighted the need for much greater Soviet involvement in the war as a way of subverting the 'reckless' and 'dangerous' Chinese influence and ensuring that communist Vietnam could absorb the hammer blows inflicted by US military power, as well as subjecting the Hanoi leadership to Soviet geopolitical concerns to contain rather than escalate US involvement in the war.[43] Finally, with the ousting of Khrushchev from the Kremlin in October 1964, the new Leonid Brezhnev–Alexei Kosygin leadership was keen to restore Soviet prestige within the international communist movement after the public humiliation caused by the withdrawal of Soviet nuclear forces from Cuba two years earlier, and in response to the increasingly virulent Chinese ideological attacks. The consolidation of a Beijing–Hanoi axis in this regard, on the back of the defeat of US imperialism in Vietnam, would have dealt a major blow to Soviet prestige and leadership of the international communist movement.

For North Vietnam, as US military intervention increased, so Hanoi became more dependent on its external allies.[44] Yet, like Kim in Korea in 1950, Ho and the North Vietnamese leadership used the political-ideological divisions and tensions to their advantage and, despite material dependence, managed to maintain a high degree of political autonomy throughout the war.[45] The relations between the communist triad, then, reflected the interconnection of domestic ideological and political struggles and how these were played out within the international communist movement, combined with military developments on the ground. With the intensification of US military involvement in 1967–68, the Soviets put evermore pressure on Hanoi to negotiate with Washington and, by making concessions, reduce the likelihood of the war escalating further and dragging the USSR and/or China into direct confrontation with the US. However, whilst recognising this, we need to recognise that Moscow did not abandon its ally, and at the same time that Moscow was offering to act as a mediator for talks between the two sides, it continued to provide military supplies to North Vietnam.

As with Cuba in Latin America, Soviet policy towards Vietnam and southeast Asia was concerned with the wider/regional 'correlation of forces', as much as it was with defending the Vietnamese Revolution and incorporating Vietnam into the Soviet bloc. Through Vietnam, as it was (in a misplaced way) hoped with regards to Cuba after 1960, the USSR – by means of an allied and dependent local leadership – would realise its wider objectives understood as expanding Soviet influence in other (mainly non-communist) states in the region, particularly Indonesia, and thus curtailing US influence in the region as well as China's ambitions as an alternative political-ideological pole within the international communist movement. Yet, the tension within this strategy was that because it was implicitly highly militarised, i.e. it rested on the containment and defeat of US military power in Vietnam, the defence of the Vietnamese Revolution undermined the possibilities of building a broader anti-imperialist front in the region. Consequently, whilst trying to *contain* the strategic consequences of the war, the USSR at the same time ended up *amplifying* the international and strategic aspects of the war by having a presence within North Vietnam through its provision of political and military support.

Soviet support for North Vietnam, then, helped realise a successful war of national liberation and contributed to the biggest military-political defeat for the US during the Cold War. This was at a relatively, and comparatively small, cost.[46] Soviet military involvement ensured that North Vietnam could maintain the strategic and political offensive despite being heavily bombed,[47] and also, ultimately, limited (alongside the Chinese conventional military threat) the possibility of a US political victory through military power. Soviet militarisation at the strategic and conventional level served to undermine US military omnipotence after the Cuban Missile Crisis. The ability of the USSR to maintain a strategic influence in Vietnam, which in the long run helped ensure a US military defeat, appeared to reflect the fact that the US, for a number of reasons, had finally recognised the strategic-military weight of the USSR, and was acting accordingly. Victory in Vietnam served to undermine US and

Chinese power in south-east Asia. It also seemed to reinforce the Soviet form of an international relations of expansion whereby the Soviet Union would consolidate and expand internationally through the successful transformation of social relations through social revolution, premised on Soviet strategic and political protection. The international vanguard of the USSR had appeared to have been realised in the successful conclusion of the Vietnamese Revolution.

DÉTENTE: THE CONTRADICTIONS OF CONTAINMENT BY DIPLOMACY

The US defeat in Vietnam was a key factor in promoting a realignment of strategic relations between the superpowers (and China) during the early 1970s. However, even before the US defeat, the strategy pursued by Nixon's National Security Adviser, Henry Kissinger, to secure withdrawal from Vietnam whilst maintaining US military prestige in large part consisted of redefining relations with the communist powers. In this sense, then, the origins of détente lay in US attempts to use a diplomatic strategy to prevent its political defeat in south-east Asia, which was to be applied more broadly to Soviet relations with the third world throughout the 1970s.

Initially, Kissinger's diplomacy concentrated on China and reflected attempts to take advantage of the Sino-Soviet split as a way of pressuring Moscow to lean on Hanoi in peace negotiations. The first signs of the new line in US Cold War thinking came with Nixon's surprise visit to China in February 1972.[48] Whilst the basis of US *rapprochement* with China derived from its increasing political-military difficulties in Vietnam, for the Chinese, improved relations with Washington would allow it to concentrate its military concerns on the USSR, and also helped provide a more stable international context for the domestic political reconstruction of China in the early 1970s after the chaos of the Cultural Revolution. In concrete terms not much came from the US opening towards China in 1972, particularly as Kissinger's diplomatic offensive failed to force Hanoi to concede to US demands, yet it was obviously an important factor in pushing Moscow to take up arms control talks with the US.

With its evacuation from Vietnam, for the first (and only) time since 1945 the US found itself in a position where its conventional military power had been severely blunted. Further, the domestic political consensus and public support that had allowed the US to deploy its military power with such effect and relative freedom since 1950 had evaporated with the débâcle in Vietnam. On top of these defensive developments, the US also confronted a Soviet Union that now matched its strategic nuclear arsenal,[49] after embarking on a massive programme of increasing its strategic nuclear weapons capacity after its humiliation in its Caribbean in 1962.[50] In short, the US was in a position where it had to devise methods – other than relying on military power – to contain Soviet-communist expansion. Détente was the outcome.

The warming of relations or easing of tension between Moscow and Washington, indicated by a series of superpower diplomatic summits, trade agreements,[51] agreements on crisis management (particularly after the 1973 Arab–Israeli War) and, most important of all, arms control agreements[52] between 1971 and 1979, reflected a new, and different conjuncture of the Cold War, characterised by US concessions to the USSR. In this respect, détente should not be considered as an episode outside of the Cold War but rather as a continuation of Cold War, but by other means, particularly on the part of the US. For the USSR, détente could be seen as the realisation of its policy of peaceful co-existence, which, at least based on Khrushchev's understanding, rested on distinguishing global competition and conflict between the two social systems of capitalism and communism from the strategic competition and the arms race between the superpowers. Thus, the social, ideological and political conflict of the Cold War would continue as social forces in shifting locales struggled for the ascendancy of one social system over the other and, correspondingly, the international power of each superpower, but decoupled from the threat of superpower nuclear confrontation. For the USSR détente meant the continuation of the Cold War without the threat of nuclear war. Prior to détente, and as exemplified by the Cuban Missile Crisis, the US advantage in possession (and use) of (strategic) nuclear weapons allowed it to contain the spread of Soviet-communist power. Détente, then, reflected the realisation that the US's post-war nuclear advantage had been neutralised, thus cancelling out (alongside its inability to deploy conventional military forces) a major element of post-war containment policy.

The most important element of détente were the moves towards arms control. The two SALT treaties sought to institutionalise arms control in specific categories of weapons. In particular SALT I checked the growth of land-based intercontinental ballistic missile (ICBM) launchers, whilst SALT II sought to extend the limits on more categories of long-range weapons. Both treaties, and détente in general, rested on a wider international political momentum and, in particular, political support from within the US. Whilst the arguments for arms control and containment by diplomacy and linkage were in the ascendant in the early–mid-1970s, by the end of the 1970s, the international political climate and, consequently, domestic political climate, had changed considerably.

Détente was, then, based on a contradiction. The substance of the changes reflected in détente concerned shifts in US policy, highlighted in Kissinger's strategy of linkage, whereby the USSR would be encouraged to moderate its behaviour by delinking Soviet support for revolutionary armed struggle in the third world and by linking this 'good' behaviour with concessions and inducements highlighted by arms control and trade agreements. Linkage did offer benefits to the USSR: the export of grain from the US (which American farmers lobbied for) helped address the endemic problems of Soviet agriculture and the two major arms control treaties provided a brief hope that the burden on the

Soviet economy of reaching parity could be lessened. However, as we shall see, the revolutionary consequences of the contradictions of international capitalism could not be addressed by détente, and although the USSR did not initiate this new wave of revolution, it did seek to take advantage of the more favourable geopolitical circumstances produced by détente.

In many respects, the idea of détente and academic discussions of its place in the wider tapestry of the Cold War reflect liberal theoretical and political assumptions. Simply put, the claim[53] was that détente reflected a broader set of developments whereby world politics was increasingly characterised by developments external to superpower strategic and military competition, alongside the increasing significance of other relationships (involving other states) and the importance of non-military forms of power, grounded in the assumption that co-operation characterised world politics as much as conflict. The fact that détente was soon to be replaced by a return to a more intense phase of Cold War – what some scholars have called the 'new' or 'second' Cold War – primarily through a reassertion of US global power in the ideological and military spheres, and a breakdown in arms control talks and other spheres of co-operation, highlights the deeper and more substantial roots and relations of conflict. This was implicit in the different understandings of détente in Washington and Moscow. For the former, détente meant the continuation of containment by other means; for the latter it implied a greater freedom to assert and spread its influence in the south.

Further, although the US was not to deploy its nuclear and conventional military power in the way that it had done between 1950 and 1973, its foreign policy, particularly under President Reagan, was highly militarised through the massive expansion in military expenditure, particularly in strategic nuclear weapons, and in its support for anti-communist governments and armed movements in many areas of the south. Finally, the 'revolutionary offensive' in many parts of the third world – Zbigniew Brzezinksi's 'arc of crisis' – not only highlighted the continuing currency of social and ideological struggle in world politics, but how these struggles were associated with the Cold War and the superpowers. I discuss this in greater depth below. Before I do so, I will discuss the impact of the end of the post-war boom and the collapse of the Bretton Woods system.

THE COLLAPSE OF BRETTON WOODS AND THE ONSET OF A NEW WAVE OF CRISIS WITHIN CAPITALISM

The transformation in the strategic-military relations of the Cold War highlighted by the US defeat in south-east Asia and détente was replicated in the crisis and changes within the political economy of international capitalism throughout the 1970s. Consequently, US international political strength was challenged not only in the strategic-military sphere, but also in the economic sphere, with the unravelling of the political and economic arrangements that had governed the capitalist world economy since the late 1940s. Whilst these developments had nothing to do directly with the USSR,[54] the onset of economic crisis triggered social conflict within the capitalist world, particularly within and between the advanced capitalist states. This shook US leadership of the western world and with it, the socio-economic foundations of the Cold War within the West.[55]

Because the Cold War was a conflict present within states, and within the two political-ideological blocs as much as between them, the fracturing of the political and economic relationships that had fuelled post-war economic growth and thus political stability not only broke up the Cold War anti-communist social contract between capital and labour, but also threatened the wider structures of capitalist power at the domestic and international levels, upon which US national security rested.[56] The intensification of social conflict within the capitalist world[57] (intra-West and north–south[58]) raised the prospect of two political scenarios, each of which would have had profound consequences for the national security and economic health of the US. One was that the advanced capitalist states of Western Europe would move towards a nationalist-statist economic stance, thus rolling back the post-war waves of economic liberalisation promoted by Washington, particularly in international trade and foreign investment.[59]

The other and far more serious scenario was that the intensification of social conflict within the advanced capitalist states would lead to a revolutionary anti-capitalist transformation within these societies, raising the prospect of explicitly anti-American social and political forces gaining political power, and expelling the US political and economic presence within these states, a prospect that US foreign policy since 1945 had been most concerned to prevent. In reality this scenario seemed highly unlikely. The closest that a major Western European state came to the 'revolutionary scenario' was in France[60] in the late spring and early summer of 1968 with the combined 'student–worker insurrection' of May 1968, and in Italy in the late 1960s–early 1970s with a combination of widespread industrial unrest and the emergence of ultra-leftist terrorism associated with the *Brigate Rosse*.

As it was, the sources of political instability in Western Europe were quickly overcome, and although the 1970s were dominated by low rates of economic growth and recession[61] and periods of intense social conflict, particularly in Britain in 1974 and 1976–79, neither scenario was to be realised and the socio-economic foundations of the Western alliance and thus the Cold War were preserved.[62] Further, during the 1970s the US embarked on a set of policies to reassert its economic leadership of the capitalist world – what came to be known as neoliberalism.[63]

To a large extent the crisis that erupted within the international capitalist economy resulted from the success of the long boom – a key ingredient in post-war stability and the strength of the capitalist world after a series of major convulsions in the early decades of the twentieth century which contributed to the outbreak of the two world wars and revolutions. Between 1950 and the early 1970s the international capitalist economy and the advanced countries in particular witnessed unprecedented economic growth – by 1973 output within these economies was 180 per cent higher than in 1950[64] and world production of manufactures quadrupled[65] – providing the material basis for major improvements in the living standards of the majority of the population.

The sources of the boom were derived from the adjustments in US foreign economic policy after the failure of the original 1944 Bretton Woods agreement, highlighted by the scrapping of plans for the rapid liberalisation of international economic relations and the introduction of Marshall Aid. The introduction of the Marshall Plan established the basic framework of the postwar international capitalist economy, of which the key features were these:

- *The Bretton Woods managed/fixed exchange rate system:* The value of currencies was agreed by public monetary authorities (finance ministers and central banks within the forum of the IMF) based on the fixed price (exchange rate) of US$35 for 1 oz of gold. This was agreed at the Bretton Woods conference in 1944, a time when the US possessed over half of all international gold reserves, and most dollars were circulating within the US. In effect, then, the value of currencies was pegged to the dollar and could only be changed by political agreement, and the US dollar became the international reserve currency and primary means of international exchange. This gave the US rights of seignorage, the benefits of which I will discuss below. This system, however, was not fully implemented until after 1959 when most European currencies finally became fully convertible for trade purposes, thus allowing businesses to use their domestic currencies to buy dollars to pay for imports, and restrictions on capital controls continued to remain in place.
- *The US export of capital:* Because of the shortage of capital (dollars) to fund reconstruction and for purchases of goods (most of which were produced in the US immediately after the war),[66] beginning with the Marshall Plan the US pumped credit into the economies of the advanced capitalist states. Consequently, from 1950 the US ran a deficit on its capital account[67] (which compensated for the massive surplus in its balance of trade with the rest of the world), as more capital flowed out of the US to provide liquidity for the other advanced capitalist countries, thus overcoming the dollar shortage and stimulating economic growth. On top of this, the export of capital was promoted by paying for US overseas military bases and troops (and military interventions in Korea and later Vietnam).
- *European regionalism:*[68] The US encouraged economic reconstruction and growth in the other major centres of the advanced capitalist world through regional co-operation and permitting trade discrimination against US

imports but in favour of European and Japanese exports to help bring the international balance of trade to some kind of equilibrium.[69] A key political aim of US foreign economic policy after 1947, then, was to build up the economies of the other advanced capitalist states as a way of promoting social and political stability and US international political legitimacy. The long-term economic consequence of this, however, was a relative decline in US economic superiority,[70] as Europe and Japan began to compete with US capital by the mid–late 1960s. US political hegemony, then, came at a cost of relative economic decline.[71]

- *Managed capitalism and welfare states:* The post-war arrangements allowed for significant domestic political-economic autonomy for the other advanced capitalist countries, whereby the impact of external economic shocks was limited (primarily through co-ordination in exchange rate policies and capital controls) and the US tolerated significant state involvement and collectivist measures, such as the welfare state, in the economy. The power of capital and international capital in particular was, then, to a significant degree restrained through relatively high and progressive levels of taxation, capital controls, a massive increase in collective social provision (in health, welfare and education), state involvement in management, planning and direct economic activity (through state-public ownership of industries), and a broader ideological consensus that collective (i.e. workers') rights and provision were legitimate.[72]

All of these elements of the 'golden age' of capitalism began to unravel during the 1970s, and in doing so undermined the social and political stability of the major capitalist states and the legitimacy of US leadership of the capitalist world. As much as the US had been the key player in constructing the framework of international capitalism after the war, so it was primarily responsible for the restructuring of the international capitalist economy after 1971. What, then, were the changes that began in the 1970s and what impact did they have on the Cold War?

As mentioned above, the source of the crisis was a product of the structures and relations that had produced the economic successes associated with the long boom. Post-war economic growth (in production and trade) rested on international liquidity based on US capital outflows, which, in the medium term, undermined the competitive economic strength of the US economy vis-à-vis the other advanced capitalist economies as capital was invested and accumulated in other advanced capitalist economies.[73] However, the stability of the international monetary system, based as it was on the dollar's (fixed) convertibility to gold, rested on the continuing competitive economic strength of the US economy reflected in the maintenance of a healthy balance in its current account.[74]

This contradiction, evident in the declining stocks of US gold reserves in Fort Knox and the accumulation of overseas dollar liabilities throughout the

1960s – the so-called 'dollar overhang' – reached crisis point in 1971.[75] In effect, the value of the dollar, and consequently the Bretton Woods system of international monetary arrangements, could no longer be sustained, as the US/gold standard could not meet its external liabilities, causing a major decline in confidence in the value of the dollar as a reserve currency. The contradiction reached a critical point in 1971 when the announcement, for the first time since before the First World War, of a US balance of trade deficit[76] combined with higher interest rates in the Euromarkets[77] triggered a massive outflow of dollars from the US as speculators – expecting a dollar devaluation – exchanged dollars for other currencies, and central banks converted dollars into gold.[78] The US response was dramatic, the so-called Nixon shock of August 1971,[79] when Nixon unilaterally suspended the Bretton Woods system by ending dollar–gold convertibility, effecting a *de facto* devaluation of the dollar, and imposing a 10 per cent surcharge on all imports.[80] The US Treasury Secretary, John Connelly, demanded that the suspension of the dollar–gold standard produce a devaluation sufficient to yield a $13 billion surplus in the US trade balance, enough for the US to cover its overseas military burdens and capital investments.[81]

With the failure of the Smithsonian Agreement of December 1971, the West Europeans and Japanese failed in their attempts to resuscitate some kind of new managed/fixed exchange rate system, mainly because the US no longer wanted to be held to the discipline of a monetary system that limited its freedom of action in monetary affairs, domestically and internationally. The collapse of the Bretton Woods system exposed not only the contradictions in the post-war international capitalist economic order but also conflict amongst the major capitalist powers. The US decision to terminate dollar–gold convertibility and introduce protectionist measures sacrificed the health and stability of the global economy on the altar of US domestic politics and political stability. Thus, rather than American citizens bearing the costs of economic adjustment to correct the imbalance that had emerged by the late 1960s through cuts in public spending and raising taxes and interest rates – the classic neoliberal solution – the US cut its overseas dollars liabilities/foreign debt through devaluation and began to undermine the monetary stability of the other advanced capitalist economies.

The disagreements between the US and the other advanced capitalist countries continued in 1973–74 as the US decided to abolish capital controls against the wishes of the West Europeans and Japanese. This decision was a move to promote the one area of US comparative economic advantage over its main economic competitors – the US financial market centred on Wall Street – which would allow US banks and financial institutions to take advantage of the surplus dollars in the international financial system, thus strengthening the power of the US financial system.[82] The US could do this because of privileges of seignorage based on the profits and advantages accrued from the issuing of dollars. As Gowan[83] suggests, the consequence of this is that the US has not faced the same balance of payments constraints that other economies face, which means that it can spend far more abroad (paying for military bases and troop deployments as well as foreign direct investment) than it earns there, and because key commodities such as oil are priced in dollars the US is far less affected by changes in the exchange rate of the dollar than are other countries. In effect, then, dollar seignorage, particularly since 1973, has meant that US monetary policy became *de facto* global monetary policy and, further, gave the US unlimited credit abroad to pay for its foreign (Cold War) expenditures without having to compensate by liquidating its assets and increasing taxation. Finally, seignorage also meant that US public debt became world debt as an increasing amount of it was held by foreigners through more dollars circulating outside the US than within. Thus, in spite of the relative decline of its economy vis-à-vis the other capitalist powers, as the surplus countries have funded the deficit by holding dollars, which are channelled back to the US through (effectively irredeemable) US Treasury 'IOUs', the US has not only managed to maintain its hegemony over the capitalist world, but also has allowed it to begin contesting Soviet advances by the end of the 1970s.

The reasons why the dollar-holding currencies acquiesced to such an unfair relationship were political – the fact that Japan and Germany were US military protectorates – and economic – their respective economic health depended on export-led growth to the US market, something that ending this monetary relationship would jeopardise. The upshot is that dollar-holding/surplus economies have indirectly contributed to US spending in armaments and other goods, through taking in – buying – unwanted/unspent dollars to prevent appreciations in their own currencies which would endanger their export-led growth.

The transition to a new international monetary regime based on US unilateralism was a major, if not determining, factor in producing a crisis of confidence that plagued the capitalist world economy throughout the 1970s. This was further aggravated by the oil crisis of October 1973 when Middle East/Arab members of the oil-exporting cartel, OPEC, raised prices and cut production in support of the joint attack by Arab armies on Israel – the Yom Kippur War – and as a way of tilting the relationship between oil producers and (western) consumers in favour of the former. The oil price rise contributed to structural changes – increased worker militancy fuelling inflation – and a breakdown in international policy co-ordination and international monetary instability to produce stagflation – rising unemployment combined with high rates of inflation which marked the global recession of 1974–75.[84]

At the time the international political outcomes of these developments on the Cold War were far from clear. In pursuing unilateralism and politicising international economic relations the US risked a rupture in the western Cold War alliance and in helping to spark international monetary instability it also risked provoking social unrest in key allied countries, which had the potential fundamentally to undermine the western Cold War system. As it was, these scenarios were not realised. Instead, the absence of a significant 'revolutionary' social constituency within the advanced capitalist states allowed the social forces of capital, spearheaded by the US, to embark on a transformation in the nature of international capitalism that would lead in the 1980s to the gradual, if uneven, overturning of the socio-economic gains that working people had secured in the earlier post-war decades. In short, the (economic) crisis of the 1970s was resolved in favour of capital, and US capital in particular.[85]

US unilateralism in ending dollar–gold convertibility in August 1971 and abolishing capital controls in January 1974, thus ushering in a new era of international capitalism, needs to be understood, however, from a wider context than that of its position within the international capitalist system alone. As the previous sections (and below) suggest, this crisis was directly linked to the Cold War struggle with the USSR and international communism in the sense that one of the major causes of US economic weakness was the burden of the economic costs of militarised containment. Whilst the US was willing to make concessions in one sphere – détente – because of domestic political expediency it was not willing to make further concessions and adjustments that would have crippled its political and economic ability to contain Soviet-communist power that the readjustments suggested by the other advanced capitalist countries would have led to.[86] In this sense, whilst US policy in the economic and strategic-military spheres had been complementary after 1947 – hegemony over the capitalist world through economic largesse and containment of Soviet communism through military power – during the 1970s this relationship came apart as the costs of militarised containment came to a head at the same time as the US and world capitalist economies entered a period of crisis.

For the US to maintain the twin objectives of hegemony over the capitalist world and containment of Soviet communism, détente and economic unilateralism were the most obvious policies given the economic and political challenges it faced at the time. However, the political-military leverage the US continued to hold over two of its major economic protagonists at this time – West Germany and Japan – meant that it could afford to sacrifice intra-western co-operation and harmony in the economic sphere knowing full well that the ruling classes in Bonn and Tokyo would only go so far in challenging US hegemony and their protectorate status in the Cold War.

A NEW WAVE OF REVOLUTIONARY CRISIS AND SOVIET INTERNATIONAL EXPANSION

Between 1974 and 1979 revolutionary movements – a number of which were communist-led – seized power in 13[87] states in a shifting assault on pro-western regimes, climaxing in 1979 – the year that the US declared détente officially dead – with the Islamic Revolution in Iran, the Sandinista Revolution in Nicaragua and the Soviet intervention in support of its communist allies in Afghanistan. The significance of these developments was not just that pro-western states were overthrown and a number of pro-Soviet regimes emerged to replace them, thus extending the political and geopolitical reach of the USSR, but that, unlike any other revolutionary conjuncture in the Cold War, the US was unable – because of the domestic political fall-out of its humiliation in south-east Asia and the Watergate crisis – to deploy its military power to contain and/or reverse these political upheavals.

The domestic constraints on US responses to revolutionary change combined with the external one highlighted by the greater strategic reach of the USSR – a consequence of the construction of a greater global naval capacity – and the achievement of approximate nuclear parity with the US. The 1974–79 period was, then, unique in the Cold War: for the one and only time revolutionary change took place within a favourable geopolitical climate, which meant that many revolutions managed to secure themselves, at least in the short term, when they may not have done so in a different, less favourable geopolitical context.[88]

One reading of these events, which gained ever greater acceptance within the US throughout the late 1970s – becoming the leitmotif of Reagan's presidential campaign in 1980 – was that this wave of revolutionary seizures of power was somehow engineered by the USSR under the cover of détente and, consequently, these events reflected a fundamental transformation in the Cold War's balance of social, political and military forces in Moscow's favour. Whilst there is an element of truth to this, in the sense the US suffered a number of significant political defeats and the USSR extended its global political and military reach, the 'conjuncture of the 1970s' produced more varied results than Reaganite propaganda would have us believe. Thus, whilst Soviet-communist influence spread to the Horn of Africa and southern Africa, creating new fronts of Cold War, it suffered a major setback in the Middle East with the defection of Anwar Sadat's Egypt after the October 1973 Arab–Israeli War from the Soviet diplomatic sphere to the US between 1973 and 1976. The eclipse of Soviet-communist influence in the Middle East combined with the Sino-American rapprochement which continued after Mao's death in 1976 evidenced in the establishment of formal diplomatic relations between Beijing and Washington in 1979 and the beginnings of China's opening to the world capitalist economy.[89] The significance of these developments for Moscow is only comparable to the US loss of Iran in 1979. Revolutionary successes elsewhere and the spread of Soviet influence in southern Africa, Latin America and elsewhere, could not repair the damage done to Soviet international influence from the loss of Egypt and the continuing *rapprochement* between the US and China.[90]

Notwithstanding these qualifications, the series of revolutionary assaults on US allies between 1974 and 1979 were significant in the evolution of the Cold

War, as they highlighted the persistence of revolutionary-communist outcomes of crises in the reproduction of localised capitalist forms of social and political order in parts of the third world, and the opening up of possibilities for Soviet international expansion. In a word, the new wave of revolution between 1974 and 1979 maintained the dynamic of Cold War initiated in 1917, where crises of capitalist forms of rule (associated with and incorporated into an international capitalist order and guaranteed by the military power of the US) were overthrown, bringing to power new political regimes committed to socio-economic and political transformation, to varying degrees at odds with the US-led international socio-political order and thus inviting superpower competition and geopolitical conflict.

What is worth noting is that the character of revolutionary change was much more heterogeneous than in previous Cold War revolutionary conjunctures. This was most evident in the Islamic rather than communist character of the 1979 Iranian Revolution and the subsequent 'neither East nor West orientation' of the new Islamic Republic. The distinct anti-western *and* anti-communist character of revolutionary Iran after 1979 contrasted with more 'typical' cases of revolutionary change – in Vietnam, Laos, Cambodia, Angola, Mozambique and Afghanistan – involving communist and communist-inspired movements playing leading roles in revolutionary struggle, and the post-revolutionary states that emerged quickly associating themselves with the wider Soviet-communist bloc and modelling their internal political-economic development on communist lines to varying degrees. However, even in this regard, as the case of Angola highlights, it was Cuban rather than Soviet external influence that prevailed in the post-revolutionary state adding a further layer of complexity in understanding the character of these revolutions and their respective place in the evolution of the Cold War during the 1970s. The significance of the varied nature of this anti-imperialism, particularly with regard to Islamic anti-imperialism, will be made clearer in the next two chapters. However, for the purposes of the remainder of this chapter I will focus on the most significant Cold War fronts that emerged from the new wave of revolution: developments in the Horn of Africa and southern Africa, Iran, Afghanistan and Nicaragua.

Cold War Fronts in Africa

Apart from the Congo crisis of 1960–61, which saw the CIA and Belgium forces involved in the assassination of the radical Congolese independence leader Patrice Lumumba in January 1961, sub-Saharan Africa remained largely outside the Cold War conflict, in spite of the waves of decolonisation that swept across the continent from the 1950s onwards. This was to change in the 1970s with the expansion of Soviet-communist influence in southern Africa and the Horn of Africa. In the former, Soviet-communist influence spread with the coming to power of revolutionary guerrilla movements in a number of former Portuguese colonies – Cape Verde, Guinea-Bissau, São Tomé,

Mozambique and Angola – as the Portuguese African empire collapsed in the wake of revolutionary change within Portugal itself with the disintegration of the right-wing dictatorship during 1974–75. In the latter, Soviet influence spread after the overthrow of the pro-western Emperor Haile Selassie in September 1974 by nationalist military officers and the coming to power of Colonel Mengistu Haile-Mariam in February 1977.

The spread of Soviet-communist influence in the former Portuguese colonies, and the crisis it induced in superpower relations, focused on the Angolan civil war between 1974 and 1976 and the victory of the Marxist-led MPLA (*Movimento Popular de Libertação de Angola*). Soviet involvement in Angola marked a watershed in superpower relations and the evolution of the Cold War. For the first time since 1945 the USSR projected its military power in a comparable way to the US use of military power, by directly intervening in an *ongoing* conflict in a decisive way that helped secure victory for its ally over US-backed forces. It was able to do this because it had developed the capacity, by air and sea, to deploy forces some distance from the Eurasian landmass, and also because it was confident that the US – still coping with the domestic political fall-out of its humiliation in Vietnam – would not be able to counter, militarily, Soviet intervention.[91] For the US, Soviet intervention in Angola was seen as a major breach of Kissinger's linkage politics – the basis of US interpretations of détente – appearing to mark a new, more aggressive dimension to Soviet foreign policy, and provided one of a number of arguments in the armoury of the critics of détente located in the right wing of the Republican Party.

Although Soviet involvement in the Angolan civil war should be seen as a major development in the evolution of the Cold War, we need to be clear about the character of the intervention. In this respect two things are particularly significant. First, that Soviet intervention was of a defensive nature; it was in response to calls for assistance from the MPLA which faced military defeat at the hands of US-backed forces (the FNLA – *Frente Nacional de Libertação de Angola* – and UNITA – *União Nacional para a Independência Total de Angola*) who were also supported by a major military intervention by South Africa forces in October 1975. Second, the fact that it was Cuba and not the USSR which drove 'communist policy' towards Angola, and it was Cuban combat troops – albeit transported by the USSR – who proved decisive in saving the MPLA and defeating South African forces.[92] In this respect, Soviet involvement in Angola was secondary to that of Cuba and its longstanding policy of supporting national liberation and social revolution in Africa that went back to the early 1960s and Che Guevera's expedition to Congo in support of revolutionary forces.[93]

With the collapse of Portuguese colonial power in Angola an attempt was made to establish a peaceful transfer of power involving all three guerrilla movements with the signing of the Alvor Accords in January 1975. However, the Accords could only paper over the cracks in the relations with the three groups and with the support of external powers, each group quickly broke the Accords by engaging in military operations in an attempt to gain power for itself. It was the MPLA which initially gained the upper hand – in part helped by Soviet arms shipments – seizing control of most of Angola's provincial capitals between February and August 1975.[94] Whilst Washington regarded these developments a result of disproportionate Soviet meddling, Piero Gleijeses has documented that, prior to October 1975, there was little between the level of military aid that each superpower provided to its Angolan clients.[95] Further, President Gerald Ford approved increased amounts of military aid to the FNLA from July 1975 through to the autumn in response to MPLA advances.[96]

The turning point in the Angolan civil war came in October with the US-backed South African invasion of southern Angola through Namibia. With the prospect of a pro-Soviet MPLA victory and unable to intervene on the ground, the US encouraged Pretoria's intervention, thus following the logic of the Nixon Doctrine of using local allies, in this case, South Africa, to contain and/or overthrow pro-Soviet regimes and movements. Making rapid progress through the bush, it looked like the MPLA's days were numbered. It was in this context – the likelihood that US-backed South African forces would destroy the MPLA and install a pro-western regime allied to the racist apartheid state that spurred Cuban to launch 'Operation Carlota'[97] – the armed Cuban intervention in defence of the MPLA.

Cuban forces began to arrive in large numbers by air and sea from early November 1975 as the phalanx of South African-led forces moved to within 150 miles of the Angolan capital, Luanda. Within days Cuban forces had helped the MPLA begin to turn the situation around and, by January 1976, when Cuban forces had reached 12,000 in number, they had destroyed the FNLA and UNITA as serious military opponents of the MPLA, and also given South Africa a very bloody nose.[98]

By any account the Cuban intervention was risky, audacious and a triumph of international revolutionary solidarity. As Gleijeses makes clear, the defeat of a 'White' army by 'Blacks' did much to destroy the myth of White racial superiority in southern Africa and spurred on other national liberation movements in Rhodesia and South Africa. Further, Cuba's decision to aid the MPLA was taken without consulting Moscow,[99] a quite amazing fact given the logistical task of moving troops thousands of miles from the Caribbean to Angola and the risk that such a dramatic intervention against US interests might provoke increased hostility from the US. There had obviously been Soviet–Cuban discussion and co-ordination on the Angolan civil war before Castro's decision to intervene,[100] but had the Soviets refused to co-operate in the Cuban operation, either by limiting arms shipments or not helping Cuba in its air/sealift of troops to Angola, 'Operation Carlota' might not have ended so favourably for Cuba and its Angolan ally.

The Angolan crisis, then, demonstrated that Moscow would not be constrained from taking advantage of strategic opportunities that might arise through US arms control and economic inducements as Kissinger had assumed. However, Soviet 'adventurism' also needs to be considered from the perspective of US strategic weakness. There was little appetite within the US, so soon after the Vietnam War, for another military intervention in the third world and with the Angolan crisis coming at a time when anti-militarist tendencies within Congress peaked, Soviet support for the Cuban initiative could come at little cost.[101]

The expansion of Soviet-communist influence in (southern) Africa through the MPLA victory in the Angolan civil war consolidated by the signing of a 22-year Treaty of Friendship between Moscow and Luanda in October 1976, and the stationing of thousands of Cuban troops (alongside thousands of aid workers, teachers, technicians and doctors) was to be extended after 1977 in the Horn of Africa. As in Angola, it was local political developments and US policy decisions that provided an opportunity for the expansion of Soviet influence rather than the USSR inducing a crisis that it took advantage of. In particular, it was the confluence of three developments during 1977 that provided a strategic-political opportunity for the USSR to extend its influence in the Horn of Africa: (1) Mengistu Haile-Mariam's seizure of power within the Dergue (the provisional military administrative committee) which had ruled Ethiopia since the overthrow of Haile Selassie in September 1974, after a shoot-out with his rivals in February; (2) Somali incursions into the Ethiopian border region of the Ogaden in June–July; and (3) the suspension of military aid by the Carter administration in protest at human rights violations carried out by the new Ethiopian regime in February.

Thus, with Somali aggression[102] and unable to secure arms from the US to repel Somali incursions, Mengistu was effectively forced to turn Moscow, thereby ensuring that a localised political crisis would quickly became a Cold War issue for the US.[103] However, this was no ordinary crisis involving a US ally in conflict with a Soviet ally, as Somalia was, nominally, a Soviet ally.[104] Initially, then, Moscow was concerned to contain the crisis not stoke it, and Castro was dispatched to try to mediate between the two sides at a summit in Aden in March 1977.[105] However, within the space of a few months, Moscow was beginning to tilt away from its former ally, Somalia, and towards Ethiopia, as the Somali leader, Mohammed Siad Barre, refused to accept anything other than the end of Ethiopian jurisdiction over the Ogaden, and also demonstrated that he was not willing to subordinate the interests of Somali nationalism to Soviet geopolitical interests. By November, not only had the USSR cut off arms supplies to Somalia and increased military aid to Ethiopia, it had also began another airlift of thousands of Cuban troops to Ethiopia to help defend its new ally.[106] The result was that in January a combined Ethiopian–Cuban offensive drove out Somali forces and destroyed much of the Somali army.[107] With the end of the war the formality of Ethiopia's new diplomatic posture was sealed in November with the signing of a Treaty of Friendship and Co-operation by Moscow and Addis Ababa.[108]

Whilst Soviet–Cuban intervention in Angola had defeated US-backed forces, the expansion of Soviet-communist influence – at least in the sense that Ethiopia was a much bigger and more important state than Somalia – in the Horn of Africa reflected less a clear-cut defeat for US interests and more how the USSR was unable to resolve tensions between radical nationalist regimes allied to it, and how the militarised nature of Soviet aid to its Somali ally provided a major ingredient in the crisis. Although US diplomacy towards Somalia had not helped the situation by dropping hints of military aid and stressing sympathy for Mogadishu's concern over the Ogaden, the US did not give a green light to the Somali invasion and did not provide arms.[109] Further, the US did nothing – it was unable to – to prevent the decisive Soviet–Cuban intervention to resolve the crisis.

The upshot of the crisis, then, was that the USSR (and its Cuban ally) had taken advantage of favourable geopolitical circumstances to capitalise on a locally induced crisis to ensure that Soviet influence was maintained and expanded in the region. While less of a US defeat than in Angola, the Horn of Africa crisis further underlined to critics of détente within the US that unless the US overcame the strategic paralysis produced by the political fall out from the Vietnam War, developments like that in the Horn of Africa would become all the more common, allowing the USSR a free hand to extend its influence in areas of interest to the US.

The Iranian Revolution and the Cold War

Whilst the consequences of revolutionary change in Africa suggested unambiguous gains for the USSR and the extension of its international power, the 1979 Iranian Revolution – a dramatic defeat for US political, economic and geopolitical interests – produced a rather different set of outcomes. Prior to the Islamic Revolution, Iran, under the autocratic regime of the Shah, had been a key US ally, dominating the Persian Gulf and a stable source of oil supplies.[110] In the post-Vietnam context it became the exemplar of the Nixon Doctrine in action through its huge arms purchases[111] from the US during the 1970s and as a regional 'policeman' and provocateur – intervening in Oman in 1972 to help the pro-western Sultan crush Dhofari rebels and using Kurdish insurgents to harass the pro-Soviet Ba'athist regime in Iraq in the early 1970s.[112]

The revolution was a major setback for the US, particularly when viewed in the wider post-Vietnam context coming at the end of a decade that had seen a succession of revolutionary upheavals against pro-US regimes. Further, as in the other cases of revolutionary change (and Soviet-communist advance), the US was prostrate, unable to prevent the fall of the Shah. On top of this, insult and humiliation were added to diplomatic defeat with the seizure of hostages in the US embassy in Tehran in November 1979 by student militants and their captivity for 444 days. If anything signified the weakened international power of the US and its inability to respond to developments beyond its borders it was the Iranian Revolution, and the hostage crisis in particular, especially after the attempted rescue of the hostages in April 1980 ended in failure and ignominy.

Whilst right-wing propagandists associated with Reagan's presidential bid attempted to blame the USSR and the machinations of the KGB in particular for the revolution, it soon became clear that the Islamic character of the revolution and the leadership of Ayatollah Ruhollah Khomeini suggested that the new regime in Tehran would be antagonistic to Soviet as much as to US interests.[113] In this respect the outcome of the Iranian Revolution represented a clear break from the revolutionary dynamic of the Cold War, introducing a heteronymous currency of conflict and anti-imperialism that persists, though in a different form, to this day. Indeed, the March 2003 invasion of Iraq by US-led forces can be traced back to the international consequences of the Iranian Revolution. Iraq became a US ally and major military power as a bulwark to Islamic Iran, evidenced in the US acquiescence to Iraq's invasion of Iran in September 1980. The subsequent Iraqi invasion of Kuwait in August 1990 was a direct consequence of the domestic economic consequences of Iraq's war with Iran and the debts it had accumulated with the Gulf states in fighting the war. Finally, a major factor that prevented western intervention in support of the popular uprising against Ba'athist rule at the end of the Gulf War in April 1991 was the concern that victory for the Shi'ite-led uprising would not only be to the benefit of Iran but might also lead to the fragmentation of Iraq.

Paradoxically, a most modern revolution[114] produced a rather reactionary outcome. As in other revolutionary ruptures that characterised the history of the Cold War, the Iranian Revolution was the product of the particularly uneven and contradictory way in which Iran under the Shah was incorporated, through its oil revenues, into the international capitalist economy. Consequently, capitalist modernisation under the Shah produced deep social antagonisms towards the state involving a range of social classes – thus laying the foundations for a broad, popular revolutionary movement – highlighted by increasing socio-economic inequality, the alienation of the traditional petty bourgeoisie of the bazaar, and compounded by the volatility of an economy dependent on revenue from oil exports.

In spite of its reactionary political, cultural and ideological dimensions, the international consequences of the revolution tended to conform to the pattern of most other revolutions, particularly in Iran's attempts to internationalise and export the revolution. Whilst this did see Islamic Iran focus some of its international revolutionary objectives against Soviet interests,[115] particularly through its radio broadcasts directed at the southern Muslim-populated republics of the USSR, and through its support of a number of anti-communist *mujahadeen* factions in Afghanistan, most of Iran's revolutionary foreign policy pitted it against US interests in the Middle East and its regional allies, particularly in the Gulf. In this respect, then, within the wider context of the Cold War, Iran introduced a distinct form of anti-imperialism which, in the case of the war with Iraq, and the support Iraq received from both Moscow and Washington, ended up pitting Iran against both superpowers for much of the 1980s.[116]

With the exceptions of Iraq and Syria, Soviet influence in the Middle East was rather limited, particularly in the Persian Gulf states. Consequently, Iranian attempts to export the revolution to these areas, especially in those countries that had sizeable Shia populations, such as Saudi Arabia and Bahrain, served to antagonise the US further as the principal external guarantor of most of these states. Whilst unsuccessful, revolutionary Iran succeeded in fomenting political instability in Saudi Arabia, which Khomeini dismissed as a state practising 'American Islam'. In November 1979 – some months after the fall of the Shah – 400 Islamist guerrillas seized control of the Grand Mosque in Mecca for two weeks and shortly after tens of thousands of Shi'ites in the oil-rich province of Al-Hasa mounted pro-Khomeini demonstrations which required 20,000 security forces to suppress. Further, in September 1981, Iranian *hajj* pilgrims fought Saudi security forces who tried to prevent their demonstrations in favour of Khomeini and condemning the al-Saud regime. [117]

Whilst US security and economic interests were being challenged, indirectly, by Iran's subversion of a number of Gulf states, in Lebanon, pro-Iranian Shi'ite forces attacked the US directly. In April 1983 dozens were killed when Islamic Jihad attacked the US embassy in Beirut, and in October 1983 suicide truck bombs targeted the US marine barracks in Lebanon (the marines were stationed there as part of a UN force to supervise the Israeli-enforced expulsion of the PLO from Lebanon) and killed over 240. These attacks, alongside Iran's sponsorship of the Hezbollah movement in south Lebanon and the taking of US hostages by pro-Iranian groups in Beirut throughout the 1980s, highlighted the impact of militant Islamic forces backed by Iran in the region and their ability to humiliate the US further.

The Iranian Revolution, then, and the Islamist internationalism that it produced and cultivated, were distinct forms of anti-imperialism outside of the Cold War dynamic. In this sense, whilst the US continued to be preoccupied with containing and rolling back the international spread of Soviet and communist influence, after 1979 in the Middle East the US confronted a different kind of political and ideological enemy. Whilst the Iranian challenge to western imperialism in the 1950s had been of a radical-nationalist character with strong communist influence, after 1979 it was Islamic and anti-communist as much as anti-western. Paradoxically, however, as we will see in regard to US policy towards Afghanistan after December 1979 (discussed in Chapter 6), at the same time that the US confronted a Shi'ite Islamic challenge in the Middle

East it cultivated Sunni-based Islamist groups – especially through Saudi Arabia – fighting Soviet forces and the communist regime in Afghanistan.

The Sandinista Revolution in Nicaragua

Whilst Brzezinski's 'arc of crisis' was primarily concerned with the threat of Soviet advances through revolutionary changes from the Horn of Africa through the Persian Gulf and central Asia, revolutionary challenge and change also extended to the US's own backyard as the more than four decades-long US-backed Somoza family dictatorship was overthrown by FSLN (*Frente Sandinista de Liberación Nacional*)-led forces in July 1979 and guerrilla war involving the revolutionary left (the *Frente Farabundo Martí para Liberación Nacional* – FMLN) against a pro-US regime raged in El Salvador. The Somoza family had been in power since June 1936 following the assassination of the revolutionary leader Augusto Sandino by pro-Somoza and US-trained National Guardsmen. After coming to power, the Somoza family dominated the political economy of Nicaragua and built a regime based on nepotism, corruption, brutality and subservience to US regional interests.

The revolution emerged from a long-drawn-out crisis associated with the corruption, illegitimacy and brutality of the Somoza dictatorship, which, by the mid-1970s, had managed to alienate – in a way similar to that of Batista in Cuba in the late 1950s – nearly all shades of political opinion and social classes in Nicaragua. With the emergence of a broad anti-Somoza front in December 1974 committed to ending the dictatorship and the resumption of FSLN military operations,[118] Somoza declared a state of emergency, in effect destroying any chances of a reformist rather than revolutionary resolution to the crisis of rule in Nicaragua. With the lifting of the state of emergency in September 1977 the recommencement of FSLN guerrilla activities and the continuing opposition to the regime from elements within the ruling class as well as popular classes intensified the crisis.[119] Throughout 1978 until the collapse of the regime in July 1979, the regime confronted a growing level of challenge and popular militancy evidenced in the September urban insurrections in most of Nicaragua's cities,[120] which resulted in the death of over 5,000 and, through air bombardment of the rebel-held areas by the National Guard, the reduction of many parts of urban Nicaragua to rubble.[121] With the National Guard increasingly acting in an arbitrary and brutal manner, the ranks of the opposition and the FSLN in particular swelled. The final push against the regime took place between March and July 1979 as the FSLN established civil defence committees throughout the country which formed the backbone of the final insurrection in June–July 1979.[122]

In many ways a repeat of its behaviour towards Cuba in the final months of the Batista dictatorship, the US tried to engineer a transfer of power that would maintain the institutional structure of power – concentrated in the US-trained and funded National Guard – in Nicaragua, thus preserving US influence and the socio-economic order within Nicaragua and, most importantly, marginalising and isolating the influence of the FSLN in any post-Somoza political dispensation. Thus, throughout the final months and weeks of the Somoza dictatorship – a period marked by widespread and brutal human rights abuses by the regime[123] – the US pressed Somoza to surrender power to a coalition of moderate political forces – including Somoza's personal fiefdom, the National Liberal Party – which either excluded the FSLN and/or sought to contain their growing popularity and political strength.[124] However, Somoza's intransigence, encouraged by the mixed signals coming from Washington,[125] meant that US plans to secure a political settlement that kept the FSLN from the levers of power began to slip away in the early months of 1979. With the FSLN moving in on Managua in the summer, the US – in a last-ditch effort to try to determine Nicaragua's post-Somoza future – proposed an OAS peacekeeping force, which was rejected by governments at an OAS meeting on June 25[126] weary of any precedent this might set that they may in future fall victim to.

With the Sandinista-led victory the US confronted revolutionary political change which it had tried to prevent. Although cautiously welcoming the new government[127] in Nicaragua, which contained a significant number of non-Sandinistas, the Carter administration also clandestinely evacuated the remnants of Somoza's National Guard to the safety of Miami where they would base themselves in the war which they would soon launch against the new Sandinista government.[128] The destruction of the political base – the Somoza family and the National Guard – of US power in Nicaragua and the coming to power of a new government dominated by a revolutionary movement committed to radical socio-economic and political change[129] was always likely to test the relationship between Washington and Managua. This was particularly the case when the Sandinistas remained sympathetic to the revolutionary struggle of the FMLN in El Salvador and when the new government began receiving humanitarian assistance from Cuba.

The Sandinista Revolution did not see the spread of Soviet influence – at least not directly – in Nicaragua in the same way that Soviet influence could be seen to have spread in the Horn of Africa and other parts of the third world during the 1970s. Rather, it was Cuban influence that spread; however, even in this respect the political and economic character of Nicaragua under the Sandinistas was significantly different from the more fundamental revolutionary break that occurred in Cuba between 1959 and 1961. However, although Nicaragua was not another Cuba, it was an example of revolutionary change – the violent overthrow of a pro-US regime against the wishes of the US – and it did see the construction of a different kind of state-society relationship at odds with the interests of the US. Further, with the spread of Cuban influence and instability in neighbouring states, particularly El Salvador, it was not difficult to see why the US would be troubled by Nicaragua after July 1979. In this respect, although the ideological orientation of the Reagan administration from

1981 onwards was a fundamental factor in US–Nicaraguan relations, there was also something objectively antagonistic between revolutionary Nicaragua and the US that troubled even the Carter administration.[130] Finally, and as in previous cases of revolutionary political change, confronted by the prospects of a relationship with the US that required either major concessions that would have fundamentally undermined the support from its key social constituencies and/or its political neutralisation, the Sandinistas turned to Havana and the Soviet bloc for economic and political support. When the US launched its militarised campaign of counter-revolution (which I will discuss in Chapter 6) the Sandinistas had little choice but to draw even closer to the enemies of Washington.[131]

Revolutionary Upheaval and Soviet Intervention in Afghanistan

The *coup de grâce* to détente – at least from Washington's point of view – came in late December 1979 with the Soviet intervention in Afghanistan involving the killing of the Afghan communist leader, Hafizullah Amin, and the imposition of a new communist leadership under Babrak Karmal. The initial Soviet intervention spearheaded by special forces quickly expanded into an occupation force of over 100,000 troops which soon became directly involved in a brutal civil war with a number of Islamist and nationalist armed groups, collectively known as the *mujahadeen*.[132] The Soviet intervention was the one and only time that the USSR deployed combat troops directly in a country outside of its 'recognised' sphere of interest in east-central Europe. Consequently, the intervention not only stimulated increased resistance to the Afghan communist regime, but also led to widespread international condemnation and hostility, particularly from Islamic states.

The US response was swift. Combined with the turmoil in Iran and the expansion of Soviet influence in the Horn of Africa, the US was gravely concerned that Soviet designs were not confined to Afghanistan but the wider region and the Persian Gulf in particular.[133] Following this logic, President Carter announced in his January 1980 State of the Union address that '[a]n attempt ... by any outside force to gain control of the Persian Gulf region will be regarded as an assault on the vital interests of the United States of America, and such an assault will be repelled by any means necessary, including military force.'[134] With this – what became known as the Carter Doctrine – the US returned to a much more militarised and confrontational approach to dealing with the USSR and laid the foundations for the intensification of militarised containment (and rollback) under the visceral critic of détente, Ronald Reagan, who assumed the presidency the following year.

As in the previous cases of revolutionary change and Soviet 'advance', it was local developments that accounted for change, and Soviet policy only became significant after a new regime had seized power in Kabul in April 1978. The April 1978 'revolution' or, more accurately, communist-led *coup*[135] overthrew the regime of Prince Daoud. The spark to revolutionary change came with the arrest of leading members of the communist PDPA (Peoples' Democratic Party of Afghanistan) after communist-organised demonstrations in Kabul opposed to the Daoud regime and, in particular, the influence of the Shah and his security agents on the Afghan government. With the arrests, PDPA elements within the army – which had been cultivated over the preceding months – attacked the presidential palace overthrowing Daoud, expelling Iranian influence and bringing Kabul much closer to Moscow.[136]

Although a Pakistani-based insurgency simmered from 1975 onwards, internal threats to the new regime were not serious until the *Khalq* (masses) faction of the PDPA, led by Amin and Taraki, seized power (and exiled Karmal of the *Parcham* [flag] faction to east-central Europe) in July 1978.[137] After marginalising the *Parcham* faction the *Khalq* embarked on a much more radical programme of socio-economic and cultural transformation. It was this attempt to impose socialism 'from above' on rural Afghanistan in a highly coercive manner using urban-based party cadres backed by the army which quickly stirred up opposition from the traditional tribal and landlord social structures which pervaded Afghan society outside of Kabul. Whilst the Soviets endorsed the harsh response of the *Khalq* to counter-revolutionary forces initially, as the counter-revolution spread,[138] they grew increasingly concerned at developments and soon began to urge Amin to moderate his policies as a way of addressing some of the grievances that the earlier reforms had created.

However, Amin ignored Soviet influence, and whilst the counter-revolution in the countryside grew with increasing support from Iran and Pakistan, the *Khalq* began to clamp down on suspected opponents within the cities – once the backbone of the party.[139] By the summer of 1979, then, Moscow confronted a situation in Afghanistan not that dissimilar from that which confronted Washington with regard to the Diem regime in Saigon in the summer of 1963. Two regimes, both of which were increasingly reliant on external military support to deal with hostile internal forces, both refused to bow to external pressure whilst acting in a way that served to increase opposition rather than defuse it. However, whilst the US was able to acquiesce to the 'local' overthrow of Diem, because of the crackdown on the *Parcham* faction, and even elements within the *Khalq*, it became increasingly clear by late 1979 that if the USSR was to 'rescue' the situation in Afghanistan, it would have to act itself.[140]

By December, then, there seemed little prospect of an internal solution other than that which would have amounted to a major setback for the USSR in the form of the continuation of an increasingly brutal civil war promoting instability, or the defeat of the Amin regime and its replacement by an Islamist regime hostile to the USSR with the prospect of instability spreading to the Muslim-populated southern republics of the USSR that bordered Afghanistan. The key element in Soviet thinking, as rightly emphasised by Halliday, was the presence and scale of the counter-revolution *supported by external forces* (unlike in east-central Europe) in Afghanistan.[141] Whilst Moscow could do nothing to prevent the overthrow of the socialist government of Salvador Allende in Chile in September 1973, it could and would act to prevent such a possibility in its own backyard, especially when the risks of any direct US response were minimal.[142]

With the intervention the USSR made itself responsible for the survival of another communist state and put itself directly in the firing line of an insurgency that was growing in strength. Further, the consequence of the intervention on the already demoralised Afghan army was dramatic. Thousands deserted, some becoming refugees in Pakistan and Iran, others joining the *mujahadeen*.[143] Finally, the intervention, and with it the intensification of the civil war, was to provoke much greater external anti-Soviet/communist involvement from the US, Saudi Arabia and Pakistan that would, as will be discussed in Chapters 6 and 7, not only play an important role in the closing stages of the Cold War, but also the character of post-Cold War international relations.

CONCLUSIONS: THE END OF DÉTENTE AND THE REVIVAL OF US MILITARISM

This chapter has covered a crucial and dynamic period in the history of the Cold War from the early 1960s, when the bedrock of US Cold War policy – militarised containment based on US strategic military power and autonomy seemed assured (evident in facing down the Soviets over Cuba in 1962) – to the profound crisis in the strategy of militarised containment in the early 1970s brought about by the political defeat of militarised containment in Vietnam War, and extending to a wave of revolutionary change in the third world that the US was unable to prevent, which encouraged an unprecedented amount of Soviet political and military activity in the periphery. In short, whilst the 1945–73 period of the Cold War was dominated by the promiscuous use of US military power and the successful militarised containment of the USSR, the period 1973–79 saw a reversal of this situation with the USSR becoming much more active in world affairs due to the transformed military-geopolitical environment consequent on the US defeat in south-east Asia. It was the Vietnamese Revolution, then, that was the most important factor in transforming the Cold War in the 1970s, as it was this that broke the domestic political consensus within the US over the use of force to contain the spread of Soviet-communist power.[144]

The historical developments during the 1970s also have significance for broader theoretical understandings of the Cold War. Specifically, détente is seen to reflect mutual interests and understanding, cooperation and compromise as characteristic of superpower relations rather than Marxist and Realist views that give greater emphasis to material power, crises and conflict. The key elements of détente, particularly the arms control agreements, did reflect common interests about the need to avoid nuclear war, but the emphasis on superpower relationship – rather than wider global developments – and on mutual interests and cooperation overlooks the complex relationships between the superpowers, revolutionary change in the periphery and political-economic developments within the western bloc and the US in particular during the 1970s.

With respect to the US, the 1970s was a watershed and conjuncture of crisis vis-à-vis its leadership of the capitalist world and its confrontation with the Soviet Union and the forces of international (communist) revolution. The important point is that these 'spheres' were interconnected. The world economic crisis of the 1970s was a contributory factor to the development of a revolutionary atmosphere in the south and the emergence of a series of revolutionary crises there. The ability of the US to address such crises – as it had done in the past, by using force – was severely constrained by the consequences of its defeat in Vietnam, and the US intervention in Vietnam was itself a major factor in the breakdown of the post-war international economic order – Bretton Woods.

The three pillars of US Cold War international relations – leadership of the capitalist world, geopolitical containment of the USSR, and the containment and rollback of international revolution – were all severely undermined by the confluence of developments in the 1970s. Whilst these three objectives had been compatible between 1945 and the mid-1960s, they were no longer so by the 1970s. Further, the pursuit of one – international counter-revolution – had come at a cost to the others.

For the US, the 1970s saw an attempt to secure the three objectives through different means. Détente was to neutralise any advantage the USSR might gain from the inability of the US to deploy armed force in a way that it had between 1945 and 1973, whilst aggressive economic unilateralism was used to restore US economic leadership over the capitalist world. In many respects one depended on the other. A relaxation of Cold War tensions allowed the US to be less concerned with unity within the capitalist bloc, unlike the early post-war period where the US made economic concessions – from a position of considerable strength and advantage it must be said – to its capitalist rivals.

The sense of crisis, however, was compounded by the wave of revolution that swept across the third world between 1973 and 1979, which détente could not prevent, because revolutionary change was a social dynamic that operated outside of but impinged on the bipolar superpower relationship. Thus, Vietnam reduced the geopolitical power of the US, whilst the arc of crises provided outlets for Soviet geopolitical expansion, effectively destroying the US strategy of détente.

Confronting a crisis within each of the three areas of US Cold War policy in the 1970s, particularly by the end of the decade, the US returned to a strategy based on militarism and confrontation. With a newly mobilised domestic political constituency that supported a more assertive and aggressive posture towards the USSR and the forces of international revolution, if not the deployment of large numbers of combat troops as in the past, the US seized upon the *objective* evidence of Soviet and revolutionary advance to launch the 'new' Cold War after 1979, and in doing so ensured that its capitalist ally-rivals were reminded of their strategic-military dependence on the US. Consequently, the US could embark on the project of neoliberal globalisation in the early 1980s, knowing that the more hostile international atmosphere, which it had helped to create, consolidated its leadership of the capitalist world, as it had done in the early period after 1945 and as it had been undermined during the 1970s.

The return of US militarism, then, was not just about the USSR; it was also an important instrument in instilling discipline and loyalty and consolidating US leadership over the capitalist world as an external military protectorate of the US. The US sought to rebuild its *economic* leadership of the capitalist world by promoting new economic policies, collectively known as neoliberalism, and sought to pressure its economic competitors to implement economic reform by emphasising their dependence on US military protection, which was made all the more important in the context of much greater superpower international tension stoked by the shift in US policy. In this sense the Cold War posture of the US was not only about addressing the geopolitical threat of the USSR and the international political threat of communist revolution, but also about the way in which this posture promoted US political *and* economic leadership over the wider capitalist world.

For the Soviet Union, the 1970s provided the one and only time in its history when it was relatively free of an external-strategic veto on its international relations and particularly its use of military instruments to realise its international objectives. However, we need to be clear that though there was something objective about Soviet 'revolutionary adventurism' during the 1970s, this pales into insignificance when compared to the length and character of US military activities during the post-war period. As Raymond Garthoff has detailed in his impressive account of superpower détente, the Soviets not only tended to be more cautious[145] in their use of military power, even during the promising geopolitical context of the 1970s, but prior to the Afghanistan intervention the number of Soviet military personnel deployed outside of the Warsaw Pact was very small – just over 5,000 in 1976 – and the casualties suffered in these deployments were very small.[146]

Further, in terms of communist-revolutionary advance, the revolutionary conjuncture of the 1970s was much more chequered than previous ones. Despite its ability to project itself beyond Eurasia, there were still limits to what the USSR was able to do in support of international revolution and the economic costs of such support – a case of being a victim of (its own) revolutionary success – meant that Moscow was unable to fund 'another Cuba', as in the case of Nicaragua after 1979. It was not just the domestic economic and military (and ideological) limits of Moscow's support for international revolution during this period, but also the character of revolutionary change, most evident in the case of Iran, that qualifies the historical record of Soviet-communist expansion during the 1970s, and which exposes the exaggerations of the many critics of détente.

The Cold War of the 1970s was, then, fundamentally based on shifting fronts of revolutionary crisis and transformation and the way in which such localised developments saw the overthrow of pro-US regimes and, consequently, setbacks for US international power and how such changes provided opportunities for the advance of Soviet influence and power. In this respect developments in the 1970s were consistent with the earlier phases of the Cold War. It was shifting localised revolutionary transformations that provided the dynamic of the Cold War. Yet, as the 1970s show, whilst the Cold War continued to spread in some parts of the world it was ending in other parts through the effective absorption of those social forces – primarily the working class – that had been its primary agency into states that were then incorporated into the structures and institutions of the advanced capitalist world, or, as in the case of parts of the Middle East, the emergence of new forms of revolutionary resistance, that were anti-communist as much as they were anti-western.

6

Ending the Cold War: From Militarised Counter-Revolution to the Collapse of Soviet Communism, 1980–91

INTRODUCTION

Chapter 5 focused on the transformation of the Cold War during the 1970s evident in the increased activity of the USSR in the third world on the back of a succession of successful revolutionary struggles, and in the post-Vietnam caution of the US concerning the use of military force to contain Soviet-communist expansion. Listening to the rhetoric of the 'Committee on the Present Danger'[1] in the late 1970s one would have thought that the US and its Western allies were losing the Cold War and that the march of Soviet advance was unstoppable. Yet, within ten years the tumultuous events of 1989 in east-central Europe would see the collapse of communist power there, and later the disintegration of the USSR in 1991. The 1980s, then, were a turbulent time in the history of the Cold War, characterised by an intensification of superpower hostility and conflict, especially after the election of Ronald Reagan to the US presidency in November 1980, to a warming of superpower relations – what some called a 'new détente' – with the accession of Mikhail Gorbachev to the Soviet leadership in March 1985, and ending with the popular and largely peaceful overthrow of communist rule.

The task of this chapter is to provide a theoretically informed historical overview of these developments, concentrating on the Reagan administration's programme of militarised counter-revolution to contest and roll back the advances made by the USSR and international communism during the 1970s, and the manner of the collapse of Soviet power between 1989 and 1991. However, although the historical and empirical focus of this chapter will be on evolving superpower relations during the 1980s and developments within the USSR and Soviet bloc, I will also examine the broader theoretical discussion concerning the nature and meaning of the ending of the Cold War.

As should be clear from the preceding chapters, my understanding of the Cold War as a form of 'systemic social conflict' amounting to something more

than the bipolar superpower relationship means that though the collapse of
Soviet power between 1989 and 1991 is crucial to any account of the Cold War
and its end, it is also important to assess the broader history of historical communism as a form of revolutionary challenge to US international capitalist
power and also the evolving character of wider non- and anti-communist forms
of anti-imperialism that emerged in the 1970s, which have become much more
prominent in recent years. For, as the previous chapter implied, during the
1970s there emerged heteronymous forms of politics and anti-imperialism –
products of Cold War to be sure – but based on different types of conflict
particularly in the Islamic world and Middle-East.

Not only did new sources of politics emerge but, in the case of the civil war
in Afghanistan during the 1980s, the US and its regional allies, Pakistan and
Saudi Arabia, actively cultivated these new social and political movements as
localised and non-western (illiberal) forms of anti-communism. The 1980s and
the character and manner of the ending of the Cold War were, then, more complex and paradoxical than prevailing and conventional accounts have tended to
recognise. Whilst the superpower conflict as a structural form of international
conflict covering all corners of the world came to a close with the collapse of
Soviet communism, not only were developments within the Soviet bloc shaped
by the wider social history of the Cold War – evident in the defeat of communist revolution (and thus the ends of other, localised Cold Wars) in other parts
of the world – but within this broader structure of Cold War new sources of
international conflict were emerging *and* being cultivated by localised Cold
Wars. This will be the focus of Chapter 7, which discusses the character of
post-Cold War international relations and the emergence of new forms of
resistance out of the ends of the Cold War.

The chapter is organised as follows: it begins with a focus on the Cold War
during the 1980s concentrating on the more confrontational stance of the
Reagan administration towards the USSR and international revolution, with a
particular focus on US counter-revolution in Afghanistan and Nicaragua. This
is followed by a critical discussion of the debate about the end of the Cold War
within the discipline of International Relations, which is followed by an examination of the collapse of Soviet communist power between 1989 and 1991.

REAGAN AND MILITARISED COUNTER-REVOLUTION

Although Reagan's assumption of the presidency in January 1981 is widely
seen as witnessing a fundamental transformation in US policy towards the
USSR – from one of détente to a 'new' Cold War – as the previous chapter
highlighted, this shift had begun in the latter stages of the Carter presidency,
evident in the creation of the Rapid Deployment Task Force between 1977 and
1979 to intervene in third world crises, and the announcement of the Carter
Doctrine in January 1980. By the end of the decade, the arms control advances

of the early 1970s, and the mutual diplomatic confidence they had helped produce, had been eclipsed by the Soviet decision to replace ageing intermediate
nuclear missiles based in eastern Europe with newer, more accurate SS-20s,
which had helped trigger the NATO decision to install a new generation of
short and intermediate range nuclear forces (Pershing II and cruise) in Western
Europe in late 1979 (to be operative from 1983). The breakdown in the strategic-nuclear sphere – the cornerstone of détente – was echoed in the political
and military spheres; brought about by the Soviet advances in the third world
and, in particular, by the Soviet intervention in Afghanistan. As much as Soviet
attempts to realise political security (in east-central Europe) through armed
force had contributed to the militarisation of superpower relations after 1945
so the use of force to *uphold* – not impose – communist.power in Afghanistan
provided an important focal point for the re-militarisation of US foreign policy
during the 1980s.[2]

The behaviour of the USSR, combined with the intensification and advances
of revolutionary struggle in many parts of the world, did, then, contribute to a
shift away from the post-Vietnam posture of the US most evident in the election of the visceral anti-communist Reagan in 1980 on a platform that committed the US to pursue a much more active and aggressive campaign, based
on military strength, to counter and roll back Soviet advances in the third
world.[3] However, as Chapter 5 highlighted, the conjuncture of the 1970s was
also characterised by a breakdown in the domestic and intra-bloc political
consensus – and the social basis that had sustained it – upon which US/western
Cold War strategy had been based since the late 1940s.[4] Thus, as much as
Truman and other western political leaders exaggerated and manipulated the
Soviet-communist threat after 1945 as a way of ensuring domestic and bloc
unity and legitimation for militarised international relations, so Reagan and
other western leaders – particularly Margaret Thatcher – did the same in the early
1980s. Further, in emphasising the military character of the Soviet threat – to
some degree borne out by the SS-20 deployment and Soviet intervention in
Afghanistan – the US sought to use its position as military protector of the
western democracies (including Japan) to secure political and economic concessions from its capitalist economic rivals as a way of addressing the question
of its relative economic decline.[5]

The 1980s, then, saw a transformation in the political economy of US global
power after the interregnum of the 1973–79 period. On the one hand, the US
returned to a more militarist approach to dealing with the USSR and international revolution, which required an investment in more military resources[6] –
both conventional and nuclear – whilst, on the other hand, the US sought to
restructure the character and relations of the international capitalist economy
to suit its domestic *and* international political needs.

A return to (intensified) Cold War confrontation rather than détente served
the political interests of the Reagan administration. A more militarised

international posture would not only allow the US to contain, and potentially roll back, the momentum of Soviet international advance, as well as putting pressure on an already lethargic Soviet economy to match the US arms build-up,[7] particularly in the area of new strategic weapons; the confrontational atmosphere this would generate, ideologically and militarily, would help restore US political leadership (or at least those social and political elements that supported the Reagan presidency) over the western bloc and within the US. Simply put, Cold War was functional for the US. The Soviet threat would bring home once again to its wayward allies – seduced by the continuing possibilities of (European) détente – and economic rivals the necessity of US military protection and leadership, thus allowing the US greater freedom to push through economic policies at home and abroad which served to promote US advantage, and which facilitated US rearmament.[8] The importance of US domestic politics, then and now, was that US external relations required domestic support and, specifically, a social constituency to replace the post-war basis of containment that had been shattered by the Vietnam War and the economic crisis of the 1970s. The strategy of the Reagan administration sought to achieve this through mobilising new social forces within the US[9] (and out-side the US in other capitalist states, especially Britain), which required the destruction of the post-war socio-economic settlement, as this was associated with both relative economic decline and, after Vietnam, a lack of political resolve in combating Soviet power.

The Reagan strategy, then, was to reassert US leadership over the capitalist world by promoting neoliberal ideological remedies to the economic problems that had surfaced in the 1970s, particularly with regard to the operations of the key international economic institutions – the IMF and World Bank – and advo-cated by some of the key social interests, concentrated in Wall Street, associated with Reagan in the US. This required reining in those tendencies, which had emerged within the main zones of capital accumulation outside of the US – in Western Europe and Japan – during the détente period, which advocated more independent economic and foreign policies,[10] which would be best secured through stressing the common external threat of the USSR, thus reuniting the western bloc and allowing the US to reassert its leadership in *all* spheres.

This is not to suggest that the Soviet-revolutionary advances of the 1970s were not real or seen as strategic and political setbacks for the US, or that the Cold War antagonism with the USSR was in some way subordinate to, or a function of, deeper inter-capitalist rivalries. Rather, the social and political interests of the US as a *capitalist* great power operated in two ways during the Cold War: first, in combating the spread of a rival (communist) social system and its attendant states that challenged the existence and reproduction of the international socio-economic system of which the US was at the heart; and, second, in maintaining its competitive position and thus political and economic leadership (hegemony) over the international capitalist economy.

With respect to the Cold War and US relations with the USSR and other communist-revolutionary states and struggles, the Reagan administration returned to a much more militarised strategy. This militarisation, as suggested in Chapter 5, had begun in the latter part of the Carter presidency, but took on a much more confrontational and ideological character under Reagan.[11] The policy of confrontation had two elements: nuclear rearmament and pressuring the Soviet Union at the strategic level; and much more military involvement in the third world to roll back some of the revolutionary success of the 1970s[12] (pro-insurgency), and to prevent further revolutions occurring (counter-insurgency).[13] Prosecuting counter-revolution in the third world was a deliberate attempt to meet head-on the challenge posed by Soviet and revolutionary advances during the 1970s. A return to a strategy that emphasised military over diplomatic and economic instruments would ensure that any more Soviet advances would risk direct military confrontation with the US, and would also come at a very painful political and economic cost for Moscow and its revolutionary allies.

In the sphere of strategic nuclear weapons Reagan's aim – at least during his first term of office – was to renew the strategic nuclear advantage that the US had lost after the early 1970s, thus allowing the US to use nuclear intimidation geopolitically to discipline any Soviet moves towards adventurism in the third world or elsewhere.[14] The objective of securing nuclear advantage over the US would not only allow the US to prosecute 'nuclear imperialism,'[15] but would also allow it, in Reagan's words, to 'negotiate from strength' with the USSR over any future arms control agreement. The strategy was based on technological innovation – an area where the US had maintained an advantage over the USSR throughout the Cold War. Military technology, however, was not confined to a new generation of more powerful and accurate nuclear weapons such as the land-based MX missile and the Trident II (D-5) submarine-launched ballistic missile system, but also the B-1 strategic bomber project which Carter had previously cancelled, and the anti-ballistic missile system – SDI (the Strategic Defence Initiative also known as 'Star Wars') – because of its operation in space.

SDI was highly controversial, not only because of the degree of scepticism within parts of the Reagan administration as to its practicality and effectiveness (Would it be able to shoot down enough Soviet ballistic missiles to make it worthwhile?), but also because it threatened to challenge fundamentally the doctrine of deterrence and 'mutually assured destruction', upon which superpower nuclear stability had been based since the mid-1960s. If it ever became operational it would have effectively allowed the US to launch a nuclear attack on the USSR without suffering a devastating (and deterrent) retaliation.

SDI was never operational – it did not even come close – but its (theoretical) existence and the other strategic policies of the first Reagan administration[16] contributed to an impasse with the USSR over arms control after the advances during the 1970s. It was to take a combination of US domestic politics – the popular response of a large anti-nuclear movement and wider concerns within the US population of the lack of progress on arms control talks – with the emergence of a new leadership in the Kremlin in March 1985 that served to spark a new round of arms control talks that would lead to a number of major agreements between 1987 and 1991 that led to the end of the Cold War, at the strategic level. I will come back to this in the next section.

The other dimension of the policy of confrontation and aggression, which became known as the 'Reagan Doctrine',[17] focused on the third world and the link between revolutionary change and Soviet advance. The aim here was to weaken Soviet power 'at the edges', or impose much higher, military, political and economic costs on Soviet support for revolutionary regimes and revolutionary change in the third world. In pursuing a much more proactive policy towards the third world that involved the deployment of combat troops, the Reagan administration attempted to overcome the 'Vietnam Syndrome'.[18] The rhetoric of Reagan suggested that the US would support, arm and intervene in support of anti-communist 'freedom fighters' wherever they may be. In reality, however, and reflecting the continuing popular aversion and hostility to the deployment of US combat troops overseas, US intervention was more limited and circumspect. The US deployed its own troops on only two occasions: in Lebanon (Beirut) between September 1982 and February 1984[19] to oversee the PLO evacuation from Lebanon after the Israeli invasion of September 1982 and siege of Beirut; and in invading the Caribbean island of Grenada and overthrowing the pro-Cuban New Jewel revolutionary government.[20]

With its hands effectively tied over the use of combat troops, the Reagan administration sought to undermine and harass revolutionary regimes and give succour to counter-revolutionary states through the selective use of its military assets and a more indirect strategy of low-intensity warfare. This strategy was based on the 'lessons' learnt by the US military in its defeat in Vietnam. Low-intensity warfare

involves maintaining a multiplicity of pressures – political, economic, diplomatic, psychological, and ideological – against the enemy, and synchronizing those pressures with permanent but low-key military aggression. At its heart is political invalidation, rather than the military defeat, of the enemy.[21]

Thus, rather than deploying combat troops to defeat a revolutionary enemy, the US used a range of instruments to destroy the ability of revolutionary regimes to function politically at a much lower economic cost and, because of the absence of the involvement of large numbers of combat troops (and casualties thereof) and its covert nature, such a strategy was much less politically controversial amongst the US public. This strategy rested on a massive expansion of the CIA and its covert operations through the 1980s[22] and also of US special forces.[23] These played a crucial role in the four main 'theatres' of low-intensity warfare: Ethiopia, Angola, Nicaragua and Afghanistan.[24] These latter two I will now discuss in more depth.[25]

Nicaragua: The Reagan Doctrine, the *Contras* and Counter-Revolution

As discussed in Chapter 5 US intervention against the Sandinistas had occurred before the July 1979 revolution when the Carter administration sought to prevent radical political change in Nicaragua carried through by social and political forces antagonistic to traditional patterns of US external influence in Nicaragua. When Reagan became president in January 1981, however, US hostility towards the new revolutionary government in Managua shifted up a gear, as Nicaragua became the template for the prosecution of the Reagan Doctrine.

The Reagan Doctrine, as applied to Nicaragua during the 1980s, consisted of three elements, two of which were directed at Nicaragua, and one at US domestic politics and public opinion. With respect to the latter, the Reagan administration used the full resources of the state alongside a wide range of private civil society groups and news media (as well as Hollywood)[26] to propagate an image of Nicaragua as a dangerous Soviet-communist outpost committed to military aggression against its neighbours and a threat to the American way of life. The first lesson, then, from Vietnam, was to win over public opinion in support of counter-revolution, even if this meant deceiving the public as to the true nature, character and policies of the Nicaraguan government.[27]

It goes without saying that most of the justifications and accusations about the Sandinistas parroted by Reagan and his allies were far from the truth. With respect to human rights, electoral democracy, the political and economic character of Nicaragua and its relations with its neighbours, Nicaragua under the Sandinistas – though far from perfect – was a 'model' state in contrast to most other Central American states,[28] the only difference being that it had very close relations with Cuba, was sympathetic to the FMLN's revolutionary struggle in neighbouring El Salvador[29] and was committed to constructing a domestic and international politics that challenged the privileged position of private capital and US influence in Nicaragua's domestic affairs.[30]

The character of the Nicaraguan Revolution was in many respects post-communist, reflecting the local specificities of the revolution and the ideology and political objectives of the Sandinistas, and highlighting the heteronymous character of international relations during the latter stages of the Cold War. The Sandinistas were committed to an anti-imperialism based on national self-determination and independence resting on a policy of non-alignment rather than any explicit linkage with the USSR, as was the case with Cuba and Vietnam and, domestically, Nicaragua was never a one-party (communist) state. It was largely because of US policies, which I will detail below, that Managua was forced to become more dependent on the provision of economic aid and military supplies from the Soviet bloc than would otherwise have been the case.[31] Further, because of the rather limited Soviet involvement in

Nicaragua, at the ideological, economic and military levels, the Reagan Doctrine towards Nicaragua, in contrast to Afghanistan, had little impact on Soviet international relations and international power. Instead US counter-revolution towards Nicaragua was used as a means to build political support for a wider strategy of global counter-revolution through emphasising the Soviet-communist threat in 'America's own backyard'.[32] The idea was to scare the American people into action, and, in doing so, make clear to any would-be revolutionaries the costs of acting against the interests of the US.

The domestic propaganda war was to supplement the two other elements of the Reagan Doctrine strategy of overthrowing the Sandinistas. The US pursued this aim through economic means – primarily starving Nicaragua of economic aid, financial credits and closing of export markets – and militarily – through creating, financing, organising and training the remnants of Somoza's National Guard that formed the backbone of the *Contras'* pro-insurgency against the Sandinistas.[33] The economic dimension of the Reagan Doctrine began within days of Reagan taking office with the termination of the remaining aid funds granted to Nicaragua by Congress.[34] Henceforth, the US gradually turned the economic screw on Nicaragua in its bilateral dealings,[35] and through its dominant position within the key multilateral lending institutions, the IMF, World Bank and the Inter-American Development Bank.[36]

Considering the dire state of the Nicaraguan economy – in part caused by the destruction wrought by the National Guard in the final months and weeks of the dictatorship – when the Sandinistas seized power, and the fact that Somoza and his cronies had looted the Nicaraguan central bank of its foreign exchange reserves,[37] US economic warfare was to impose a severe strain on Nicaragua during the 1980s, making it much harder for the Sandinistas to realise their socio-economic objectives. The economic burden of withstanding US counter-revolution was also compounded by the increasing costs of dealing with the economic destruction caused by *Contra* attacks[38] and the use of scarce economic resources in fighting the *Contras*.[39]

This economic strategy complemented a more direct and coercive strategy of counter-revolution through US support for covert war waged by the *Contras* from bases in Honduras and Costa Rica. As William Leogrande comments, the military assistance provided by the US served to transform 'a ragtag collection' of anti-Sandinista exiles numbering approximately 1,000 into a well-equipped military force of 4,500 by July 1982.[40] The CIA played the key co-ordinating role in collaboration with Central American governments, especially Honduras, in organising and directing the *Contra* war against the Sandinistas. This dimension of the Reagan Doctrine consisted of three elements. First was the massive increase in US military support for the 'frontline states' of El Salvador and Honduras. This saw a massive increase in the military capacity of Honduras and El Salvador,[41] as well as the regular deployment of US troops in military exercises with Honduran forces close to the Nicaraguan border, which amounted to a deliberate attempt to intimidate the Sandinistas with the threat of a US invasion.[42] Second, the US employed CIA-managed Latin American right-wing mercenaries (known as unilaterally controlled Latino Assets) to attack Nicaragua's infrastructure. The most infamous case was the mining of Nicaraguan harbours between February and April 1984, which was declared illegal by the World Court and widely condemned – even by US allies.

Finally, the US organised, funded, trained and directed *Contra* attacks on Nicaragua. At their peak the *Contras* numbered 15,000 and launched regular raids into Nicaragua. However, despite the claims of the Reagan administration that the *Contras* were 'freedom fighters' committed to freedom, democracy and human rights, most commentators agree that not only did the *Contras* not pose much of a military challenge to the Sandinistas, they also targeted civilians and were guilty of gross human rights violations.[43]

As applied to Nicaragua, the Reagan Doctrine imposed massive human and economic costs on the Nicaraguan people[44] but ultimately failed to realise its twin objectives of swaying the American public to support a policy of militarised counter-revolution – including the deployment of US troops – and, the overthrow of the Sandinistas by the *Contras*. Instead, the US–Sandinista conflict was to end in 1990 with the confluence of developments – domestic, regional and international. Internationally, the superpower conflict was coming to an end, and with this Soviet bloc support (and, no doubt Cuban, as well) for Nicaragua could no longer be guaranteed. Regionally, the peace proposals associated with the Contadora process[45] and then, later, Costa Rica's President Oscar Arias provided a means for negotiations between Managua and the *Contras* (who could no longer rely on the same level of US support after the Iran–*Contra* scandal broke). Finally, the 1990 Nicaraguan election provided a 'choice' for the Nicaraguan people: either continue supporting the Sandinistas and risk more US hostility and continued war and economic stagnation,[46] or vote for the pro-US opposition and end US hostility and hope for an improvement in their economic fortunes. Unsurprisingly, the Nicaraguan people chose peace and voted the right into power. Unfortunately, this did not lead to economic improvement, at least not for the majority.

Afghanistan: The US and Islamic Anti-Communism[47]

With the Soviet intervention to address the crisis within the leadership and rule of the PDPA regime in Afghanistan in December 1979, the US, along with some of its key allies in the region – Saudi Arabia, Pakistan and Egypt – initiated a major programme of support for the anti-communist (and largely Islamist) resistance against Soviet forces and their local communist allies.[48] In contrast to Nicaragua, however, whereas the CIA had effectively created and organised the *Contras* as a counter-revolutionary army, in Afghanistan an indigenous anti-communist counter-revolutionary insurgency existed before Afghanistan became a flashpoint of superpower conflict after December 1979.

The Afghan anti-communist Islamist insurgency emerged from a revolt by traditional and reactionary elements within a deeply traditional and insular Afghan society in response to an authoritarian project of secular modernisation carried through by the PDPA after the 'April Revolution' of 1978. Further, the key external actor involved in the Afghan–Soviet war was not the US but Pakistan.[49] For it was Pakistan and the Islamisation that it underwent, particularly in the military and intelligence services and the cultivation of madrassas in the Pashtun tribal belt, under the dictatorship of General Zia al-Haq, who came to power in a US-backed *coup d'état* in July 1977, that provided the infrastructure of military and economic support for the Afghan *mujahadeen*. The relative autonomy of Pakistan's support for the Afghan *jihad* and the fact that US policy and power were mediated via the Pakistani national security apparatus and wider Islamist social forces within Pakistan would have important consequences for the post-Cold War era, which I will come back to in Chapter 7.

The US, then, was presented with a unique opportunity, indeed, the only opportunity during the history of the Cold War where it could support armed resistance against the USSR because of the presence of up to 100,000 Soviet troops involved in combat outside of the Soviet bloc. Indeed, the US – at least according to the revelations of Carter's National Security Adviser, Zbigniew Brzezisnki, in an interview in 1998 – had sensed the opportunity offered, in July 1979, by the anti-communist insurgency in Afghanistan before the Soviet intervention when Carter authorised clandestine aid to the *mujahadeen*, which, according to Brzezinski, would help provoke a Soviet intervention.[50]

According to Charles Cogan, one of the principal CIA agents overseeing US aid to the *mujahadeen* in Pakistan, the first consignment of arms arrived two weeks after the Soviet intervention.[51] This would be the initial shipment in a massive programme of military aid that would amount to $2 billion in official US aid between 1981 and 1987,[52] supplemented by further millions of dollars of military aid from Egypt, Saudi Arabia and Pakistan. The significance of US counter-revolution in Afghanistan was not just the provision of aid, but also the facilitation, organised by Pakistan, of an international network of armed Islamists numbering approximately 35,000 from 43 countries, who were to provide the backbone of the post-Cold War Islamist terrorist movements in a number of different locales.[53]

The international support for the *mujahadeen* was a major factor in tying down Soviet forces, contributing to over 14,000 Soviet combat deaths and sapping the resources and morale of the PDPA regime and its Soviet ally, thus providing some substance to the claim that Afghanistan was the USSR's 'Vietnam'.[54] However, despite the losses incurred by the Soviets and the inability of the PDPA regime to maintain control of most of rural Afghanistan, it was to take the accession of Gorbachev to the Soviet leadership and his commitment to a fundamental rethinking of the USSR's international commitments[55] before Moscow would begin to move towards withdrawing its forces.[56] In this respect, US policy had succeeded, as the Soviet withdrawal would leave a highly vulnerable PDPA regime.[57] The combination of US funding, alongside allies like Saudi Arabia, for the insurgency combined with the emergence of a reactionary Islamist internationalism[58] allowed the US to 'bleed' the USSR, fulfilling the Reagan Doctrine's goals of imposing a painful lesson in human and material terms for Soviet 'adventurism' and undermining third world revolution.

The Afghan episode, which I will return to in Chapter 7, allowed the US to combine its objective of rolling back revolutionary change and imposing strains on the USSR directly through the losses the Red Army incurred and the promotion of Islamist currents within the Muslim-populated southern border republics of the USSR. However, although the US played an important role – through the training provided to the *mujahadeen* by its special forces and the advanced military equipment like the Stinger surface-to-air missile to cancel out any Soviet advantage – the important point to stress was that the Afghan *jihad* was an Islamist operation promoted by regional US allies to realise their domestic and international objectives. The US was obviously crucial because without its involvement and strategic umbrella the USSR might have invaded Pakistan, yet Islamist currents pre-dated the US involvement. The success of the Reagan Doctrine as applied to Afghanistan was, then, qualified and this became particularly evident with developments after the final defeat of the PDPA regime in 1992 by Pakistani and Saudi-backed Islamist forces.

THE DEBATE ABOUT THE END OF THE COLD WAR

The debate about the end of the Cold War has involved two sets of theoretical questions. First is the relationship between endogenous factors promoting political change within the USSR/Soviet bloc and exogenous sources of change. Simply put, did communism collapse because of the internal contradictions and weaknesses associated with the communist political and economic system – the lack of political legitimacy for communist leaderships, particularly in east-central Europe, and relative economic decline and stagnation, which had become much more acute in the 1980s – or were external influences (coercive and/or persuasive) more significant? The second question concerns the role played by material and ideational factors in accounting for the collapse of Soviet-communist power. That is, was the Soviet leadership, and Gorbachev in particular, forced to make strategic and geopolitical concessions to preponderant US material/military power – a consequence of Reagan's rearmament programme and policy of aggressive counter-revolution – thus ending the post-war competition for global ascendancy, or was Gorbachev's reform trilogy of *glasnost*, *perestroika* and new foreign policy thinking part of an ideological transformation within the Soviet leadership that was domestic rather than international in origin?

There is a huge literature on the end of the Cold War that addresses these questions giving emphasis to any one or more of these factors, and because of considerations of space I cannot do justice to such debates.[59] I will spell out my own explanation for the collapse of Soviet-communist power below. In this section I will concentrate on the two dominant theoretical explanations within the discipline of International Relations for the end of the Cold War. The mainstream debate has been dominated by Realist and Neorealist scholars, who have tended to explain the end of the Cold War as the USSR making strategic concessions (arms reductions, withdrawal from east-central Europe and the cutting back of political and military involvement in the third world) to preponderant US material power,[60] and Ideas-based approaches that tend to emphasise the importance of ideas and values – as opposed to external material power – in shaping the decisions of Gorbachev's leadership.[61] In a word, whilst Realists focus on exogenous and material factors that have a coercive edge to explain the collapse of Soviet-communist power, ideational explanations give greater emphasis to endogenous and non-material factors that have a more persuasive edge.

Whilst the differences between these two accounts are significant, they share a basic understanding of what needs to be accounted for. Thus, the Cold War is seen as a post-war conflict between the superpowers combing ideological and geopolitical competition and, consequently, what needs to be explained is the transformation of the bipolar relationship. As should be clear from previous chapters, my understanding of the Cold War and what needs to be explained is significantly different. Accordingly, I will offer a critique of the mainstream debate before discussing my own explanation for the collapse of Soviet-communist power and my understanding of the nature and consequences of the Cold War's end, which will also be addressed in the final chapter.

Realism and Neorealism

Realist-informed explanations of the end of the Cold War focus on the general formula of the balance of power to account for change within the international system. Hence, the decisions of the Soviet leadership and developments between 1987 and 1991 are the product of power calculations and adjustments by the Kremlin in the face of preponderant US material power. Whilst more partisan commentators claim that the aggressive and confrontational policies of the Reagan administration accelerated the end of the Soviet challenge,[62] most Realists emphasise the longer-term consequences of containment combined with the deep-rooted economic problems within the Soviet bloc. Consequently, the Soviets, faced with a domestic political and economic crisis, opted for strategic retrenchment by ending the Cold War through withdrawing Soviet forces from east-central Europe and ending the global competition for strategic ascendancy with the US, thus allowing for much needed economic resources to be directed towards domestic political and economic challenges.

The focus is largely on the military dimensions of the Cold War with particular emphasis given to the arms control and reduction agreements between 1987 and 1991, and the withdrawal of Soviet military forces from east-central Europe. Although Realist explanations do not ignore economic and ideological developments, these are seen as being of secondary importance. Thus, the question of the ending of communist rule in east-central Europe and then the USSR, alongside Moscow's (or more accurately the international department of the CPSUs) decision to stop supporting international revolution do not really matter. Indeed, the Cold War could have ended with the preservation of domestic communist polities, yet without the external militarised challenge to the US.

The ending of superpower competition and the Soviet geopolitical challenge to the US is obviously a major element in the story of the ending of the Cold War. However, it is not only a partial account, it also fails properly to connect socio-economic and ideological change in the domestic politics of the USSR/Soviet bloc with the transformation in the external relations of the USSR. Further, because of their implicit determinism – the USSR was bound to make strategic concessions because of greater US power with or without Gorbachev – Realist accounts of the Cold War's end ultimately overlook the dynamics associated with Gorbachev and the changes that he helped unleash, particularly with respect to the *character* of change within east-central Europe in 1989. The question here is about timing and why the situation that confronted Gorbachev resulted in fundamental change, when a similar domestic and international context did not lead earlier Soviet leaders to pursue Gorbachev-like policies. Indeed, the early 1980s provided for a much more hostile international environment with respect to the character of US policy towards the USSR yet did not invoke Soviet concessions.[63]

In concentrating on the military-strategic dimension of the Cold War, Realist accounts decouple the militarised domestic political constitution of Soviet power from the external relations of the USSR and Soviet bloc. Consequently, external change – understood as the end of a militarised international relations based on its military occupation of east-central Europe – rested upon the reconstitution of domestic communist power. This was the key decision of Gorbachev – the attempt to redefine communism as a social system and the relations between the USSR and east-central Europe – and it was the failure of this due to the popular pressure and uprisings against 'naked' communist authorities in east-central Europe that could no longer call upon the Red Army, that sealed the fate of communist rule and effectively ended the Cold War.

The partial nature of the Realist account fails to connect the attempt to reconstitute communist power from within, free of military force, from its international relations. The strategic retrenchment, then, simultaneously amounted to a domestic 'revolution' in the nature of Soviet power in east-central Europe; a power that was undermined not only by the popular revolutions, but also by the incorporation of these states into the structures and institutions of the US-led capitalist international order after 1989. It was not a question of change in *matériel* – reductions in nuclear missiles, tanks and movements of troops[64] – but the socio-economic and ideological defeat of communist forms of rule and their replacement by liberal democratic and capitalist forms of rule that ended the Cold War because communist power was premised on coercive-militarised relations of power. Without the (unexpected) revolutionary domestic political changes within the USSR and Soviet bloc which were a consequence of Gorbachev's attempt to redefine the domestic basis of communist rule, the arms agreements and so forth may have served to lessen the strategic aspect of the Cold War, but the social and ideological elements would have remained. Finally, it was an *internal* rather than an external dynamic – the deep-rooted political illegitimacy of communist governments and increasingly acute economic problems – and not western military pressure that accounts for the popular overthrow of communist rule. In the final instance, then, it was not external pressure that ended Soviet communism, but domestic political change rooted in domestic *not* international political dynamics.

Ideational Approaches

Inverting the focus of Realist-informed explanations, ideational approaches emphasise the domestic and ideological developments within the Soviet leadership under Gorbachev. Thus, whereas Realists emphasise international structures and material power with little space for a discussion of agency (Gorbachev and social movements in east-central Europe) and contingency (revolutionary uprisings and change), ideational approaches stress the ideas that informed Gorbachev's new thinking and how this was complemented by shifts in the ideological mindset, away from Cold War, of the western leaders. Indeed, they tend to dismiss the claim that 'Reagan won the Cold War' by claiming that the hostility and confrontation Reagan promoted actually prevented an earlier accommodation between the superpowers.

The Cold War ended because when the ideas and norms that shaped Soviet policy-making were transformed during Gorbachev's leadership – the final phase of de-Stalinisation – these changes were recognised as such and were reciprocated by the West. Thus, whereas previous Soviet leaders had either been hostile and/or fearful of the West, Gorbachev saw things differently. In particular, he and his colleagues, such as his foreign minister, Eduard Shevardnadze, recognised the profound transformation of Western Europe, and Germany in particular, to a stable, liberal and pacific state that could not be seen as a threat to Soviet security as it had been in the past. In sum, the Soviet leadership became influenced by liberal political and normative assumptions rather than Marxist-Leninist ones.

Consequently, what mattered in ending the Cold War were not the relative levels of economic development, or the calculations and adjustments associated with the balance of military power, but rather the adoption of a particular way of defining the norms and values on which to base policy. Once Moscow had recognised the non-threatening and positive features of western liberalism, the Soviet Union could, to quote a classic phrase of Cold War fiction, 'come in from the cold'.[65]

Ideational approaches obviously provide an important alternative to Realist-based explanations of the Cold War's end. However, as much as Realists divorce strategic relations from the domestic socio-economic constitution of Soviet power, so ideational explanations end up reifying the power of ideas and exaggerating their explanatory power. Whilst on strong ground in emphasising the changes in ideas and norms that shaped Gorbachev's worldview and reform programme, it is far from clear that Gorbachev viewed the world through a liberal prism. Further, the objective of his reform programme, at least until 1989, was to preserve communist power within the Soviet bloc and especially within the USSR,[66] but without relying on military power, not to dismantle it. Thus, whilst communist power did collapse, this was because of the intervention of social forces within east-central Europe via revolutionary forms of popular pressure and later the penetration of these societies by the combined power of Western (capitalist) civil society and states that served to destroy the socio-economic bases of communist rule, which the 'velvet revolutions' had succeeded in achieving at the political level through ending the communist parties' monopoly on power backed by military force.

The ideational account also tends to conflate the manner of political change within east-central Europe with that of the USSR. Whilst communist power was destroyed from below by social forces outside party-state structures in east-central Europe,[67] in the USSR communist power was dismantled from 'within and above' as Gorbachev's 'revolution from above' split party-state structures and allowed local/regional *apparatchiks* to seize property and/or campaign on nationalist platforms thus weakening the central power of Moscow between 1989 and 1991. Although there was some popular dimension to the end of communist rule in the USSR, particularly in the Caucases and the Baltic Republics, what ultimately mattered were the splits within the party, the inertia of the security organs and emergence of local/regional party fiefdoms legitimised on nationalist rather than communist grounds. Thus, the end of communist power within the USSR allowed former communists to continue to control the levers of power, though the socio-economic and ideological basis of that power was changed as the centralised command economy was plundered and broken up and economic assets seized by the *nomenklatura*.

The ending of the Cold War was driven by ideological factors, but their influence and agency were played out within political and economic structures within and across state boundaries that were contingent on the balance of social forces. Hence, whilst liberal and democratic ideas captured the imagination of large numbers of people in east-central Europe providing the ideological glue that bound social movements together against communist power in 1989, the influence and power of such ideas were much less pronounced within the USSR. Thus, by concentrating on elite decision-making ideational approaches neglect the wider structures and relations of society that ultimately determine the influence of any currency of ideas. Finally, the Cold War did not end with an accommodation indicated by a mutual shift in ideological mindsets between East and West. Rather, the end of the Cold War was a one-way process based on the collapse of communist power and the spread of western liberal democratic and capitalist structures, institutions and relations.

CONCLUSIONS: ENDING THE COLD WAR – THE COLLAPSE OF COMMUNISM IN THE SOVIET BLOC AND THE INTERNATIONAL DEFEAT OF HISTORICAL COMMUNISM

What I intend to do in this section is link the external and internal dynamic of change alongside relating the material with the socio-economic and ideological dimensions, thus providing an explanation that goes some way to overcoming the weaknesses in the mainstream account. I will do this by focusing on the internal contradictions within Soviet-communist forms of rule and then examining the international context of the 1980s.

Contradictions and Collapse in the Political Economy of Communist States

As has been well documented in the accounts of the collapse of communist power in the Soviet bloc,[68] communist power, particularly in east-central Europe, suffered from a number of long-term structural frailties. The two key ones were the lack of political legitimacy of communist regimes stemming from their authoritarian character and their nature as *de facto* one-party states, combined with the historical legacy of the external imposition of these regimes and their maintenance by the Red Army; and the economic problems that emerged – becoming particularly acute from the late 1970s – after their initial impressive economic growth through the 1950s.[69] These economic problems also afflicted the USSR.[70]

These structural difficulties were brought into the open during the periodic bouts of 'revolutionary' crises that dominated the history of communist regimes in east-central Europe throughout their existence. Each of these crises involved a number of common factors that brought to the fore the structural contradictions in the constitution of Soviet-communist power: economic problems and concerns about stagnating living standards – particularly acute in centrally planned states where economic provision was the *direct* and *political* responsibility of the party-state authorities rather than the economic responsibility of the market;[71] leadership change – both locally and in Moscow; and the unintended consequences of attempts at reform. Reform – to address political and/or economic problems – within the communist states in the Soviet bloc was always problematic and exposed these regimes to challenges from below.[72] Moreover, as Chris Harman argued some two decades before the dissolution of Soviet power, any attempts to pursue major reform required the overcoming of conservative sections of the bureaucracy who opposed reform. The problem, however, of pushing through 'reform from above', as the postwar episodes in east-central Europe highlighted, was that '[m]uch of the conservative resistance could not be overcome without the danger arising of the repressive apparatus vis-à-vis the rest of society being paralysed, thus unleashing forces that might easily turn against the bureaucracy as a whole'.[73] In sum, communist forms of rule were systematically prone to crisis where the maintenance of communist rule tended to require the use of force.

Yet, these long-term and structural problems do not adequately explain why change occurred in the late 1980s and not before. The convergence of a number of factors in the 1980s were crucial to the survival of Soviet-communist power. Thus, with respect to the economic performance of communist states, things had deteriorated significantly by the 1980s and this decline was a consequence of the combined failure of domestic reforms[74] and how these were linked to the greater integration of all the Soviet-communist economies into the capitalist world market.

Most of the east-central European economies were connected to the world market through an unhealthy relationship based on asymmetric trade and debt. By 1989 over half the trade of Poland, Hungary and East Germany was with the major western economies; Czechoslovakia's share had increased from 28 per cent in 1980 to 34 per cent in 1989;[75] and the USSR's international trade had recorded a more than 13-fold increase by the early 1980s from its 1950 level.[76] The problem with the trading relationship was that it rested on the export of raw materials[77] and the import of higher-value technological goods. This uneven relationship related to the accumulation of debt by east-central European economies in particular. Thus, foreign debt increased to fund consumption and living standards because these economies were unable to pay for more imports through increasing (the value) of their exports, due to the competition from the low-wage, low-cost 'newly industrialising countries' of south-east and east Asia and Latin America. By 1987 the burden of foreign debt – and the east-central European communist economies' increasing dependence on it – had reached $76 billion, with Poland alone owing $36 billion.[78] Whilst the communist economies of east-central Europe exposed themselves to greater debt to try to maintain their standards of living, the USSR was forced to introduce rationing in the provision of basic consumer goods by the late 1980s.[79]

Consequently, by the 1980s the relationship of the communist economies to the wider capitalist world economy had been transformed from one of competition and relative isolation and hostility to one of increasing structural economic dependence with the official blessing of each state's party-state leadership.

In effect, the 'Great Contest' was essentially over, because these types of state were no longer able to challenge the economic superiority of the West.[80] Furthermore, though politically different, from the 1970s onwards, the socio-economic properties of these regimes were transformed to resemble increasingly those of capitalist states due to their growing exposure to the logic and discipline of the world market.

By the late 1980s, the material project of the rapid development of the productive forces of the Soviet Union/Soviet bloc appeared exhausted. The earlier expectations of surpassing capitalist levels of material development were far from being realised. Moreover, because of the exposure of countries like Poland and Hungary to western debt, these economies had a *political* interest in western economic stability, thus ensuring manageable rates of interest payments and the possibility of more credit. The Soviet Union, indirectly, was also concerned to see that economic problems, particularly in Poland, did not spill over into outright political contestation of communist rule as had occurred in the 1970s and more seriously in 1980–81 with the formation of the free trade union, Solidarity.

It was in this context that Gorbachev assumed power, ensuring that economic restructuring – *perestroika* – was to be a fundamental political priority. The policies that Gorbachev initially outlined in the mid-1980s to address Soviet economic problems were similar to previous attempts by Soviet leaders and other states in the Soviet bloc to deal with internal economic problems. Gorbachev's strategy related to longer-term historical developments within the Soviet economy in the post-Stalin era which were dominated by two interrelated issues. The first was the gradual reduction in the role of force and pressure in the management of the command economy. The second, which was a consequence of the reduction of the role of coercion and pressure in economic management, was an increase in the areas of 'relative autonomy' in economic decision-making, which reduced the relative power of the centre over local economic enterprises.[81] This had begun with Khrushchev and was continued in a much more 'stop-go' manner under Brezhnev.[82] The main goal of economic reform was to stimulate economic productivity. However, whereas Gorbachev's predecessors had sought to 'tinker at the edges' by trying to improve economic performance by encouraging local initiative, but within the structure of centralised control, Gorbachev attempted to go a step further by fundamentally shifting the balance of economic power away from the central party-state apparatus in Moscow to local enterprises and their managers.[83]

The reforms initiated by Gorbachev were unique in that, because of their radical anti-Stalinist nature, they required an officially sanctioned political attack on what Gorbachev saw as the obstacles to change within significant sections of the party-state apparatus, which also implicitly undermined communist leaderships in east-central Europe.[84] Consequently, because of the source of domestic opposition and the structural power of the *apparat*, especially with respect to the coercive organs, the international context was even more important. Previous attempts at reform within the USSR and the wider Soviet bloc had taken place within the context of a relatively stable and unified set of party-state structures. Gorbachev's reforms, then, required external stability if not support from some western states, thus ensuring the best chance of 'controlled change' yet without having to call upon the 'forces of conservatism' within the *apparat* and Red Army.

However, what is important to recognise about the direction of Soviet policy under Gorbachev after 1985 was that the relationship between domestic economic reform and foreign policy was not always consistent. Indeed, the initial orientation of Gorbachev towards improving Soviet economic performance was not 'liberalisation', but rather a focus on discipline and enforcing the rule of the party over the economy in a similar manner to that championed by Yuri Andropov in the 1970s.[85] It was only after this policy had failed to achieve its expected results that Gorbachev opted after 1987 for a different strategy. Even when Gorbachev did begin to move towards decentralising economic power, Soviet economic policy continued to favour those sectors of the economy that were essential to the production of *matériel*.[86] Moreover, the Soviet defence budget remained stable until 1987, as did Soviet support for its revolutionary allies.[87] Thus, it was only *after* initial attempts at economic reform had proved unsuccessful that economic reform shifted in a more radical direction combined with the need to restructure Soviet international relations so as to support domestic economic reform that the continued burden of military competition and geopolitical conflict could only undermine.

The character and eventual outcome of Soviet policy in the late 1980s was, profoundly conditioned by the social constitution of Soviet politics. What defined the politics of the Soviet bloc was that it was premised on the coercive-militarised authority of the party-state. The coercive-militarised nature of the Soviet bloc not only defined the production and reproduction of internal socio-political order, but also, and more importantly, its international relations. Because of this not only was reform always likely to be problematic as it had been in the past (especially in east-central Europe), but because of the relationship of military power with internal socio-political order, the relationship between domestic change and international relations was likely to be mutually reinforcing.

The objective of the policies of the Gorbachev leadership was to reconstitute the basis of social power within the Soviet bloc by reducing, and then removing, the role of coercion and force as the basis of political order. Through such 'liberalisation' the Soviet leadership sought not only to revitalise socialism within the bloc, but also undermine the assumptions that guided western policy towards the USSR. This was not, then, at least in the initial stages of Gorbachev's leadership, about ending Soviet socialism, but rather its coercive-militarised character, thus not only reconstituting domestic/bloc politics but also transforming the nature of 'East–West' conflict, as the removal of military power from internal bloc politics would necessarily transform the international power and relations of the USSR.

The role of coercive-military power was determining in this respect. With the revoking of the Brezhnev Doctrine and the implicit acceptance of what became known as the 'Sinatra Doctrine'[88] the Soviet-socialist political barrier to change was removed, thus allowing the flourishing of autonomous cultural, national, ethnic, political and economic relations within the Soviet bloc and with the West. With the removal of the threat of force, communist regimes in east-central Europe had a choice: negotiate with the opposition or use force on their own to maintain power. However, with the former option being taken by Poland and Hungary in January and June 1989[89] respectively, the option of using force to uphold communist power became much less likely for the other regimes.[90] The upshot was that communist power was effectively dissolved through negotiation (Poland, Hungary and Bulgaria) and forced from power by popular revolt from below (Czechoslovakia) or, in the case of East Germany, by the combined forces of revolt from below and external pressure from West Germany.

Developments in east-central Europe contrasted with the USSR where the death throes of communist power was more protracted. Whereas Gorbachev and the Soviet leadership could tolerate the end of communist rule in east-central Europe, until the watershed of the August 1991 *coup*, they would not tolerate it at home. Yet, because of the reforms, and their ambivalent character,[91] implemented by Gorbachev, the structures and institutions of party rule were destroyed from within through the combination of conflict within different levels of the party-state, and how this led to the inertia of the security organs, the ultimate arbiter of communist power. Yet, rather than promoting widespread popular revolt from below, it facilitated the implosion of the communist party from within as it broke up into national-republican fiefdoms,[92] as state property was seized by leading *nomenklatura*, and Moscow's grip on the political structures and economic assets within the USSR was finally broken.

Because of the decoupling of politics and economics that these developments triggered, the possibility of the party-state controlling these developments, and thus preventing them from undermining the institutions and sources of communist power, was reduced. The Soviet leadership had exposed the brittleness of its authority by removing the structural political veto of military power combined with direct political authority over the control of economic assets and economic relations. The collapse of Soviet communism was almost inevitable once the floodgates had been opened which allowed the emergence of internal political freedoms. Moreover, the impact of these internal changes, and the possibility of the party-state supervising them as Gorbachev expected, were compounded by the rapid imbrication of these internal political and economic changes with international relations.[93]

The International Context and the Soviet Collapse

As indicated above, whilst it is useful, analytically, to separate the internal/bloc factors that caused the collapse of Soviet-communist power, in practice these developments were conditioned by, and influenced, international factors. Much of the discussion of the international dimensions to the collapse of communist power has focused on the transformation in the superpower relationship highlighted in a number of military-strategic agreements between 1987 and 1991.[94] These agreements reflected a profound transformation in the bipolar relationship from one dominated by suspicion, hostility and confrontation – particularly on the US side – which characterised the first half of the decade, to one of cooperation, trust and agreement in a range of areas, not just strategic arms agreements.[95]

The improvement in superpower relations – quite unforeseen in the early 1980s – was a result of shifts in the US position based upon a greater willingness to enter into arms control negotiations, and the coming to power of Gorbachev. Domestic factors obviously influenced Soviet policy under Gorbachev, particularly the need to reduce the economic burden associated with the arms race[96] and confrontational relationship with the US, but domestic factors also influenced Reagan's position, though to a much lesser degree.[97]

The agreements signed between 1987 and 1991 were certainly significant and contributed to political developments within the Soviet bloc, as any attempt to uphold communist power through force, as in the past, would, in all likelihood, have prevented the US signing these agreements.[98] Further, these agreements facilitated, and to some degree rested upon, the removal of militarised relations of power from the political constitution of communist rule within the Soviet bloc. Yet, in themselves, they did not signal the end of the Cold War as the agreements did not require the dissolution of communist rule; nor did they amount to the end of international social conflict involving communist movements. With respect to the former, it was to take domestic political developments within the USSR and Soviet bloc to dissolve communist power. And with regard to the global social systemic conflict between Soviet-communism and international capitalism, its termination was much more shifting and uneven than the singular end of the transformation of the USSR's support for international revolution under Gorbachev and the subsequent collapse of the Soviet Union. Gorbachev could not, and did not, end the Cold War because the Cold War was an international social conflict which was not reducible to the history of the USSR.

The significance of this point, as should be clear from the preceding analysis, is that the history and international relations of the USSR were *symptomatic* of a specific form of politics and state. Thus, the history of the Cold War concerned the history of the emergence, spread and decline of historical communism in its challenge to international capitalism. This socio-economic challenge emerged out of shifting – temporally – conjunctures of international crises associated with capitalist socio-economic development leading to revolutionary seizures of power carried through by distinct (communist) forms of political agency committed to realising particular social, economic and political objectives and involving the mobilisation of specific social constituencies in support of such projects. Whilst the USSR was the most important revolutionary-communist state providing military and economic support for other communist states and movements – in some cases of crucial significance to their survival and success – there were other communist states and movements of significance for the history of the Cold War.

Consequently, their history – how far such states remained 'communist' in their domestic political constitution and socio-economic reproduction, and to what extent they remained part of the Soviet bloc and committed to contesting international capitalist power and supporting the forces of international communist revolution – and the history of communist and other radical-nationalist movements as agents of resistance and revolutionary change, also need to be factored into an account of the ending of the Cold War. If we reduce the Cold War to the bipolar conflict, as many mainstream approaches do, then such concerns are marginal. Yet, in doing so we would end up overlooking the relationship between revolutionary change and the superpowers, a major part of the history of the Cold War.

This broader historical and empirical canvass raises two issues for our consideration of the international context of the end of the Cold War and the defeat of historical communism as a form of revolutionary anti-capitalist politics and state.[99] First, the significance of the role of the USSR in supporting international (communist) revolution and challenging US-capitalist power; and, second, the continuation of (communist) revolutionary outcomes of international capitalist crises that were not reducible to the behaviour of the USSR. That is, what of the 'autonomous' dynamic of Cold War evident in the waves of revolutionary crises and successful communist revolutionary seizures of power in the post-1917 era?

With respect to the first, the transformation of Soviet foreign policy under Gorbachev was significant in tempering Soviet support for allied communist regimes and communist/revolutionary movements, indicated by the withdrawal from Afghanistan and moves towards negotiations to address a number of conflicts involving its allies. In this sense, Gorbachev's 'new thinking' went beyond the idea of 'peaceful co-existence' in that it was a further attempt to demilitarise regional conflicts and the competition between social forces and social systems, even if this meant that some revolutionary regimes were removed from power, as was the case in Nicaragua. Yet, it was not a refutation of support for revolutionary political change carried out by local political forces *tout court*, as Gorbachev continued to believe in the possibility of states with different social systems co-existing, freed from the threat of military conflict and nuclear war. Consequently, it was only after the August *coup* and the dissolution of the USSR that the Soviet Union broke its links with its erstwhile revolutionary allies – North Korea, Vietnam and Cuba in particular – and its support for other revolutionary movements.

One cannot be precise about the direction of Soviet policy under Gorbachev had there been no *coup* attempt and had the USSR not disintegrated, but with the prioritising of domestic concerns which required a new *modus vivendi* with the US and the West, in all likelihood the USSR, following earlier patterns of foreign policy – especially notable under Stalin, and evident in the earlier debates (i.e. before Gorbachev became leader) about the costs and benefits of supporting revolutionary states in the third world[100] – would have sacrificed international revolution for the domestic survival of the regime. In this sense, Gorbachev's policies of tempering Soviet support for other revolutionary states and movements, particularly if such support jeopardised the USSR's *rapprochement* with Washington, should be seen as the realisation of a tendency present within Soviet foreign policy since 1917.

Yet, this tendency of caution and, for some critics of the USSR, counter-revolution[101] was not consistent, and co-existed with tendencies supportive of international revolution.[102] What tended to determine the dominance of one over the other was the combination of the regime's domestic security and the external – read, geopolitical opportunities – environment and, in particular, the degree to which 'conservatism' or 'adventurism' in Soviet international relations threatened to undermine the regime's domestic security. Obviously, Gorbachev's policies went considerably further than any of his predecessors'; indeed, his questioning of the centrality of the Marxist-Leninist idea of class struggle in a world of nuclear weapons could be seen as a fundamental ditching of the core framework which had guided Soviet international relations.[103] However, notwithstanding Gorbachev's ideological differences with previous Soviet leaders, the key turning point in the relationship between the USSR and international revolution was not the new superpower détente evident after 1987 or the ending of communist rule in east-central Europe, but rather the dissolution of communist rule within the USSR. It was this and not the earlier developments that forced a change in the political economy of other communist states, like Cuba and Vietnam, allied to the USSR.

Yet, because the international history of communist revolution was not reducible to the USSR, our account of the end of the Cold War also needs to look at international communist revolution more broadly as a form of politics, and as a product of international crises. Thus, whilst Stalin on a number of occasions did act against the forces of local communist revolution, some of these forces – as in China, Yugoslavia and Indochina – were ultimately successful in establishing communist rule. In this sense, throughout the history of the Cold War, an autonomous dynamic of (communist) revolution was present.

However, this was not the case when Gorbachev assumed power. Rather, two developments had emerged, both of which informed Soviet thinking about international revolution. The first concerned the economic and political costs of supporting revolutionary states in the third world and the degree to which these states – particularly in sub-Saharan Africa – could ever mature into industrialised communist states, particularly when they were subject to US-assisted counter-revolution. The question here, then, was how viable these states were with and without external (Soviet) support and the political and economic costs the USSR incurred from such support. This was a question that concerned all Soviet leaders such that throughout the history of the USSR, revolutionary states or movements that had managed to seize power in one instance were also overthrown, in part because of the absence of any Soviet assistance.[104]

Because of the pressing domestic political and economic demands that confronted Gorbachev, combined with the historical learning associated with the problems of building socialism in the third world in the context of counter-revolutionary hostility, he went further than any other Soviet leader in reducing Soviet commitments. But, as I mentioned above, this was not abandonment but retrenchment. What ultimately mattered for the forces of international revolution was the domestic strength of individual revolutionary states with or without Soviet support.

The history of the Cold War, shifting as it was across time and space saw defeats and victories for the forces and movements of historical communism within the same historical timeframe. Indeed, the beginning of the Cold War in the founding of the USSR in 1917 reflected this paradox – the Bolshevik Revolution and the emergence and survival of the USSR, which contrasted with the strangling and then defeat of the German and wider European revolution. The successful expansion of Soviet-communist power into east-central Europe through war, and the strengthening of the forces of international revolution in Asia and later the Middle East, Latin America and Africa – understood as the spread of the Cold War through the dynamic of revolutionary struggle and success – contrasted with the ending of Cold War through the containment and defeat of the forces of communist revolution in Western Europe. This continued throughout the history of the Cold War. By the 1980s, then, the historical record highlighted the end of other/most Cold Wars as much as the continuation of the central, superpower conflict, notably in the post-Mao reforms in China and its opening towards the West and its active opposition to the international spread of Soviet power. Consequently, whilst the superpower dimension of Cold War continued in the 1980s, many other former fronts of Cold War had changed with the defeat of (communist) revolutionary movements and states[105] or, as in the case of China, the termination of hostility towards international capitalism as the means to uphold an increasingly nominal form of *communist* power.

This brings me to the second issue relating to the broader history of communist revolution and the end of the Cold War which concerns the degree to which revolutionary crises emergent from capitalist development continued to result in communist revolution or the establishment of regimes in some way connected to the political tradition and programme founded in 1917. Thus, prior to the 1980s, whilst the dynamic of the Cold War witnessed multiple beginnings as much as ends – evidenced in the continued (communist) revolutionary outcomes of international crises engendered by capitalist development – this was no longer the case by the 1980s. This is significant on its own terms, but also has a bearing on the policies of the USSR in the later 1980s and any explanation for Gorbachev's 'new thinking'. The irony here is that at the moment when the USSR was able to contest US power geopolitically (during the 1970s) in a way that it was unable to before or after, the consequences of international crises associated with capitalist development were producing very diverse outcomes, some of which involved communist movements committed to historical communist objectives allied to the USSR, whilst others (most cases) involved post-communist (Nicaragua), and anti-communist (Iran) social forces.

Whilst the uneven, contradictory and conflictual character of international capitalist development across uneven geographical space continued – and continues – to provide a socio-economic context for political ruptures that see fundamental transformations in the basis of state power, it was no longer promoting the formation of social movements and revolutionary political agency committed to the historical goals of communist revolution and mobilising those social constituencies that tended to form the backbone of communist movements – radicalised intellectuals, the industrial and agrarian proletariat and the peasantry.

The 'revolutionary' outcomes of capitalist development, then, have become more varied, such that heteronymous sources of conflict and resistance – and as was indicated in Chapter 5 – outside of the Cold War global social-systemic conflict between historical communism and capitalism have increasingly emerged, sometimes on the back of the historical defeat of the social and political forces associated with historical communism. This is something that I will discuss in more detail in Chapter 7 as these new sources of resistance and conflict, which emerged out of the endings of Cold Wars, are crucial to accounting for the current conjuncture in world politics associated with the war on terror. For our account of the end of the Cold War, it was not only that Gorbachev confronted a world where other Cold Wars had ended with the defeat and socialisation of other revolutionary states, but that the social dynamic that sustained the historical communist challenge to western capitalism and which sustained the ideological and doctrinal basis of the USSR was in terminal decline, if not already dead.

7

Conclusions: Tracing the Paradoxical Ends of the Cold War and the Origins of Contemporary Conflict in World Politics[1]

INTRODUCTION

The collapse of Soviet communism and disintegration of the USSR ushered in a systemic transformation in the structure and political character of the international system. The socio-economic and ideological challenge to capitalism and the capitalist great powers that had originated in 1917, and the geopolitical and strategic arrangements that had emerged after 1945, were replaced with the termination of the USSR's strategic and geopolitical challenge to the US, and the extinguishing of the social and political forces that had fuelled the flames of communist-inspired revolution. Whilst the US was no longer subject to a geopolitical check on its projection of military force, the further (global) entrenchment and spread of the social relations of capitalism – and those social and political forces that most benefited from the spread of capitalism – no longer faced a challenge in the form of the revolutionary guerrilla or communist cadre. The consequences of this came to dominate international relations during the 1990s: the US and its Western allies were able to use military power free from the threat of igniting a major war,[2] and these same states were able to promote the expansion of capitalism in former communist states and elsewhere through what became known as the 'Washington Consensus'.

At first glance, then, the 1990s did appear promising for the realisation of a 'New World Order,' based on the promotion of the US-sponsored harmonious triad of liberal democracy, economic liberalisation and human rights, into which states outside of the 'victorious' liberal zone of peace and prosperity – with the US at its centre – could be incorporated and integrated. The key assumption that informed the hopes of a New World Order was that the end of the Cold War had come about through the triumph of the combined forces of liberal democracy and capitalism, and that the forces of 'freedom' over 'totalitarianism' could provide the foundations for a new, more harmonious international order.[3]

Such hopes were realised to some degree with the planting of the seeds of liberal democracy and capitalist markets into east-central Europe culminating in the accession of former communist states (and parts of the former Soviet Union – the Baltic states) to the European Union in 2004. The ongoing economic transformation of China along capitalist lines and its integration into the world market, though still under the rule of the (nominally) communist one-party state, suggest a further successful extension of the liberal zone of peace. More broadly, US-sponsored neoliberal economic globalisation through the structural adjustment policies of the IMF and World Bank[4] and the creation of the World Trade Organisation (WTO) in 1995 suggested that in the sphere of the global economic relations the world was becoming increasingly inter-connected and homogenised along liberal lines.[5]

However, even before the Islamist terrorist attacks on the US on 11 September 2001 and, before that, the (highly controversial) election of the right-wing George W. Bush to the US presidency in November 2000, there were already indications that the liberal hopes of 1989–91 were unlikely to be realised at a global level. Thus, whilst some parts of the world were joining the liberal zone of peace, other areas, notably in sub-Saharan Africa, the Middle East and central Asia, continued to remain on the outside whilst yet other areas, particularly parts of Latin America – based on their experience of over a decade of neoliberal economic medicine – began to question their acceptance of such policies.

The reasons for the failure of the New World Order lay in a number of historical and more contemporary developments, whilst the emergence of the conjuncture of the War on Terror was directly associated with the (uneven) manner of the end of the Cold War. As was suggested in Chapters 5 and 6, the Cold War had endings shifting in time and space and, most importantly, in *form*. Consequently, rather than laying the foundations for the globalised spread of liberalism under a benign US hegemony, it was more contradictory. The para-doxical character of the Cold War's ending is revealed in that whilst a number of communist (militarised-authoritarian) states in east-central Europe were overthrown by 'popular revolution' carried through by a re-emergent liberal civil society which provided the seeds for the successful transplanting of liberal democracy and capitalism, the manner of the Cold War's ending in different parts of the world was quite different. In these locales, centred in the Middle East, central and (parts) of south-east Asia, the political challenge from com-munist and revolutionary forces was defeated not by the triumph of liberal civil society but rather the ascendancy of highly illiberal, reactionary social and political forces which had participated in the US-sponsored bloody and violent smashing of the revolutionary left. What this suggests is that the origins of Islamist terrorism – the most visible expression of the failure of liberal hopes of a New World Order and the focus of the War on Terror – lie in the Cold War and its endings in areas of the Islamic world and the roles played by the US and its key regional allies in countering pro-Soviet and leftist forces in these areas.

The manner of the Cold War's ending in some locales did not, then, provide the social and political forces necessary for the construction of liberal democratic societies that could be integrated into the liberal zone of peace. On the contrary, with the smashing of the secular left, moderate and revolutionary alike, through US Cold War strategies that promoted *il*liberal and reactionary forms of anti-communism, the social and political fabric of many societies, especially in the Middle East and wider Islamic world, became antithetical and openly hostile to liberal modernisation and incorporation into the liberal zone of peace. The upshot was that the defeat of the left in these locales rested on the strengthening of political forces committed to transforming their societies in a direction at odds not only with existing regimes, but also with the US and its commitment to promoting the secular universalisms of human rights, liberal democracy and capitalist markets.

The ends of Cold War, then, bequeathed new forms of conflict and 'resistance' to the global projection of US power. The focus of this chapter, then, is the temporal-political linkage between the shifting and uneven (in time, space *and* form) ends of the Cold War, and the emergence of the conjuncture of the 'War on Terror' – what many scholars and commentators see as the end of the post-Cold War era or interregnum, and the beginning of a new era in world politics. Its focus is not just the 1990s – the conventional temporal framework of the post-Cold War era – but rather shifting historical moments (in the 1970–1980s) in different parts of the world, where heteronymous forms of conflict and resistance emerged, which became much more manifest with the collapse of communism and Soviet power, literally exploding into world politics on 11 September 2001.

This chapter is organised as follows. First, I will offer a brief survey of different theoretical explanations of the post-Cold War world to assess how these characterise the post-Cold War era and how far the concepts associated with each of these theories help us explain the rise of reactionary Islam. Second, I will discuss the socio-economic, cultural, political and ideological characteristics of what I regard as reactionary forms of resistance and anti-imperialism that have emerged over the last two decades. Finally, the chapter will examine the manner and consequences of the ending of the Cold War in three geographical locales – the Middle East, central Asia and south-east Asia – that have formed the main geographical sources of reactionary resistance to the expansion of the liberal zone of peace.

CONTEMPORARY CONFLICT AND THE THEORISATION OF POST-COLD WAR WORLD POLITICS

With the 9/11 Islamist terrorist attacks on the US and the subsequent declaration of the War on Terror, post-Cold War world politics appeared to enter a new phase highlighted by the security threat to Western societies by fanatical Islamist terrorists, and the adoption by the Bush administration of a new national security strategy that committed the US to a more unilateralist and militarist posture than had been the case since the collapse of Soviet power.[6] The origins of the 9/11 attacks and the political forces that the attacks reflected and represented were a product of a very *particular type* of post-Cold War politics defined by developments – social, economic, cultural, ideological and political – within different parts of the world, and the Islamic world in particular out of which terrorist groups emerged and grew. What this suggests is that if we are to trace the origins of contemporary conflict in world politics we need to look at a number of issues associated with the rise of political Islam and its terrorist offshoots:

- the manner in which the Cold War ended within these (Islamic) locales;
- the balance of social and political forces, and their ideological make-up, resultant from the ending of these localised Cold Wars;
- the role of US policy, and the nature of US global power, both in the ending of Cold War within these locales and in determining the character of post-Cold War politics.

Through such an investigation we should be able to understand better the character of post-Cold War international relations[7] and the relationship between the ending of the Cold War, US unipolarity, economic globalisation and rise of new forms of Islamist anti-western, anti-imperialist movements.

Before I go on to outline my response to the three issues it is necessary to consider – albeit briefly – wider theoretical debates about the character of post-Cold War international relations and the degree to which they have addressed the issue of the consequences of the end of the Cold War and the emergence of new sources of conflict in world politics. I will discuss the major theoretical currents that emerged during the 1990s.

Liberalism and the New World Order

I have highlighted above some of the key themes associated with liberal explanations of the end of the Cold War and the character of the post-Cold War order. Liberals[8] argue that the Cold War ended with the spread of liberal democratic values and institutions and capitalist markets into former communist states and the post-Cold War order witnessed their consolidation and spread. The 1990s, then, was the decade of (neoliberal) globalisation. This position has been criticised in two major ways. First, as a number of commentators have argued,[9] drawing on well-founded empirical studies, the global spread of liberalism has been much more limited spatially than liberals have recognised. Consequently, the character of post-Cold War international relations has been more heterogeneous, with many areas of the world still defined by the absence of liberal democratic values and institutions, and a very limited involvement in the world market.

This spatial criticism is accompanied by a more telling criticism of the socio-economic and political consequences of neoliberal globalisation during the 1990s. Thus, whilst liberals have tended to celebrate globalisation, seeing it as a process whereby the spread and consolidation of liberal democracy is complemented by the widening and deepening of capitalist markets, others have pointed to the contradiction between strengthening the social power wielded by market forces against the weakening of collective-public authority vested in democratic institutions.[10] Further, the spread of neoliberal economic globalisation has resulted in the break-up of post-war patterns of social solidarity institutionalised in progressive-redistributive taxation, the welfare state and limits on market power. The result has been widening socio-economic inequality, which – in light of the fragmentation and realignment of the political left – has fed the rise of populist and far-right political movements which have targeted the most visible features of the new economic and cultural landscape – foreign companies operating in the domestic economy and 'alien' cultural influences especially in the form of ethnic minorities and immigrants.

The significance of these criticisms is that they point to the failure of liberal explanations of the end of the Cold War/post-Cold War era to recognise the differentiated nature of the Cold War's ending and the contradictions within the project of neoliberal globalisation, particularly as they relate to helping to trigger social and political conflict. Whilst one should be careful not to exaggerate the consequences of neoliberal globalisation, particularly in parts of the Islamic world, the evidence points to the way in which the policies associated with liberal triumphalism have contributed to the rise of reactionary and Islamist politics and terrorism. Thus, whilst liberals regard the rise of political Islam as a consequence of the policies of corrupt and authoritarian states that require heavy doses of cultural, political and economic modernisation, in doing so they have tended to overlook the ways in which western policies, during and after the Cold War, have contributed to a socio-economic and political context, not least the smashing of the secular left and secular sources of solidarity, which have provided fertile openings for an Islamist revival. This is something I will discuss in more depth in the following sections.

Realism and the Return of Great Power Conflict

Realist approaches have provided the primary theoretical foil to liberal explanations of post-Cold War world politics. Whilst liberals have tended to offer a rather optimistic and positive survey of post-Cold War developments, Realists have been more circumspect, questioning the spatial, political and normative consequences of globalisation. It should come as no surprise, then, that Realist commentators have tended to focus on the state and state-to-state relations and, in particular, the persistence of hierarchy, competition and conflict between states for power and influence.[11]

With their 'top-down' state-centric ontology Realists have difficulty in accommodating the 'external' political consequences of transnational and domestic socio-economic, cultural and political-ideological changes that have characterised international relations during the 1990s, especially in the Islamic world. Indeed, the whole idea that (Islamic) cultural and ideological factors can condition the behaviour of political actors in the international sphere is something that Realists are highly sceptical about, believing in the secular and rational power motivations of states and political actions in general. Consequently, Realist accounts of the end of the Cold War and the character of post-Cold War international relations have tended to marginalise or even ignore the significance of the political challenge of Islamist political currents, as partly reflected in the criticisms of the Bush administration's prosecution of the war on terror by a number of leading Realist scholars within the US.

Obviously, political developments relating to the relations between the major powers, notably the rise of China as a regional power, US relations with its European allies and the uneven distribution of political and economic benefits flowing from globalisation, are important features of post-Cold War international relations, but this focus on state-to-state relations has tended to rest on a rather one-dimensional theory of the state and a failure to realise the transformations unleashed by the end of the Cold War and globalisation, particularly in the way that political agency, other than states and the great powers, in the form of (Islamist) social and political movements played a significant role in the end of the Cold War in parts of the world and in shaping the character of post-Cold War politics in these regions and beyond. Thus, whilst the Realist stress on hierarchy, conflict and the uneven distribution of benefits from the existing international order is useful, their neglect of the international consequences of transnational and domestic political developments and conflicts means that they are unable to shed much light on the rise of reactionary Islamist resistance to US power.

Huntington and Inter-Civilisational Conflict

Superficially, Samuel Huntington's 'clash of civilisations' thesis, published in the early 1990s and later expanded into a book,[12] seems to have been borne out with the 9/11 attacks and the US response, suggesting that his work would be helpful in explaining the character of post-Cold War international relations. Indeed, for Osama bin Laden and his ilk, as well as some elements within the Bush administration, contemporary international relations are characterised by a clash of civilisations between the West and Islam. For Huntington the major fissures in world politics are not economic or political, but cultural, and are particularly acute in the clash between Western societies and Islam.

Huntington's argument provoked a fierce response, in part based on his crude generalisations as to what constitutes a civilisation, and also because of the way in which it seemed to promote static descriptions and understandings of different cultures. Huntington's argument certainly tapped into xenophobic and racist prejudices present within western societies, but its focus on the increasing role played by cultural and ethnic identity in informing political choices and as a key factor in accounting for political conflict after the collapse of Soviet power cannot be easily dismissed. However, it is one thing to accept that since the end of the Cold War conflict based on 'identity' has become more significant and quite another to accept Huntington's explanation of why this has happened, and his policy prescriptions to address it.

Huntington provides a very superficial and static overview of Islamic societies which fails to recognise the differences within and between them which highlight their distinct political character, their relations with the West, and the degree to which Islamic cultural/ethnic identity informs politics amongst their populations. Further, his overview fails properly to factor in the role of the West, and US policy in particular, during and after the Cold War on political developments within these societies, most obviously through the sponsoring of particularly anti-democratic and anti-liberal social and political forces against communist and radical nationalist movements and states. His discussion fails to recognise the ideological similarities between the new social and political forces that have emerged in the Islamic world, but also in parts of the West, that draw on reactionary ideological discourse and seek to mobilise similarly marginalised social groups. Consequently, rather than recognising the link between the rise of reactionary Islamist political movements and the Cold War (and US policy), Huntington's argument treats Islamic societies, and the political forces within them, as fundamentally different and separate from developments within the West. This is a gross simplification, which informs his policy prescriptions. For our purposes, whilst Huntington has identified – along with many other commentators who do not share his conservative political views – something important about the character of post-Cold War world politics, his explanation is highly problematic.

Marxism and the Contradictions of Globalising Capitalism

The final part of this brief survey of how post-Cold War international relations has been theorised looks at explanations drawing on a Marxist framework of analysis. What has tended to characterise Marxist explanations of post-Cold War international order are the focus upon contradictions present within ever-expanding globalised capitalist social relations, the administrative and political authority of states that regulate those relations, and the hierarchy within the geopolitical order. Thus, whilst during the Cold War inter-capitalist conflict was reduced through the acceptance by (weakened and more pacific) advanced capitalist states of US hegemony based on the presence of the Soviet-communist threat, the disappearance of that threat and the opening up of new markets have provoked tensions and splits within the liberal zone of peace.[13]

More widely, and again following the pattern established during the Cold War, US imperial power is seen as being characterised by the shifting relationship between force and consent as instruments of US global power projection. Marxists who emphasise the coercive properties of US global power spar with others who highlight the structural imperative of the US to use more consensual and collectivist instruments of global power projection that, to some extent, extend the bourgeois interest beyond that of the US capitalist class.[14] In this account there is a pay-off between the legitimacy of US global political leadership at the head of the advanced capitalist states and relative economic decline of the US's position of economic dominance within the advanced capitalist world. The concern is less with north–south relations and more with how the US manages its leadership over the other capitalist powers, and its ability to maintain this whilst incorporating other (challenging) centres of capital accumulation into the system.

If Marxist explanations of post-Cold War world politics emphasise hierarchy and conflict – the key concerns are relations amongst the major capitalist powers – as well as the importance of neoliberal globalisation on the capacities of states and ruling classes to realise their objectives, how do they? Or do they adequately explain the rise of Islamic resistance to the post-war projection of the US-promoted universalisms of liberal democracy, human rights and capitalist social-property relations within Islamic locales?

Marxist-informed analysis of the inequities of neoliberal globalisation and the way in which it has broken post-war values, bonds and institutions of social solidarity has shed important explanatory light on the rise of right-wing and reactionary-xenophobic political movements throughout the western world (and beyond) during the 1990s and their mobilisation of marginalised social constituencies – the petit-bourgeoisie, the unskilled and non-unionised and the young unemployed – based on a rhetoric and ideology that draw on symbols and discourse that are hierarchical, atavistic and exclusivist.[15] In short, the ideology of the far right in the West is as hostile to liberal universalism as the ideology of reactionary Islamist movements. The other commonality with the rise of reactionary Islam is that, like the far right in much of the western world, extreme right-wing political movements have prospered in the absence of an organised radical left-wing alternative – the legacy of the end of Cold Wars combined with intensified neoliberal globalisation in the 1980–1990s. Whilst in no way able to address fundamentally the socio-economic needs of the people they seek to mobilise, the far right in the West and the Islamic world have provided a potent and in some cases effective counter-narrative of solidarity based on nation, faith, ethnicity and shared cultural values to the weightless, ungrounded values they associate with liberal universalism and rationalism.

However, whilst Marxist (and other left-leaning) analysis has rightly traced the socio-economic roots and properties of the new forms of politics, it has not fully integrated this analysis with a discussion of the uneven and paradoxical character of Cold War endings. This is particularly the case with the ends of Cold War in the Islamic world. Further, in some cases elements on the left have adopted a warped anti-imperialism by giving legitimacy to the reactionary and terrorist resistance to the projection of US power in the Middle East and Iraq in particular.[16] The preoccupation with US imperialism has led to a neglect of the significance of the politics of reactionary Islam. Instead, there has been a tendency to reduce reactionary Islam – especially in the form of its terrorist offshoots led by al-Qaeda – as a largely western creation which has come back to haunt the US and its allies and/or a functional instrument that has allowed the US to reassert the imperial character of its global power through the launching of the War on Terror. Consequently, whilst the *deus ex machina* of the Soviet-communist threat facilitated US 'empire-building' after 1945, so, thanks to al-Qaeda, the US has embarked on another imperial project based on 'scaring the hell' out of its civilian population to ensure that they support the more coercive and militaristic projection of US power.

The significance of the 9/11 attacks, like Soviet actions in east-central Europe – manipulated and exaggerated though they have been – is that without such a *casus belli* it is difficult to see how the US could bring its population with it in projecting its power overseas in a coercive manner. The requirement of a *casus belli* – unless one accepts the conspiracy theory that the neocons planned the attacks – means that the liberal and mediated nature of the US empire needs to be recognised perhaps more than some on the left have accepted. This also relates to arguments over the creation of 'reactionary blow-back', which was a more complex phenomenon than those who emphasise US imperial structures in a north–south direction suggest.

THE SOCIAL AND IDEOLOGICAL CHARACTER OF REACTIONARY RESISTANCE

As I have stressed in this and the previous chapter, the end of the Cold War amounted to more than just a reconfiguration of geopolitical order and the balance of strategic-military power. Further, the manner and timing of the ends of Cold War differed. Although the Cold War was most visible in the nuclear arsenals of the superpowers and the way in which they supported rival political movements and states, at its essence the Cold War was a conflict over how societies should be organised (particularly the relationship between political authority and socio-economic reproduction) and the distribution of socio-economic benefits from such organisation. The Cold War or, more accurately, the states and social and political movements that contested it, were based on distinct forms of social organisation and the mobilisation of particular social groups in support of rival ideological visions. Consequently, the end(s) of Cold War resulted in socio-economic transformation as the social and political forces that benefited from and were associated with communist and radical nationalist forms of state and political movement were broken-up and defeated.

The debris of the end of the Cold War, then, included not the just state officials, party leaders and military staff of the Soviet bloc and other revolutionary states, but also, and ultimately more importantly, those individuals and groups who had once formed the membership of social movements, political parties and revolutionary guerrilla armies mobilised by an ideological commitment to transform their societies in an anti-capitalist direction and motivated by a range of socialist-inspired ideas. Whilst post-communist social and political movement have emerged – not least the global anti-capitalist movement as well as a number of left-wing nationalist governments – the social forces behind such movements have not carried anywhere near the political weight that historical communism, in the form of the USSR and its allied states and the wider international communist movement, carried for most of the twentieth century and, subsequently, have failed to secure major political victories at a global level.

The relationship between the collapse of movements committed to building a socialist-inspired future and the entrenchment and spread of neoliberal globalisation is not coincidental, as the social forces behind the neoliberal project have not had to contend with organised, mass-based political movements armed with a clear and coherent ideological alternative. Instead, the political and ideological opposition to both US (imperial) global power and neoliberalism after the Cold War has been both fragmented and disoriented, reflecting the new configuration of social power. Whilst in the advanced capitalist states and parts of the south (particularly in the Americas), movements have emerged that espouse a politics associated with the secular universalisms of democracy, human rights, internationalism and social justice – most evident in the global anti-capitalist movement – other movements, also found within parts of the advanced capitalist world (Europe) and especially in the Islamic world, have emerged espousing a very different political-ideological vision based on intense hostility towards secular universalisms, and instead a defence of cultural and national/ethnic exclusivity, and social and political practices and institutions that preserve hierarchy, and are anti-democratic and anti-egalitarian. The significance of this reactionary form of 'anti-imperialism' is not only that it has become the dominant political force of opposition and resistance in much of the Islamic world; it is out of such political and ideological currents that the terrorist attacks on the US came, which triggered the War on Terror.

The rise of the reactionary right, then, is a product of the defeat and fragmentation of the left brought about by the ends of Cold War[17] and the crisis of cultural identity, political representation and socio-economic welfare triggered by neoliberal globalisation. Social constituencies have been mobilised, based on similar ideological appeals that emphasise the corrupt and decadent nature of governments, pursuing 'foreign'-inspired programmes of political and economic reform, whether IMF/World Bank structural adjustment policies and the promotion of universal human rights in the Middle East and other parts of the Islamic world, or the intrusion and dilution of cultural and national identity through immigration, the break-up of traditional patterns of male employment, and moves towards political integration within Europe.

On such an ideological platform the reactionary right has sought to mobilise particular social groups. Within the Islamic world reactionary political movements have succeeded in mobilising two main sources of support that share similarities with the social constituencies that have been drawn to the far right in Europe. On the one hand they have attracted the socially marginalised – usually young, male and poorly educated – unemployed or those at the margins of the labour market, whilst the leadership cadres have tended to be drawn from more petit-bourgeois elements, well-educated (scientists, engineers, teachers and civil servants) middle-class strata that traditionally provided the bedrock of the capitalist social order and, in the past, the main beneficiaries in the Middle East[18] and elsewhere of revolutionary-statist modernisation programmes.

The mobilisation of these social groups highlights a number of issues relating to contemporary reactionary political movements and Islamist ones in particular. First, that their religious appearance and rhetoric obscure their more modern features in providing a political identity and worldview for individuals confronting social and psychological crises of a very modern persuasion. Second, whilst they have succeeded in securing some support from people who formerly identified with the political left,[19] far right political movements have also taken advantage of the weakness of the left to capture the ideological terrain of social (or, more accurately, ethnic/faith) solidarity as a way of marginalising class differences and antagonism. This (vulgar) notion of solidarity has in parts of the Europe and the Islamic world replaced the formerly dominant idea of solidarity and collectivity associated with communist and revolutionary movements, and has managed to provide a powerful and populist mobilising pull in contradistinction to the ideological discourses of liberal universalism which talks of free and equal individuals removed from any obligations and responsibilities to any (ethnic, religious or national) collective. In this sense, there does seem to be a correlation between the deepening and spreading of neoliberalism and a particular type of political response associated with the rise of far right political movements.

The ends of the Cold War have been central to the rise of reactionary political forces through the defeat and splintering of the left and how the end of the Soviet-communist challenge has helped propel neoliberalism. However, the rise of reactionary politics in the post-Cold War era, especially within the Islamic world, also concerns the pervasive, organic presence of reservoirs of ideological support for reactionary political visions foundered on faith, highlighted in the continuing strength of religiously inspired values, practices and institutions in public and private life – something very different from the influence of religion and faith in the western world – as well as the *strengthening* of such ideological reservoirs *against* secular-universalist political currents in the closing phases of Cold War within the Islamic world in the Middle East, south-east Asia and central Asia in particular. Consequently, the crucial difference between the rise of the reactionary right in the Islamic world as opposed to elsewhere, particularly in Europe, has been the longer-term historical legacy of these societies and the residual strength of Islamic culture, ideas and social practices within them, combined with their strengthening in a violent and reactionary direction during the 1970s and 1980s by the US and its regional allies, Pakistan and Saudi Arabia in particular, as part of its anti-communist strategy.

The upshot is that whilst the end of the Cold War was perceived as a victory for the forces of (neo)liberal capitalism in east-central Europe, in many parts of the Islamic world the defeat of Soviet communism was seen as a victory for (armed and militant) Islamist political forces, thus laying the foundations for such political movements to become the primary sources of opposition to ruling regimes in the region and also US/western influence and interference. In short, whilst secular political doctrines of nationalism, socialism and communism mobilised people against corrupt and authoritarian regimes and their western patrons in the 1950s through to the 1970s, they no longer do so. Instead, the social and political movements that can mobilise large numbers of people and that have persuasive, though deeply flawed, ideological visions are religious/Islamic-inspired.[20] It is no longer the colour red that dominates banners on popular demonstrations but the green of Islam.

In this sense although we can describe these movements as reactionary in their political-ideological outlook, we also need to recognise that they are modern movements, not only in the way that they function in their organisation and use of (information) technology, but also in their political tactics, notably through terrorism and the propaganda gained from the 'spectacle of violence'. Furthermore, their political objectives, dressed up in religious rhetoric though they may be, can be seen as typical of 'third worldist' national liberation movements in the removal of western influence from the Islamic world. Thus, whilst radical nationalists and communists identified the western presence in primarily political and economic terms seeing its expulsion as the first step in building independent national, democratic and socialist republics, Islamists emphasise the cultural as much as the political and economic dimensions of western influence.[21]

The character of western – and in particular US – influence in the post-Cold War Middle East provides an important context for the rise of a very violent form of reactionary politics. Thus, although the region has been influenced by neoliberal economic globalisation in the form of IMF-directed structural adjustment policies and the perception of its relative economic stagnation in comparison to the economic growth of other parts of the south (and east Asia in particular), the economies of the Middle East have not been integrated into the world market and societies transformed in the way that other parts of the world have. In this sense the impact of neoliberal economic globalisation on the rise of reactionary political movements is more ambivalent than is the case with the rise of the far right elsewhere, as in Europe. Yet whilst the impact of western, neoliberal economic forces has been more muted, the spectre and actuality of US imperialism has been much more pronounced through its support for a number of key Arab states (notably Egypt and Saudi Arabia) and its continued acquiescence to Israeli policies, alongside its (ongoing) military interventions in Iraq since 1991. In this region, then, the political-ideological outcomes of the end of Cold War have been exaggerated by a combination of the economic dislocation caused by IMF/World Bank-inspired policies alongside the continuing spectre of great power interference in the area, with the latter being a key ingredient in fostering a politics of violence.

The proclivity to use violence for political ends based on religious justification is certainly not confined to Islamist groups. However, the social and political context out of which reactionary Islam has emerged has made violence a more obvious means of securing political ends than in other social contexts. This is something that I will focus on in the next section. To summarise what will follow: the historical context has been crucial in those parts of the world – the Middle-East, central Asia and parts of south-east Asia – where violence and reactionary politics have become most interconnected, primarily in Islamic-inspired reactionary political movements. Islamist terrorist movements emerged out of a political context of patronage from both local and external states during the Cold War, where violence was not only tolerated in the achievement of political objectives, but was actively encouraged.[22] On top of this, civil society within many of these states has been deeply fractured and fragmented by the consequences of neoliberal globalisation, thus exacerbating existing social and cultural tensions within these already fragile states, and providing a new foundation on which reactionary political movements can base their ideological and political appeals.

THE PARADOXICAL ENDS OF COLD WAR, REACTIONARY POLITICS AND US STRATEGY

The understanding of the end of the Cold War and hence discussion of the prospects for post-Cold War international relations within the discipline of IR have given scant if any consideration to the role of extreme right-wing anti-communist social and political forces in the political defeat of the forces of radical nationalism and communism. It has only been more recently – since the 9/11 attacks – that these political forces have come under the analytical and political spotlight, particularly the degree to which these movements should be regarded as 'US creations' as part of the 'new' Cold War strategy of rollback and counter-revolution associated with the Reagan administration during the 1980s, and, consequently, the degree to which the contemporary Islamic terrorist menace can be considered a form of violent political blowback for the short-sightedness and morally bankrupt nature of US foreign policy.[23]

The focus of this section is to examine the relationship between US anti-communist strategy, particularly during the latter phases of the Cold War, and its cultivation and support for right-wing anti-communist political movements[24] in those locales – the Middle East, central Asia and south-east Asia – that have become the geographical focus of the War on Terror. Through examining the manner and timing of the ends of Cold War within the three locales, I aim to highlight the relationship between the character of US global power – during and after the Cold War, the rise of reactionary political forces in the temporally and geographically shifting ends of Cold War, and the origins of Islamist terrorism.

The Local Origins of Reactionary Islam in the Middle East and the 'Saudi–Egyptian Axis'

The conditioning power of the Cold War, in the form of superpower support for particular states and the role of communist and radical nationalist movements, to shape political developments in the Middle East was tempered by the Arab–Israeli conflict and, after 1979, the Iranian Revolution. The significance of this is that both developments within the Arab–Israeli conflict – particularly the Six-Day War of June 1967 and the Yom Kippur War of October 1973 – and the Iranian Revolution played a very important role in determining the outcome of the Cold War struggle in the region and in shaping the nature of post-Cold War politics.

Until the early 1970s secular and radical left-wing forces to varying degrees allied with Moscow committed to statist models of economic development and the expulsion of any remaining western-imperial presence were politically ascendant, most evidently in Nasser's Egypt. The nationalist and communist lefts were opposed by pro-US regimes, particularly the oil-rich monarchies in the Gulf led by Saudi Arabia, and in this sense an intra-Arab Cold War existed. Under the military protection of the US and organised and supported by the same social forces that had been overthrown in Egypt and elsewhere,[25] these regimes staked their political legitimacy upon upholding traditional patterns of social reproduction anchored in the Islamic faith and buttressed, in the case of Saudi Arabia, by its role as custodian of the two Islamic holy sites, Mecca and Medina.[26]

The significance of the intra-Arab Cold War was not only that a common political and military front against Israel was difficult to establish amongst the Arab states, but also that the social and ideological basis of the Saudi regime and its allies rested on propagating a highly illiberal and reactionary ideological discourse. Whilst during the Cold War this suited US political purposes in containing and attacking leftist political forces allied to varying degrees with the USSR, it also meant that the nature of the ideological conflict of the Cold War in the Middle East was of a very different character from that elsewhere.

The Cold War in the Middle East, at least between the leading 'revolutionary' state, Egypt, and the leading conservative state, Saudi Arabia, was not a conflict over capitalism versus communism or 'freedom versus totalitarianism', but rather one between secular modernisation in a statist-socialist direction and traditionalist and reactionary anti-secularism centred on the puritanical Wahhabi version of Islam. Thus, whilst Nasser's Egypt sought leadership of the Arab world and sponsored radical anti-conservative forces in the region, most notably through its (unsuccessful) intervention in the civil war in Yemen between royalist and republican forces during the mid-1960s, the Saudis, with US endorsement, supported anti-Nasserite forces throughout the region, including Yemen.[27] In effect, then, under the geopolitical protection of the US, throughout the Cold War, and particularly with the financial bounty provided by the oil price hikes in the 1970s and the political opportunities presented by the Soviet intervention in Afghanistan in 1979, Saudi Arabia became a key player, in terms of funding, organisation and ideology, in cultivating distinctly *il*liberal and anti-universalist forms of anti-communism[28] which would provide the foundations for contemporary reactionary Islamist movements[29] and their terrorist offshoots.

Although the political and ideological pull of Saudi-sponsored reactionary Islam was a significant force in the region, it was wider developments in the Middle East, particularly with respect to the Arab-Israeli conflict and how this influenced political developments within Egypt, that would ultimately determine the political outcome of the Cold War in the region in the 1970s. In this respect the turning point for the fate of radical nationalist forces in the Middle East – which was to open the door to a revival of political Islam throughout the region – came with the military humiliation inflicted on the Arab nationalist armies by Israel in the Six Day War. The defeat exposed not only the failings of Nasser's strategy to defeat Israel – the key factor in regional politics – but also the ineffectiveness of Egypt's alliance with the USSR.

Although the Egyptian/Arab defeat was primarily a regional political issue it soon had an impact on the Cold War as, with Nasser's death in 1970 and his replacement by Anwar Sadat, Egypt began to move away from its diplomatic and military alliance with Moscow, and its support for radical nationalist social and political forces throughout the region. The consequences of these shifts were not to be fully revealed until after the Yom Kippur War, which ironically – considering Sadat's cynical manipulation of Soviet support and his diplomatic objective of moving towards the US – provoked a superpower crisis which saw US nuclear forces put on worldwide alert and the brief spectre of Soviet military intervention in support of its Egyptian ally.

Under Sadat Egypt moved to cooperate with Saudi Arabia in its planning for the Yom Kippur War, which was to act as a means to force Israel into negotiations with Egypt primarily over Egyptian land occupied by Israel in June 1967. The diplomatic success of the war for Sadat – all the more evident in that the superpower crisis provoked by the war made the US much less tolerant of Israeli objections to negotiations – meant that Sadat could terminate the alliance with Moscow, which he did[30] in 1974. These external developments were complemented by domestic political change within Egypt. Whereas Nasserism had been based on an international relations of anti-imperialism alongside a commitment to the destruction of Israel, which was supported by a domestic policy that attacked the traditional landholding classes and promoted statist economic development that benefited the petit bourgeoisie and subaltern social layers, ensuring the support of the political left, Sadat's domestic policies focused on reconstituting the social and political basis of the regime centred on breaking the power of leftist forces.[31]

Sadat began his domestic programme soon after coming to power with an internal *coup* against the socialist-leaning Al Sabri section of the ruling party – the Arab Socialist Union. At the same time that he attacked the left the new regime also began to cultivate the Islamic clerical establishment located in al-Azhar University through providing state support for mosque construction and permitting the establishment of Islamic student association (and harassing leftist student groups).[32] The result was that Islamists rose to prominence in Egypt through the 1970s as the state clamped down on the organised political left and 'used' Islamic militants as its foot soldiers, particularly in the universities.[33]

Overall, throughout the 1970s Sadat encouraged a much greater public profile and legitimacy for Islam, even associating it with the 'success' of the Yom Kippur War. The irony was that Sadat's policies of moving into the diplomatic embrace of the US and subsequently making peace with Israel at Camp David in 1979, alongside his attempts at dismantling the statist economic framework,[34] established under Nasser, put him increasingly at odds with the Islamic militants, which was to culminate in his assassination in 1981.

The consequences of the changes initiated by Sadat after 1970 indicate that by the early 1970s the Cold War had effectively ended in the Middle East. Egypt, the key Arab state, which had once formed the core source of anti-imperialism within the region and the USSR's principal ally, had shifted its foreign policy towards accommodation with the West and opposition to the USSR. The weakening of Soviet influence in the region and of Egypt's support for leftist political struggle combined with the transformation in the balance of social and political forces within Egypt and, correspondingly, the wider region.[35] With the encouragement of the Egyptian state, reactionary Islamist forces emerged and grew in organisational and political strength. Further, as John Cooley and others[36] have documented, with the beginning of the Afghan *jihad* these forces were to grow even stronger as the Egyptian state became a 'transmission belt' (with US endorsement) for sending Islamic militants, many of whom (including bin Laden's *aide-de-camp*, Ayman al-Zawahiri) had been convicted of offences in Egypt, to the Pakistan/Afghan border to be trained in guerrilla warfare and terrorism for use in Afghanistan.

With the political failure of the pro-Soviet radical Arab nationalist project both internally – in terms of the construction of a stable basis of socio-economic support for the regime – and externally – with respect to the failure to 'deal' effectively with the problem of Israel – the Middle Eastern regional front of the social-systemic conflict of Cold War fizzled out to be replaced by new forms of resistance initially cultivated locally as an alternative social and political basis for Sadat's Egypt. The upshot was that the defining political conflict with the region had become (by the mid-1970s) heteronomous of the Cold War; it was a conflict no longer waged between the forces of western capital and its local allies against radical nationalist/communist forms of modernity, but a new one, which to a significant degree continues to define the region, between pro-western authoritarian states committed to capitalist development and integration into the 'civilised' West against reactionary Islamist forces committed to a regressive politics based on expelling western social and cultural as much as political and economic influence.

What is important about these developments was that they were largely locally driven. Whilst the US supported Sadat and other sources of anti-communism in the region, particularly Saudi Arabia, the *Islamic* (and reactionary) character rather than the liberal or bourgeois character of opposition and resistance to Soviet/leftist influence was of local origin and locally promoted.[37] Consequently, it was not liberal universalism that won the Cold War in the Middle East in contrast to how the Cold War ended in Western Europe in the late 1940s and east-central Europe in the late 1980s, but illiberal and reactionary anti-(communist) universalism. Further, the US's Cold War strategy and the nature of its imperial power was mediated by local political and ideological structures which Washington promoted in Cairo, Riyadh and elsewhere in the region. By encouraging Saudi autonomy and supporting Sadat's reforms the US promoted political spaces that it did not dominate or control, in spite of its geopolitical dominance in the region, effectively allowing Saudi Arabia (or elements within it) to cultivate an ideological agenda and political network that would come to challenge western interests after the defeat of communist-socialist universalism, whilst in Egypt the US did nothing to prevent the strengthening of social and political forces as antagonistic to its ideological vision as that of the USSR. It was out of such social and political forces that the contemporary menace of Islamist terrorism emerged.

Pakistan and the Afghan Anti-Communist Jihad

Whilst the Middle East had become a front of Cold War conflict soon after the end of the Second World War,[38] the central Asian region – and Pakistan and

Afghanistan in particular – had to wait until the 1970s before becoming hotbeds of social systemic conflict that came to draw in the superpowers. Again, as in the Middle East and elsewhere in the history of the Cold War it was local socio-economic and political dynamics that sparked the emergence of a Cold War crisis in the region which would provide a defining theatre of conflict for the rise of a reactionary Islamist politics of violent resistance. In this respect, although the US took advantage and contributed to the strengthening of reactionary Islamist militias in 'revolt against a modernising secular state',[39] it did not create them. I have discussed this in Chapters 5 and 6 with regard to the origins of the Afghan War, but it is important to emphasise that social and political developments in Pakistan were crucial not only to political developments within Afghanistan from the early 1970s onwards, but also with respect to Pakistan's role in cultivating the political forces of reactionary Islam, primarily through its key logistical, organisational, co-ordinating and political role in the Afghan *jihad* against the PDPA government and its Soviet ally.[40]

In Pakistan the financial clout of Saudi Arabia was also important as, with the humiliation of the loss of East Pakistan in 1971, the secular-nationalist-leaning government of Zulfiqar Ali Bhutto turned to Saudi Arabia for economic assistance, which came at the cost of branding government policies as a form of 'Islamic socialism'.[41] The creeping Islamisation of Pakistan, which went beyond economic policies to include a greater role in Pakistani law and the education system – the beginnings of what has become the infamous networks of madrassas – was also revealed in Bhutto's support for Islamist guerrilla movements in neighbouring Afghanistan.[42]

It was to be through a combination of developments, within Pakistan and Afghanistan, that the simmering political tensions and conflicts between Pakistan and Afghanistan were to open up a key front in the latter stages of the Cold War. Further, it was to be this Cold War front that would provide the most important avenue for the emergence of an international network of Islamist militants, many of whom ended up providing the key ideological, political and armed personnel of the reactionary Islamist terrorist groups that rose to prominence in the Middle East, the Caucases, south-east and central Asia in the 1990s. The two developments were the US-backed *coup d'état* in Pakistan which overthrew Bhutto and brought General Zia ul-Haq to power in July 1977 and the communist-led April (1978) Revolution in Afghanistan. With a revolutionary government installed in Kabul, confronting a growing Islamist-inspired insurgency that secured significant support from Pakistan, the new Pakistani government became increasingly involved in the Afghan civil war. With Soviet intervention in December 1979, not only did the stakes rise for Pakistan's support for an Islamist-dominated resistance, so the US and other states – and Saudi Arabia and Egypt in particular – become increasingly involved in the Pakistani-initiated and led operation.[43]

Zia's involvement in Afghanistan, especially Pakistani support for an Islamist rather than a secular/nationalist-based resistance to the PDPA regime, was directly linked to the basis of social and political support for the military dictatorship in Pakistan. Accordingly, Zia accelerated, intensified and expanded Islamist currents within Pakistan as a way of securing support for his regime and of reducing ethnic and secessionist tendencies within the country. The Islamisation of Pakistan under Zia was reflected in the growth of Saudi-financed madrassas,[44] many of which promoted the most reactionary (Wahabbite and Deobandi) tendencies within Islam, alongside the promotion of Islamist tendencies within key institutions of the Pakistani state notably the army and the Inter-Services Intelligence (ISI) directorate, which was cemented through support from and cultivation of the *Jamaat-e-Islami* (Islamic Party) and the Afghan *Hezb-e-Isalmi* (Islamic Party) led by the notorious Gulbuddin Heymatyar as the main conduit for arming the Afghan *mujahadeen*.[45]

Local and regional dynamics, then, were crucial to the development of Cold War in central Asia and in this respect, as in the Middle East, the US was less a direct instigator but certainly a beneficiary of the rise of reactionary Islam. With the openings provided by Pakistan's support for the *mujahideen* and the Soviet intervention, Afghanistan became a key theatre of operations for the Reagan Doctrine as the US funnelled US$4–5 billion in aid between 1980 and 1992, funds that were equalled by support from Saudi Arabia,[46] amounting to a massive level of international support and promotion for reactionary Islam. Indeed, it was the provision of international support that was crucial in determining the conduct of the war. US intervention and its alliance with Pakistan limited Soviet military options, particularly any thoughts about attacking the *mujahideen* camps dotted along the Pakistani side of the border, whilst the CIA's provision of Stinger anti-aircraft missiles in the later stages of the conflict helped neutralise Soviet air power.

The significance of the Afghan conflict and external – not just US – involvement in it obviously went far beyond Afghanistan. The creation of an international Islamic army involving upwards of 35,000 combatants from 43 countries[47] inculcated with a particularly virulent, puritanical and reactionary interpretation of Islam and committed to realising their political aims though violence have come to dominate political conflicts in many parts of the Islamic world during the 1990s. In all of these cases it has been veterans of the Afghan *jihad* who have been the key personalities. The nature and ending of Cold War in central Asia, then, has been of global significance for the character of post-Cold War politics and the paradoxical nature of the US victory.

The End of the Suharto Dictatorship and the Emergence of Reactionary Islam in Indonesia

The final element of our political-geography of the roots of reactionary Islamist violence takes us to south-east Asia and the archipelago of Indonesia in particular. In contrast to the cases already surveyed, the relationship between the ends of Cold War in Indonesia and the rise of reactionary Islam are less pronounced. Although the social-systemic conflict of Cold War ended violently with the *coup d'état* of 1965 that overthrew the radical nationalist regime of Achmad Sukarno and the subsequent mass murder of tens of thousands of cadres – and suspected members – of the Indonesian communist party (the PKI, a major pillar of the Sukarno regime)[48] there was less Islamist involvement in these events in contrast to the two other cases and certainly less obvious benefit or strengthening of Islamist forces, at least in the short and medium term. The *coup* and destruction of the social and political constituencies of radical nationalism and communism provided the domestic basis for the shift in Indonesian foreign policy away from anti-imperialism and alliance with China towards the diplomatic sphere of the US.

The main beneficiaries of the *coup* were right-wing elements within the military and those social forces opposed to the left-leaning and statist orientation of the Sukarno regime, as well as those (racist) elements within Indonesia opposed to ethnic Chinese influence on the regime. Although Islamic forces and groups did not benefit directly from the *coup*, traditional Muslim leaders, especially the *Dewan Dakwah Islamiyah Indonesia* (Indonesian Council for Islamic Prediction),[49] did play an important role in the anti-leftist pogrom in helping to identify and round-up suspected PKI militants. Instead of becoming a central pillar of the regime (as in Pakistan) or being cultivated by the state as an alternative source of popular mobilisation (as in Egypt), the Suharto regime was committed to maintaining an apolitical Islam in Indonesia loyal to the regime's ethnic-nationalist ideology of *Pancasila*.[50] Indeed, this was helped by the indigenous character of Islam within the archipelago infused as it was with pre-Islamic mystic traditions anathema to the purist forms of Islam specifically associated with Wahabbite doctrine.

In contrast to the other two cases, reactionary Islam emerged in a post-Cold War rather than Cold War context, in particular, the socio-economic and political contradictions and conflicts that emerged in the mid-late 1990s that came to undermine the stability of the Suharto dictatorship, which came to a head through the devastating socio-economic impact of the Asian financial crisis of 1997–98.[51] Consequently, the key explanatory context for the rise of reactionary Islam was not the social-systemic conflict of the Cold War but rather the twin consequences of neoliberal economic globalisation and the post-Cold War promotion of liberal universalism in the form of human rights and the institutions of liberal democracy.

However, the legacy of the ending of the Cold War in Indonesia in the late 1960s and the smashing of the secular left inevitably promoted those indigenous and permitted social institutions – mosques and madrassas and Islamic publications – as the primary institutions that incubated and ultimately provided the political infrastructure of the anti-Suharto movement when it emerged in the 1990s rather than secular and leftist movements as during the Cold War era.[52] The context for the rise of *reactionary*[53] Islam, then, emerged from a socio-economic crisis triggered in the long term by Indonesia's opening up to the capitalist world economy which fundamentally undermined a right-wing authoritarian state already under pressure to democratise and improve its human rights record.

Challenged from below by mass-based movements, many of which were led by moderate Islamic leaders, and under pressure from without by western states to implement radical (neoliberal) economic reform and end political restrictions, Suharto, like Sadat in Egypt and a number of post-Soviet leaders in central Asia, turned to Islam as an alternative social and ideological basis for the regime. In this sense whilst the anti-Suharto democracy movement was dominated by Muslim intellectuals and Muslim popular movements[54] committed to a moderate form of Islamic-inspired government, Suharto was effectively forced to cultivate extremist, violent and reactionary Islamist tendencies through such organisations as the KISDI (Indonesian Committee for Solidarity with the World of Islam) and the DDII (Indonesian Council for Islamic Prediction), both of which claimed that democracy was an alien conspiracy. In this sense elements within the Suharto state played a key role in creating reactionary Islamist groups in Indonesia.[55]

The Suharto regime, then, helped create a deeply reactionary and, in the main, largely non-organic Islamist current within Indonesia that drew on Wahabbi-influenced doctrines of Islam[56] rather than mainstream and traditional Islamic practices within Indonesia. Both the KISDI and DDII promoted anti-Semitic, anti-Christian, anti-Chinese and anti-western political positions and with support of elements within the military, especially Suharto's son-in-law, Prabowo Subianto, these movements led violent attacks on Christian and Chinese minorities, allowing the regime to talk up a state of crisis and emergency caused by 'outside elements' and thus allowing the state to take extraordinary measures – in the form of a violent clampdown – to restore order.[57]

As in the other cases examined here, the groups cultivated by the Suharto regime had their own agenda and after Suharto's ousting in 1998 and the beginnings of democratisation continued to spread their poisonous propaganda and support terrorist groups such as *Laskar Jihad* and *Jeemah Islamiyah*[58] which have been responsible for a number of terrorist attacks in recent years. Whilst US influence on these developments was indirect – primarily in the way that its policies contributed to the socio-economic crisis – the shadow of the Afghan *jihad* also cast its shadow over Indonesia as many of the key figures in the Islamist terrorist movements in the region were veterans of the Afghan war.[59]

CONCLUSIONS

This chapter has sought to highlight the connections between the shifting ends of Cold War and the rise of reactionary forms of politics and violence, particularly within those parts of the world that have formed the political geography of the War on Terror. The survey has shown that the collapse of Soviet-communist power was not only a more gradual and variable phenomenon than most studies of the Cold War suggest, but also that this victory was carried through by a range of social forces and political actors. The endings of other Cold Wars suggest, then, a heteronomy in the socio-economic, ideological and political character of conflicts within world politics from the 1970s. Such differences are identifiable with respect to the social forces and political movements that were contesting the existing political order – at a local and international level – how they were challenging it, and the objectives they sought.

The US obviously played a considerable part in these developments, particularly in the way that it supported and cultivated anti-leftist political movements. However, the cultivation from without *and* through other state apparatuses – especially Pakistan and Saudi Arabia – highlights US dependence on local actors in securing US political objectives and also the mediated way in which US power is realised, and the impact of local political struggles and agendas on the projection of US global power. This external dimension to the character and impact of US global power projection is paralleled – particularly in the context of the post-Vietnam Cold War – by a domestic politics that limited the scope and form of US power projection. The consequences of this – how US material power is constituted – have tended to reduce the ability of the US to direct and determine political outcomes across the world, partly because such power has promoted political spaces for local actors and issues to make the outcomes of US policy more contingent and politically subjective. The three cases viewed in this chapter have shown this.

The importance accorded to local rather than global or US conditioning on the ends of Cold War and rise of reactionary political movements is also central to an understanding of the relationship between the Cold War and globalisation. Economic globalisation was a major process within the history of the Cold War after 1945 with respect to political and economic developments within the West – through the development of multilateral forms of political cooperation and, from the early 1970s, the rise of neoliberalism – and the way in which such developments contributed to the social-systemic conflict of Cold War by allowing the US to marshal economic resources beyond its national economy, and in the way that it undermined the more autarchic forms of economic development associated with the Soviet bloc and similarly constituted states across the world.

The paradox in the relationship between globalisation and the projection of US power especially so during the 1990s, however, is that whilst during the Cold War political *and* economic developments were *always* defined in national security terms, in the post-Cold War era (prior to 9/11) the degree to which the US was concerned with involving itself in the domestic affairs of far and distant countries was transformed. Consequently, the political spaces available to local political actors and issues to determine and/or promote contrary policy outcomes due to the refining of US power projection and reordering of national security priorities expanded.

During the 1990s, then, there was a reduction in the scope and form of US influence in a number of states that – because of the Cold War – had previously been seen as US national security priorities. In a *global* sense, then, and against some conventional wisdom, the 1990s witnessed a reduction in the projection of US power and influence in determining political developments in all parts of the world. This perspective was fundamentally different from the Cold War era when developments *across* the world tended to be viewed through the prism of the global systemic struggle against the USSR and international communism. In contrast to this the era of globalisation after the Cold War saw a more pristine economic dynamic govern US power projection, which has resulted in practice in a reduction of a US global political presence, mainly because significant parts of the world are not part of this process. The 9/11 attacks brought an end to this 'moment', transforming US global (security) priorities such that US global concerns now involved the US busying itself in the domestic affairs of countries outside of the zones of globalisation (the Middle East and central Asia being second only to sub-Saharan Africa in this respect).

With the declaration of the War on Terror not only have US post-Cold War priorities changed – bringing about a return of Cold War concerns about national security and the need to reconstruct the international order to meet the 'terrorist challenge' – it has also seen the US confronting an enemy which it played a significant role in cultivating. Whilst the US did not create these movements and their terrorist offshoots, its historical mission, during the Cold War, to crush the social and political forces of the radical left and its *ongoing* hostility to those forces has provided a key international stimulus to the rise of the banner of reactionary Islam. Further, the social and political fragility of many states in the Islamic world consequent upon the endings of Cold War have been compounded by neoliberal globalisation, producing a crisis of political identity which the reactionary right has, in part, successfully filled. It is not then that reactionary politics was an inevitable outcome of the ends of Cold War, but rather how the ascendancy of reactionary social, ideological and political forces brought about by the ends of Cold War in parts of the world have become more pronounced due to the changes associated with neoliberal globalisation during the 1990s.

Notes

1 INTRODUCTION: HISTORY AND THEORY IN THE COLD WAR

1. Socio-economic properties refer to the way in which societies are organised to realise their material production, specifically, the evolving relationship between formal structures of political-coercive authority – the state – and the realm of economic production and the way in which this domestic relationship regulates relations between different social classes and determines the *form* of a state's international relations.
2. The leading realist thinkers on the Cold War are Gaddis (1987, 1992, 1997); Kennan (1947, 1982, 1984); Kissinger (1994); Waltz (1979); and on the end of the Cold War specifically, Brooks and Wohlforth (2000); Mearsheimer (1990, 2001); Wohlforth (1994).
3. With their emphasis on the (bipolar) structural character of post-war international politics, Realists also (over)emphasise the geopolitical stability of the Cold War system captured in Gaddis's (1987) idea of the 'long peace', which not only reduces the Cold War to the structure of the international system (i.e. the number of great powers), but also means that Realism remains trapped within a theoretical framework that is insensitive to sub-macro international changes.
4. Although a number of 'Realist historians', led by George Kennan, Henry Kissinger and John Lewis Gaddis, have provided accounts of the historical evolution of the Cold War – including events beyond the theoretical lens of Realist theory – in theoretical terms these historical accounts remain trapped in the realist cage that state behaviour is best conceptualised as a struggle for security and power under conditions of anarchy and that this is how the superpowers behaved and the Cold War should be understood. *Plus ça change*; for all of the historical and empirical detail the theoretical payback is that much remains the same as it ever was.
5. Key Ideational thinkers are Checkel (1997); Crockatt (1995); Forsberg (2000); Koslowski and Kratochwil (1994); Lebow (1994); Risse-Kappen (1994).
6. See Campbell (1998).
7. This section draws from Saull (2001: 15–24; 111–19).
8. The fact that large areas of the world under communist control were effectively removed from participating in, and being subject to, capitalist exploitation and combined with the promotion of an alternative socio-economic system was obviously of concern to the leading capitalist powers meaning that the advanced capitalist states were never reconciled to the existence of Soviet-communist states.
9. The best statement that emphasises the internal dimensions of conflict downplaying the external aspects is Cox (1986). See also Gowan (2002, 2005) for an argument that the Cold War system served the material interests of the US.
10. The state capitalist argument – a variant of Trotskyism derived from Trotsky's critique of Stalinism as an exploitative bureaucratic form of state – was developed by Cliff (1988) and also informs the argument of Callinicos (1991); and Harman (1988). For critiques of the state capitalist argument see Anderson (1983); Blackburn (1980).
11. Lenin (1934).

12. This understanding of the USSR as an inherently conservative power is also found in the arguments of the American Cold War Revisionists who, from the mid-1960s, began to contest the Orthodox historical interpretation for the origins of the Cold War. The Revisionists argued that after the war and throughout the post-war period the USSR was much more concerned with domestic issues focused on economic reconstruction, and was very hesitant about supporting the forces of international revolution. Consequently, rather than blaming Stalin and the USSR for causing the Cold War, the Revisionists tend to lay the blame for the Cold War at the door of the US and its expansive need to find more markets. Further, and following those Marxists that emphasise intra-bloc conflict, the Revisionists have highlighted antagonisms and conflicts within each bloc, particularly the US concern to dismantle the British empire. See Horowitz (1967, 1969); Kolko (1969a, 1969b); Kolko and Kolko (1972); LaFeber (1993); and Paterson (1979).

13. The focus of Horowitz and others on American counter-revolution policies in the western hemisphere before the Second World War also highlights an important continuity in US foreign policy, suggesting that the ideological and political predisposition of antagonism towards revolutionary change – a defining characteristic of US foreign policy and presidential national security doctrines after 1945 – was well-established before the conventional understanding of the Cold War's origins.

14. See Deutscher (1960, 1966a, 1967, 1970).

15. See Halliday (1982, 1986, 1994).

16. Saull (2001, 2005a).

17. See Westad (2005) for the most comprehensive account (in a single volume) of the role of the USSR and its ideological model in the third world.

18. See Halliday (1986: 24–5, 1994: 170–80).

19. Thus Halliday refers to the 'first' Cold War as characterising world politics and superpower relations between 1946 and 1953, whilst the period 1953–69 is one of 'oscillatory antagonism' rather than Cold War, and the period 1969–70 one of détente, with the period 1979–85 as the 'second' Cold War. See Halliday (1986: 3).

20. Thus the Soviet system was based on the suppression and destruction of the socio-economic foundations – private property as the organisational form of production, the market as the means of distributing goods and services, and the separation of the political and economic spheres of social life under the rule of law – integral to the US capitalist system. Likewise, the international expansion of the Soviet system required the destruction of these socio-economic institutions and relations.

21. Leffler (1994a). The consequence was the same for the US as a liberal-republican form of capitalist state with regard to Soviet expansion: the elimination of potential and actual markets for the US economy and the requirement that the US respond to such developments in kind, which – taken to its logical end – would have involved a serious undermining of the American liberal-republican way of life. On the liberal and republican character of American capitalism see Agnew (2005).

22. Labour camps and forced labour played an important role in the construction of the Soviet economy under Stalin. See Conquest (1992); Davies et al. (1994); Lewin (2005: 113–26).

23. According to Nove (1992: 274) armaments production accounted for 52 per cent of Soviet national income in 1942, the highest reached anywhere by any state. Further, most scholars agree that the USSR spent twice as much on all aspects of military defence as the US after 1945 where major areas of the 'civilian economy' – machine tools, metallurgy and chemicals – were devoted to military production. See Dibb (1986: 80–9).

24. Whilst all states have a coercive and military component – this is what partly defines them as states – this component was particularly pronounced and distinct in Soviet-communist types of states compared to *advanced* capitalist states because of the revolutionary and violent origins of these states combined with the radical social, economic and political transformations

pursued by these states – and the requirement of force in such transformations – and the external hostility such developments triggered.

25. In recognising this distinction, however, we also need to recognise that US external power projection has not just been realised through persuasion or consent but also significant amounts of coercion and violence, and – in the case of the western hemisphere – much of which pre-dated the post-war conjuncture. Yet the use of military power by the US associated with a prolonged commitment to the deployment of large amounts of troops and *matériel* overseas – has usually required some kind of *casus belli* to enable the US political leadership to convince the public that a threat exists that would warrant such a commitment. The announcement of the Truman Doctrine in 1947 and the National Security Strategy of the Bush administration announced in the wake of the terrorist attacks of 11 September 2001 suggest as much.

26. As long as West European states did not challenge US military leadership and that these societies remained capitalist and committed to open participation in a US-led international capitalist economy. However, the 'price' of such an 'empire by invitation' was that there was always the possibility that democratic social forces within Western Europe could withdraw the invitation by embarking on radical socio-economic change in a socialist direction. When such developments occurred in other parts of the world, the US was more often than not willing to deploy coercive and military force to prevent such threats to the capitalist social order, highlighting the iron fist that most of the time remains hidden within the velvet glove of bourgeois democracy.

27. See Colás and Saull (2005: 12–17).

28. As Gindin and Panitch (2005: 24–43) insist, US global power is '[c]haracterised by the penetration of borders, not their dissolution', with a preference for global domination *through* rather than *over* states and peoples (emphasis added).

29. The March 1918 Treaty of Brest-Litovsk that saw the young Bolshevik regime forced to make concessions to the superior military power of imperial Germany out of revolutionary political expediency to ensure the regime's political survival was one such episode. Whereas the geopolitical circumstances of early 1918 induced caution, by 1920 – under conditions of internationally supported civil war and political chaos and instability in much of east-central Europe – the Bolsheviks attempted to expand Soviet power westwards with the 1920 war with Poland, and later successfully used force to expand the writ of Soviet power in the other hinterlands of the old Russian Empire, bringing Georgia and Mongolia under communist Soviet-communist rule by the mid-1920s.

30. Such as Vietnam, Cuba and Iran.

31. We also need to recognise the very distinct local/regional political and ideological characteristics and objectives of these revolutionary states. Thus, in the Middle East revolutionary states were much more defined by a commitment to radical nationalism than association with the international communist movement, highlighted by the role of the Arab-Israeli conflict in their respective domestic and international politics. In Latin America, the longer historical legacy of US imperialism in this region ensured that revolutionary struggles were informed by pre and non-communist ideological currents and political movements as well as pro-Soviet forces. Consequently, the character of revolutionary change and the states that emerged here – in Cuba, Nicaragua, El Salvador and Guatemala – reflected this. The survival of revolutionary Cuba after the Soviet collapse is testament to the very particular anti-imperialism and revolutionary character of Cuba.

2   THE INTERNATIONAL IMPACT OF THE BOLSHEVIK REVOLUTION AND THE EARLY COLD WAR, 1917–45

1. Nazi Germany's ideological and geopolitical hostility towards Bolshevism and the USSR, evidenced in the domestic policies of the Third Reich and its policy of *lebensraum* through eastward

territorial expansion, and the hostility of the liberal capitalist powers, evidenced in their domestic worries over the role of communist parties and their inability to form a military alliance with the USSR against fascism even after the numerous acts of aggression carried out by Berlin.

2. One might add that the USSR was, indeed, transformed by the war, but in a way that made its coercive and militarised nature even more, not less, pronounced, and even more preoccupied after the devastation of the war on its military security.

3. However, the rebellion by the naval garrison on the island of Krondstadt, near Petrograd, in March 1921 continued to highlight the military vulnerabilities of the revolution.

4. Carr (1979: 28–30); Lewin (1985); Nove (1992).

5. Highlighted by strikes, urban depopulation (due to the scarcity of food and resulting privations), peasant unrest over state requisitioning of grain, and in March 1921 an armed rebellion by the garrison at the naval base of Krondstadt.

6. The NEP worked through a 'mixed economy' in the countryside whereby the peasantry were bound to supply a fixed amount of crops to state authorities, allowing them to sell any surplus on the open market.

7. The reference to scissors refers to the diagram presented in Trotsky's report to the twelfth party congress in April 1923 which depicted the growing divergence in the prices of agricultural and industrial goods. See Carr (1979: 56); Service (1997: 155).

8. Deutscher (1966b: 301–18).

9. Lewin (1985: 142–77).

10. Service (1997: 181).

11. Service (1997: 170).

12. In this sense there was an indirect capitalist economic pressure on the USSR throughout its existence based on the need to catch up and, ultimately, realise the historical mission of socialism as set out by Marx, in surpassing the economic potential of capitalism. This argument is most associated with the state-capitalist understanding of the USSR. See Cliff (1988).

13. Mazower (1998: 126) states, 'Starting with the mass arrests during collectivization, and fluctuating in intensity throughout the 1930s, the security organs gained control of millions of prisoners in a complex network of prisons, "corrective labour camps", labour colonies and special settlements: latest estimates put the total number of prisoners as rising from 2.5 m in 1933 to 3.3 m by mid-1941.'

14. The Stalinist solution was not, then, the only option. As a number of scholars (Bettelheim, 1978; Corrigan et al., 1978; Lewin, 1985, 2005) have recognised, the Soviet leadership overlooked other ways of promoting industrialisation through socialising agriculture drawing on anti-capitalist possibilities within the peasantry. However, such arguments necessarily play down the role of external necessity and Stalin's correct anticipation of imminent future military aggression. This is significant because the non-Stalinist strategy would have inevitably required (more) time, something that, as history would prove, the USSR did not have.

15. As Stalin made clear in 1929, '[d]o you want our Socialist fatherland to be beaten and to lose its independence? If you do not ... [we] must put an end to its backwardness in the shortest possible time'. Cited in Holloway (1984: 6–7).

16. This was particularly the case with respect to the vicissitudes of the USSR's support for international revolution. Here the USSR was highly cautious about committing itself to supporting international revolution in contexts of geopolitical vulnerability, whilst much less so during those moments of geopolitical opportunity.

17. Dergas (1978: 221–2).

18. The British intervened in northern Russia at Murmansk and Archangel, Siberia and in the Crimea, the US in northern Russia and Siberia, the Japanese at Vladivostock and the French in the Crimea.

19. Leffler (1994a: 9).

20. The best analysis of these diplomatic manoeuvrings remains Mayer (1967).
21. Westoby (1989: 42–5); Davies (1972).
22. See Borkenau (1962: 134–60).
23. Leffler (1994a: 3–32) provides an insightful discussion of US domestic anti-communism between 1917 and 1941 highlighting this distinction in the perception of the communist threat.
24. See Westoby (1989: 63–7).
25. Carr (1979: 84–94).
26. However, the US did not establish diplomatic relations with the USSR until 1933.
27. Carr (1979: 43).
28. Carr (1979: 92).
29. Deutscher (1966b: 402).
30. The obvious cases were Italy, Germany and Spain, where fascist movements came to power. One could also include France in this list. On the eve of the Second World War France was wracked by political and class divisions amounting to a simmering 'civil war' between the political representatives of the working class and the fascist right. This social and political polarisation was a contributing factor not only to the French military collapse in 1940, but also the emergence of civil war within France after 1940 between the communist-led Resistance and the fascist-collaborationist Vichy regime and its Nazi overseer. On fascism in France, see Paxton (2004: 68–73).
31. In the case of Mussolini's 'seizure of power' in Italy, as Mazower (1998: 13) suggests, this was not the product of a revolutionary crisis but rather the fear of Italy's traditional ruling class of the consequences of universal suffrage, which led them to invite Mussolini to form a government as a way of preventing a socialist government coming to power via the ballot box.
32. In the two defining cases in Europe – Germany and Italy – Mussolini and Hitler were co-opted to govern by elements within the traditional political elite and ruling class. In each case the traditional social power of the ruling class was being challenged by the revolutionary left, but state power had not collapsed, hence, both cases could be seen as preventative forms of counter-revolution. See Paxton (2004).
33. It is also possible to see post-war developments in a number of states – South Korea, Argentina, Chile, Indonesia, etc. – as resembling this inter-war context of crisis where local ruling classes, supported by the US, allied themselves with right-wing and neo-fascist political forces – usually concentrated in the military – to overthrow left-wing governments or prevent such movements from coming to power.
34. See Mayer (1971).
35. Thus following the logic of Lenin's understanding of peaceful co-existence' as outlined; see Dergas (1978: 221–2).
36. The Czechoslovaks were caught between the proverbial 'rock and a hard place' – Soviet military assistance against Nazi Germany may have come at the cost of political dependence and/or military subordination to Moscow, at least if one considers the way in which the USSR realised similar security concerns with regard to Poland in 1939.
37. Roberts (1992: 73).
38. Deutscher (1966b: 402).
39. See Preston and Mackenzie (1996: 87–105).
40. McDermott and Agnew (1996: 142).
41. Claudin (1975: 63).
42. As discussed in depth in McDermott and Agnew (1996: 81–157); Borkenau (1962: 332–412); Claudin (1975: 103–242).
43. Borkenau (1962: 386–400).
44. McDermott and Agnew (1996: 121–30).
45. McDermott and Agnew (1996: 130–42).
46. Carr (1979: 101–2).

47. Westoby (1989: 75).
48. Westoby (1989: 75–7).
49. Smith (1998: 267).
50. See Saull (2001:125–31).
51. See Duiker (1973: 186–98).
52. Saull (2001: 125–31).
53. Kim Khánh (1982: 152–4).
54. This is what Leffler (1994a) concentrates on.
55. Leffler (1994a: 3–32).
56. This concern was a major impetus behind the establishment of the Organisation of American States (OAS) in 1948, which was meant to reduce the need for US military intervention to prevent 'foreign' political ideas and movements overthrowing political order in the region, by all member states making a pledge to oppose communism.
57. For Williams (1972) the intervention in Cuba heralded a policy of 'imperial anti-colonialism' or the 'open door' where the US used a range of instruments to force open economies to accept US goods, which continued to be the basis for US policy after 1945.
58. Williams (1972).
59. However, communist parties were instrumental in insurrections in El Salvador in 1932 and Brazil in 1935. See Caballero (1986: 9).
60. Saull (2001: 121–5)
61. See the costs discussed by Deutscher (1984). Mandel (1986: 127) states that Soviet casualties at Stalingrad were greater than all US casualties in the Second World War.
62. See the discussions in Kolko (1969a); Thorne (1978: 384–93); Pollard (1985); and Mandel (1986: 106–49).
63. See Mandel (1986: 144).

3   THE COLD WAR TRANSFORMED: GEOPOLITICAL RESTRUCTURING AND A NEW WAVE OF SOCIAL REVOLUTION, 1945–49

1. Initial Soviet policy after the war rested on the assumption of future inter-imperialist conflict, which, as in the past, the USSR hoped to take advantage of. See Westad (2005: 57–66).
2. On Soviet thinking about the future of the grand alliance, see Pechatnov (1995).
3. The one exception was Austria, where all foreign troops, including the Red Army (and consequently Soviet power), were evacuated in 1955 with the establishment of a neutral, non-aligned, but capitalist Austria with the 1955 peace treaty.
4. The orthodox account emerged in the 1940s. It was particularly associated with the diplomatic dispatches of Kennan (1947) and later the work of Feis ([1957] 1967; 1970); Rostow (1960); and Schlesinger Jr (1967). A solid overview of the evolution of this account of the origins of the Cold War can be found in Melanson (1983).
5. The initial source of opposition to the orthodox account of the origins of the Cold War came from the 'Realist Revisionists' (Lippman, 1947; Morgenthau, 1948; McNeil, [1953] 1976), who argued for a much more limited form of containment based on the assumption that the USSR was more of a traditional form of great power rather than an ideologically-driven power as the orthodox account suggested.
6. The main contributions to the Revisionist approach are Williams ([1959] 1972); Kolko (1969a, 1969b); Kolko and Kolko (1972); Horowitz (1967, 1969) and Gardner (1976).
7. An exception to this is the work of Alperovitz (1966), who argues that an atmosphere of hostility emerged between Moscow and Washington from the attempt by the Truman administration to use its atomic monopoly to intimidate the Soviets into making concessions in east-central Europe.

8. See Saull (2001: 111–19) for an extended critique of the revisionist position.

9. Figures provided by Leffler (1994a: 35) detail that the USSR lost between 10 and 11 million soldiers; in addition, over half (3½ million) of Soviet soldiers in German prisoner of war camps perished. A further 10 million civilians died from hunger and/or through imprisonment in the Soviet Gulag system. On top of this immense human cost, the Germans destroyed 1,700 cities and towns, more than 70,000 villages and demolished 31,000 factories and slaughtered millions of livestock – a catalogue of barbarism unsurpassed in modern warfare.

10. Lundestad (1998) describes the character of US power in Western Europe in contrast to Soviet power in east-central Europe as an 'empire by invitation'.

11. This is not to suggest that the evolution and maintenance of the liberal-capitalist form of state has not required the use of coercion and violence, nor that such states are immune from requiring the use of 'organised violence' to maintain social order in times of revolutionary crisis. Rather, the point is that the constitution of such states is based upon circumscribing the writ and organisational authority of the state over society and the economy in particular.

12. Stalin, quoted in Djilas (1962).

13. On discussions over Poland's future between Stalin and Gomulka, see Werblen (1998).

14. Deutscher (1966b: 510).

15. Mark (1995–96) argues that this strategy echoed 'popular frontism' as well as demonstrating that Stalin was proactive rather than reactive in establishing communist power in east-central Europe.

16. Mazower (1998: 238).

17. The *coup de grâce* to the communist takeover in east-central Europe being the *coup* in Czechoslovakia where communist forces, backed by a communist militia, forced non-communists out of the government in February 1948.

18. See Wagner (1980).

19. Leffler (1994a: 50–1).

20. Roberts (1999: 30–2).

21. Kuniholm (1980).

22. Keylor (2001: 256–7).

23. Kuniholm (1980: 255–70).

24. Keylor (2001: 256–7); Kuniholm (1980: 355–78). Paterson (1979: 55) cites a memorandum from Truman: '[t]he United States would resist any Soviet "aggression," by "force of arms" if necessary.'

25. Brett (1985: 63) states that in 1945 the US controlled some 70 per cent of the world's gold and foreign exchange reserves and more than 40 per cent of its industrial output.

26. Spero (1997: 8–48).

27. Cited in Pollard (2001: 103).

28. Playing a major role in scuppering prospects for a new global trading system based on the International Trade Organisation. The ITO was replaced with the much less ambitious GATT in 1948, which allowed forms of protectionism. See Pollard (2001); Brett (1985).

29. Pollard (1985: 10–32).

30. Pollard (1985: 69–70).

31. See Wyatt-Walter (1996).

32. Pollard (2001: 107–8).

33. Leffler (1994a: 57).

34. Carew (1987: 6) stresses that the 16 countries that signed up to the Marshall Plan also committed themselves to four core aims: a focus on increasing production effort; expanding foreign trade; maintaining financial stability; and the development of European economic co-operation.

35. The outflow of US dollars to Western Europe was also significantly boosted by the US response to the Korean War in 1950, which saw the US commit itself to strengthening NATO and German rearmament, both of which added to the outflow of dollars.

36. See Lundestad (1998).
37. On the Soviet response to the Marshall Plan, see Narinsky (1994).
38. Carew (1987: 6–18).
39. Brett (1985: 62–79)
40. For a discussion of the how far Marshall Aid contributed to European economic recovery, see Milward (1984); Hogan (1987).
41. Maier (1987); Cox (1987).
42. Maier (1987: 121–52). See Carew (1987: 40–6) for a discussion of the influential role of 'New Deal' business leaders on Truman foreign economic policy.
43. See van der Pijl (1984) for an emphasis on the transnational dimensions to this new class dispensation.
44. Such 'successes', however, rested on a very narrow economistic conception of class struggle confined to the 'point of production'. This not only undermined the potential for wider political alliances against the rule of capital, but also screened out any linkages with ongoing anti-imperialist struggles taking place in the third world, which in some cases challenged the political and economic assumptions about the nature of anti-capitalism held by the dominant elements within the post-war Western left. See Harvey (2005b: 169–80).
45. Rupert (1995: 43–4).
46. Maier (1987: 121–52).
47. Rupert (1995: 44).
48. See Carew (1987: 70–9). Rupert (1995: 170–1) produces figures for the US that highlight the gap between rates of growth in capital accumulation compared to rates of growth in real wages: between 1951 and 1966, real average hourly earnings in manufacturing increased by about 39 per cent, while output per worker/hour grew by 65 per cent and real value-added per worker/hour grew by nearly 52 per cent.
49. Rupert (1995: 45–6).
50. Rupert (1995: 46).
51. Rupert (1995: 48).
52. Rupert (1995: 49).
53. According to Mortimer (1984: 346), the PCF (*Parti Communiste Français*) had over 800,000 members by the end of 1946, making it the largest political party alongside its leading role within the CGT, trade union confederation which could mobilise millions of workers. Kolko (1969a) estimates that by the end of 1946 the PCI (*Partito Communiste Italiano*) had two million members, again significantly more than any other political party in Italy.
54. Influential voices within the Truman administration such as George Kennan were so concerned over the prospects of the PCI coming to power via the ballot box that they spoke of the better scenario of a bloody communist seizure of power and the north–south division of Italy, which would have at least prevented a complete communist takeover. See Urban (1986: 180). What this suggests is that had the Italian and French communists been foolhardy enough to pursue an insurrectionary strategy, a bloody and vicious civil war, involving western intervention in support of the forces of 'order' would have likely resulted, ending with the violent destruction of the communist left, as occurred in Greece.
55. Ross (1982: 31) highlights the industrial policy of the communist-led CGT between 1945 and 1947, which had the slogans 'produce, produce' and 'work hard first, then ask for concessions'. See Carew (1987: 19–39), Wegs and Ladrech (1996: 49–57), Mortimer (1984: 326–60).
56. Cox (1984; 1986).
57. Carew (1987: 34); Mortimer (1984: 359).
58. Ross (1982: 56–8).
59. Filippelli (1989: 103–4).
60. Filippelli (1989: 146).
61. Wittner (1982: 5).

62. Wittner (1982: 5). Kuniholm (1980: 88) claims that some elements within EDES actually collaborated with the Germans out of a shared anti-communism in 1944. Thomas (1987: 384) suggests EDES forces fought ELAS as early as 1942.

63. The geopolitical division was as follows: Greece – (UK) 90/(USSR) 10; Romania – 10/90; Hungary – 20/80; Bulgaria – 20/80; Yugoslavia – 50/50.

64. According to Iatrides (2005: 10–16) it was not until December 1943 that Moscow began to cultivate meaningful political contacts with the KKE.

65. On relations between the USSR and the Yugoslav communists during and after the war, see Löwy (1981: 108–14).

66. What Stalin and his successors in the Kremlin regarded as 'reckless' and 'irresponsible' conduct through 'provoking' the Western powers was behaviour that others regarded as 'revolutionary internationalism'. This is precisely what Tito did with respect to Greece between 1945 and 1949 and Mao in the 1950s. Although Tito's support for the KKE during the civil war reflected his project of creating a Yugoslav-centred Balkan communist confederation including Greece (which would challenge the Soviet position in Bulgaria), as much as communist solidarity, its ideological consequences were crucial in stoking up British and US suspicions towards the USSR and propelling an increasingly militarised response to what the West saw as communist aggression.

67. According to Zubok and Pleshakor (1996: 56–7) Stalin purportedly told Georgi Dimitrov that Britain and the US 'would never tolerate a "red" Greece threatening their vital communications in the Middle East'.

68. Wittner (1982: 29).

69. British troops played a key role in the early period of the civil war, and although the US did not commit troops to Greece, it did provide significant quantities of military aid through its military mission in Athens. The US came very close to sending ground troops in the winter of 1947–48. See Wittner (1982: 237).

70. Iatrides (2005) suggests otherwise, but the *matériel* he mentions was of negligible consequence for the armed struggle.

71. Tensions between Moscow and Belgrade were dominated by differences over Greece. These divisions reached breaking point in June 1948 when the USSR succeeded in expelling Yugoslavia from the Cominform.

72. Wittner (1982: 267–9); Iatrides (2005).

73. For discussions of the 'Huk insurgency', see Kerkvliet (1977); Richardson (1978).

74. After agreeing to enter the war against Japan at the Yalta meeting of February 1945, the USSR finally entered the war on 9 August 1945.

75. Following Stalin's instrumentalist approach to communist revolution, at Potsdam the USSR indicated its interest in communist revolution in south-east Asia by agreeing to a division of geopolitical responsibilities in Vietnam which would see the British assume responsibilities for the south of the 16th parallel and the Kuomintang for north of the 16th parallel. See Löwy (1981: 134).

76. See Kahin (1977: 347–8).

77. Kolko (1986: 37).

78. Duiker (1996: 99).

79. See Hunt and Levine (1994: 267–8).

80. Duiker (1996: 124).

81. Papp (1981: 4).

82. Chiang was so concerned with containing communist influence during the war that he concentrated his best military resources *not* on confronting the Japanese invaders but rather on surrounding the communist stronghold of Yenan. See Chassin (1965: 17).

83. Bianco (1971: 149–50).

84. These figures (cited in Bianco, 1971: 150) highlight the point: by the time of Japan's surrender the communists had established 19 base areas behind Japanese lines. The strength of the

Red Army had grown from 80,000 in 1937 to 900,000 in 1945. Thomson et al. (1981: 220) states that CCP membership had increased from 40,000 in 1937 to 1.2 million in 1945 and that by the war's end it was responsible for the well-being of approximately 100 million Chinese.

85. Paterson (1988: 58) suggests that between 1945 and 1947 US assistance to China topped $3 billion.

86. Kolko (1969a: 202) states that a US mission in China led by General Wedemeyer after the war estimated that less than 2 per cent of the army could be considered effective military units. Paterson (1988: 68) cites George C. Marshall, who labelled the Kuomintang 'a reactionary clique, much like "corroded machinery that does not function" '.

87. The USSR signed an agreement with the Kuomintang government one day before the Japanese surrender which saw it gain significant territorial concessions including access/control of Port Arthur, and the port of Dairen, joint operation of the Changchun railway and China's recognition of Outer Mongolia's independence. See Mineo (1977: 208). Furthermore, as in east-central Europe, the Soviets took advantage of their temporary military presence in Manchuria to strip the area of as many portable industrial assets as possible. See Bianco (1971: 173); Paterson (1988: 61).

88. After the Japanese surrender the US provided equipment and helped train 39 Chinese divisions, and US planes transported one and a half million Kuomintang troops to North China and Manchuria. See Paterson (1988: 58–9).

89. See Chassin (1965: 71–90) for an analysis of the Marshall mission.

90. Bianco (1971: 170).

91. Between August 1946 and May 1947 the US reduced its military supplies to Chiang to try to pressure him, unsuccessfully, to implement reforms. Paterson (1988: 60).

4 THE MILITARISATION OF COLD WAR: THE CONTAINMENT OF THE USSR AND THE EMERGENCE OF NEW REVOLUTIONARY FRONTS, 1950–62

1. See Dibb (1986).

2. Gaddis (1987).

3. Leffler (1994a: 103) estimates that in the middle of 1950, in spite of the surprise successful Soviet atomic test in August 1949, the US continued to hold a decisive advantage in nuclear weapons: the Soviets had fewer than 25 atomic bombs and no means to deliver them against the US; the US had over 500 atomic bombs, 264 nuclear capable aircraft, and access to bases and airfields in the Middle East and Asia within easy striking distance of the USSR.

4. Its formal title was the Warsaw Treaty Organisation.

5. See Lundestad (1998).

6. See Crockatt (1995: 80–2).

7. As it was, the US increased military aid to Western Europe after 1950, amounting to over $25 billion between 1950 and 1954, which contributed to a significant increase in the alliance's troop strength and air power. See Leffler (1994a: 114).

8. Named after the French Foreign Minister Robert Schuman, and which provided the outline of the European Coal and Steel Community (ECSC).

9. At the time, however, the prevailing view within the Truman administration (and subsequent US presidencies), based on developments within east-central Europe between 1945 and 1948, was that communist expansion and aggression was directed from Moscow even when Soviet forces were not directly involved, as in China and Indochina. There was an inability on the part of US decision-makers to recognise local sources of conflict and the agency of local communist forces who, as in the case of Mao and Tito, sometimes acted against Soviet advice.

10. For analysis of US Presidential National Security Directives, see National Security Archive (2005).

11. Leffler (1994b: 118).
12. See Richter (1992) for a discussion of the possibilities of a resolution of the 'German problem' in the immediate years after Stalin's death.
13. Within three months of Stalin's death the new leadership had also renounced all territorial claims on Turkey and re-established diplomatic ties with Yugoslavia and Israel. See Richter (1992).
14. This related to Soviet concerns either to prevent or limit any (West) German rearmament and the domestic political need to channel economic resources away from armaments towards civilian goods as a way of promoting political stability. See Bekes (1996: 2–5).
15. As Lenin had done in the early 1920s.
16. See Roberts (1999: 44–6).
17. Roberts (1999: 51) suggests that during the 1950s until the Berlin Wall was built the flows were between 100,000 and 200,000 annually.
18. Zubok (1993) goes further in suggesting that the USSR was also concerned that an emboldened West Germany would sign a peace treaty with Poland behind Moscow's back with the result that 'the Polish government would no longer be interested in hosting Soviet troops on Polish territory'.
19. Zubok (1996: 248–58).
20. The outcome was not decided until June 1957, when the so-called 'Anti-Party group' led by Molotov (foreign minister in 1939–49 and 1953–6) and Malenkov failed in their attempt to depose Khrushchev.
21. Kramer (1999b).
22. Zubok (1996: 161); Richter (1992).
23. Kramer (1999b); Zubok (1996: 163).
24. Ostermann (1995).
25. Richter (1992); Ostermann (1995).
26. Ostermann (1995).
27. Kramer (1996/7).
28. Gomulka had been purged as a 'national communist' by Stalinists in the late 1940s.
29. Gluchowski (1995).
30. Roberts (1999: 46–7); Kramer (1996/7).
31. Kramer (1996/7).
32. Kramer (1996/7).
33. On Soviet concerns over Titoist tendencies with the Soviet bloc, see Bekes (1996); Kramer (1996/7: 362–3).
34. Halliday (1999b: 133–60).
35. Roberts (1999: 48).
36. Kramer (1996/7).
37. Roberts (1999: 49).
38. For analysis of the making of the Sino-Soviet Alliance, see Goncharov et al. (1993: 36–129); Zubok (1994: 54–62); and Westad (1998a; 1996–97).
39. However, Westad (2005: 69) suggests that after Stalin's death up to 1960 Soviet aid became much more generous, amounting to 7 per cent of Soviet national income – significantly more generous than US assistance through Marshall Aid and suggesting a massive attempt to construct Soviet-style socialism in China.
40. See Westad (1996/7).
41. See the documents and commentary on the Korean War in the *Cold War International History Project Bulletin 6–7* (Winter 1995/6) in particular. See also Goncharov (1993).
42. See Zubok (2001) for discussion of the impact of the Mao–Khrushchev personality clash.
43. Zubok (1996: 215), with a touch of exaggeration, summarises the different paths of the USSR and China after 1957–8: '[o]ne country shut the doors of concentration camps and the other opened them.'

44. See Saull (2001: 144–5).
45. Zhai (1995/6).
46. One of the best analyses of the role of international developments on the Sino-Soviet split is to be found in Zubok (1996: 210–35).
47. Kramer (1995/6).
48. Roberts (1999: 52).
49. Kramer (1995/6).
50. The withdrawal of Soviet advisers came at a critical time for the Chinese. China was in the midst of great economic difficulties, including widespread famine affecting millions of peasants in the countryside caused by Mao's 'Great Leap Forward'. With the withdrawal of Soviet advisers, Mao was quick to link China's domestic economic difficulties with the Soviet withdrawal.
51. Jian (1996/7).
52. Zubok (1996: 232).
53. See Prozumenschikov (1996/7).
54. Prozumenschikov (1996/7).
55. Prozumenschikov (1996/7).
56. See Jian and Wilson (1998).
57. Leffler (1994a). His argument focuses on developments within the major advanced economies rather than the third world.
58. Cumings (1981; 1990).
59. See Lee (2001: 21–35) for a succinct analysis of the problems in establishing a trusteeship for Korea after the war.
60. Lee (2001: 22–3).
61. See Cumings (1981; 1990).
62. Communists in the south had attempted to overthrow the Rhee regime with insurrections on the island of Chenju and Yosu on the mainland in 1949, both of which were bloodily repressed by South Korean military forces.
63. Although, as documentary evidence (Jian, 1992, 1995/96; Mansourov, 1995–96) suggests, the Chinese leadership was far from united in supporting North Korean aims. With the American landings at Inchon in September 1950 and the possibility that Chinese forces, in defence of North Korea, might end up fighting US forces, such divisions increased within the Chinese leadership.
64. See Weathersby (1993b: 35–6).
65. The documentary evidence on the trilateral correspondence between Kim, Mao and Stalin after US forces had landed on the peninsula shows how Stalin was keen to ensure that Soviet forces were removed from the frontline of combat and where they were involved in air combat with US forces they did not fight over enemy-controlled territory and also fought under North Korean 'colours'. Indeed, until Mao finally agreed to dispatch Chinese forces to assist the North Koreans in mid-October, the evidence suggests that Stalin would have accepted the loss of North Korea rather than the possibility of Soviet forces engaging US forces on the peninsula to save the Korean communists from defeat. See Mansourov (1995–96); Weathersby (1995; 1995–96).
66. For detailed analysis of the documentary evidence, see Bajanov (1995–96); Weathersby (1993a; 1993b; 1995; 1995/96)
67. According to Lee (2001: 98), between 1950 and 1953 US military spending more than quadrupled. By the summer of 1951 US armed forces had doubled to over 3.2 million with army divisions increasing from ten to 18, whilst the air force went from 42 to 72 wing groups and navy ships almost doubling to 1,000.
68. See Saull (2001: 189–92).
69. Indeed, it was largely due to the demand provided by the Korean War to supply the US-led forces with a range of industrial goods that the Japanese economy begin to pick up and in 1954 Japanese industrial production finally surpassed pre-war levels. See Lee (2001: 103–4).

70. See Iriye (1974); Lee (1995).
71. Kahin (1986: 36–8).
72. For discussion of the relationship between the agrarian social property relations and the war in Vietnam, see Wiegersma (1988); Post (1989, 1990); Murray (1980); Kolko (1986); Duiker (1996).
73. Reaching 90,000 by 1952. See Crockatt (1995: 184).
74. Borer (1999: 58–60, 95–7).
75. Crockatt (1995: 186).
76. The political-military situation in Laos in 1960 was even more precarious for US interests than South Vietnam. Since gaining independence the country had been wracked by civil war between Soviet and Chinese-backed communist and nationalist armed groups and the pro-US government, which was overthrown in 1960 by non-communist nationalists. The continuing instability and civil war in Laos, with the US furnishing military aid to its allies and breaking an agreement signed in June 1962 at Geneva between the US, China and the USSR to end the civil war, was an important factor that helped the NLF in the south, particularly through the supply of arms to the NLF by Hanoi along the 'Ho Chi Minh trail'.
77. This section draws on Saull (2001: 122–5, 146–57, 179–89).
78. The US had communicated its recognition of the necessity of political change in Cuba in 1958 through severing its military ties with the Batista regime and calling for political reform in Cuba.
79. See Miller (1989); Westad (2005).
80. See Blackburn (1963); Farber (1976); Pérez-Stable (1999).
81. See Perez (1990); Morley (1987).
82. Citing official US figures, Wood (1970: 17) suggests that by the 1950s 40 per cent of raw sugar production was US-owned, along with 23 per cent of non-sugar production, 90 per cent of telephone and electrical services, and 50 per cent of the public railways. Johnson (1965: 441) calculated that the 'book value' of US enterprises in Cuba at the time of the revolution was over three times the value for the rest of Latin America.
83. Initially, US capitalist hostility expressed itself in the capitalist economic form, through a combination of economic inducements (loans), to tie the Cubans to the rule of capital and limit the scope of socio-economic transformation and coercive measures highlighted by the suspension of sugar imports into the US from Cuba in July 1960 – an export the Cuban economy was almost completely dependent on for its hard currency earnings. See Saull (2001: 179–84).
84. For the Cubans the most recent and ominous case was that of Guatemala in June 1954 where a CIA-sponsored military *coup* had overthrown the Arbenz government whose package of socio-economic change was of a decidedly more moderate nature than that being carried out in Cuba. Further, Che Guevara had been in Guatemala at the time of the *coup*. For details, see Anderson (1997).
85. See Morley (1987); Blasier (1976); Bender (1975: 13–31); Johnson (1965: 440–59) for discussions of the economic measures taken by the US state and capital in response to revolutionary developments within Cuba between 1959 and 1961.
86. See Pavlov (1994); Duncan (1985).
87. Economic problems within the USSR at the time forced the regime to double the price of meat and butter, which provoked civil disturbances, the most serious occurring in Novocherkassk in southern Russia where dozens were killed. Gidwitz (1982: 25–42); Zubok (1996: 262–5).
88. See Saull (2001: 141–57).
89. This was particularly important in the context of Khrushchev's failure – in spite of issuing a number of threats – of squeezing concessions out of Washington over the status and future of Berlin. Furthermore, the installation and targeting of intermediate nuclear weapons on the US from Cuba would give the USSR a first-strike capability on the US mainland for the first time, going some way to addressing the massive strategic-nuclear advantage possessed by the US through its larger ICBM force and numerous nuclear missile bases bordering the USSR.

90. At the same time that Moscow was negotiating the dispatch and installation of nuclear missiles, the Soviets were trying to increase their influence within Cuba through the Cuban communist party and Castro's increasing dependence on the PCC. In particular the Soviets were concerned that Cuban support and training for revolutionary guerrillas (using Soviet supplied arms) autonomous of any Soviet involvement and in contradiction to the official doctrinal line of pro-Moscow Latin American communist parties who opposed revolution through armed struggle threatened to undermine Soviet leadership of the international revolution and provoke a US military attack. See Saull (2001: 151–7).
91. Crockatt (1995: 159).
92. See Holloway (1983).
93. And further afield in Africa. See Gleijeses (2002); Westad (2005: 208–49).
94. See Debray (1967).
95. Cuba organised a number of meetings that challenged Soviet revolutionary doctrine and that of Latin American pro-Soviet communist parties after 1962: the January 1966 Tricontinental Conference of communist parties and the August 1967 meeting of the Latin American Solidarity Organisation. The Soviets, on the other hand, sought to curtail Cuban dissent by promoting factions within the Cuban leadership closer to the Moscow line, which came to a head with the arrest and trial of the leading pro-Soviet Anibal Escalante in 1961. On the tensions in Cuban–Soviet relations before, during and after the missile crisis, see Brenner (1995); Saull (2001: 151–7).

5   THE FINAL GASP OF COLD WAR: THE DECLINE OF US MILITARY SUPERIORITY AND THE EXPANSION OF INTERNATIONAL COMMUNIST POWER, 1962–80

1. For an extended discussion of US (and Soviet) strategy towards the Vietnamese Revolution, see Saull (2001: 157–66, 189–99).
2. The focus of this section is Vietnam, that part of former French Indochina where US military power and concern were most concentrated. However, it is important to recognise that the US played a major role in political and military developments in the other two successor states of French Indochina – Laos and Cambodia. Both countries had communist insurgencies and both received US diplomatic and military support in combating them. In Laos US military involvement was at its most intense between 1964 and 1969 through the air bombardment of communist (Pathet Lao)-controlled areas and the Laotian parts of the Ho Chi Minh trail. In Cambodia, US intervention came later, but involved the deployment of combat troops in the invasion of Cambodia in April 1970, as well as the covert use of air power between February 1969 and April 1970, known as 'Operation MENU' and later, in July–August 1973.
3. There were insurgencies involving communist forces elsewhere in the region (Malaysia and the Philippines) and, until 1965, the Indonesian Communist Party (PKI) was a major political force within Indonesia and formed part of the governing nationalist coalition under Achmed Sukarno's leadership.
4. In strictly legal terms, based on the 1954 Geneva Accords, Vietnam was a single state and the division into communist north and capitalist south at the 17th parallel was supposed to be temporary, ended by unification referendum in July 1956. North Vietnamese intervention was not, then, international but rather an 'internal' affair to unify a divided state.
5. Kolko (1986); Young (1991).
6. Whilst there is general agreement on the number of US casualties – over 57,000 killed – there is less certainty about communist (North Vietnamese and Vietcong) and civilian casualties, in the north and south. Estimates vary between 500,000 and one million deaths, where even the conservative estimate dwarfs the US figure. On civilian casualties, figures again vary, with some consensus over the figure of approximately 500,000 South Vietnamese civilian deaths

between 1965 and 1975. No figures are available for civilian casualties in the north, but a common estimate is that around 2 million Vietnamese (north and south, military and civilian) were killed during the war out of a population of around 17 million.

7. Diem was seen as a credible alternative to Bao Dai, as he had nationalist credentials and refused to be associated with either Bao Dai or the Viet Minh during the first Vietnam War. However, it was his uncompromising anti-communism and commitment not to negotiate with Hanoi over implementing the Geneva Accords which curried particular favour with Washington. See Young (1991: 44).

8. However, because the war was largely fought in the countryside and because of US military strategy, the South Vietnamese countryside was transformed in both population and environmental terms. The countryside was emptied of its population as peasants were killed or fled to the relative safety of urban areas from the horrors of napalm and Agent Orange. Kolko (1994: 432) suggests that by 1971 the urban population had more than doubled within ten years making up 43 per cent of the overall population due to the ravages of the war and the use of these and other biological-chemical weapons destroyed much of the rural eco-system.

9. Young (1991: 57).

10. Young (1991: 60–3); Kolko (1994: 420) suggests that up to two-thirds of the party in the south had been killed or arrested by 1959.

11. See Turley (1986: 47–8); Young (1991: 82–6).

12. The most infamous was 'Operation Ranch Hand', which ran from 1962 to 1971 and involved the spraying of over 17 million gallons of Agent Orange over 3.6 million hectares of South Vietnam, with devastating environmental and human consequences. See Schulzinger (1997: 193) and Young (1991: 82). Further, according to Borer (1999: 81–2), by 1970 US bombing had destroyed about half the crops in the south, about 12 million hectares of forests and hills, and because of this South Vietnam had become a net importer of rice, having formerly been a major exporter.

13. Areas forcibly cleared of civilians, allowing US and South Vietnamese forces 'free fire' on those remaining.

14. The Commercial Import Programme (CIP) paid the salaries of the primary urban social constituency of the South Vietnamese state – civil servants, police and soldiers – thus ensuring the acquiescence of the middle class. See Saull (2001: 196–7) for discussion of the CIP on the political economy of South Vietnam.

15. Between 1961 and 1962 the number of US military personnel in South Vietnam more than tripled from 3,000 to 11,000, increasing to over 16,000 in 1963 and more than 23,000 before the formal introduction of combat troops in March 1965. By the end of 1965 there were 184,000 US military personnel in South Vietnam. See Young (1991: 332–3).

16. Army of the Republic of Vietnam.

17. Most graphically (and horrifically) illustrated in the self-immolation of a Buddhist monk broadcast on US television channels in June 1963.

18. For documentary evidence on US involvement see Prados (2003).

19. Over the duration of the air war, on an area a little larger than France, the US dropped 7.8 million tonnes of bombs, more than the total amount dropped by all aircraft in the Second World War. See Turley (1986: 87).

20. A very different explanation of the incident emerged in 1971 when Daniel Ellsberg leaked the Pentagon Papers (see Sheehan, 1971), secret Department of Defense materials related to the Vietnam War. In the Pentagon Papers, Ellsberg claimed that the *Maddox* and *Turner Joy* had illegally entered North Vietnamese territorial waters in a deliberate act of provocation (alongside US-directed South Vietnamese commando raids in the Gulf of Tonkin area at the same time) thus providing the *casus belli* that Johnson required to convince the US Congress and public of the aggressive intent of North Vietnam. See Prados (2004) for further examination of US explanations.

21. US troop numbers rapidly increased from 184,000 at the end of 1965 reaching a peak of 535,000 at the time of the Tet Offensive. See Young (1991: 333–4).
22. The launching of the CIA-sponsored Phoenix programme in 1968 was an attempt by the US and its South Vietnamese allies to decapitate the NLF through intelligence work and led to the capture and assassination of NLF cadres. According to Young (1991: 213) between 1968 and 1971 28,000 Vietcong were captured and 20,000 assassinated alongside the widespread use of rape and torture against suspected NLF cadres. Young (1991: 213) details some of the horrific 'interrogation techniques' used on NLF suspects. Whilst Operation Phoenix did weaken the NLF it was not enough to destroy its political and military structure.
23. Cited in Kolko (1994: 431).
24. Young (1991: 217).
25. However, the success of NLF strategy in taking over so many urban areas during Tet did suggest that they had the support of a significant portion, if not a majority of urban population of South Vietnam.
26. As the soon-to-be US National Security Adviser, Henry Kissinger, said at the time, 'the prevalent strategy could no longer achieve its objectives within a period or with force levels politically acceptable to the American people'. Cited in Goodman (1978: 83).
27. The notorious massacre of a whole Vietnamese village, including women and children, by US troops – the My Lai massacre – took place in March 1968, after the first phase of the Tet Offensive. The massacre received major media coverage, but was not an isolated incident. The testimony of soldiers who had served in Vietnam in the hearings of the Vietnam Veterans Against the War (VVAW) suggests that rape, torture and killing by US forces was commonplace.
28. More broadly, this was known as the Nixon Doctrine, announced by Nixon on Guam in June 1969. Although its main focus was south-east Asia where large numbers of US forces were involved in combat, the Nixon Doctrine did not refer only to a greater role for the South Vietnamese forces in the war, but also to greater military burden-sharing by other US allies, including those in western Europe.
29. Young (1991: 240).
30. Even before US military intervention was at its height in 1968, by 1967 the annual cost of the war had reached US$20 billion. See Young (1991: 210–11).
31. This crisis was evidenced by a combination of factors, from the killing of student anti-war demonstrators by National Guardsmen at Kent State University and Jackson State College in Mississippi in May 1970, to the corruption and skulduggery at the heart of the US government exposed by the Watergate scandal and Nixon's subsequent threatened impeachment and resignation in August 1974, and the mounting economic problems in the US.
32. Marked by Congress's ban on despatching US combat troops to Laos and Cambodia. However, the legal loopholes secured by Nixon's supporters on Capitol Hill meant that it was not until the passing of the War Powers Resolution in November 1973 that the executive power in deploying US armed forces overseas was seriously constrained. See Young (1991: 252–4).
33. The reassertion of Congressional authority over the President reached its high point with the Clark Amendment in January 1976 which banned covert CIA assistance to (Angolan) anti-communist guerrillas. This ban was overturned during the Reagan presidency.
34. When it looked like Nixon might hesitate about making peace with Hanoi in late 1972 Congress voted in January 1973 to cut off all funding for the war as soon as troop withdrawal and repatriation of prisoners could be arranged. See Young (1991: 279).
35. The Saigon government of Nguyen Van Thieu was effectively forced to accept the agreement by Washington. The agreement resulted in the withdrawal of US forces and the recognition of two 'administrative entities' in the south (the Saigon regime and the NLF's provisional revolutionary government), which were to negotiate after the ceasefire to form a transitional authority to oversee new elections in the south.
36. See Zhai (1995/6: 237).

37. See Saull (2001: 157–66) for an extended discussion of Soviet and Chinese involvement in the Vietnam War.
38. See Kuisong (2002) for an overview of Chinese policy towards the Vietnamese revolution and war.
39. By 1968–69 relations with Moscow had deteriorated to such a degree that between March and August 1969 the PLA was engaged in armed clashes with Soviet troops over disputed parts of the Sino-Soviet border.
40. Thus, by the end of the 1950s, Beijing provided about 60 per cent and Moscow 30 per cent of socialist aid to North Vietnam. See Gaiduk (1998: 139). For an assessment of China's involvement in the Vietnam War, see Jian (1995).
41. Further, and to an extent following the pattern of the Korean War, whist the USSR dispatched military *matériel*, in increasingly large quantities after 1965, the Chinese played a more direct role in the conflict with 300,000 PLA troops stationed in North Vietnam and making it clear to Washington that any invasion of the north by US forces would provoke a Chinese response. See Zhai (1995/6).
42. Vulnerabilities exposed by the consequences of US military escalation. Thus after Kosygin's visit to Hanoi in February 1965 and the subsequent US military escalation, the Soviets proposed to China a policy for 'united action' against the US. This proposal included allowing Soviet forces and weapons to have transit rights through China, the use of airfields and the stationing of Soviet personnel there, a free air corridor over China to facilitate the supply of North Vietnam, and finally talks between the leaders of the three communist powers to decide on future strategy. Not surprisingly, the proposal for 'united action' was quickly rejected by Beijing, but Beijing did acquiesce to the transhipment of Soviet weapons through China. See Sung An (1998: 404, n. 41); Kuisong (2002: 25–41).
43. See Gaiduk (1995/6: 232, 250–8).
44. By 1968, overall Soviet assistance grew to over 50 per cent of all socialist aid to the DRV, and was worth more than US$500 million compared to US$370 million in 1964. See Gaiduk (1998: 143–4).
45. See Gaiduk (1995/6: 250–1) for disagreements between Moscow and Hanoi on the conduct of the war.
46. Papp (1981: 207) suggests the figures of approximately US$1 billion cost per year for Soviet involvement and as high as US$30 billion per year for the US.
47. Indeed, the final victory of communist forces in April 1975 to a significant degree rested on the provision of armour and heavy weaponry from Moscow that allowed North Vietnamese forces to counter the military *matériel* provided to the Saigon regime by Washington.
48. After Kissinger's secret visit to Beijing in July 1971.
49. It was not until 1957 that the USSR acquired the capacity to strike US territory with its nuclear weapons, and not until the end of the 1960s that the USSR secured an approximate parity with the US in terms of delivery systems, numbers of warheads and megatonnage. Prior to the late 1960s the US had the psychological advantage of confidence that a first strike would have destroyed Soviet nuclear forces, thus discounting any Soviet retaliation. For details on the strategic nuclear balance at the end of the 1960s, see Crockatt (1995: 215–16).
50. Halliday (1986: 50–1) documents 19 occasions when the US has deployed nuclear weapons on moments of international tension, and on four occasions (Suez, 1956; Lebanon, 1958; Cuba, 1962; and Arab-Israeli War, 1973) actually made threats that such weapons would be used.
51. See Crockatt (1995: 224–6) for a discussion of the trade, cultural and scientific dimensions of détente.
52. The most important being the Strategic Arms Limitation Treaty (SALT I) of May 1972, and SALT II of June 1979, and the Anti-Ballistic Missile (ABM) Treaty of May 1972. The most wide-ranging agreement was the Basic Principles of Relations Between the US and the USSR

signed in May 1972. This committed both parties to the goal of creating 'conditions which promote the reduction of tensions in the world and the strengthening of universal security and international co-operation'. For details on each of the treaties, see Grenville and Wasserstein (1987).

53. Articulated at a general level in Keohane and Nye (1971, 1977) and specifically on the Cold War by Crockatt (1995). For a critique of this position, see Saull (2001: 11–15).

54. Indeed, as history would reveal, at the same time that the western-dominated international capitalist economy was about to enter a decade of crisis, conflict and recession, the economies of the Soviet bloc were entering a period of long-term crisis (which was to be a major factor in the collapse of communist power in the late 1980s).

55. As mentioned earlier, the origins of both world wars were, to a significant degree, derived from inter-imperialist conflict between the major capitalist states. Whilst in the first case the USSR emerged, in the second, the USSR and international revolution spread. In this case, the inter-capitalist conflict was of a different magnitude than the two earlier ones, but the consequences were similar: the spread of Soviet-communist power.

56. For a ruling class perspective on this crisis, see Crozier et al. (1975).

57. See Armstrong et al. (1991: 192–220).

58. Evident in two developments: the OPEC-induced oil crisis of 1973 and the call for a 'New International Economic Order' in 1974 by the 'Group of 77' in a special session of the UN General Assembly.

59. This was a serious prospect in Britain in the mid-1970s in the form of the Alternative Economic Strategy promoted by the left wing of the Labour Party in response to the harsh austerity measures that were attached to the conditions of an IMF loan to deal with Britain's balance of payments crisis. See Helleiner (1994: 124–30).

60. Two other cases – on the periphery of Western Europe on the Iberian peninsula – concerned the end of two longstanding right-wing authoritarian dictatorships. The Portuguese dictatorship collapsed in April 1974, sparked by a rebellion amongst sections of the armed forces mainly against Portuguese policy towards its southern African colonies. For a brief period in 1974–75, Portugal seemed to be on the brink of social revolution, but splits in the left and the appeal of membership of the EEC helped dampen down any revolutionary tendencies. In the case of Spain, the death of Franco in November 1975 provided the trigger to a transition to constitutional liberal democratic rule again with the prospect of membership of the EEC. In this case, the spectre of revolution was less evident, but there was a moment where the combined forces of the left had an opportunity, which they failed to take, fundamentally to weaken the social interests of capital. On Portugal, see Blackburn (1974); on Spain, see Maravall (1982).

61. At the height of the first crash in the autumn of 1975 around 11 per cent of fixed capital was not being utilised in the advanced capitalist economies and unemployment had reached 15 million, averaging 4.2 per cent throughout the 1970s in Western Europe whilst it averaged only 1.5 per cent during the 1960s. See Armstrong (1991: 228–9, 234–41).

62. However, the expectation that they would be resolved in the manner in which they were, and that their consequences would see a strengthening of US capitalist power, were far from certain at the time.

63. See Gowan (1999: 19–38) for an excellent analysis of these developments; and Harvey (2005a).

64. Armstrong (1991: 117).

65. Hobsbawm (1994: 261).

66. Hobsbawm (1994: 258) suggests that the by the end of the war the US was responsible for as much as two-thirds of the world's industrial production.

67. By 1961, the value of dollars held overseas exceeded the value of US gold reserves, thus threatening (in theory if not in practice) the basis of the Bretton Woods system. By 1965 US foreign currency reserves were $15.45 billion and liabilities $25.18 billion; by 1971 reserves were $13.9 billion and liabilities $67.81 billion. See Brett (1985: 119).

68. This framework also applied to Japan.

69. As Brett (1985: 105–10) suggests, the combination of an undervalued exchange rate, generous US aid and positive trade discrimination all helped generate the so-called post-war 'economic miracles' in Germany and Japan.

70. Evidenced in the decline of US exports as part of world exports (from 18.2 per cent in 1960 to 15.4 per cent in 1970) and as a share of world manufactured exports (from 22.8 per cent in 1960 to 18.4 per cent in 1970). Figures cited in Calleo (1982: 65).

71. See Bromley (2005: 44–64).

72. These socialist gains were in large part a consequence of the 'revolutionary' changes in economic management produced by the war in countries such as Britain, and also the political strength of the organised working class. The irony of these socialist gains was that capitalist profits increased during this period and did so at a higher rate than they have tended to do since the rolling back of these socialist gains from the mid-1970s onwards. The most comprehensive survey of these developments is Brenner (1998).

73. The competitive position of the US economy was also undermined by the heavy economic burden of fighting the war in Vietnam, combined with the longer-term structural costs of the militarisation of large sections of the US economy.

74. Whilst the US capital account deficit from 1950 had been compensated by a large surplus in its balance of trade, by the late 1960s this had shrunk whilst capital outflows continued, thus exposing a fundamental weakness in the US economic position vis-à-vis the rest of the advanced capitalist world. See Armstrong (1991: 151–68), Brett (1985: 111–25); Block (1977: 164–202).

75. Between 1967 and 1971 US foreign liabilities increased from $33.2 billion to $67.8. See Brett (1991: 119).

76. Robinson (1973: 413–16).

77. On the development of the Euromarket, see Helleiner (1994: 81–100).

78. Whilst US gold reserves could cover 32 per cent of US external dollar liabilities at the beginning of 1971, by the end of that year this had fallen to only 18 per cent. Further, the capital outflow from the US between May and August 1971 was the equivalent to a staggering annualised $35 billion. See Armstrong (1991: 209); Robinson (1973: 414).

79. For a concise narrative of the build-up to the August 1971 crisis, see Strange (1972: 198–209).

80. As Robinson (1973; 416–17) suggests, the aim was to return the external position of the US economy to some kind of balance through a return to a trade surplus, thus allowing the continuation of capital outflows – the key financial basis of US imperialism. Further, as Hudson (2003: 340) suggests, 'the $61 billion of liquid debt owed to foreigners would be paid only in the form of other paper evidences of debt. Not only were gold payments suspended, the overseas debt of the United States was, in effect, repudiated.'

81. Cited in Calleo (1982: 63).

82. See Gowan (1999: 24–30).

83. Gowan (1999: 25). De Gaulle called this 'the exorbitant privilege' in that the US could pay for its defence spending and FDI through issuing paper IOUs rather than through exports. See Strange (1997: 6–9).

84. See Armstrong (1991: 234–61) for a concise analysis of the causes and nature of the 'great slowdown'.

85. See Harvey (2005a) for an excellent discussion of the class consequences of this transformation.

86. Yet the context of superpower détente was also important because the reduction in tensions with the USSR and with hopes of constraining Soviet expansion through détente, the US had a window of opportunity that allowed it to be more assertive and unilateralist in its dealings with its allies.

87. The 13 were Ethiopia (1974), Cambodia, Laos, Vietnam, Guinea-Bissau, Mozambique, Cape Verde, São Tomé, Angola (all in 1975), Afghanistan (1978–79), Iran, Grenada and Nicaragua (all in 1979).

88. As Kissinger argued, until the 1960s the 'USA had used its strategic superiority to limit the assistance given by the USSR and China to third world movements: the possibility of direct US nuclear attacks, as well as of conventional assaults backed by nuclear power, played their role in this'. Kissinger, cited in Halliday (1986: 102).

89. On top of these developments the hopes of non-violent revolutionary socialist transformation were shattered with the overthrow, through US-backed military *coup d'état*, of the Popular Socialist Unity government headed by Salvador Allende in Chile in 1973. Not only did the 'Chilean September 11' (the date of the *coup*) highlight the problem of carrying through radical social transformation, in the face of local and international opposition, but the *coup* also initiated a wave of savage repression against the left – radical and moderate alike – involving the torture and murder of thousands in Chile and Argentina, unleashing what became known as the 'Dirty War'.

90. Further, the failure of 'revolutionary conjunctures' that emerged after the collapse of right-wing military dictatorships in southern Europe – particularly in Portugal and Spain – to produce left-wing and pro-Soviet regimes, and instead the consolidation of these states into the pro-US bloc, and the increasingly critical posture of West European communist parties towards Moscow based on the doctrine of Eurocommunism were also major blows to Soviet international interests.

91. In Kissinger's words, 'Angola represents the first time that the Soviets have moved militarily at long distance to impose a regime of their choice. It is [also] the first time that the United States has failed to respond to Soviet military moves outside the immediate Soviet orbit.' Cited in Garthoff (1994a: 579–80).

92. The most authoritative explanation of communist involvement in the Angolan civil war, based on a comprehensive survey of documentary evidence, is the magisterial account provided by Gleijeses (2002). Other impressive accounts are provided by Garthoff (1994a: 556–93); Porter (1984: 147–81); Westad (2005).

93. On Guevara's African expedition, see Gott (1996). Cuban involvement in African liberation struggles, with a particular focus on the Portuguese empire, continued throughout the 1960s with the provision of guerrilla training schools and arms. See Gleijeses (2002); Westad (2005: 208–18).

94. Porter (1988: 149).

95. Gleijeses (2002: 350).

96. Garthoff (1994a: 564).

97. For the 'official' Cuban version of 'Operation Carlota', see Garciá-Marquéz (1977).

98. Garthoff (1994a: 567).

99. Gleijeses (2002: 307).

100. Indeed, Castro had proposed a Soviet airlift of Cuban troops to assist the MPLA in August 1975, which Moscow had rejected. See Gleijeses (2002: 307).

101. Just when the scale of Soviet-Cuban intervention began to increase dramatically, CIA funds for its Angolan operation ran out, and the request by the Ford administration for another $28 million was rejected by Congress with the Clark Amendment of 12 December 1975 which effectively ended US involvement in Angola. See Garthoff (1994a: 570).

102. Backed by a number of key US allies, including Egypt and conservative Arab states. See Halliday (1981a: 98–9).

103. The primary spark to the crisis in the Horn of Africa was through Somali aggression, yet we also need to recognise autonomous political and economic developments within Ethiopia and the more radical direction that the Dergue regime was beginning to move in under Mengistu, particularly with respect to agrarian reforms. See Halliday and Molyneux (1981); Westad (2005: 253–72) for discussion of the Ethiopian revolution.

104. As Porter (1984: 183) notes, Moscow had cultivated Somalia for nearly 15 years as a major regional ally with military and economic assistance totalling $285 million, alongside

1,700 Soviet military advisers in Somalia at the beginning of the crisis, and the Soviet fleet having access to naval facilities at a number of Red Sea ports.

105. Garthoff (1994a: 695–6).

106. Porter (1984: 183–6); Garthoff (1994a: 698–706). According to Westad (2005: 252, 276) the USSR delivered weapons to the value of around $1 billion to Ethiopia between March 1977 and May 1978.

107. Havana dispatched over 11,000 combat troops in support of Ethiopia and over 6,000 advisers and technical experts whilst Moscow sent almost a 1,000 military personnel making the intervention the most important Soviet-led military operation outside the Warsaw Pact since the Korean War. See Westad (2005: 276–7).

108. Soviet involvement continued after the Ogaden War with more than 7,000 Soviet bloc personnel working to construct Soviet-style socialism in Ethiopia. According to Westad (2005: 279), this was the largest Soviet foreign assistance programme since China in the 1950s.

109. However, Halliday (1981a: 106–7) notes that the US was aware that its ally, the Shah of Iran, had encouraged Siad Barre and provided arms.

110. Iran had refused to participate in the Arab boycott of oil sales to the US in 1973 and was also the principal oil supplier to Israel. See Bill (1988: 226–7).

111. Bill (1988: 202) and Rubin (1980: 158–60) note that Iranian purchases of US military hardware during the 1970s was a huge source of US export earnings, amounting to $16.2 billion between 1972 and 1977 (over a third of all US foreign military sales) absorbing approximately 40 per cent of Iran's budget by 1977, making it the largest purchaser of arms in the developing world.

112. As Bill (1988: 205) notes, between 1972 and 1975, the CIA funnelled $16 million to the Kurds through Iran in their struggle with Iraq, thus helping tie down pro-Soviet Iraqi forces, yet with little support for the Kurdish political objective of independence.

113. Initially, the wrath of the new Islamic regime was focused on the US – the main external ally of the Shah – however, with Soviet intervention in Afghanistan and Khomeini's concerns about the activities of the radical left, notably a number of armed groups, which had launched bomb attacks against Islamist political forces in 1981, the Islamists turned against the left, banning the pro-Soviet *Tudeh* party and crushing left-wing urban guerrillas. On the conflict between Islamists and the leftist *Mujahedin –e Khalq*, see Hiro (1985: 186–221); Behrooz (1999); Zabih (1986).

114. As Halliday's (1988: 31–63; 1996: 42–75) excellent account of the causes of the revolution highlights the revolution was modern – more so than either the Bolshevik or Chinese Revolutions – in the sense that Iran was a relatively developed capitalist state, with most of the population urbanised and where the revolution took place in the cities rather than the countryside involving mass mobilisations of proletarians and other urban-based classes through the use of the general strike and mass demonstrations that eventually forced the collapse of the Shah's rule.

115. On relations between Islamic Iran and the USSR, see Hiro (1985: 282–93); Yodfat (1984).

116. The Soviets restored arms shipments to Iraq in late 1982 after Iran launched a counter-attack of Iraq, which was to see Soviet-supplied missiles raining down on the residents of Dezful. See Bakhash (1984: 237–8).

117. Hiro (1985: 335).

118. The FSLN had been active since 1961 waging a periodic guerrilla struggle against the dictatorship, throughout its existence receiving arms and training from Cuba.

119. See Weber (1981: 38–41).

120. The regime was ultimately topped by the sustained onslaught of a wave of mass insurrections beginning in early 1978 with the isolated rebellions in the Indian neighbourhoods of Monimbo and Subtiava on the outskirts of the cities of Masaya and Leon early in 1978, followed by a massive insurgency in a half-dozen cities in September 1978 following the daring FSLN

seizure of the Legislative Palace the previous month; and ending with the final nationally co-ordinated FSLN-led insurrection of May through July 1979. See Walker (1991: 78–9).

121. See Sklar (1988: 17); Walker (1985: 21).

122. See Walker (1991: 79).

123. Most commentators calculate that as many as 50,000 Nicaraguans died in the war of liberation, the overwhelming majority civilians. For a country with a population of only 2.5 million, this figure is huge, the equivalent of 4.5 million deaths in a country with the population size of the US. See Walker (1985: 22).

124. Curiously, and in contrast to US policy towards the Batista regime in its final months, the Carter administration, whilst condemning the human rights abuses of the Somoza regime, did not prevent Somoza receiving more arms (from Israel) with which to continue its war against the Sandinistas and, by implication, the population of Nicaragua. See Sklar (1988: 17–32).

125. Indicated by the withdrawal and/or withholding of aid being accompanied by the signing of military assistance agreements and other 'basic human needs' loans in 1978. See Morley (1988: 162).

126. Kornbluh (1987: 15).

127. Demonstrated through its advance of $15 million in aid to the new government. Kornbluh (1987: 18–19).

128. Walker (1987: 21).

129. Right-wing propaganda, particularly associated with the Reagan presidential campaign, quickly claimed that the new Sandinista government would introduce a Soviet-type state in Nicaragua based on one-party dictatorship and a command economy. On both counts such claims were nonsense. Throughout the period of Sandinista rule, although the government did implement major socio-economic programmes (including the nationalisation of certain sectors of the economy, government control of exports and a big increase in state spending) which shifted resources away from the traditional social elite the economy continued to have a significant private sector and the political system, in spite of being in a war during the 1980s, remained relatively plural and open. For assessment of the political economy of Nicaragua under the Sandinistas, see Walker (1985, 1987, 1991); Harris (1985).

130. See Walker (1991: 189–3) for an alternative view that stresses how there was nothing inevitable about the breakdown of relations between the US and Nicaragua after 1979.

131. Indeed Soviet assistance to Nicaragua was initially moderate and only became significant after the Contra war intensified in the mid-1980s. See Walker (1991: 295–320).

132. Prior to the Soviet intervention in December 1979 Moscow had already become increasingly involved in the civil war – in an organisational and tactical way – through its 4,000 military advisers throughout the country. See Bowker (1988: 238). Further, the Soviets were also directly involved in combating the *mujahadeen* through the use of air power. Steele (1983: 124).

133. Halliday (1981a: 16–24) and Steele (1983: 120–1) ridicule such claims.

134. And a 5 per cent increase in military spending, see Garthoff (1994a: 1064).

135. Although the actual seizure of power did not involve a popular uprising, and in this sense was not a revolution, the revolutionary nature of the regime soon became apparent through the policies that the new regime sought to implement – sometimes in a highly coercive fashion – involving attacks on the traditional landlord class, and a radical programme of secularisation. As Garthoff (1994a: 990) notes, 'All in all, the domestic socialist program of the new regime violated practically every Afghan cultural norm, and strayed far beyond the allowable bands of deviance in the social, economic and political institutions'.

136. Consummated in the signing of a Soviet–Afghan Treaty of Friendship in December 1978. See Halliday (1981: 90); Garthoff (1994a: 735); Westad (2005).

137. See Halliday (1980a: 23–7) on the factional conflicts within the PDPA.

138. Garthoff (1994a: 990–1) states that by the winter of 1978–9 armed resistance to the regime had spread to 28 provinces, and in March 1979 the city of Herat was seized by rebels who

held out for three days and killed a number of *Khalq* and Soviet officials in the city. See also Steele (1983: 124).

139. Halliday (1980a: 29–32).

140. This was particularly so after Moscow had encouraged Amin's *Khalq* colleague Nur Muhammad Taraki to seize power in September 1979 resulting in a shootout which failed to kill Amin leading to Taraki's murder by Amin's agents. For details see Halliday (1980a: 34–5); Garthoff (1994a: 1004–6).

141. Halliday (1980a: 35–9). Garthoff (1994a: 1029–30) suggests that the main sources of external support for the counter-revolution came from Saudi Arabia, Egypt and Pakistan.

142. Further, as Bowker and Williams (1988: 243) emphasises, any negative impact on SALT II from the Afghan intervention was not seen as a concern, particularly because the benefits Moscow secured from SALT II seemed much less attractive by late 1979 after the NATO decision to deploy intermediate nuclear forces (cruise and Pershing missiles) in western Europe and the introduction of the MX-missile by the US.

143. Bowker and Williams (1988: 246) claims that the size of the Afghan army quickly fell by two-thirds.

144. Whilst the USSR's reaching of approximate strategic nuclear parity with the US by the late 1960s should not be overlooked as a factor in reducing US strategic-military autonomy, what best explains the 'conjuncture of the 1970s' was the confluence of a new wave of revolution allowing the expansion of Soviet-communist power at a time when the US was domestically unable to mobilise to prevent the spread of Soviet influence. Thus, whilst the strategic-nuclear equation, on the whole, remained constant – despite a massive programme of US rearmament in the 1980s – it was the emergence of a new social and political constituency supportive of a return to militarised Cold War within the United States that accounts for the character of the Cold War in the early–mid-1980s.

145. Garthoff (1994a: 745).

146. Garthoff (1994a: 753). The military personnel were present in 37 countries.

6 ENDING THE COLD WAR: FROM MILITARISED COUNTER-REVOLUTION TO THE COLLAPSE OF SOVIET COMMUNISM, 1980–91

1. Initially formed in 1950 to support the proposals in NSC'68 its activity quickly declined. It was revived by Democratic Senator Henry 'Scoop' Jackson in 1976 and quickly became a leading campaigning group of intellectuals and former officials that attacked détente and Carter's foreign policy as being too soft towards the USSR. For more information on the CPD see Sanders (1983).

2. In his first press conference as president in January 1981 an off-the-cuff comment indicated the new direction of US foreign policy with Reagan declaring that '[d]étente [had been] a one-way street that the Soviet Union had used to pursue its own aims'. Cited in Garthoff (1994b: 8).

3. See Scott (1996) for an impressive survey of the Reagan Doctrine.

4. The best survey of the social and political basis of the Western alliance and its relationship to the superpower conflict is Cox (1986).

5. On US relations with Western Europe under Reagan, see Morley (1988: 46–79).

6. Higher military spending had begun under Carter (with increases of 4 per cent, 3.1 per cent and 4.8 per cent respectively for 1979–81) in response to what the US saw as Soviet-communist advances, but increased to a much higher level under Reagan. Thus, even if one discounts inflation, whilst Carter's last military budget proposed $171.4 billion of spending, Reagan's final budget for fiscal year 1990 was more than $300 billion, not far off a 100 per cent increase

in eight years based on annual increases in spending of a much higher level than under Carter. See Crockatt (1995: 306–7).

7. See Bodenheimer and Gould (1989: 44–5); McMahan (1984: 42).
8. With its commitment to cutting public expenditure and inflation, as parts of its attack on the social constituencies associated with social democracy, the Reagan administration focused on cutting state-welfare spending whilst at the same time increasing military spending without raising taxes. This was achieved through a policy of high interest rates and net capital inflows – itself part of the new international economic architecture created by the US out of the ashes of Bretton Woods – which indirectly funded US rearmament. In effect, US rearmament was funded by the global capitalist system rather than the US economy alone. See Arrighi (2005).
9. Associated with the military-industrial-complex, and also new industries and regions that were non-unionised and free from the ideological grip of the 'New Deal' located in the south and south-west of the country. See Davis (1984); Halliday (1986: 105–33).
10. Evident in the different approaches put forward for managing the international monetary system after the collapse of the Bretton Woods by the Western Europeans and the Americans, the conflicting views on international trade, as well as the distinct dynamic of European détente and German *Ostpolitik*, the Helsinki process, and the different responses to the Iranian Revolution and Soviet intervention in Afghanistan. See Palmer (1988); DePorte (1986); Helleiner (1994); Gowan (1999).
11. Reagan's manichean worldview, evidenced in his calling the USSR the 'evil empire' and the 'source of all disorder and trouble in the world' was one such aspect. It was also indicated in the ideological tenor of his administration in contrast to Carter, where 'hawks' and 'doves' – at least until the resignation of Cyrus Vance in April 1980 – tended to cancel each other out, with the naming of 50 members of the Committee on the Present Danger to senior positions within the new Reagan administration. See Garthoff (1994b: 14).
12. However, as Garthoff (1994b: 31–2) has highlighted, the 'rollback' of communist-revolutionary states extended to older communist states such as Poland where – in cooperation with the Vatican – the CIA, working through the AFL-CIO and the National Endowment for Democracy, funded a major programme to destabilise the Polish government and support the oppositional Solidarity movement.
13. This policy was associated with Reagan's notorious ambassador to the United Nations, Jeanne Kirkpatrick, and her distinction between 'totalitarian' (i.e. communist) and 'authoritarian' (right-wing/capitalist) regimes, outlined in 'Dictatorships and Double-Standards', *Commentary* 68/5 (November 1979). This helped legitimise US support for a number of brutal regimes, which tortured and murdered thousands of civilians in the name of 'anti-communism', notably in central America, with Guatemala and El Salvador standing out.
14. Some nuclear strategists within the Reagan administration, particularly those close to Reagan's Assistant Secretary of Defense, Richard Perle, also advocated going beyond deterrence to a policy based on 'winning' any nuclear exchange with the USSR. This aggressive (and dangerous) thinking is most clearly stated in Gray and Payne (1980). For a critical discussion, see McMahan (1984: 18–47); Scheer (1982).
15. See Davis (1982).
16. On taking office Reagan was committed to following the twin-track policy agreed by NATO in December which consisted of the future deployment of new intermediate nuclear forces (Pershing II and Cruise) in Western Europe and negotiations with Moscow to reduce or eliminate this class of weapon. Negotiations with the USSR began in November 1981 in Geneva. The US proposed the 'zero-option' – the elimination of all intermediate range missiles. Unsurprisingly, the Soviets rejected this proposal as it would have required them to have dismantled their INF forces in the east (targeting China) and would have also involved a *de facto* act of unilateral disarmament as NATO had not yet deployed its new missiles. Further, Reagan's 'zero-option' made no reference to the nuclear arsenals of Britain and France, which

obviously had a bearing on the nuclear balance in Europe. When NATO did begin the deployment in November 1983, the Soviets walked out of the Geneva talks.

17. For extended discussions, see Halliday (1989: 52–96); Klare and Kornbluh (1989: 2–20).

18. However, the Reagan administration was unable to return the US to its pre-détente use of military power, because of the increased military power of the USSR and, more importantly, the continuing opposition of most of the US population to the deployment of US combat troops overseas. Consequently, the US was forced to use covert means and local agents. As Bodenheimer (1989: 53–79); Mamdani (2004: 63–177); Sklar (1988: 236–42; 251–79); Robinson and Norsworthy (1987: 87–94) have detailed, this led to a policy of lies, deceit, lawbreaking and criminality within the US, and also the US associating with criminals and terrorists in its efforts to harass and attack revolutionary states in southern Africa, south-east Asia, Afghanistan and Central America.

19. This intervention soon turned to humiliation as over 240 US marines were killed by a suicide car-bomb attack on their barracks just outside Beirut in retaliation for a US naval bombardment of pro-Syrian Druze militia forces earlier. Prior to 9/11 this was the single biggest loss of life suffered by the US in a terrorist attack.

20. The other significant use of force – air power rather than combat troops – was the bombing of Libya in April 1986 in retaliation for Libya's alleged involvement in terrorist attacks on US forces in Europe.

21. Robinson (1987: 16). For a more extended discussion, see Molloy (2001).

22. As Klare (1989: 95–6) notes, during the 1980s the US intelligence budget tripled to about $25 billion and CIA personnel increased from 14,000 in 1980 to 19,000 by 1986, which included a tripling of CIA covert operatives from 300 under Carter to over 1,000 under Reagan. See also Bodenheimer (1986).

23. After 1981 money for operations involving US special forces more than tripled, reaching $1.5 billion by 1986, helping to increase the number of US special forces troops by 80 per cent – to just under 35,000 by the end of the decade. By 1988 Special Operations Forces had more than tripled with total FY 1986 funds for special operations at about $1.5 billion. Future Pentagon plans call for spending $7.6 billion in the five years beginning in 1988. See Klare (1989: 82, 102).

24. For a discussion of the problem of maintaining Congressional oversight of CIA covert and special forces operations during the 1980s, see Klare (1989: 95–7).

25. According to Robinson (1987: 337) by 1986 the US was sponsoring approximately 210,000 'Contras' – 150,000 in Afghanistan, 25,000 in Angola, 20,000 in Cambodia and 15,000 in Nicaragua.

26. The notorious (and awful) film *Red Dawn* released in 1984 depicted the US invaded by Soviet forces through Central America, which, when connected with the anti-Sandinista propaganda of the Reagan administration, left little to the (ill-informed) imagination of viewers as to which Central American state the Soviet forces had come from.

27. For discussions of the domestic 'propaganda war' over Nicaragua and the role of the US media and private organisations in support of the Reagan doctrine towards the Sandinistas, see Walker (1985; 1987; 1991; 2003); Kornbluh (1987); Robinson (1987); Sklar (1988).

28. In stark contrast – and exposing the lie of Jeanne Kirkpatrick's arguments concerning the political characteristics of right-wing dictatorships – US allies in the region (Honduras, Guatemala and El Salvador – especially the latter two) had atrocious human rights records based on state and para-state murder and torture of thousands of civilians in the name of anti-communism. The Orwellian nature of US policy, praising these states as 'democratic' and 'defenders of freedom', could not have been clearer. Vilas (1995: 8) calculates that there were over 300,000 deaths, most of which were caused by (pro-US) state and parastate forces, resulting from revolutionary/counter-revolutionary political conflict from the late 1970s to the early 1990s.

29. There is much controversy over the degree and character of Sandinsta support for the FMLN after the Sandinista's seized power. What seems clear, however, amongst most commentators is that the level of support was nowhere near the level the Reagan administration claimed it to be and, further, neither was the level of *matériel* support significant for the military fortunes of the FMLN.

30. Made clear by US Secretary of State George Schultz in March 1986, 'If the Sandinistas "succeed in consolidating their power, *all* the countries in Latin America, who *all* face serious internal economic problems, will see radical forces emboldened to exploit these problems" '. Cited in Kornbluh (1987: 3), original emphasis.

31. See Walker (1985: 447–66; 1991: 247–73, 295–320); Westad (2005: 339–48) for details on Soviet bloc aid. Indeed, Soviet-bloc aid – military and economic – only became significant after US-sponsored *Contra* attacks intensified after 1982.

32. The propaganda war was also very important in deflecting attempts by some members of Congress to limit US intervention in Nicaragua by curtailing Congressional appropriations of funds the administration requested for the *Contras*, as in the case of the Boland–Zabloki amendment of July 1984 which cut off US funds for the *Contras'* covert war. In response to this Congressional activism the Reagan administration developed a network of private, right-wing civil society groups to fund raise for the *Contras*, and also secured the support of its allies – notably Saudi Arabia, Israel, Chile, Taiwan and others – to help plug any funding gap. The most notorious case in this regard was the Iran–*Contra* scandal where the US government used the proceeds of illegal arms sales to Iran to fund the *Contras*. See Sklar (1988: 236–42); Kornbluh (1987: 74).

33. By 1986 the US had provided $130 million in official aid, and in June 1986 Congress authorised another $100 million for the *Contra* war effort. See Walker (1987: 33–4).

34. Kornbluh (1987: 98).

35. In May 1983 the US cut Nicaragua's sugar quota by 90 per cent – depriving it of a major source of hard currency, and, two years later in May 1985, imposed a full economic embargo. See Kornbluh (1987: 95–121) for an extended discussion of the economic dimensions of US counter-revolutionary strategy.

36. From November 1981 the US vetoed all Nicaraguan loan applications to the Inter-American Development Bank and World Bank (Walker, 1985: 434). See Kornbluh (1987: 103–15); Walker (1987: 57–79) for a discussion of US economic aggression towards Nicaragua.

37. According to the World Bank in the last months of the Somoza dictatorship there was $500 million of capital flight from Nicaragua, and with the looting of the central bank, Nicaragua was virtually decapitalised and left close to insolvency, with a foreign debt of $1.6 billion. See Walker (1987: 62).

38. A key element in *Contra* strategy was to destroy health and welfare facilities provided by the Sandinistas, as well as assassinating health and other key workers. See Kornbluh (1987); Robinson (1987); Walker (1987).

39. By 1985 over half of Nicaragua's national budget was going on defence spending. See Walker (2003: 95).

40. Walker (1985: 444).

41. By US fiscal year (FY) 1986 US military assistance to El Salvador, Guatemala, Honduras and Costa Rica had skyrocketed to $233.8 million from a figure of $10 million in FY 1980, with just under two-thirds going to El Salvador and a third going to Honduras. See Robinson (1987: 189); Vilas (1995: 133).

42. Which was made all the more threatening after the US invasion of Grenada in October 1983.

43. The torturing and killing of civilians emulated the even worse human rights records of the US-sponsored counter-insurgencies waged by the governments of El Salvador and Guatemala. See Sklar (1988).

44. According to Walker (1991: 34–5) over 30,000 Nicaraguans (military, civilian and *Contra*) were killed, whilst tens of thousands more were wounded, orphaned or left homeless. Further,

as of 1987, property destruction from *Contra* attacks totalled $221.6 million, whilst the estimated loss of $2.5 billion of development potential.

45. The Contadora (an island off the Panamanian coast) peace process was initiated by Mexico, Columbia, Panama and Venezuela in January 1983. Whilst the Sandinistas had responded favourably to its peace proposals the Reagan administration focused on sabotaging anything that allowed the Sandinistas to remain in power.

46. Domestic economic problems associated with the growing conflict between the Nicaraguan bourgeoisie and the Sandinista government compounded by the war had resulted in declining rates of growth and hyper-inflation (of over 33,000 per cent by 1989) forcing the government to sack thousands of public sector employees – a major social constituency of the Sandinistas. See Walker (2003: 55).

47. This section draws on Saull (2005b: 77–80).

48. The best survey of US involvement in the Afghan conflict remains Cooley (2002).

49. See Yousaf and Adkin (2001) for a Pakistani military perspective on the Afghan war.

50. Soviet concerns about US involvement in Afghanistan were a major factor in the Soviet decision to intervene and remove Amin from power – particularly as some in the Soviet leadership had suspicions that Amin was flirting with the US, yet the key reason was the need to reduce the domestic resistance to the PDPA stoked by Amin's policies. Brzezinki's interview was in *Le Nouvel Observateur*, cited in Cooley (2002); Mamdani (2004: 123–4).

51. Cooley (2002: 10).

52. Halliday (1989: 77).

53. Rashid (2001: 130).

54. The parallel is particularly evident in two aspects. First in the inability of the PDPA, like governments in Saigon, to secure widespread popular support; and secondly, in the friction between the external ally and the local regime. As much as relations between Washington and Saigon were plagued by the obstruction and the refusal of the local ally to follow guidance offered by the superpower ally – inspite of the latter's military and economic dependence on the superpower – so this was the pattern in relations between Moscow and Kabul. See Halliday (1998) for an examination of the communist regime in Afghanistan up until its defeat in 1992.

55. However, it appears that the US decision to supply Stinger missiles in 1986 was decisive in making up Gorbachev's mind about a Soviet withdrawal from Afghanistan. See Crockatt (1995: 362).

56. See Halliday (1999b).

57. This was especially so as both Pakistan and the US reneged on their commitments in the Geneva Agreement of April 1988 with the USSR to end external military involvement in Afghanistan, as they continued to aid the *mujahadeen* after the Soviet withdrawal.

58. Ironically for the US, strongly influenced by the Iranian Revolution.

59. A good anthology of a range of different views is Hogan (1992). Lebow and Risse-Kappen (1995) nicely captures the mainstream debate within IR.

60. See Waltz (1993); Wohlforth (1994); Brooks and Wohlforth (2000) for a representative sample.

61. See Koslowski and Kratochwil (1994); Risse-Kappen (1994); Checkel (1997); Forsberg (2000) for a representative sample.

62. See Pipes (1995). Evidence suggests that with respect to timing when the Reagan arms build-up and intervention in the third world were at their peak, between 1981 and 1985, the USSR continued to maintain its spending levels on military outlays and support for its allies. Only in the later part of the (second) Reagan term, when the earlier hostility had lessened and when defence spending had stabilised did Soviet policy shift. This suggests that the impact of Reagan's policies were far from clear and may have delayed reform rather than accelerated Gorbacher's reform programme. See Halliday (1994); Garthoff (1994b).

63. See Kramer (1999).

64. It was not the missiles and troops that were problematic, as the US had no problems in having good relations with other militarised societies, but rather the fact that these missiles and troops

were central to preserving antagonistic (communist) forms of rule, and permitting the international expansion of such forms of rule through the use of force.

65. See Koslowski and Kratochwil (1994: 228); Checkel (1997).
66. Note the use of lethal force against nationalist demonstrators in the Baltic Republics, Georgia and Azerbaijan during 1989–91 when Gorbachev was not willing to sanction such actions in east-central Europe.
67. With the exception of Romania.
68. See Batt (1991); Brown (1991); Fowkes (1995); Crockatt (1995: 338–68).
69. Fowkes (1995: 174) notes that average growth was between 6 and 7 per cent per annum in the 1950s, falling to 2–3 per cent p.a. in the early 1960s and despite a pick-up afterwards set in for long-term decline after 1975.
70. Dibb (1986: 68–73) highlights that Soviet statistics showed a slowing in Soviet economic performance from an average high of 10 per cent in the 1950s to an average of only 3 per cent by the early 1980s. This combined with declining rates of personal consumption from increases of 5.9 per cent in 1956–60, 5.2 per cent in 1966–70 to 2.7 per cent in 1970–80 and 1981–2. See also Ellman and Kantorrivich (1992: 1–39).
71. Indeed the whole *political* legitimacy of communist centrally planned states rested on the continuation of economic growth rates that sustained improvements in living standards.
72. As noted by Callinicos (1991: 49) '[t]he dilemma confronting the regime is that the changes it attempts are likely to be too radical for many of its own supporters but too moderate for the mass of the population. The resulting paralysis of an internally divided ruling class creates the conditions in which a popular revolution from below can take place.'
73. Harman (1970: 14). See also Kramer (1999b) for a discussion of the role of the coercive apparatus of the Soviet state in earlier internal political struggles.
74. One might argue that this failure reflected the end of the extensive model of industrialisation based on the use of excess economic resources and the failure of reforms to successfully adopt to a more intensive, technologically led, model of industrial development. See Kaser and Radice (1986); Kornai (1982).
75. Fowkes (1995: 174).
76. Dibb (1986: 219–32).
77. This was particularly significant for the USSR. Whilst its oil exports were a major source of hard currency – allowing it to purchase hi-tech goods from the West – particularly after the massive oil price rises in 1973 and 1979, the dramatic fall in oil prices in the 1980s obviously exposed the other, negative side to its international trading position.
78. Fowkes (1995: 175). This foreign debt amounted to over 48 per cent of Poland's GNP. World Bank figures cited in Lane (1996: 65).
79. See Ellman and Kontorrivich (1992: 1–2).
80. Cemented by the increased productive potential of capitalist social relations of production highlighted in the 'third industrial revolution' based upon the use of intensive hi-tech and micro-electronic forms of production and organised increasingly in a transnational manner through the operations of multinational companies. See Callinicos (1991: 21–50); Solomon (1999: 25–50, 76–94).
81. See Lane (1996); Ellman (1992).
82. Nove (1992: 334–93).
83. Indicated by the 1987 reforms permitting private farming and business cooperatives and the January 1988 Enterprise Law which shifted economic decision-making from the central planning ministries to local enterprises. See Ellman (1992: 1–39); Ticktin (1992: 154–81).
84. Indeed, it was resistance from conservative-Brezhnevite forces within the Soviet leadership that probably accounts for the limited nature of Gorbachev's reforms between 1985 and 1987. Things changed in 1988; in May Gorbachev effectively abandoned the Brezhnev Doctrine by announcing at the 19th Party Conference that 'other countries are free to choose their own

social systems', and in September he consolidated his position over the conservatives with Andrei Gromyko's demotion in September. See Fowkes (1995: 171).

85. Ellman (1992: 15–16).

86. Ellman (1992: 19).

87. See Bova (1992: 43–58); Halliday (1989: 97–135).

88. This phrase was coined by Soviet foreign ministry spokesman Gennadi Gerasimov in October 1989 and indicated that Moscow recognised and encouraged different paths to socialism and that it would not use force to uphold communist power as it had done in the past, to the concern of hard-line leaders like Erich Honecker of East Germany, Miloš Jakeš of Czechoslovakia and Todor Zhivkov of Bulgaria.

89. With the coming to power of a non-communist/Solidarity prime minister, Tadeuz Mazowiecki, in Poland in August 1989.

90. The two regimes most likely to use force – East Germany and Czechoslovakia – were undermined from doing so by the opening of the Hungarian border in the summer of 1989 which allowed East Germans to cross to the West, and, in the case of Czechoslovakia, that Poland, Hungary and East Germany had all already made political concessions without resorting to force, leaving it rather isolated.

91. Gorbachev reforms triggered hostility from both conservative (the August 1991 *coup*-plotters) and more liberal forces – those, led by Boris Yeltsin, that defeated the August *coup* attempt – such that his attempt to ensure the continuation of communist rule through some degree of consent and popular mandate could never be realised.

92. Indeed, the immediate backdrop of the August *coup* was the imminent signing of a new 'Union Treaty' which gave substantial autonomy to each of the fifteen republics. See Crockatt (1995: 347).

93. This was most evident in the GDR, where a combination of population movement and the domestic disintegration of local communist rule alongside the emergence of West German political parties in the East saw what was in effect the 'swallowing up' of the GDR within a year by the Federal Republic. See Kopstein (1997).

94. The key ones being the INF Treaty signed in Washington in December 1987, which eliminated intermediate nuclear forces from Europe, and was largely based on Reagan's 'zero-option' (see note 16, above); the Soviet withdrawal from Afghanistan agreed in April 1988 at Geneva; Gorbachev's announcement in his speech to the UN General Assembly in December 1988 of a unilateral reduction in Soviet military power in Europe, amounting to the withdrawal of 10,000 tanks, 8,500 artillery pieces and 800 combat aircraft, and a 500,000 cut in the strength of the Red Army; and the signing of the Strategic Arms Reduction Treaty (START) in July 1991, which saw significant cuts in the strategic nuclear arsenals of the superpowers.

95. The warming of relations at the strategic level was reproduced in negotiations and the signing of a number of agreements after 1987 to try to end – not always successively – regional conflicts involving the superpowers. The key ones concerned Angola, with the signing of an agreement between UNITA and the MPLA government based on the withdrawal of Cuban troops by May 1991; Vietnam's agreement (under pressure from Moscow) to withdraw its troops from Cambodia by September 1989, and the final end of the war in October 1991 after a UN peacekeeping operation; and the brokering of a peace agreement between the FMLN and the Salvadoran government by the UN in the autumn of 1991, after the electoral defeat of the Sandinistas in February 1990.

96. It is estimated that by 1987 Soviet military expenditure was twice as much (13 per cent of GDP) as the US level of spending. See Callinicos (1991: 44); and details available at http://www.globalsecurity.org/military/world/russia/mo-budget.htm.

97. As mentioned above, the degree to which Reagan could maintain the same high levels of military expenditure of his first term was open to dispute with Congressional concerns about the growing budget deficit. Further, the US public were committed to pursuing arms control

agreements and negotiating from a 'position of strength' so that the Reagan administration was much more favourable to negotiating agreements than in the early 1980s.

98. Indeed, some members of the Reagan and Bush administrations (from January 1989) continued to be suspicious of Soviet intentions, and hence were cautious about making agreements with the USSR if those agreements helped bolster communist rule. It was only after the effective collapse of communist power in east-central Europe during 1989 that the US became much more enthused about reaching an agreement. See Crockatt (1995: 363).

99. See Callinicos (1991); Blackburn (1991); Halliday (1999a); Saull (2002) for discussions of the international consequences of the defeat of communist revolution.

100. On this, see Hough (1985); Valkenier (1983).

101. See Callinicos (1991).

102. Thus, whilst Stalin was notorious for subordinating foreign policy and the international communist movement to the domestic interests of the regime, Khrushchev was willing to take risks in support of international revolution, whilst Brezhnev took advantage of the geopolitical context of the 1970s to advance Soviet influence beyond Eurasia in an unprecedented fashion.

103. Gorbachev laid much more stress on universal human interests than interests associated with class and recognised that in a world of nuclear weapons there 'had to be an objective limit to "class confrontation in the international arena." ' See Gorbachev (1988: 137; 146–7).

104. The first case concerned the Hungarian Soviet Republic between March and August 1919. Other cases where revolutionary states were overthrown, in part because of the lack of Soviet support in the face of externally assisted counter-revolution were Spain between 1936 and 1939; Guatemala in 1954, Congo in 1960, Chile in 1973, and Grenada in 1983.

105. The most significant being the defeat of any prospects of communist advance in Western Europe between 1945 and 1948 (and later in southern Europe with the transformation of the right-wing authoritarian dictatorships to liberal democracy during the late 1970s); the destruction of the PKI in Indonesia between 1965 and 1968; the overthrow of the Allende government in Chile in 1973, among others in Asia, Africa and the Americas.

7 CONCLUSIONS: TRACING THE PARADOXICAL ENDS OF THE COLD WAR AND THE ORIGINS OF CONTEMPORARY CONFLICT IN WORLD POLITICS[1]

1. Parts of this chapter draw heavily from Saull (2005b).

2. The US used military power against the following states: the Noriega regime in Panama (1989), the Ba'athist regime in Iraq (1991 and after), Somalia (1992), Haiti (1994), and against Yugoslavian (Serbian) forces in Bosnia (1995) and Kosovo (1999). In most of these cases the use of force was justified in terms of upholding human rights, yet they were also highly controversial – in part because of such normative considerations undermined the non-intervention norm – and in light of the absence of unambiguous legal sanction from the UN Security Council. The main point, however, was that the US and its allies were able to use force in a highly contested way, because there was no state powerful enough to prevent the US from doing so.

3. Primarily associated with Fukuyama's (1993) 'end of history' thesis. See also Friedman (2000).

4. Structural adjustment policies emerged in the context of the third world debt crisis in the 1980s based upon countries agreeing to implement major macro-economic reform in return for IMF credits and support in response to the debt crisis. The (dogmatic) neoliberal formula that the IMF and World Bank proscribed rested on the key assumption that the long-term economic health of countries in such economic difficulties required them to reduce state involvement in the economy thus promoting private-capitalist economic activity and also opening up

formerly sheltered economies to the world market. The key policies prescribed to achieve these ends were: raising interest rates (to curb inflation and attract (foreign) capital inflows); privatising public assets (to secure foreign investment and reducing the public sector in the economy); reducing trade barriers; and cutting public spending. These policies formed the 'Washington Consensus' and became the template for macro-economic policy across the world during the 1990s, not just in the south. For a critical survey of neoliberal economic doctrine, see Saad-Filho and Johnston (2005).

5. These constituents of the New World Order were supplemented by the ending of regional conflicts in the early 1990s in the improved international climate caused by the end of the Cold War. Thus, the political situation in a number of countries has improved through the 1990s, in part caused by the localised impacts of the end of the superpower conflict, as in Cambodia, northern Ireland, southern Africa and central America. For a discussion of the impact of the end of the Cold War on conflicts in the South see Ayoob (1995).

6. See Whitehouse (2002).

7. Whilst the Cold War could be considered a global conflict after 1945 within which other political developments and conflicts were filtered, post-Cold War international relations – ironically, when the idea of globalisation suggests uniformity and homogeneity – have been characterised by much greater unevenness, variation and fragmentation. Consequently, the rise of Islamist terrorism is not a global phenomenon in the way in which the Cold War was. Rather, it is largely a regional trend associated with Islamic societies and those other societies that have significant Muslim minorities and/or immigrant populations. The rise of Islamist terrorism is but one major factor that defines post-Cold War international relations that also includes China's integration into the capitalist world economy, European integration, and expansion and the expansion of international human rights norms. The significance of political Islam as a form of political resistance and terrorism, however, is that it's social, political and ideological character is comparable to political-ideological developments in other parts of the world also associated with the end of the Cold War and the impact of neoliberal globalisation, which I will discuss in a moment.

8. See note 3 for references. See also Bobbitt (2002).

9. In particular see Hirst and Thompson (1999).

10. See Saad-Filho and Johnston (2005); Harvey (2005a) on this.

11. The key Realist commentators on the post-Cold War international order are Mearsheimer (2001); Walt, (2002; 2005). See also Bacevich (2002).

12. Huntington (1996).

13. The best representative of this view is Gowan (1999; 2002; 2005). See also Arrighi (2005); Callinicos (2003); Harvey (2005b).

14. See Bromley (2005); Panitch and Gindin (2003); Colás and Saull (2005).

15. An excellent survey is provided by Leys and Panitch (2002). See also Rupert (2000).

16. See the editorial 'Vichy of the Tigris', *New Left Review*, II, no. 28 (July–August 2004) and the positions of the Respect party leader, George Galloway.

17. And, with the end of the binary ideological division the promotion of ideological fragmentation and the emergence of new individual and group political identities.

18. In Egypt after 1962 all university graduates were guaranteed a job in the public service upon graduation. See Yapp (1991: 215). The end of this provision is not coincidental with the rise of militant Islam.

19. Most evident in those former supporters of the PCF in France who have voted for the Front National during the 1990s. See Simmons (1996).

20. Most recently highlighted by the electoral successes of the Muslim Brotherhood in Egypt and Hamas in Palestine.

21. In this regard the claim by advocates of the War on Terror and the interventions in Afghanistan and Iraq are justified because Islamist terrorists want to destroy 'our' civilisation seems highly

dubious. It seems clear, based on the pronouncements of al-Qaeda and the targets attacked, that the primary objective of Islamists political movements and their terrorist offshoots is not the destruction of 'western civilisation' but the expulsion of the dominant western presence, made all the more problematic by these two interventions and continued support for Israel.

22. See Mamdani (2004: 63–177).

23. Mamdani (2004: 63–118), highlights the impact of the US defeat in south-east Asia manifested in the fusing of terrorist and criminal elements organised by sections of the US national security state apparatus who co-ordinated covert and illegal anti-leftist activities outside of congressional and democratic oversight.

24. See Halliday (1989); Klare and Kornbluh (1989).

25. The other notable examples of radical and revolutionary change in the region in the post-war period that overthrew the power of traditional social and political forces were: Iraq (1958); Algeria (1954–62); Syria (1954 and 1966); Yemen (1962); Libya (1968); and Iran (1979). Many other countries within the region went through periods of political instability involving radical social and political forces such as Lebanon and Jordan in 1958.

26. See Hiro (2002: 144).

27. There were a number of Saudi initiatives throughout the 1960s to counter the pervasive influence of Nasser's pan-Arab socialism. In 1969 a Saudi initiative established the first official pan-Islamic organisation of inter-governmental co-operation amongst Muslim states, the Organisation of Islamic Conference. See Hiro (1988: 145); Esposito (2002: 106–7).

28. The importance of Saudi Arabia as a regional ally of the US went beyond its virulent anti-communism as Saudi Arabia was also hostile to Shia Iran. Indeed, after 1979 Iranian Revolution Saudi Arabia saw its support for anti-Shi'ite forces in Afghanistan, as a way of undermining Iran's claim to leadership of the Islamic world. See Talhami (2003: 119). The Saudi's also provided a great deal of financial support to Iraq, a secular state, in its war with Iran between 1981 and 1988.

29. Saudi funding for such bodies as the World Islamic League based in Mecca has also seen the spread of Wahhabite doctrine and practice to mosques in Europe and the US. See Ruthven (2002: 176–7).

30. Prior to the Yom Kippur War Sadat had expelled Soviet military advisers in 1972, upon which Egypt's military planning and defence had been heavily dependent. One reason suggested to explain this was that Sadat's decision was meant as a signal to the US of Egypt's openness to US influence. When the US did not respond by pressuring Israel to the negotiating table, Sadat, cynically turned to Moscow again for arms, and then finally ended the 'alliance' in 1974 after securing his diplomatic objectives. See Al-Sayyid Marsot (1985: 133–4).

31. See Esposito (2002: 83–4).

32. Hiro (1988).

33. See Heikal (1983: 140–7, 220).

34. This was known as *intifah* or opening. It rested on encouraging foreign investment and ending the state's dominance over the economy through tax-breaks and other instruments to promote domestic private capital accumulation.

35. In this respect the international impact of the Iranian Revolution was also significant, as Iran contributed to a move away from radical nationalism in the region to that of a pro-Iranian Islamist anti-imperialism.

36. Cooley (2002); Mamdani (2004); Talhami (2003); Heikal (1983).

37. Again highlighted by the role of the Iranian Revolution in ending the Cold War in the Middle East. Thus, whilst the US was able to marshal, fund, train, arm and provide diplomatic and ideological cover for Islamist forces as 'freedom fighters' through its local allies against the USSR during the 1980s, it also had to contend with Iranian-inspired Islamists committed to challenging US influence in the region.

38. Indeed one of the earliest post-war crisis that put Washington and Moscow at loggerheads involved Iran in 1945–46. See chapter 3.

39. For Halliday (2002: 37) it was the actions of specific factions within the Afghan PDPA that were largely to blame for provoking this resistance.

40. In this respect whilst Saudi Arabia, arguably, could be seen as holding primary responsibility for promoting reactionary Islam in the Middle East, Pakistan carries a great deal of responsibility for the rise of reactionary Islamist forces in south Asia – notably with regard to the Islamist dimension of anti-Indian Kashmiri 'nationalist' forces – and central Asia.

41. See Esposito (2002: 109).

42. Most commentators stress that Bhutto and Pakistan's support for Islamist rather than nationalist guerrillas in the early 1970s, and later after the Soviet intervention was largely down to concerns about stability and the need to contain any secessionist tendencies from the Pashtuns who not only lived in large numbers in the North-West Frontier Province that bordered Afghanistan, but were also the largest ethnic group within Afghanistan and from which there were political tendencies that did not recognise the Pakistani border. See Griffin (2001: 17–32); Talhami (2002: 120–1).

43. The reactionary orientation of the politics that emerged within this social milieu was not only a product of the reactionary Wahhabi and Deobandi interpretations of Islam that gained widespread appeal through the madrassas, but was also due to the pervasive influence of personal identities based upon tribal loyalties. The issue of tribal loyalty was key in the fragmentation of the Islamic resistance to the Red Army and the subsequent civil war and provided an important ingredient in the reactionary political cocktail that characterised most of the groups within the Afghan *mujahadeen* during and after the war against the Soviets.

44. By the time of Zia's death in 1988 the number of madrassas had increased to approximately 8,000 with over 25,000 unregistered ones educating tens of thousands of students. See Rashid (2000: 89).

45. See Ali (2002: 189–95) Rashid (2000: 82–94); Weinbaum (1994: 29–52); Burke (2004).

46. See Rashid (2001: 18).

47. Rashid (2001: 130); Griffin (2001: 128–40).

48. The consequences of the Suharto *coup* led to the most tragic case in the history of the international communist movement after the Second World War as the right-wing military junta launched a vicious and brutal campaign of torture and mass murder leading to the deaths of approximately 300,000 Indonesian leftists, many of whom were ethnic Chinese. A similar pogrom was launched in Chile and Argentina during the 1970s as part of Washington-backed 'Dirty War' against the left and resulted in the torture and murder of tens of thousands of leftists. Documentary evidence indicates that both the British and US governments were not only aware of the *coup* plot against Sukarno, but also assisted right-wing forces in their murderous campaign against the left. See Easter (2005); The National Security Archive, (2001).

49. Hefner (2000: 107–9).

50. Vatikiatis (1993: 128).

51. Between August 1997 and February 1998 the Indonesian currency lost 70 per cent of its value vis-à-vis the dollar provoking a debt crisis, which caused factories to close and the shedding of jobs all of which contributed to the ballooning of the levels of poverty from 14 per cent to over 40 per cent of the population. See Hefner (2000: 198).

52. Hefner (1999: 43).

53. It is important to note that the influence of Islamic-inspired political movements in Indonesia in the 1990s went beyond the reactionary and violent strands of Islam to include a number of mass-based movements, notably the United Development Party which sought to promote a distinctly Indonesian brand of Islam far removed from Wahhabite interpretations and officially committed to some form of parliamentary democracy. Furthermore, the mobilisation of moderate Muslims played a key role in the toppling of Suharto in 1998. See Hefner (2000).

54. Including Amien Rais of the *Muhammadiyah* (Followers of Muhammad) and Abdullah Wahid of the *Nahalatul Ulama*, as well as the many thousands of Muslims who supported Megawati's Indonesian Democratic Party.

55. Such tendencies not only played a role in trying to split the anti-Suharto democracy movement, they were also important as the 'foot soldiers' in the pogroms against non-Muslims in
the Moluccas islands of the archipelago and in the anti-Christian militias in East Timor. See
Abuza (2003).
56. Both were also sponsored and funded by Saudi-based charities and groups. See Davis (2002).
57. See Hefner (1999, 2000); Davis (2002). The blaming of outside forces of course focused on
an internal element as well, and conformed to a classic 'Hitlerite' conspiracy formula of blaming local communists and left-wing forces *in alliance with* international Jewry and finance
capital aimed at the destruction of Indonesia's Muslim way of life.
58. See Davis (2002); Abuza (2003).
59. See Abuza (2003).

Select Bibliography

Abuza, Z. *Militant Islam in Southeast Asia* (Boulder, CO: Lynne Rienner, 2003).

Agnew, J. *Hegemony: The New Shape of Global Power* (Philadelphia: Temple University Press, 2005).

Ali, T. *Clash of Fundamentalisms* (London: Verso, 2002).

Alperovitz, G. *Atomic Diplomacy: Hiroshima to Potsdam* (London: Secker & Warburg, 1966).

Al-Sayyid Marsot, A. *A Short History of Modern Egypt* (Cambridge: Cambridge University Press, 1985).

Anderson, J. L. *Che Guevara: A Revolutionary Life* (New York: Grove Press, 1997).

Anderson, P. 'Trotsky's Interpretation of Stalinism', *New Left Review*, 139 (1983).

Armstrong, P. et al. *Capitalism since 1945*, second edition (Oxford: Basil Blackwell, 1991).

Arrighi, G. 'Hegemony Unravelling Part I', *New Left Review, II*, 32 (March–April 2005).

Ayoob, M. *The Third World Security Predicament: State Making, Regional Conflict and the International System* (Boulder, CO: Lynne Rienner, 1995).

Bacevich, A. *American Empire: The Realities and Consequences of US Diplomacy* (Cambridge, MA: Harvard University Press, 2002).

Bajanov, E. 'Assessing the Politics of the Korean War, 1949–51', *Cold War International History Project Bulletin*, 6–7 (Washington DC: Woodrow Wilson International Center for Scholars, Winter 1995–96), http://wwics.si.edu/index.cfm?topic_id=1409&fuseaction=library.document&id=71

Bakhash, S. *The Reign of the Ayatollahs: Iran and the Islamic Revolution* (New York: Basic Books, 1984).

Batt, J. *East Central Europe from Reform to Transformation* (London: RIIA, 1991).

Behrooz, M. *Rebels with a Cause: The Failure of the Left in Iran* (London: I. B. Tauris, 1999).

Bekes, C. 'The Hungarian Revolution and World Politics', *Cold War International History Working Paper*, 16 (Washington DC: Woodrow Wilson International Center for Scholars, 1996) http://www.wilsoncenter.org/index.cfm?topic_id=1409&fuseaction=topics.publications&group_id=11901

Bender, L. *The Politics of Hostility: Castro's Revolution and United States Policy* (Hato Rey, Puerto Rico: Inter American University Press, 1975).

Bethell, L. and Roxborough, I. (eds.) *Latin America between the Second World War and the Cold War, 1944–48* (Cambridge: Cambridge University Press, 1992).

Bettelheim, C. *Class Struggles in the USSR, Second Period: 1923–1930* (Hassocks: Harvester Press, 1978).

Bianco, L. *The Origins of the Chinese Revolution, 1915–1949* (Stanford, CA: Stanford University Press, 1971).

Bill, J. *The Eagle and the Lion: The Tragedy of American–Iranian Relations* (New Haven, CT: Yale University Press, 1988).

Blackburn, R. 'Prologue to the Cuban Revolution', *New Left Review*, 21 (October 1963).

Blackburn, R. 'The Test in Portugal', *New Left Review*, 87–88 (September–December 1974).

Blackburn, R. 'Class Forces in the Cuban Revolution: A Reply to Binns and Gonzalez', *International Socialism*, 2/9 (1980).

Blackburn, R. (ed.) *After the Fall: The Failure of Communism and the Future of Socialism* (London: Verso, 1991).

Blasier, C. *Hovering Giant: US Responses to Revolutionary Change in Latin America* (Pittsburgh: University of Pittsburgh Press, 1976).

Block, F. *The Origins of the International Economic Disorder: A Study of United States International Monetary Policy from World War II to the Present* (Berkeley, CA: University of California Press, 1977).

Bobbitt, P. *Shield of Achilles: War, Peace and the Course of History* (London: Allen Lane, 2002).

Bodenheimer, T. and Gould, R. *Rollback! Right Wing Power in US Foreign Policy* (Boston, MA: South End Press, 1989).

Borer, D. *Superpowers Defeated: Vietnam and Afghanistan Compared* (London: Frank Cass, 1999).

Borkenau, F. *World Communism: A History of the Communist International* (Ann Arbor, MI: University of Michigan Press, 1962).

Bova, R. 'The Soviet Economy and International Politics', in Ellman, M. and Kontorovich, V. (eds.) *The Disintegration of the Soviet Economic System* (London: Routledge, 1992).

Bowker, M. and Williams, P. *Superpower Détente: A Reappraisal* (London: Sage Publications/ RIIA, 1988).

Brenner, P. and Blight, J. 'Cuba 1962. The Crisis and Cuban–Soviet Relations: Fidel Castro's 1968 Speech', *Cold War International History Project Bulletin*, 5 (Washington DC: Woodrow Wilson International Center for Scholars, Spring 1995), http://www.wilsoncenter.org/ index.cfm?topic_id= 1409&fuseaction=topics.publications&group_id=15142

Brenner, R. 'The Economics of Global Turbulence: A Special Report on the World Economy, 1950–98', *New Left Review*, 229 (May–June 1998).

Brett, E. A. *The World Economy since the War: The Politics of Uneven Development* (Basingstoke: Macmillan, 1985).

Bromley, S. 'The Logic of American Power in the International Capitalist Order', in Colás, A. and Saull, R. G. (eds.) *The War on Terror and the American Empire after the Cold War* (London: Routledge, 2005).

Brooks, S. and Wohlforth, W. 'Power, Globalization, and the End of the Cold War: Reevaluating a Landmark Case for Ideas', *International Security*, 25/3 (2000).

Brown, J. F. *Surge to Freedom: The End of Communist Rule in Eastern Europe* (Twickenham: Adamanite Press, 1991).

Burke, J. *Al-Qaeda: The True Story of Radical Islam* (Harmondsworth: Penguin Books, 2004).

Caballero, M. *Latin America and the Comintern 1919–1943* (Cambridge: Cambridge University Press, 1986).

Calleo, D. *The Imperious Economy* (Cambridge, MA: Harvard University Press, 1982).

Callinicos, A. *The Revenge of History: Marxism and the East European Revolutions* (Cambridge: Polity, 1991).

Callinicos, A. *The New Mandarins of American Power* (Cambridge: Polity, 2003).

Campbell, D. *Writing Security: United States Foreign Policy and the Politics of Identity* (Manchester: Manchester University Press, 1998).

Carew, A. *Labour Under the Marshall Plan: The Politics of Productivity and the Marketing of Management Science* (Manchester: Manchester University Press, 1987).

Carr, E. H. *The Russian Revolution: From Lenin to Stalin (1917–1929)* (Basingstoke: Macmillan, 1979).

Chassin, L. *The Communist Conquest of China: A History of the Civil War 1945–49* (London: Weidenfeld & Nicolson, 1965).

Checkel, J. *Ideas and Political Change: Soviet/Russian Behaviour and the End of the Cold War* (New Haven, CT: Yale University Press, 1997).

Chernyaev, A. *My Six Years with Gorbachev*, trans. and ed. R. English and E. Tucker (University Park, PA: Pennsylvania State University Press, 2000).

Claudin, F. *The Communist International: From Comintern to Cominform* (Harmondsworth: Penguin Books, 1975).

Cliff, T. *State Capitalism in Russia Today* (London: Bookmarks, 1988).

Colás, A. and Saull, R. G. (eds.) *The War on Terror and the American 'Empire' after the Cold War* (London: Routledge, 2005).

Colls, S. *Ghost Wars: The Secret History of the CIA, Afghanistan, and Bin Laden, from the Soviet Invasion to September 11, 2001* (Harmondsworth: Penguin Books, 2004).

Conquest, R. *The Harvest of Sorrow: Soviet Collectivization and the Terror-Famine* (London: Pimlico, 1986).

Conquest, R. *The Great Terror: A Reassessment* (London: Pimlico, 1992).

Cooley, J. *Unholy Wars: Afghanistan, America and International Terrorism* (London: Pluto Press, 2002).

Corrigan, P. et al. *Socialist Construction and Marxist Theory: Bolshevism and its Critique* (London: Macmillan, 1978).

Cox, M. 'Western Capitalism and the Cold War System', in M. Shaw (ed.) *War, State and Society*. (London: Macmillan, 1984).

Cox, M. 'The Cold War in the Age of Capitalist Decline', *Critique*, 17 (1986).

Cox, M. 'The Revolutionary Betrayed: The New Left Review and Leon Trotsky', in M. Cox and H. Ticktin (eds.) *The Ideas of Leon Trotsky* (London: Porcupine Press, 1995).

Cox, R. *Production, Power, and World Order: Social Forces in the Making of History* (New York: Columbia University Press, 1987).

Crockatt, R. *The Fifty Years War: The United States and the Soviet Union in World Politics, 1941–1991* (London: Routledge, 1995).

Crozier, M. et al. *The Crisis of Democracy: Report on the Governability of Democracies to the Trilateral Commission* (New York: New York University Press, 1975).

Cumings, B. *The Origins of the Korean War*, 2 vols. (Princeton, NJ: Princeton University Press, 1981 and 1990).

Davies, N. *White Eagle, Red Star: The Polish–Soviet War, 1919–20* (London: Macdonald, 1972).

Davies, R. W. et al. (eds.) *The Economic Transformation of the USSR, 1913–1945* (Cambridge: Cambridge University Press, 1994).

Davis, M. 'Nuclear Imperialism and Extended Deterrence', in New Left Review (ed.) *Exterminism and Cold War* (London: New Left Books, 1982).

Davis, M. 'The Political Economy of Late Imperial America', *New Left Review*, 143 (January–February 1984).

Davis, M. 'Laskar Jihad and the Political Position of Conservative Islam in Indonesia', *Contemporary Southeast Asia*, 24/1 (2002).

Debray, R. *Revolution in the Revolution? Armed Struggle and Political Struggle in Latin America* (London: Monthly Review Press, 1967).

DePorte, A. *Europe between the Superpowers: The Enduring Balance* (New Haven, CT: Yale University Press, 1986).

Dergas, J. *Soviet Documents on Foreign Policy*, Vol. I (New York: Octagon Books, 1978).

Deutscher, I. *The Great Contest: Russia and the West* (London: Oxford University Press, 1960).

Deutscher, I. *Ironies of History: Essays on Contemporary Communism* (London: Oxford University Press, 1966a).

Deutscher, I. *Stalin: A Political Biography* (Harmondsworth: Penguin Books, 1966b).

Deutscher, I. *The Unfinished Revolution, Russia 1917–1967* (London: Oxford University Press, 1967).

Deutscher, I. *Russia, China, and the West*, ed. Fred Halliday (Harmondsworth: Penguin Books, 1970).

Deutscher, I. *Marxism, Wars and Revolutions: Essays from Four Decades*, ed. and intro. Tamara Deutscher (London: Verso, 1984).

Dibb, P. *The Soviet Union: Incomplete Superpower* (Basingstoke: Macmillan, 1986).

Djilas, M. *Conversations with Stalin* (New York: Harcourt, Brace & World, 1962).

Duiker, W. 'The Red Soviets of Nghe Tinh: An Early Communist Rebellion in Vietnam', *Journal of Southeast Asian Studies*, 4/2 (September 1973).

Duiker, W. *The Communist Road to Power in Vietnam* (Boulder, CO: Westview Press, 1996).

Duncan, W.R. *The Soviet Union and Cuba: Interests and Influence* (New York: Praeger, 1985).

Easter, D. 'Keeping the Indonesian Pot Boiling: Western Covert Intervention in Indonesia, October 1965–March 1966,' *Cold War History*, 5/1 (February 2005).

Ellman, M. and Kontorrivich, V. (eds.) *The Disintegration of the Soviet Economic System* (London: Routledge, 1992).

Esposito, J. (ed.) *The Iranian Revolution: Its Global Impact* (Miami, FL: Florida International University Press, 1990).

Esposito, J. *Unholy War: Terror in the Name of Islam* (Oxford: Oxford University Press, 2002).

Farber, S. *Revolution and Reaction in Cuba, 1933–1960: A Political Sociology from Machado to Castro* (Middletown, CT: Weslyan University Press, 1976).

Feis, H. *Churchill, Roosevelt, Stalin: The War They Waged and the Peace They Sought* [1957] (Princeton, NJ: Princeton University Press, 1967).

Feis, H. *From Trust to Terror: The Onset of the Cold War, 1945–1950* (London: Blond, 1970).

Filippelli, R. *American Labor and Postwar Italy, 1943–1953: A Study of Cold War Politics* (Stanford, CA: Stanford University Press, 1989).

Forsberg, T. 'Power, Interests, and Trust: Explaining Gorbachev's Choices at the End of the Cold War', *Review of International Studies*, 25/4 (2000).

Fowkes, B. *The Rise and Fall of Communism in Eastern Europe* (Basingstoke: Macmillan, 1995).

Friedman, T. *The Lexus and the Olive Tree* (New York: HarperCollins, 2000).

Fukuyama, F. *The End of History and the Last Man* (Harmondsworth: Penguin Books, 1993).

Gaddis, J. Lewis. *The Long Peace: Enquiries into the History of the Cold War* (New York: Oxford University Press, 1987).

Gaddis, J. Lewis *The United States and the End of the Cold War: Implications, Reconsiderations, Provocations* (New York: Oxford University Press, 1992).

Gaddis, J. Lewis. *We Now Know: Rethinking Cold War History* (Oxford: Clarendon Press, 1997).

Gaiduk, I. 'The Vietnam War and Soviet-American Relations, 1964–73: New Evidence', *Cold War International History Project Bulletin*, 6–7 (Washington DC: Woodrow Wilson International Center for Scholars, winter 1995–96), http://www.wilsoncenter.org/index.cfm?topic_id=1409&fuseaction=topics.publications&group_id=15127

Gaiduk, I. 'Developing an Alliance: The Soviet Union and Vietnam, 1954–75', in P. Lowe (ed.) *The Vietnam War* (Basingstoke: Macmillan, 1998).

García-Marquéz, G. 'Operation Carlota', *New Left Review*, 101–2 (January–April 1977).

Gardner, L. *Imperial America: American Foreign Policy since 1898* (New York: Harcourt Brace Jovanovich, 1976).

Garthoff, R. *Détente and Confrontation: American–Soviet Relations from Nixon to Reagan*, revised edition (Washington DC, The Brookings Institution, 1994a).

Garthoff, R. *The Great Transition: American–Soviet Relations and the End of the Cold War* (Washington DC: The Brookings Institution, 1994b).

Gidwitz, B. 'Labour Unrest in the Soviet Union', *Problems of Communism*, XXXI/6 (November–December 1982).

Gindin, S. and Panitch, L. 'The Unique American Empire', in Colás, A. and Saull, R. G. (eds.) *The War on Terror and the American 'Empire' After the Cold War* (London: Routledge, 2005).

Gleijeses, P. *Conflicting Missions: Havana, Washington, and Africa, 1959–1976* (Chapel Hill, NC: University of North Carolina Press, 2002).

Gluchowski, L. 'Poland 1956: Khrushchev, Gomulka and the "Polish October" ', *Cold War International History Project Bulletin*, 5 (Washington DC: Woodrow Wilson International Center for Scholars, Spring 1995), http://www.wilsoncenter.org/index.cfm?topic_id=1409&fuseaction=topics.publications&group_id=15142.

Goncharov, S. et al. *Uncertain Partners: Stalin, Mao and the Korean War* (Stanford, CA: Stanford University Press, 1993).

Goodman, A. *Lost Peace: America's Search for a Negotiated Settlement* (Stanford, CA: Hoover Institute, 1978).

Gorbachev, M. *Perestroika: New Thinking for Our Country and the World* (London: Collins, 1988).

Gott, R. 'Che Guevera and the Congo', *New Left Review*, 220 (November–December 1996).

Gowan, P. *Global Gamble: Washington's Faustian Bid for World Dominance* (London: Verso, 1999).

Gowan, P. 'The American Campaign for Global Sovereignty', in Leys, C. and Panitch, L. (eds.) *Socialist Register 2003: Fighting Identities. Race, Religion and Ethno-Nationalism* (London: Merlin, 2002).

Gowan, P. 'The Bush Turn and the Drive for Primacy', in Colás, A. and Saull, R. G. (eds.) *The War on Terror and the American Empire After the Cold War* (London: Routledge, 2005).

Gray, C. and Payne, K. 'Victory is Possible', *Foreign Policy*, 39 (Summer 1980).

Grenville, J. and Wasserstein, B. (eds.) *The Major International Treaties since 1945: A History and Guide with Texts* (London: Methuen, 1987).

Gribkov, A. and Smith, W. *Operation Anadyr: US and Soviet Generals Recount the Cuban Missile Crisis* (Chicago: Edition Q, 1994).

Griffin, M. *Reaping the Whirlwind: The Taliban Movement in Afghanistan* (London: Pluto Press, 2001).

Halliday, F. 'War and Revolution in Afghanistan', *New Left Review*, 119 (January–February 1980a).

Halliday, F. 'The Iranian Revolution in International Affairs: Programme and Practice', *Millennium: Journal of International Studies*, 9/2 (Autumn 1980b).

Halliday, F. *Threat from the East? Soviet Policy from Afghanistan and Iran to the Horn of Africa* (Harmondsworth: Penguin Books, 1981).

Halliday, F. 'Sources of the New Cold War', in New Left Review (ed.) *Exterminism and Cold War* (London: Verso/NLB, 1982).

Halliday, F. *The Making of the Second Cold War* (London: Verso, 1986).

Halliday, F. 'The Iranian Revolution: Uneven Development and Religious Populism', in Halliday, F. and Alavi, H. (eds.) *State and Ideology in the Middle East and Pakistan* (Basingstoke: Macmillan, 1988).

Halliday, F. *From Kabul to Managua: Soviet–American Relations in the 1980s* (New York: Pantheon Books, 1989).

Halliday, F. *Rethinking International Relations* (Basingstoke: Macmillan, 1994).

Halliday, F. *Islam and the Myth of Confrontation: Religion and Politics in the Middle East* (London: I. B. Tauris, 1996).

Halliday, F. *Revolution and World Politics: The Rise and Fall of the Sixth Great Power* (Basingstoke: Macmillan, 1999a).

Halliday, F. 'Soviet Foreign Policymaking and the Afghanistan War: From "Second Mongolia" to "Bleeding Wound" ', *Review of International Studies,* 25/4 (October 1999b).

Halliday, F. *Two Hours That Shook the World* (London: Saqi Books, 2002).

Halliday, F. and Molyneux, M. *The Ethiopian Revolution* (London: New Left Books, 1981).

Halliday, F. and Tannin, Z. 'The Communist Regime in Afghanistan 1978–1992: Institutions and Conflicts', *Europe–Asia Studies*, 50/8 (1998).

Harman, C. 'Prospects for the Seventies: The Stalinist States', *International Socialism*, 42 (1970).

Harman, C. *Class Struggles in Eastern Europe, 1945–83* (London: Bookmarks, 1988).

Harris, R. and Vilas, C. (eds.) *Nicaragua: A Revolution under Siege* (London: Zed Books, 1985).

Harvey, D. *A Brief History of Neoliberalism* (Oxford: Oxford University Press, 2005a).

Harvey, D. *The New Imperialism* (Oxford: Oxford University Press, 2005b).

Hefner, R. 'Islam and Nation in the Post-Suharto Era', in A. Schwarz and J. Paris (eds.) *The Politics of Post-Suharto Indonesia* (New York: Council on Foreign Relations, 1999).

Hefner, R. *Civil Islam: Muslims and Democratization in Indonesia* (Princeton, NJ: Princeton University Press, 2000).

Heikal, M. *The Reign of the Ayatollah: The Iranian Revolution from Mossadeq to Khomeini* (London: André Deutsch, 1981).

Heikal, M. *Autumn of Fury* (London: André Deutsch, 1983).

Helleiner, E. *States and the Reemergence of Global Finance: From Bretton Woods to the 1990s* (Ithaca, NY: Cornell University Press, 1994).

Hiro, D. *Iran Under the Ayatollahs* (London: Routledge & Kegan Paul, 1985).

Hiro, D. *Islamic Fundamentalism* (London: Paladin Books, 1988).

Hiro, D. *War Without End* (London: Routledge, 2002).

Hirst, P. and Thompson, G. *Globalization in Question: The International Economy and the Possibility of Governance*, second edition (Cambridge: Polity, 1999).

Hobsbawm, E. *Age of Extremes: The Short Twentieth Century 1914–1991* (London: Michael Joseph, 1994).

Hogan, M. *The Marshall Plan: America, Britain and the Reconstruction of Western Europe, 1947–1952* (Cambridge: Cambridge University Press, 1987).

Hogan, M. (ed.) *The End of the Cold War: Its Meaning and Implications* (Cambridge: Cambridge University Press, 1992).

Holloway, D. *The Soviet Union and the Arms Race* (New Haven, CT: Yale University Press, 1984).

Horowitz, D. *From Yalta to Vietnam: American Foreign Policy in the Cold War* (Harmondsworth: Penguin Books, 1967).

Horowitz, D. *Imperialism and Revolution* (London: Allen Lane, 1969).

Hough, J. *The Struggle for the Third World: Soviet Debates and American Options* (Washington DC: The Brookings Institution, 1985).

Hudson, M. *Superimperialism: The Origin and Fundamentals of US World Dominance*, second edition (London: Pluto Books, 2003).

Hunt, M. and Levine, S. 'Revolutionary Movements in Asia and the Cold War', in Leffler, M. and Painter, D. (eds.) *Origins of the Cold War: An International History* (London: Routledge, 1994).

Huntington, S. *The Clash of Civilizations and the Remaking of World Order* (New York: Simon & Schuster, 1996).

Iatrides, J. 'Revolution of Self-Defense? Communist Goals, Strategy and Tactics in the Greek Civil War', *Journal of Cold War Studies*, 7/3 (Summer 2005).

Iriye, A. *The Cold War in Asia: A Historical Introduction* (Englewood, NJ: Prentice-Hall, 1974).

Jian, C. 'The Sino-Soviet Alliance and China's Entry into the Korean War', *Cold War International History Project Working Paper*, 1 (Washington DC: Woodrow Wilson International Center for Scholars, 1992), http://wwics.si.edu/index.cfm?topic_id=1409&fuseaction=library.document&id=468

Jian, C. 'China's Involvement in the Vietnam War, 1964–69', *China Quarterly*, 142 (June 1995).

Jian, C. 'China's Road to the Korean War', *Cold War International History Project Bulletin*, 6–7 (Washington DC: Woodrow Wilson International Center for Scholars, Winter 1995–96), http://wwics.si.edu/index.cfm?topic_id=1409&fuseaction=library.document&id=241

Jian, C. 'A Crucial Step towards the Sino-Soviet Schism: The Withdrawal of Soviet Advisers from China, July 1960', *Cold War International History Project Bulletin*, 8–9 (Washington DC: Woodrow Wilson International Center for Scolars, Winter 1996/7), http://wwics.si.edu/index.cfm?topic_id=1409&fuseaction=library.document&id=176

Jian, C. and Wilson, D. 'All under the Heaven is Great Chaos: Beijing, the Sino-Soviet Border Clashes, and the Turn Towards Sino-American Rapprochement, 1968–69', *Cold War International History Project Bulletin*, 11 (Washington DC: Woodrow Wilson International Center for Scholars, Winter 1998), http://www.wilsoncenter.org/index.cfm?topic_id=1409&fuseaction=topics.publications&group_id=13422

Johnson, L. 'US Business Interests in Cuba and the Rise of Castro', *World Politics*, XVII/3 (April 1965).

Kahin, G. 'The United States and the Anti-Colonial Revolutions in Southeast Asia, 1945–50', in Nagai, Y. and Iriye, A. (eds.) *The Origins of the Cold War in Asia* (New York: Columbia University Press, 1977).

Kahin, G. *Intervention: How America Became Involved in Vietnam* (New York: Alfred A. Knopf, 1986).

Kaser, M. C. and Radice, E. A (eds.) *An Economic History of Eastern Europe, 1919–1975* (Oxford: Clarendon Press, 1986).

Kennan, G. ' "X" Article The Sources of Soviet Conduct', *Foreign Affairs*, 25/4 (July 1947).

Kennan, G. 'The Long Telegram,' in the *Foreign Relations of the United States: 1946*, Volume VI (Washington DC: US Government Printing Office, 1969).

Kennan, G. *The Nuclear Delusion: Soviet–American Relations in the Atomic Age* (New York: Pantheon Books, 1982).

Kennan, G. *American Diplomacy* (Chicago: University of Chicago Press, 1984).

Keohane, R. and Nye, J. (eds.) *Transnational Relations and World Politics* (Cambridge, MA: Harvard University Press, 1971).

Keohane, R. and Nye, J. (eds.) *Power and Interdependence: World Politics in Transition* (Boston, MA: Little, Brown, 1977).

Kerkvliet, B. *The Huk Rebellion: A Study of Peasant Revolt in the Philippines* (Berkeley, CA: University of California Press, 1977).

Keylor, W. *The Twentieth Century World: An International History* (New York: Oxford University Press, 2001).

Kim Khánh, H. *Vietnamese Communism, 1925–45* (Ithaca, NY: Cornell University Press, 1982).

Kissinger, H. *Diplomacy* (New York: Simon & Schuster, 1994).

Klare, M. & Kornbluh, P. (eds.) *Low-Intensity Warfare: How the US Fights Wars without Declaring Them* (London: Methuen, 1989).

Kolko, G. *The Politics of War: Allied Diplomacy and the World Crisis of 1943–1945* (London: Weidenfeld & Nicolson, 1969a).

Kolko, G. *The Roots of American Foreign Policy: An Analysis of Power and Purpose* (Boston, MA: Beacon Press, 1969b).

Kolko, G. and Kolko, J. *The Limits of Power: The World and United States Foreign Policy, 1945–1954* (New York: Harper & Row, 1972).

Kolko, G. *Vietnam: Anatomy of a War, 1940–75* (London: Allen & Unwin, 1986).

Kolko, G. *Century of War: Politics, Conflicts, and Society Since 1914* (New York: New Press, 1994).

Kopstein, J. *The Politics of Economic Decline in East Germany, 1945–1989* (Chapel Hill, NC: University of North Carolina Press, 1997).

Kornai, J. *Growth, Shortage and Efficiency: A Macroeconomic Model of the Socialist Economy*, trans. I. Lukács (Oxford: Blackwell, 1982).

Kornbluh, P. *Nicaragua: The Price of Intervention* (Washington DC: Institute for Policy Studies, 1987).

Kornbluh, P. 'Chile and the United States: Declassified Documents Relating to the Military Coup, September 11 1973', *National Security Archive Briefing* no. 8 available; http://www.gwu.edu/~nsarchiv/NSAEBB/NSAEBB8/nsaebb8i.htm

Koslowski, R. and Kratochwil, F. 'Understanding Change in International Politics: The Soviet Empire's Demise and the International System', *International Organization*, 48/2 (1994).

Kramer, M. 'The Soviet Foreign Ministry Appraisal of Sino-Soviet Relations on the Eve of the Split', *Cold War International History Project Bulletin*, 6–7 (Washington DC: Woodrow Wilson International Center for Scholars, Winter 1995–6), http://wwics.si.edu/index.cfm?topic_id=1409&fuseaction=library.document&id=328

Kramer, M. 'New Evidence on Soviet Decision-Making and the 1956 Polish and Hungarian Crises', *Cold War International History Project Bulletin*, 8–9 (Washington DC: Woodrow Wilson Centre for International Scholars, 1996–7), http://wwics.si.edu/index.cfm?topic_id=1409&fuseaction=library.document&id=130

Kramer, M. 'Ideology and the Cold War', *Review of International Studies*, 25, 4 (October 1999a).

Kramer, M. 'The Early Post-Stalin Succession Struggle and Upheavals in East-Central Europe: Internal–External Linkages in Soviet Foreign Policy Making', *Journal of Cold War Studies,* 1/3 (1999b).

Kuisong, Y. 'Changes in Mao Zedong's Attitude to the Indochina War, 1949–1973', trans. Q. Zhai, *Cold War International History Working Paper*, 34 (Washington DC: Woodrow Wilson Centre for International Scholars, 2002), http://www.wilsoncenter.org/index.cfm?topic_id=1409&fuseaction=topics.publications&group_id=11901

Kuniholm, B. *The Origins of the Cold War in the Near East: Great Power Conflict and Diplomacy in Iran, Turkey and Greece* (Princeton, NJ: Princeton University Press, 1980).

LaFeber, W. *America, Russia and the Cold War 1945–1992*, 7th edition (New York: McGraw-Hill, 1993).

Lane, D. *The Rise and Fall of State Socialism: Industrial Society and Socialist State* (Cambridge: Polity, 1996).

Lebow, R. N. 'The Long Peace, the End of the Cold War and the Failure of Realism', *International Organization*, 48/2 (Spring 1994).

Lebow, R. N. and Risse-Kappen, T. (eds.) *International Relations Theory and the End of the Cold War* (New York: Columbia University Press, 1995).

Lee, S. *Outposts of Empire: Korea, Vietnam and the Origins of the Cold War in Asia, 1949–1954* (Montreal: McGill-Queens University Press, 1995).

Lee, S. *The Korean War* (Harlow: Pearson Education, 2001).

Leffler, M. *A Preponderance of Power: National Security, the Truman Administration and the Cold War* (Stanford, CA: Stanford University Press, 1992).

Leffler, M. *The Specter of Communism: The United States and the Origins of the Cold War, 1917–1953* (New York: Hill & Wang, 1994a).

Leffler, M. and Painter, D. (eds.) *Origins of the Cold War: An International History* (London: Routledge, 1994b).

Lenin, V. I. *Imperialism: The Highest Stage of Capitalism* [1916] (Moscow: Progress Publishers, 1934).

Lewin, M. *The Making the Soviet System: Essays in the Social History of Interwar Russia* (London: Methuen, 1985).

Lewin, M. *The Soviet Century* (London: Verso, 2005).

Leys, C. and Panitch, L. (eds.) *Socialist Register 2003: Fighting Identities: Race, Religion and Ethnonationalism* (London: Merlin, 2002).

Lippmann, W. *The Cold War: A Study in US Foreign Policy* (London: Hamilton, 1947).

Löwy M. *The Politics of Combined and Uneven Development: The Theory of Permanent Revolution* (London: New Left Books, 1981).

Lundestad, G. *'Empire' by Invitation: The United States and European Integration, 1945–1997* (Oxford: Oxford University Press, 1998).

Maier, C. *In Search of Stability* (Cambridge: Cambridge University Press, 1987).

Mamdani, M. *Good Muslim, Bad Muslin: America, the Cold War and the Roots of Terror* (New York: Pantheon Books, 2004).

Mandel, E. *The Meaning of the Second World War* (London: Verso, 1986).

Mansourov, A. 'Stalin, Mao, Kim and China's Decision to Enter the Korean War, September 16–October 15 1950: New Evidence from the Russian Archives', *Cold War International History Bulletin*, 6–7 (Washington DC: Woodrow Wilson International Center for Scholars, Winter 1995–96), http://wwics.si.edu/index.cfm?topic_id=1409&fuseaction=library.document&id=373

Maravall, J. A. *The Transition to Democracy in Spain* (London: Croom Helm, 1982).

Mark, E. 'Revolution by Degrees: Stalin's National Front Strategy for Europe, 1941–47', *Cold War International History Project Working Paper*, 31 (Washington DC: Woodrow Wilson

International Center for Scholars, Winter 1995–96), http://www.wilsoncenter.org/index.cfm?topic_id=1409&fuseaction=topics.publications&group_id=11901

Mayer, A. *The Politics and Diplomacy of Peacemaking* (London: Weidenfeld & Nicolson, 1967).

Mayer, A. *Dynamics of Counter-Revolution in Europe: 1870–1956* (New York: Harper & Row, 1971).

Mazower, M. *Dark Continent: Europe's Twentieth Century* (Harmondsworth: Penguin Books, 1998).

McDermott, K. and Agnew, J. *The Comintern: A History of International Communism from Lenin to Stalin* (Basingstoke: Macmillan, 1996).

McMahan, J. *Reagan and the World: Imperial Policy in the New Cold War* (London: Pluto Press, 1984).

McNeil, W. *America, Britain and Russia: their Co-operation and Conflict, 1941–1946* [1953] (New York: Johnson Reprint Corp., 1976).

Mearsheimer, J. 'Back to the Future: Instability in Europe after the Cold War', *International Security*, 15/1 (Summer 1990).

Mearsheimer, J. *The Tragedy of Great Power Politics* (New York: W. W. Norton, 2001).

Melanson, R. *Writing History and Making Policy: The Cold War, Vietnam and Revisionism* (Lanham, MD: University Press of America, 1983).

Miller, N. *Soviet Relations with Latin America* (Cambridge: Cambridge University Press, 1989).

Milward, A. *The Reconstruction of Western Europe, 1945–1951* (London: Methuen, 1984).

Mineo, N. 'The Sino-Soviet Confrontation in Historical Perspective', in Nagai, Y. and Iriye, A. (eds.) *The Origins of the Cold War in Asia* (New York: Columbia University Press, 1977).

Molloy, I. *Rolling Back Revolution: The Emergence of Low Intensity Conflict* (London: Pluto Press, 2001).

Morgenthau, H. *Politics among Nations: The Struggle for Power and Peace* (New York: Alfred A. Knopf, 1948).

Morley, M. *Imperial State and Revolution: The United States and Cuba, 1952–1986* (Cambridge: Cambridge University Press, 1987).

Morley, M. (ed.) *Crisis and Confrontation: Ronald Reagan's Foreign Policy* (Totowa, NJ: Rowman & Littlefield, 1988).

Morris, S. 'The Soviet–Chinese–Vietnamese Triangle in the 1970s: The View from Moscow', *Cold War International History Project Working Paper*, 25 (Washington DC: Woodrow Wilson Center for International Scholars, 1999), http://www.wilsoncenter.org/index.cfm?topic_id=1409&fuseaction=topics.publications&group_id=11901

Mortimer, E. *The Rise of the French Communist Party, 1920–1947* (London: Faber, 1984).

Murray, M. *The Development of Capitalism in Colonial Indochina* (Los Angeles: University of California Press, 1980).

Narinsky, M. 'New Evidence on Soviet Rejection of the Marshall Plan', *Cold War International History Project Working Paper*, 9 (Washington DC: Woodrow Wilson Center for International Scholars, 1994), http://www.wilsoncenter.org/index.cfm?topic_id=1409&fuseaction=topics.publications&group_id=11901

National Security Archive. 'CIA Stalling State Department Histories' (July 2001), http://www.gwu.edu/~nsarchiv/NSAEBB/NSAEBB52/

National Security Archive. 'The Case against Pinochet: Ex-Dictator Indicted for Condor Crimes' (December 2004), http://www.gwu.edu/~nsarchiv/NSAEBB/NSAEBB125/index2.htm

National Security Archive. 'Presidential Directives on National Security from Truman to Clinton' (2005), http://nsarchive.chadwyck.com/pdessayx.htm

Nove, A. *An Economic History of the USSR, 1917–1991* (Harmondsworth: Penguin Books, 1992).

Ostermann, C. 'New Documents on the East German Uprising of 1953', *Cold War International History Project Bulletin*, 5 (Washington DC: Woodrow Wilson Center for International Scholars, 1995), http://wwics.si.edu/index.cfm?topic_id=1409&fuseaction=library.document&id=494

Palmer, J. *Europe without America? The Crisis in Atlantic Relations* (Oxford: Oxford University Press, 1988).

Panitch, L. and Gindin, S. 'Global Capitalism and American Empire', in Leys, C. and Panitch, L. (eds.) *Socialist Register 2004: The New Imperial Challenge* (London: Merlin Press, 2003).

Papp, D. *Vietnam: The View from Moscow, Peking, Washington* (Jefferson, NC: McFarland, 1981).

Paterson, T. *On Every Front: The Making and Unmaking of the Cold War* (New York: W. W. Norton, 1979).

Paterson, T. *Meeting the Communist Threat: Truman to Reagan* (New York: Oxford University Press, 1988).

Pavlov, Y. *Soviet–Cuban Alliance, 1959–1991* (Miami, FL: North-South Centre/University of Miami Press, 1994).

Paxton, R. O. *The Anatomy of Fascism* (Harmondsworth: Penguin Books, 2004).

Pechatnov, V. 'The Big Three after the War', *Cold War International History Working Paper*, 13 (Washington DC: Woodrow Wilson Center for International Scholars, 1995), http://www.wilsoncenter.org/index.cfm?topic_id=1409&fuseaction=topics.publications&group_id=11901

Pérez, L. *Cuba and the United States: Ties of Singular Intimacy* (Athens, GA: Georgia University Press, 1990).

Pérez-Stable, M. *The Cuban Revolution: Origins, Course and Legacy* (New York: Oxford University Press, 1999).

Pipes, R. 'Misinterpreting the Cold War: The Hardliners Got it Right', *Foreign Affairs*, 74/1 (1995).

Pollard, R. *Economic Security and the Origins of the Cold War: The Strategic Ends of US Foreign Policy, 1945–1950* (New York: Columbia University Press, 1985).

Pollard, R. 'Economic Security and the Origins of the Cold War: Bretton Woods, the Marshall Plan, and American Rearmament, 1944–50', in L. Bogle (ed.) *The Cold War. Volume One: The Origins of the Cold War – The Great Historical Debate* (New York: Routledge, 2001).

Porter, B. *The USSR in Third World Conflicts: Soviet Arms and Diplomacy in Local Wars 1945–1980* (Cambridge: Cambridge University Press, 1984).

Post, K. *Revolution, Socialism and Nationalism in Viet Nam. Volume Two: Viet Nam Divided* (Aldershot: Dartmouth, 1989).

Post, K. *Revolution, Socialism and Nationalism in Viet Nam. Volume Four: The Failure of Counter-Insurgency in the South* (Aldershot: Dartmouth, 1990).

Prados, J. 'JFK and the Diem Coup', *National Security Archive* (November 2003), http://www.gwu.edu/~nsarchiv/NSAEBB/NSAEBB101/index.htm

Prados, J. '40th Anniversary of the Gulf of Tonkin Incident', *National Security Archive* (August 2004), http://www.gwu.edu/~nsarchiv/NSAEBB/NSAEBB132/essay.htm

Preston, P. and Mackenzie, A. *The Republic Besieged: The Spanish Civil War, 1936–1939* (Edinburgh: Edinburgh University Press, 1996).

Prozumenschikov, M. 'The Sino-Indian Conflict, the Cuban Missile Crisis and the Sino-Soviet Split, October 1962: New Evidence from the Russian Archives', *Cold War International History Project Bulletin*, 8–9 (Washington DC: Woodrow Wilson International Centre for Scholars, Winter 1996–7), http://wwics.si.edu/index.cfm?topic_id=1409&fuseaction=library.document&id=358

Rashid, A. *Taliban* (New Haven, CT: Yale University Press, 2000).

Rashid, A. *Taliban: The Story of the Afghan Warlords* (Basingstoke: Pan Books, 2001).

Richardson, J. 'The Huk Rebellion', *Journal of Contemporary Asia*, 8/2 (1978) pp. 231–7.

Richter, J. 'Reexamining Soviet Policy Towards Germany During the Beria Interregnum', *Cold War International History Project Working Paper*, 3 (Washington DC: Woodrow Wilson Center for International Scholars, 1992), http://wwics.si.edu/index.cfm?topic_id=1409&fuseaction=library.document&id=286

Risse-Kappen, T. 'Ideas do not Float Freely: Transnational Coalitions, Domestic Structures and the End of the Cold War', *International Organization*, 48/2 (1994).

Roberts, G. 'The Soviet Decision for a Pact With Nazi Germany', *Soviet Studies*, 44 (1992).

Roberts, G. *The Soviet Union in World Politics: Coexistence, Revolution and Cold War, 1945–1991* (London: Routledge, 1999).

Robinson, H. 'The Decline of the Dollar', in Miliband, R. and Saville, J. (eds.) *The Socialist Register* (London: Merlin Press, 1973).

Robinson, W. I. and Norsworthy, K. *David and Goliath: Washington's War against Nicaragua* (London: Zed Books, 1987).

Ross, G. *Workers and Communist in France: From Popular Front to Eurocommunism* (Berkeley, CA: University of California Press, 1982).

Rostow, W. *The United States in the World Arena: An Essay in Recent History* (New York: Harper, 1960).

Rubin, B. *Paved with Good Intentions: The American Experiences and Iran* (New York: Oxford University Press, 1980).

Rupert, M. *Producing Hegemony: The Politics of Mass Production and American Global Power* (Cambridge: Cambridge University Press, 1995).

Rupert, M. *Ideologies of Globalization* (London: Routledge, 2000).

Ruthven, M. *A Fury for God*, revised edition (London: Granta, 2002).

Saad-Filho, A. and Johnston, D. (eds.) *Neoliberalism: A Critical Reader* (London: Pluto Press, 2005).

Sanders, J. *Peddlers of Crisis: The Committee on the Present Danger and the Politics of Containment* (London: Pluto Press, 1983).

Saull, R. G. *Rethinking Theory and History in the Cold War: The State, Military Power, and Social Revolution* (London: Frank Cass, 2001).

Saull, R. G. 'The Rise and Fall of Revolution?', *Historical Materialism: Research in Critical Marxist Theory*, 10/1 (Summer 2002).

Saull, R. G. 'Locating the Global South in the Theorisation of the Cold War: Capitalist Development, Social Revolution and Geopolitical Conflict', *Third World Quarterly*, 26/2 (June 2005a).

Saull, R. G. 'Reactionary Blowback: The Uneven Ends of the Cold War and Origins of Contemporary Conflict in World Politics', in Colás, A. and Saull, R. G. (eds.) *The War on Terror and the American Empire after the Cold War* (London: Routledge, 2005b).

Scheer, R. *With Enough Shovels: Reagan, Bush, and Nuclear War* (New York: Random House, 1982).

Schlesinger Jr, A. 'Origins of the Cold War', *Foreign Affairs*, 46 (1967).

Schulzinger, R. *A Time for War: The United States and Vietnam, 1941–1975* (New York: Oxford University Press, 1997).

Scott, J. *Deciding to Intervene: The Reagan Doctrine and American Foreign Policy* (Durham, NC: Duke University Press, 1996).

Service, R. *A History of Twentieth Century Russia* (Harmondsworth: Penguin Book, 1997).

Sheehan, N. *The 'Pentagon Papers': As Published by the New York Times* (London: Routledge & Kegan Paul, 1971).

Simmons, H. *The French National Front: The Extremist Challenge to Democracy* (Boulder, CO: Westview Press, 1996).

Sklar, H. *Washington's War on Nicaragua* (Boston, MA: South End Press, 1988).

Smith, S. A. 'The Comintern, the Chinese Communist Party and the Three Armed Uprisings in Shanghai, 1926–27', in T. Rees and A. Thorpe (eds.) *International Communism and the Communist International 1919–43* (Manchester: Manchester University Press, 1998).

Solomon, R. *The Transformation of the World Economy* (London: St. Martin's Press, 1999).

Spero, J. *The Politics of International Economic Relations* (London: Routledge, 1997).

Steele, J. *World Power: Soviet Foreign Policy under Brezhnev and Andropov* (London: Michael Joseph, 1983).

Strange, S. 'The Dollar Crisis', *International Affairs*, 48/2 (April 1972).

Strange, S. *Casino Capitalism* (Manchester: Manchester University Press, 1997).

Sung An, T. *The Vietnam War* (London: Associated University Press, 1998).

Talhami, G. H. 'Muslims, Islamists, and the Cold War', *Small Wars and Insurgencies*, 14/1 (2003).

Taubman, W. 'Khrushchev vs Mao: A Preliminary Sketch of the Role of Personality in the Sino-Soviet Split', *Cold War International History Project Bulletin*, 8–9 (Washington DC: Woodrow Wilson International Center for Scholars, Winter 1996–7), http://wwics.si.edu/index.cfm?topic_id=1409&fuseaction=library.document&id=45

Thomas, H. *Armed Truce: The Beginnings of the Cold War 1945–46* (New York: Atheneum, 1987).

Thomson, J. et al. *Sentimental Imperialists: The American Experience in East Asia* (New York: Harper & Row, 1981).

Thorne, C. *Allies of a Kind: The United States, Britain and the War against Japan, 1941–1945* (London: Hamish Hamilton, 1978).

Ticktin. H. *Origins of the Crisis in the USSR: Essays on the Political Economy of a Disintegrating System* (Armonk, NY: Myron Sharpe, 1992).

Turley, W. S. *The Second Indochina War: A Short Political and Military History, 1954–1975* (Boulder, CO: Westview Press, 1986).

Urban, J. B. *Moscow and the Italian Communist Party: From Togliatti to Berlinguer* (London: I. B. Tauris, 1986).

Valkenier, E. *The Soviet Union and the Third World: An Economic Bind* (New York: Praeger, 1983).

van der Pijl, K. *The Making of an Atlantic Ruling Class* (London: Verso, 1984).

Vatikiatis, M. *Indonesian Politics under Suharto* (London: Routledge, 1993).

Vilas, C. *Between Earthquakes and Volcanoes: Market, State, and the Revolutions in Central America*, trans. Ted Kuster (New York: Monthly Review Press, 1995).

Wagner, R. H. 'The Decision to Divide Germany and the Origins of the Cold War', *International Studies Quarterly*, 24 (June 1980): 162–73.

Walker, T. (ed.) *Nicaragua: The First Five Years* (New York: Praeger, 1985).

Walker, T. (ed.) *Reagan versus the Sandanistas: The Undeclared War on Nicaragua* (Boulder, CO: Westview Press, 1987).

Walker. T. (ed.) *Revolution and Counterrevolution in Nicaragua* (Boulder, CO: Westview Press, 1991).

Walt, S. 'American Primacy: Its Promises and Pitfalls', *Naval War College Review*, 55 (2002).

Walt, S. 'Taming American Power', *Foreign Affairs*, 84/5 (September–October 2005).

Waltz, K. 'The Emerging Structure of International Politics', *International Security*, 18/2 (1993).

Weathersby, K. 'New Findings on the Korean War', *Cold War International History Project Bulletin*, 3 (Washington DC: Woodrow Wilson International Center for Scholars, 1993a), http://wwics.si.edu/index.cfm?topic_id=1409&fuseaction=library.document&id=426

Weathersby, K. 'Soviet Aims in North Korea and the Origins of the Korean War, 1945–50: New Evidence from the Russian Archives', *Cold War International History Project Working Paper*, 8 (Washington D C: Woodrow Wilson International Center for Scholars, 1993b), http://wwics.si.edu/index.cfm?topic_id=1409&fuseaction=library.document&id=445

Weathersby, K. 'To Attack or Not Attack: Stalin, Kim Il Sung and the Prelude to War', *Cold War International History Project Bulletin*, 5 (Washington DC: Woodrow Wilson International Center for Scholars, Spring 1995), http://wwics.si.edu/index.cfm?topic_id=1409&fuseaction=library.document&id=169

Weathersby, K. 'New Russian Documents on the Korean War,' *Cold War International History Project Bulletin*, 6–7 (Washington DC: Woodrow Wilson International Center for Scholars, Winter 1995–96), http://wwics.si.edu/index.cfm?topic_id=1409&fuseaction=library.document&id=466

Weber, H. *Nicaragua: The Sandanista Reveolution*, trans. Patrick Camiller (London: New Left Books, 1981).

Wegs, J. R. and Ladrech, J. *Europe since 1945: A Concise History* (New York: St. Martin's Press, 1996).

Weinbaum, M. *Pakistan and Afghanistan: Resistance and Reconstruction* (Boulder, CO: Westview Press, 1994).

Werblan, A. 'The Conversation between Władysław Gomulka and Josef Stalin on 14 November 1945', *Cold War International History Project Bulletin*, 11 (Washington DC: Woodrow Wilson International Center for Scholars, Winter 1998), http://www.wilsoncenter.org/ index.cfm? topic_id=1409&fuseaction=topics.publications&group_id=13422

Westad, O. A. 'Fighting for Friendship: Mao, Stalin and the Sino-Soviet Friendship Treaty of 1950', *Cold War International History Project Bulletin*, 8–9 (Washington DC: Woodrow Wilson International Center for Scholars, Winter 1996/7), http://www.wilsoncenter.org/ index.cfm? topic_id=1409&fuseaction=topics.publications&group_id=14051

Westad, O. A. (ed.) *Brothers in Arms: The Rise and Fall in the Sino-Soviet Alliance, 1945–63* (Stanford, CA: Stanford University Press, 1998a).

Westad, O. A. *The Global Cold War: Third World Interventions in the Making of Our Times* (Cambridge: Cambridge University Press, 2005).

Westad, O. A. et al. (eds.) '77 Conversations between Chinese and Foreign Leaders on the Wars in Indochina', *Cold War International History Project Working Paper*, 22 (Washington DC: Woodrow Wilson International Center for Scholars, 1998b), http://www.wilsoncenter. org/ index.cfm?topic_id=1409&fuseaction=topics.publications&group_id=11901

Westoby, A. *The Evolution of Communism* (Cambridge: Polity, 1989).

Whitehouse. *The National Security Strategy of the United States* (2002), http://www.whitehouse. gov/nsc/nss.html

Wiegersma, N. *Vietnam: Peasant Land, Peasant Revolution. Patriarchy and Collectivity in the Rural Economy* (London: Macmillan, 1988).

Williams, W. A. *The Tragedy of American Diplomacy* [1959] (New York: W. W. Norton, 1972).

Wittner. L. *The American Intervention in Greece, 1943–1949: A Study in Counter-Revolution* (New York: Columbia University Press, 1982).

Wohlforth, W. 'Realism and the End of the Cold War', *International Security*, 19/3 (1994).

Wood, D. 'The Long Revolution: Class Relations and Political Conflict in Cuba, 1868–1968', *Science and Society: An Independent Journal of Marxism*, XXXIV/1 (Spring 1970).

Wyatt-Walter, A. 'The United States and Western Europe: The Theory of Hegemonic Stability', in N. Woods (ed.) *Explaining International Relations since 1945* (Oxford: Oxford University Press, 1996).

Yapp, M. *The Near East since the First World War* (London: Longman, 1991).

Yodfat, A. *The Soviet Union and Revolutionary Iran* (London: Croom Helm, 1984).

Young, M. *The Vietnam Wars, 1945–1990* (New York: HarperCollins, 1991).

Yousaf, M. and Adkin, M. *Afghanistan: The Bear Trap. The Defeat of a Superpower* (Barnsley: Leo Cooper, 2001).

Zabih, S. *The Left in Contemporary Iran: Ideology, Organization and Soviet Connection* (London: Croom Helm, 1986).

Zhai, Q. 'Beijing and the Vietnam Conflict, 1964–65: New Chinese Evidence', *Cold War International History Project Bulletin*, 6–7 (Washington DC: Woodrow Wilson International Center for Scholars, Winter 1995–96), http://wwics.si.edu/index.cfm?topic_id=1409&fuseaction= library.document&id=244

Zubok, V. 'Khruschev and the Berlin Crisis, 1958–62', *Cold War International History Project Working Paper*, 6 (Washington DC: Woodrow Wilson Center for International Scholars, 1993), http://wwics.si.edu/index.cfm?topic_id=1409&fuseaction=library.document&id=362

Zubok, V. and Pleshakov, C. *Inside the Kremlin's Cold War: From Stalin to Khrushchev* (Cambridge, MA: Harvard University Press, 1996).

Index

Compiled by Sue Carlton